TO FIX OR TO HEAL

BIOPOLITICS: MEDICINE, TECHNOSCIENCE,
AND HEALTH IN THE 21ST CENTURY
General Editors: Monica J. Casper and Lisa Jean Moore

To Fix or to Heal

Patient Care, Public Health,
and the Limits of Biomedicine

Edited by
Joseph E. Davis *and*
Ana Marta González

NEW YORK UNIVERSITY PRESS
New York and London

NEW YORK UNIVERSITY PRESS
New York and London
www.nyupress.org

References to Internet websites (URLs) were accurate at the time of writing. Neither the author nor New York University Press is responsible for URLs that may have expired or changed since the manuscript was prepared.

ISBN: 978-1-4798-7824-6 (hardback)
ISBN: 978-1-4798-0958-5 (paperback)

For Library of Congress Cataloging-in-Publication data, please contact the Library of Congress.

New York University Press books are printed on acid-free paper, and their binding materials are chosen for strength and durability. We strive to use environmentally responsible suppliers and materials to the greatest extent possible in publishing our books.

Manufactured in the United States of America

10 9 8 7 6 5 4 3 2 1

Also available as an ebook

CONTENTS

ACKNOWLEDGMENTS

The impetus for this book was a conference on "Construction of New Realities in Medicine," held in Barcelona, Spain, on April 16–17, 2010. Ana Marta González organized the meeting on behalf of the Social Trends Institute, a nonprofit research center dedicated to the analysis of globally significant social trends. By promoting research and scholarship of the highest academic standard within four subject areas—family, bioethics, culture and lifestyles, and corporate governance—STI aims to make a scholarly contribution toward understanding the varying and complex trends that characterize the modern world. Early drafts of the chapters by Bruce K. Alexander, Jon Arrizabalaga, John Evans, and Anne Hardy were presented at the STI meeting. We thank STI both for hosting that initial meeting and for other financial support of this book.

We also thank Ilene Kalish, Executive Editor of New York University Press, along with the Biopolitics series editors, Monica J. Casper and Lisa Jean Moore, for their embrace of the project. The two sets of anonymous reviewers for the Press provided invaluable feedback, including important suggestions for how to enlarge and sharpen the contribution. To them, for their thorough and thoughtful engagement, we are deeply appreciative. Caelyn Cobb, Assistant Editor, was a pleasure to work with, as was Dorothea S. Halliday, Managing Editor, who moved the book through the production process.

Joseph Davis thanks, in particular, Brooke Lea and Jaine Strauss for their generosity and kindness in hosting his annual summers-in-residence at Macalester College; the Institute for Culture and Society at the University of Navarra for a terrific semester in Pamplona, Spain; and, most especially, his academic home, the Institute for Advanced Studies in Culture (IASC) at the University of Virginia. These are the places, where, over a period of several years, he wrote his chapters and edited the book. Once again, he greatly benefited from the skillful research and painstaking editorial assistance of Susannah Myers and the wise advice of Jay Tolson, both of the IASC. Vincent Ercolano provided very careful copy editing of several of the chapters, and Robert Dingwall, who read the entire manuscript, offered timely advice and unerring suggestions. Bert Hansen generously provided images of the editorial cartoons that appear here as figures 1.1 and 1.2; these were originally reprinted in his marvelous *Picturing Medical Progress from Pasteur to Polio*. To each of them, and to each of the contributors—models of cooperation and understanding—he extends his gratitude and thanks.

Introduction

Holism against Reductionism

JOSEPH E. DAVIS

In its relationship with society, contemporary medicine is beset by a deep tension. It is an old tension and familiar to all those who work in and study medicine. It has long been observed, for example, that the instrumental stance of scientific medicine can entail a loss of consideration for the person of the patient.[1] The ideal-type of the biomedical physician is a kind of applied scientist, guided by objective diagnostic criteria and deploying an armament of specific technical interventions against nature's "real" diseases. Taking this role involves a depersonalization, a setting aside of the emotional and moral aspects of distress, and a technological focus that has in the past and continues in the present to generate considerable patient dissatisfaction and alienation.[2] Perhaps one small measure of popular unease can be seen in the plethora of recent American apocalyptic films and TV shows—*The X-Files*, *Falling Skies*, *The Walking Dead*—wherein hospitals are without exception portrayed as menacing and *in*hospitable.[3] To address this tension, clinicians, bioethicists, and other scholars have proposed over the years any number of strategies to "humanize" biomedicine, and fields such as nursing and bioethics define themselves, somewhat oppositionally, as patient-centered and oriented toward care.

Similarly, observers have long argued that the mainstream conceptual model of disease, the "biomedical model," for all its technical successes, tends to marginalize or exclude the crucial social and environmental determinants of illness. The model reduces the causes of disease and disorder to specific somatic malfunctions in the individual that respond to specific technological interventions and individual-level preventive measures. Against this narrowly individualistic and highly biological approach, alternative models have aimed to integrate or supplement somatic explanations with broader factors, whether psychological, cultural, ecological, political, or economic, that affect health and illness, both on an individual and a collective level. Much of the burden of disease and its variability, argue critics in public health, social epidemiology, anthropology, sociology, and other fields, cannot be explained or effectively addressed with the mechanism-oriented biomedical model.

Historians have explored this tension as a contrast between "reductionistic" and "holistic" approaches to health and illness. Philosophically, reductionism and holism represent different stances with respect to the relation between "parts" and "wholes." In a reductionist approach, higher-order properties of phenomena can be completely explained by—that is, reduced to—lower-order properties. So, for instance, disease (higher level of complexity) can be accounted for solely in terms of molecular biology and genetics (lower level). A holist approach, by contrast, typically treats higher-order properties ("wholes") as emergent phenomena that are irreducible to the lower-order properties ("parts") that make them up. However, in historical terms, medical reductionism and holism are not philosophical concepts but orientations of thought, typically defined in opposition to each other.[4] Reductionism has often meant those defining features of scientific medicine against which holism, in its various forms, has aligned itself.

In popular usage the term *holistic* is often used by practitioners and participants to designate particular mind–body practices—such as acupuncture and healing touch; the use of natural substances, such as botanicals and probiotics; and healing systems, such as homeopathy and naturopathy—that are alternative or complementary to mainstream medicine.[5] It can also refer to a larger, critical orientation that accompanies and informs the use of these practices. This orientation often has a premodern, non-Western, spiritual, and anti-bureaucratic ethos that is set against conventional "allopathic" medicine and wants to replace it. If the biomedical model amplifies the division between mind and body with an overemphasis on the somatic, holistic health practitioners often make the opposite error, granting the mind a nearly boundless power over the ailing body.

However, our concern is with a sensibility and a set of interlinked ideas articulated *within* the mainstream (though certainly with influence from alternative practices) of medicine and social science. Holism, in this sense, was never a self-conscious movement; few proponents even used the term. The shared feature, expressed in many different forms, is a *contextual* understanding of disease causation, intervention, or practice. A systemic concern with the whole organism (including the emotional/psychological), a focus on the interconnected effects of the larger physical or social environment, and attention to population-level variation can all be characterized as holistic. So too can more synthetic ways of knowing—supplementing the narrowness of scientific analysis with other modes and disciplines of thought—and ethical concerns with the quality of human relations in the clinical encounter and wider society.[6]

Because the biomedical literature generally lacks explicit discussion of its underlying assumptions, it has been holistic-oriented critics rather than proponents who typically articulate the more or less tacit meanings of reductionism in medicine. Over time, reductionism has been used to characterize a mechanistic and narrowly somatic understanding of disease, monocausal theories of disease, an excessive focus on localized pathology, an exclusive preoccupation with cure to the neglect of prevention, and even an overspecialization and fragmentation of medical practice.[7]

We have sought to capture the contrasting orientations and the tension between reductionism and holism in our title, "to fix *or* to heal," but the *or* is not meant to indicate any absolute distinction. Like the historians, we are talking not about polar opposites but orientations and ways of thinking that are often negotiated in practice. By *heal* we mean a broadly integrative and humanistic orientation that opposes the sufficiency of a mechanistic, individualistic, and overly technological biomedical orientation, rooted in the metaphor of the body as a machine that can be "fixed." Sufficiency is the crux of the matter. The elements of the "fix" orientation can have their appropriate place. Somatic reductionism, for instance, can be a valid explanatory strategy as adjudged in terms of scientific productivity. What we stand against is a larger, one-sided orientation, with problematic ontological (what is real) and epistemological (what we can know) implications. Our argument, consistent with the holistic tradition, is that the contemporary practice of medicine is based on both prodigious knowledge and technical skills *and* on very real limitations and blind spots.

Critically, we also argue that the "fix" orientation has powerful sources outside biomedicine that are shaping its role within. In fact, "medicine" is not a static or homogeneous category, and many areas of medicine resist a narrow physicalism, attend to the person of the patient, and recognize social and environmental contributions to illness and disorder. And, as I discuss more in the following pages and the chapters in this book will demonstrate, there are strong scientific, clinical, ethical, and public health reasons to move further in this direction. If holistic, integrative orientations remain marginal, and they do, forces well beyond the sound practice of medicine are at work. The historian Charles Rosenberg, for instance, has written: "The dominance of reductionist styles has a long history in the explanation of human behavior . . . but it has an extraordinarily salient place today. We have never been more infatuated with visions of molecular and neurochemical—ultimately genetic—truth."[8] Reductionism of this kind and other aspects of the biomedical model, including its putative value-neutrality, mind–body dualism, and decontextualized individualistic orientation, are prized for social, cultural, political, and economic reasons of their own, and medicine is being positioned in the contemporary social order accordingly. In resisting the fix orientation, our goal is to explore its sources as well as its limitations and ethical inadequacies.

There are grounds for cautious optimism as new challenges are arising that may loosen some of the hold of reductionism. While reductionism was the ascendant model throughout the twentieth century, the relative influence of holistic thinking has waxed and waned with changing social conditions, moments of cultural crisis, and the shifting nature of the disease burden. If marginalized, holism has remained alive in select pockets of the medical professions and social sciences. In the next section I briefly touch on this history as a backdrop for situating the contributions of the book, with a guide to some of the important literature provided in the endnotes. From a more holistic perspective, each chapter calls into question the adequacy of reductionist and individualistic modes in medicine, public health, or bioethics. Part I explores the role of medicine in the moral/cultural agendas of contemporary society; part II takes up the challenges to the biomedical model represented by new regimes of disease and disorder; and part III investigates bioethics and, in light of the dominance of the "fix" orientation, the urgent need for richer, more substantive ethical reflection.

The Holistic Challenge to Reductionist Medicine

Under the long reign of humoral theory, all of medicine before about 1850 was holistic. Ill health and disease reflected an imbalance or disharmony in a mutually constitutive economy of bodily, personality, and environmental factors. Yet, even as medicine was being swept up into the scientific revolution, prominent scientists and physicians continued to emphasize the importance of what are now called the "social determinants of health" and resisted the increasingly sharp distinction between mind and body. Rudolf Virchow, for example, a pioneer of microscopy and the founder of cellular pathology, is primarily remembered today for his medical achievements. But while a strong proponent of scientific medicine and experimentation, Virchow recognized the social, political, and economic dimensions of health. In 1848 the Prussian government sent him to investigate a typhus epidemic in Upper Silesia; in his report, Virchow blamed the outbreak not primarily on individual microbes and diseased bodies but on the region's poverty and social despair:

> [T]here can now no longer be any doubt that such an epidemic dissemination of typhus had only been possible under the wretched conditions of life that poverty and lack of culture had created in Upper Silesia. If these conditions were removed, I am sure that epidemic typhus would not recur. Whosoever wishes to learn from history will find many examples.
>
> The logical answer to the question as to how conditions similar to those that have unfolded before our eyes in Upper Silesia can be prevented in the future is, therefore, very easy and simple: education, with her daughters, liberty and prosperity. . . . Medicine has imperceptibly led us into the social field and placed us in a position of confronting directly the great problems of our time. . . . If we therefore wish to intervene in Upper Silesia, we must begin to promote the advancement of the entire population, and to stimulate a common general effort.[9]

Since Virchow's time, many have tried to resist medicine's seemingly inexorable reductionizing trend by proposing social models of sickness and health that take into account the mind and the larger social and political context in which we live. These holistic efforts were most powerful at two points in the twentieth century. First, major contributions were made, primarily in Europe, in the interwar years of the 1920s–1940s; indeed, the word *holism* was coined at this time.[10] Second, the late 1960s–1970s saw a revival of holistic thought, in both Europe and the Americas, that generated biting critiques of the biomedical model. Important elements of these legacies remain alive and contribute to the paradoxical situation in which we now find ourselves.

Holism of the Person

In both periods, the major holistic approaches may be roughly divided into two categories. The first is a *holism of the person*, which addresses the whole patient, not merely a particular disease process within the patient. On the physical level, this means being aware of the patient as a complete and integrated organism, not as a collection of parts. Usually, it also means taking into account other aspects of the patient, such as her mental, emotional, and social life; her family situation; and features of the larger external environment. In the interwar period in the United States, the most visible expression of this mind–body holism was in the psychosomatic movement with roots in the work of pioneers at Johns Hopkins, such as Adolph Meyer, and the groundbreaking investigations of the physiology of emotion by Walter Cannon.[11] In the 1930s the Austrian-Canadian endocrinologist Hans Seyle built on this work to develop his theory of "general adaptation syndrome," one of the earliest attempts to show the physiological action of stress.[12] The journal *Psychosomatic Medicine* first appeared in 1939; although the journal is still being published, the movement, after flourishing in the 1930s and '40s, went into decline in the postwar years. It was revived during the crisis years of the 1970s in the influential "biopsychosocial" model of the internist George Engel.

For Engel, the stripping away of social context, the effacing of the patient, and the sole focus on biology were together the linchpin of the biomedical model. Against it, he proposed an alternative scientific framework, a biopsychosocial model, which offered, he argued, a unified concept that involved "evaluating all the factors contributing to both illness and patienthood, rather than giving primacy to biological factors alone."[13] While some who articulated holistic positions downplayed the achievements of medicine, Engel was not among them. He saw the biomedical model as a powerful scientific framework for discovering and understanding the disordered bodily processes involved in disease. The problem, in his view, is when this instrumental framework is generalized as a model for a human practice like medicine. In this broader context, it is deeply inadequate. Its biological reductionism and sharp mind–body dualism lead to the downplaying or exclusion of the social, psychological, and behavioral aspects of health and illness; to an overreliance on technology; and to narrow professional specialization. The physician's clinical gaze is directed to the somatic features of disease and away from the complex environmental context that can affect the onset, course, therapeutic response, and outcome of illness and that typically holds the key to devising potential means of prevention.

Engel's writing in the late 1970s had an enormous impact, but its influence was uneven and has waned.[14] In psychiatry, for example, where Engel's ideas received the greatest attention (outside primary care), there has been a strong reassertion of the biomedical model[15] and a heavy reliance on medication treatment. In 2005, the president of the American Psychiatric Association, Steven Sharfstein, argued, "As a profession, we have allowed the biopsychosocial model to become the bio-bio-bio model. In a time of economic constraint, a 'pill and an appointment' has dominated treatment."[16] Newer psychosocial approaches have appeared since Engel's. Perhaps the best-known is the "status syndrome" theory of the British epidemiologist Michael Marmot, which identifies the primary source of stress as social status relative to peers.[17] All this work has contributed to a body of well-recognized scientific evidence on the role of stressful life events in modulating vulnerability to illness of almost every kind. Although the influence of psychosocial models is limited in medicine today, this valuable legacy remains critical to understanding social differences in health and illness.

Holism of the Environment

For Marmot, Engel, and others in the psychosocial tradition, the psychological is but one of the multiple factors at work in disease. Their holism of the person overlaps in some measure with what might be called, for simplicity's sake, a *holism of the environment*. The many varieties of this holism center not on the patient's individual traits and psychologically mediated social experience but on features of a society—cultural systems and norms, political and economic policies and relationships—that can affect the distribution of disease and health. In the period from the 1930s to the early 1950s, this holism was generally termed "social medicine." A predominantly European approach to public health, social medicine emerged, in part, in resistance to the growing dominance of the biomedical model, and in an age of population-wide programs. Its exponents saw health, too, as something existing first within populations, not individuals. During this period, social approaches to health commanded wide respect, and some highly prominent figures within the medical community—such as the medical historian Henry Sigerist and the public health statistician Edgar Sydenstricker—were affiliated with the social medicine movement. Proponents of social medicine were aware of and identified with the tradition of nineteenth-century holism (not far distant in the 1940s). Sigerist's *Medicine and Human Welfare*, for instance, approvingly quoted Virchow's famous pronouncement "Medicine is a social science and politics is nothing else but medicine on a large scale."[18]

One of the major exponents of social medicine was the Scottish epidemiologist Jerry Morris, who worked toward the end of the period. Morris's work might now seem focused on "lifestyle"-related factors of health. In the 1950s he was the first person to investigate the connection between cardiovascular activity and health; in 1962 he was one of nine doctors to write the first Royal College of Physicians report on smoking and health. But he always understood health on a social level,[19] was highly skeptical of individualistic approaches to prevention, and wrote a 1957 textbook, *Uses of Epidemiology*, that was enormously influential in establishing programs to foster public health.[20] His work suggests, as discussed in the following pages, that there was nothing inevitable in the shift toward individual behavior change that would come to characterize the "new" lifestyle epidemiology of the postwar years.

Despite Morris's work, with the end of the war and the sense of cultural crisis the war created, the 1950s and early '60s were a quiet time for social and other holistic approaches to medicine. This is doubtless partly, as Nancy Krieger observes, because social medicine was often linked to radical political programs of social change, at a time when these were suspect.[21] But it is at least equally likely that holistic accounts were simply eclipsed by the extraordinary success of biomedicine during this period.[22] In the 1950s—with the appearance of penicillin, cortisone, and the first effective antipsychotics and the eradication of polio all within roughly a decade—the explanatory power of the biomedical model was apparently complete. And the rapid rise of federal funding for laboratory research brought biology and medicine together into a new and reductionist juggernaut. Further, as Alan Brandt and Martha Gardner argue, in the postwar years the rise of the risk-factor approach to systemic chronic illnesses—an increasingly dominant aspect of the disease burden as infections were controlled—brought a rapprochement between public health and biomedicine, as public health began to shift away from a sociomedical model of disease focused on life conditions to emphasize prevention strategies aimed at the modification of individual lifestyles.[23]

But holistic approaches revived strongly with the social ferment of the late 1960s and '70s. If ever there was a moment when the dominance of biological reductionism was under assault, it was in these years. A whole range of humanistic physicians like Engel, as well as social scientists, ethicists, and others, launched trenchant criticisms of the biomedical model. Thomas McKeown, for example, argued that much of the positive change in patterns of morbidity and mortality in the twentieth century was the result of nonspecific factors, especially rising standards of living, and downplayed the role of specific medical achievements.[24] In their different ways, Ivan Illich, Irving Zola, and Michel Foucault offered stinging critiques of medicalization and the deployment of the individualistic and technology-driven medical model in the service of widening forms of social engineering and control.[25] Feminists and other minority activists questioned the politics by which health, illness, and the fundamental experience of the body were defined.[26] And after the thalidomide debacle and the infamous Tuskegee experiments, bioethicists and others called for stricter scrutiny of medicine, and a more humane doctor–patient relationship.[27]

A social medicine approach also revived, reconstituted in the Anglo-American context as the "social production of disease" and the closely related "political economy of health" (in Latin America, "social medicine"). In these approaches poverty and inequality are the ultimate structural sources of disease—risk factors underlying all other risk factors—and the solution is, first, reform of economic and political systems that produce health disparities and, second, redistributive policies to reduce inequality.[28] Sharing some features with the old social medicine, they also differed in two significant ways. First, they were characterized by a new suspicion of and pessimism about medicine and science generally; in Krieger's words, theorists of the political economy of health questioned "not only the application but the basic assumptions and theoretical orientation of mainstream science."[29] Second, and perhaps unsurprisingly, though they met with considerable success in the academy, and sometimes with policymakers, they got little hearing within the medical community.

The suspicion and social location outside of medicine, characteristic of many of the social medicine critiques offered in the 1970s, limited their impact. More important was another development, noted earlier, that had been steadily growing in influence after 1960. In the postwar period, a critical turn came in the wake of the so-called epidemiological transition in the disease burden from acute, infectious to degenerative, chronic diseases.[30] Chronic illnesses, highly dependent on circumstances, resisted explanation in deterministic, monocausal theories, and the work of researchers, such as Jerry Morris, in the 1950s was instrumental in the formulation of more complex, multicausal, and probabilistic models of disease causation. These researchers' work on what came to be called "risk factors"—including both exposures, such as to lead, and behaviors, such as cigarette smoking—and the emphasis on prevention it inspired seemed to represent a break with reductionist approaches. The role of individual and social context was now front and center, portending a necessarily more holistic orientation. What happened instead was that the risk factor—a quantitative, statistical concept—was brought within a theory of health promotion directed to individual lifestyle changes.

In this theory, risk factors, according to Robert Aronowitz, though derived from epidemiological observations, "are understood—and legitimated—only as they contribute to the specific, localized pathogenic processes that cause disease."[31] The primary concern is not with disease distribution but with disease mechanisms in individual bodies, and the only "eligible risk factors" are the "discrete, quantifiable features of individuals."[32] Thus, poverty, for instance, despite its high correlation with every sort of illness, is not eligible. There is, in fact, little attention to the larger context of pathogenic exposures, and behaviors are conceptualized as individual-level, independently modifiable, and voluntary lifestyle choices. Prevention is therefore directed to the promotion of healthy lifestyles of personal care and attention. Rather than holistic, then, lifestyle theory is of a piece with the reductionist, mechanism-oriented biomedical model. Risk factors defined in these terms fit smoothly with both the promise of drug therapy and, because the risk levels can be quantified, routine medical practice.[33] In lifestyle theory, a new public health was joined to the mainstream approach in medicine with but the barest reference to holistic context.[34]

Social medicine approaches have not disappeared and have, in fact, been developed and extended to a broader range of issues and forms of inequality. Over the past two decades, an especially prominent expression has been the "social determinants of health" framework.[35] Like earlier social medicine approaches, it is based on the tenet that the social patterning of health and disease cannot be explained on the basis of intrinsic characteristics—biological or behavioral—of individuals. Rather, disparities in health, to quote the World Health Organization (WHO), "arise from the societal conditions in which people are born, grow, live, work and age. . . . These include early years' experiences, education, economic status, employment and decent work, housing and environment, and effective systems of preventing and treating ill health."[36]

The social determinants perspective rose to prominence in the late 1990s when the WHO adopted its concepts and language.[37] The WHO has continued to promote this perspective. In 2008 its Commission on Social Determinants of Health released *Closing the Gap in a Generation: Health Equity through Action on the Social Determinants of Health*, a comprehensive action report to encourage the development of healthy (i.e., health-promoting) societies. And in 2011 the WHO convened a global conference, representing 125 member states and culminating in the Rio Political Declaration on Social Determinants of Health, which expressed formal political commitment to the sorts of corrective measures proposed in *Closing the Gap*.

The WHO's imprimatur has helped popularize both the term and the theory of social determinants of health, and this framework is today the primary holistic alternative to the biomedical model. There are other reasons, besides the WHO's patronage, for its influence. In particular, unlike its precursors in the 1960s and '70s, the social determinants of health perspective does not go beyond its central insight—the necessity of healing the patient's environment as well as the patient—to make sharp political and economic judgments. Relatedly, it also attends more closely to biology—it is interested in the *mechanisms whereby* poor social conditions affect the body's health, not exclusively in the conditions themselves.[38] (In both these tendencies, it is a partial return to the social medicine tradition of the mid–twentieth century.) By minimizing the political and emphasizing the physical aspects of medical holism, the framework is more broadly acceptable, not only across the political spectrum but also within the medical community itself: An emphasis on the social determinants of health may modify aspects of the biomedical model without explicitly challenging it.[39]

Challenging Reductionism

Speaking of holism can sound mystical and romantic, a yearning for a simpler time or an earnest concern for improving the art of medicine. Or it can sound reactionary and politicized, oppositional to the hard but fruitful achievements of bioscience or demanding of doctors a social role they cannot, and should not, assume. Even my brief and incomplete overview suggests that something larger is at stake. Holistic and integrative thinking, though it has taken an eclectic and uneven variety of forms, has contributed a large body of work—from stress research in the psychosocial tradition to the elucidation of complex social determinants of health in social medicine—that bears importantly on the health of individuals and communities. Some of this integrative thinking is now commonplace, of course, and taken up directly in new programs, the emerging field of global health being one example.

Furthermore, developments in the larger world make the holistic contribution more relevant than ever. Much of the current work in medical sociology and anthropology, social epidemiology, public health in the social medicine tradition, and so on makes this case. From the increasing concern with ecology, climate, agriculture, and food production to the rising cost of health care and the indeterminate payoff from intensive reliance on high technology, to the extraordinary and unexpected resurgence of infectious diseases, both new and old, we are confronted with the need for integrative, multidimensional, and environmental approaches like never before. In light of a globalized world, one-dimensional and reductionist approaches seem anachronistic. Several new areas of science potentially push in the same direction, including the growing field of systems biology, the study of epigenetics and the groundbreaking work on bidirectional gene–environment interaction, and neuroscientific findings on the plasticity of the brain in response to environmental diversity.[40] Each of these emphasizes interactivity and context: the body as historically and environmentally situated.

Throughout the twentieth century, holistic and integrative thinking was shaped by crises in society and discontents in and with medical practice. These too have contemporary expressions. The popular dissatisfaction that George Engel saw creating a crisis in medicine in the 1970s remains strong, a paradoxical skepticism about technological progress is pervasive, and the use of so-called complementary and alternative medicine is widespread. Critics observe that even as medical capabilities have become more sophisticated, health disparities have grown wider.[41] Humanistic physicians challenge enthusiastic talk of "personalized medicine" (prevention and treatment based on individual genetic susceptibilities), "comparative effectiveness research," and "evidence-based medicine" for yet again touting technology and a rationalized, quantitative, algorithmic logic to displace clinical judgment.[42] And on it goes, with complaints and a sense of crisis at every turn.

Despite these and other developments, which have made holistic conceptualizations more urgent for clinical practice and public health, the hold of the reductionist biomedical model remains firm and the obstacles to reforming it remain formidable. Especially in elite practice and basic medical science there has been a muscular reassertion of the model in the name of a more rigorous science. I have characterized holism in its various forms as oppositional to reductionism, and it is, but the reverse is also true. The biomedical model is central to the canonical story of medical progress from its pre-scientific past to its benevolent present and open future. Holistic reservations and alternative models can represent challenges to this story and, when not simply ignored, have often been met with serious resistance. Not all of this reaction is misplaced, of course; it can be part of a necessary negotiation, as I noted at the outset. But we are again living in a moment of antagonism. We have to begin by asking how we got here.

Part I: Reductionist Medicine in Cultural Context

The persistence of reductionism is typically explained as a basic requirement of good science. The physicalist ontology and reductionist logic of the biomedical model simply are how good science is done and genuine medical progress secured. But in chapter 1, I explore another appeal of reductionism that is only tangentially related to scientific productivity or therapeutic success, or to the current and increasingly insistent bureaucratic imperatives of commensurability, impersonality, and control that depend on a specific-entity, mechanism-oriented approach. The reductionist biomedical model, I argue, has a *cultural* authority that shapes the social positioning of medicine and gives it, as several other chapters further develop, an increasingly important moral role in contemporary liberal society. I trace the origins of this role to two sources: first the humanitarian impulse that made the relief of suffering, and the fostering of self-determination, foundational to natural science from its roots in the seventeenth century, and second the physicalism, enshrined in the biomedical model, that imbues medicine with its putative objectivity and moral neutrality. The open-ended humanitarian commitment trumps alternative moral frameworks, while the physicalism and putative neutrality allow reductionist medicine to itself become an "objective" basis for social and moral judgments. This moral role, added to the demands of bureaucratic health care delivery, commercial pressures, and the generalized orientation of natural science, greatly complicates the adoption of alternative approaches that are less technological and more integrated and socially oriented.

I also explore some of the "appropriations and dispossessions" of the biomedical model. Rather than answers to existential questions, I argue, the specific disease model provides an account that explains problematic experience, validates it as real with a somatic etiology, legitimates intervention, and reduces implications of moral culpability. All these features are in evidence, as Christina Simko shows in chapter 2, in the new genre of depression memoirs. Most authors of these memoirs draw upon the biomedical model to explain their experiences. They attest to the power of an amoral conceptualization of disease to decrease or neutralize moral responsibility (though questions of responsibility remain and reassert themselves[43]). It is partly that power, paradoxically, which makes the self-adoption of the reductionist biomedical approach so appealing.

The model offers an account that can bring assurance that something is "really" wrong, along with a sense of control. But it cannot address questions of personal transformation or theodicy. Nor, it is important to note, can it fully suppress these questions. While some reject the reductionist account, others embrace it, at least in part, even as they struggle to resist its implicit determinism. Talk of somatic etiologies, Simko finds, cannot address our larger, holistic need to find some meaning in suffering. The memoirists draw on other traditions and resources (or what's left of them), and these larger frameworks can represent a challenge to the biomedical model. At a minimum, these accounts provide narrative models of working not only "with" and "through" but also "around" the biomedical model, and they contradict the facile line, implicit in the model and further encouraged by pharmaceutical advertising, that existential issues are irrelevant.

In my discussion of the appropriations and dispossessions of the biomedical model, I also explore some reasons why medicine is ineffective in setting limits on its own expansion. Medicalization—the redefinition and treatment of problems previously outside the jurisdiction of medicine in a medical framework—typically begins with some sort of problem and is legitimated within the conventional framework of treating disease, remedying a deficit, easing pain, and the like.[44] Its end or telos, in other words, is the relief of some felt suffering or disability. But there are uses of medical technology that have as their end cultural concerns with furthering self-determination. Some aspects of dermatology and reproductive, cosmetic, and sports medicine, for example, involve technologies that are directed to healthy people. The frontier in the development of such technologies, as Luis E. Echarte argues in chapter 3, is in the exploding field of neuroscience. Existing and emerging "neurotechnologies"—psychoactive medications, functional brain imaging, cerebral stimulation, and others—are creating new abilities to alter brain function. Whatever uses they might have for treating disease and disability, these technologies also open up other possibilities, including "quality of life" interventions with respect to mood, libido, sleep, cognitive functioning, and more.

Although bioethical discussion of these nontherapeutic interventions typically classes them together as "neurocognitive enhancements," Echarte distinguishes between enhancement and cosmetic uses. Enhancement, he argues, retains at least in theory a sense of objective improvement: "better" study or sleep or mood. Cosmetic uses, on the other hand, move even further away from any sort of objective problem. They are governed by the desires of individuals pursuing their self-defined interests and goals. The distinction is valuable because most actual cases of "enhancement," by intention or by effect, are probably cosmetic. Driving the bioethical promotion of these nontherapeutic interventions, Echarte argues, is an ever more vigorous reduction of mind to brain (and body to machine) and a nearly unqualified assertion of patient autonomy. Paradoxically, neuroscientific reductionism and libertarian individualism, while consistent with the biomedical model, also constitute a challenge to it. Should these interventions be justified without some recourse to the rhetoric of suffering, they move away from the model entirely and, despite the scientific trappings, introduce a deep subjectivism that leaves psychiatry ever more captive to popular trends.

The growing role of individual preferences and judgments in medicine is also being driven by consumer culture. Echarte does not discuss the question of payment for enhancement/cosmetic uses of medicine, but an important part of the drive to medicalize everyday life problems is commercial and activist pressure. The treatment specificity in the biomedical model, as I note in chapter 1, has meant that patient response to pharmaceuticals has played an important role in the very definition of disease and disorder categories. Pharmaceutical and device manufacturers' promotion efforts—an intricate network of advertising, scientific publication plans, continuing education courses, and much more—has also led to a vast increase in diagnoses and sales. For instance, drugs for recently medicalized conditions and risk factors—social phobia, erectile dysfunction, elevated cholesterol—now generate billions in sales. Lay advocacy groups, often working hand-in-hand with companies, as noted by Robert Dingwall in chapter 4, lobby for new conditions, treatments, research funding, and the like, on precisely the ontological terms of the biomedical model. Part of what is at stake is legitimacy and with it payment through insurance schemes, public and private.[45]

Holistic critics have long argued against viewing medical care as simply a series of market transactions. Rather, it must be seen, as Dingwall depicts it in chapter 4, in terms of "mutual obligation" and "burden sharing" within the larger community. While before World War II, medicine was provided on a market model in the United Kingdom (and the United States), a mutual obligation model, Dingwall argues, informed the system established by the National Health Service after the war. Then, in both the United Kingdom and the United States in the 1960s, activist movements for patient autonomy and self-determination began to establish a new kind of consumer rhetoric. Later, and also in light of financial crises and new economic thinking, the structures for the provision of medical care were revised. These structures are highly individualized and driven by patient choice. This health consumerism, framed in terms of rights rather than mutual obligation, is synergistic with the reductionist biomedical model, and like the model is appealing because it suppresses the moral and collective dimensions of medicine.

Questions of responsibility and dependency, however, do not disappear, as many other chapters in this book also demonstrate. Drawing out implications of Talcott Parson's famous analysis of the conditional legitimacy of the sick role, Dingwall argues that the dilemmas of dependency cannot be "legislated away." Because there are financial costs and other goods at issue, the problem of constraints on individual preferences and entitlements is not eliminated by the state's adoption of a consumerist orientation. Rather it is relocated, making other stakeholders adjudicate the legitimacy of claims for care and support. The obdurate moral and collective dimensions of medicine challenge the consumer vision of the patient and suggest that a viable model of medical provision must reincorporate an understanding of mutual obligation.

Part II: Reductionist Medicine and the Disease Burden

Part I explores why reductionist medicine has been drawn deeply into key cultural priorities and projects and identifies some of the resulting paradoxes and potential openings for more holistic approaches. Part II proceeds in a similar manner, examining changes in the burden of disease and disorder, the reductionistic and individualistic medical response to them, and some possibilities for moving in a more socially integrated direction.

In the first instance, as Anne Hardy reminds us in chapter 5, the dominant regime is now one of chronic illness and diseases of aging and degeneration. Chronic illness has meant a critical shift of resources toward care and management, amidst growing economic constraints. At the same time, the absence of new curative therapeutics in recent decades has brought a return to prevention. State policy has accordingly shifted, Hardy argues, toward a new regime of disease management. While the return to a prevention strategy represents a return to the historical norm, it is now conducted through the medium of individual lifestyles. It is thus limited in all but the most extreme circumstances to steps, from tax policy to the promotion of a health-focused subjectivity, that urge or pressure individuals to change how they live. Paradoxically, even in the more holistic context of prevention, which necessarily directs our attention to a wider context, disease remains an individual problem just as in the biomedical model, abstracted from the pathogenic aspects of particular social, physical, and economic environments.

The synergy of biomedicine and the lifestyle approach, already robust, is growing even stronger, Deborah Lupton argues in chapter 6, as health promotion and preventive medicine are increasingly joined to new technologies. Like Anne Hardy, Lupton discusses the important holistic, social medicine movements of earlier decades, such as "the new public health" and social epidemiology, that emerged to challenge the individualistic approach to prevention and health promotion. These movements, as noted earlier, have not disappeared; Hardy even describes the social determinants of health as "big epidemiological business." However, Lupton observes, a changed economic and political climate has brought a renewed emphasis on individual lifestyle and personal responsibility, irrespective of social circumstances. The lifestyle approach is being transformed and accelerated with the deployment of new interactive digital technologies for health communication and with devices—wearable, implantable, even ingestible—for measuring and monitoring the body.

Health promotion endeavors, public and private, Lupton argues, have embraced digital technologies for several strategic reasons. The most important concerns are reducing costs by increased health attentiveness and prevention efforts on the part of individuals and generating new data that might contribute to health gains. The data come from amassing people's interactions with digital technologies. The accumulated information on exercise, consumption habits, biometric readings, medical treatments, illnesses, and other experience could potentially be used to identify at-risk groups, track infectious disease outbreaks, improve health services, generate predictive patterns and new risk factors, and so on. As with other promotions directed at lifestyle, the new technologies represent tools for fostering a new subjectivity. Neither Lupton nor Hardy uses the term, but it is a kind of "biomedical subjectivity."[46] Individuals, as Lupton notes, are incited to make health their top priority, conceive of themselves and their bodies in reductionist and objectivized terms, continually monitor their bodily functions, stay aware of and manage their susceptibility to illness, and keep informed of the latest developments. While the aim is generally to encourage self-surveillance, the new digital technologies also make possible new kinds of social pressure on those targeted as at risk. And yet again, because the technologies and their effects are assumed to be neutral and objective, the moral, political, and ethical are suppressed.

Another critical shift in the disease burden, also noted by Hardy, is the dramatic and totally unanticipated return of infectious diseases. If the shift to prevention in health promotion is incongruous with the relentless optimism about medicine's power to control nature, even more so is the outbreak of infectious diseases, both new (such as HIV/AIDS) and old (such as tuberculosis). In fact, as Jon Arrizabalaga argues in chapter 7, our confidence in technological success has, paradoxically, delayed effective responses to these new and incurable killers. However, several decades into the era of "(re)emerging diseases," the profound threat they represent is challenging the biomedical model by forcing attention to the complex local and global human factors—urban concentration, industrial use of new biotechnologies, land use and food production, migration, and so on—that are critical to the origins, spread, and response to these diseases. There is now some movement away from universalistic and one-dimensional biomedical approaches. Still, the global burden of these diseases is highly unequal, and their spread goes largely unchecked in many parts of the world. A more comprehensive, integrative, and holistic approach to infectious disease is urgently needed, one which fully recognizes, as Arrizabalaga writes, that "epidemics are social as much as biological events." Infectious disease, whose control has been biomedicine's greatest success, has returned as one of its greatest challenges.

Our time of chronic illness and (re)emerging diseases draws our attention to the relationships between pathology and particular social practices and arrangements. In chapter 8, Bruce K. Alexander explores the rapidly proliferating number of new addictions—compulsive and destructive pursuits that encompass far more than the traditional categories of excessive drinking and recreational drug use. In the "official" paradigm of addiction, based on the biomedical model, the disease of addiction is limited to alcohol and various drugs, treated as a chronic problem of individuals, and designated as a failure of personal agency. Various theories have been proposed over the years to explain the disease, with the current etiology conceived in terms of brain mechanisms. Though the history of treatment is poor, therapeutic optimism has been and remains high—successful intervention is only a matter of time.

Against this specific entity model, Alexander argues, stand new forms of addiction—gambling, consumption, Internet games, and much more—that implicate social breakdown itself as pathogenic. And, he believes, the many new forms of addiction are finally undermining the scientifically untenable and implicitly moralistic official view and opening a space for the emergence of a more holistic and social conceptualization of addiction. His "dislocation theory" does not concentrate on single individuals or inevitable chronicity, though it allows for genetic and other personal differences. The etiology of addiction, rather, is located in the stress of profound and dislocating social transformations, and its incidence and outcomes vary with the relative obstacles to social reconnection. The medicalization of addiction is being undermined, according to Alexander, by the inability of the specific disease model to contain it.

Part III: The Need for a More Holistic Ethical Discourse

We argue in this book that matters of morality and value are inescapable for medicine as a human practice and as a social institution. Too often such matters remain implicit, and in going unspoken they sustain the notion that medicine is value-free. This is clear in all the chapters of part I. In part II, Lupton shows how prevention focused on individuals, where risk is defined in terms of decontextualized habits and individual choices, becomes the source for introducing attributions of moral failure that biomedicine supposedly banishes. Similarly, as Arrizabalaga and Alexander emphasize, AIDS and addiction are fraught with value judgments, despite their framing within biomedical discourse. Further, parts I and II argue that the individualized biomedical framework obscures both the role of social structures and inequality in creating the conditions for problems to arise, and the role that structural change might play in ameliorating them. While there are important challenges to this regime, as the chapters have also stressed, the need for a more holistic ethical reflection on medicine is more urgent than ever. Part III takes up this issue.

Since the 1960s, a new field, bioethics, has arisen to carry on that reflection and articulate ethical standards for guiding medicine and medical research.[47] According to John H. Evans in chapter 9, bioethics initially represented a challenge to reductionist medicine: It was critical of medicalization, such as in reproductive and genetic medicine; it offered a holistic and socially oriented framework for making substantive critiques; and it had some institutional homes that were outside medicine. While important aspects of this work continue, the challenge represented by the field itself, argues Evans, "ended . . . nearly as soon as it started."

The story Evans tells is one of an opportunity missed. The dominant framework that has come to guide bioethics, and that has been institutionalized in the administration of medicine and research with human subjects, is an ethical system known as principlism. This system, Evans argues, cannot challenge reductionist medicine, despite its typically holistic-sounding talk. If briefly an outsider, bioethics has since been absorbed as a subsidiary to medicine; it has few free-standing institutional centers and little professional independence. Its four principles are relatively noncontroversial because they either articulate goals already integral to medicine—such as the relief of suffering and avoidance of harm (beneficence, nonmaleficence)—or possess little specific content (autonomy, justice). Their primary appeal is that they function as easy-to-apply procedural rules in centralized, bureaucratic, and regulatory settings. While this rationalizing and managing role is not a trivial one, its ethical minimalism provides no grounds for resistance to the extension of medicine into new areas and, significantly, supplants alternative, more substantive critiques that do. For this reason, bioethics serves, paradoxically, as a driver rather than restrainer of medicalization. Only through a "severing of the symbiotic relationship" with medicine might bioethics once again constitute a challenge.

If anything, Jeffrey P. Bishop suggests in chapter 10 an even more symbiotic relationship between bioethics and biomedicine. He begins with the early critiques of reductionist medicine by the mid-twentieth-century theologians Joseph Fletcher, Paul Ramsey, and Richard Mc-Cormick. Their theologically grounded treatments of ethical dilemmas in medicine initially worked from an ontology and teleology that were radically different from those of biomedicine. But, in an attempt to gain a hearing, Bishop argues, they became less oppositional, speaking a "thinner" language, one less challenging of the fundamental assumptions of biomedicine. At the same time, as Evans in chapter 9 also notes, concerted efforts were made by scientists to marginalize these critical theological voices. To fill the resulting void, and in terms acceptable to both government agencies and the research and medical establishment, philosophers created common morality theories, the most successful of which was principlism. Thus in Bishop's reading, principlism was from the beginning synergistic with the ontological commitments and ends of biomedicine; principlist bioethics attends to the efficiency and effectiveness of means but always within the ambit of biomedicine's frames of reference.

Furthermore, Bishop argues, subsequent holistic efforts, drawing upon the social sciences (such as the biopsychosocial model) and the humanities (e.g., narrative medicine), have attempted to reform and "humanize" the clinical practice of medicine. These efforts, however, have not challenged biomedicine's fundamental premises but, if anything, extended them. In Bishop's view, there are still some who offer richer, holistic critiques, but only on the margins of the field. If bioethics is ever to work as a strong counterbalancing force to reductionist approaches, it must recover an ethics that challenges the mechanistic, "fix" orientation rather than reproduces it.

Even if, as Evans and Bishop argue, bioethics as currently constituted does not represent a challenge to reductionist medicine, it does represent an opportunity. As Evans briefly mentions, new developments in medicine must now pass through a public ethical analysis. If, as seems to happen now, nothing technologically possible and allowably safe ever gets rejected by this process, the process itself still might be important. The very fact of bioethics, the fact that scientists and doctors do not fully control the ethics of science and medicine, opens a space for reflection that might not otherwise exist. And, as Bishop suggests, and this book seeks to foster, making the implicit ontological and moral commitments of biomedicine more transparent is an important first step.

We need a richer reflection on the human good and the place of health in a well-lived life and a good society. As this book documents, powerful and accelerating trends in modern society, influencing and influenced by medicine, contribute to the "naturalization" of the ethical dimension of life, putatively replacing a moral register with an organic one. There are pragmatic advantages to this naturalization. The "fix" orientation is attractive at the personal level, for deflecting guilt and stigma; at the social level, for avoiding controversy and public debate; and at the political level, because adapting individuals to their social environment is far easier than the other way around. As the criminologist Barbara Wootton once observed: "Always it is easier to put up a clinic than to pull down a slum."[48] Yet, as Ana Marta González shows in chapter 11, conflating ethical questions with health questions creates serious problems.

To reduce questions of the good to the healthy, González argues, is to efface questions of justice, inequality, rights, and the common good and remove them from the public sphere. Naturalizing the good risks turning health into an ideology that can justify inequality—always the danger of naturalizing discourses—and, "precisely because it easily excites our approval," legitimate the ruthless enforcement of narrow standards of normality. "Health" provides no grounds for dissent or appeal, and biomedical reductionism and individualism distort the nature and complexity of human experience. Similarly, González observes, the terms of proper care and the allocation of health resources require notions of justice and the common good, including on a global level, which cannot be found in the naturalist framework. Avoiding controversy and debate does not justify naturalization. Ethical questions, she argues, "need to be addressed in ethical terms." The good that is health, in the polity and in a meaningful life, can be understood only within the context of reflection on the human good as such.

Conclusion

Biomedicine's individualistic and reductionist orientation is pervasive and culturally powerful, the repository of some of modernity's most fervent hopes. But it is not absolute or monolithic. This book analyzes real-world developments and explores failed responses that show, we argue, the insufficiency of the biomedical model on its own. They show the need for balancing and countervailing values, practices, and institutions that can limit the model's practical, theoretical, and ideological reach. They show, in brief, the urgent need for a richer, holistic orientation, and in my Conclusion to the book I trace out the arguments and the critical implications of the book for moving further in this direction. There are no assured paths; time and again, the biomedical paradigm has demonstrated its power to marginalize or co-opt alternative visions, and the reductionist project is now tightly interwoven with both bureaucratic organization and many aspects of contemporary life and culture. We have no illusions. At the same time, we are not without traditions of thought and research on which to build. In fact, some are available in the very fields—medicine, bioethics, and public health—that are the subject of much of our critique. In all these fields, retrieving the neglected, the marginalized, and the half-forgotten is the place to begin.

NOTES

1 See Joseph E. Davis, "Reductionist Medicine and Its Cultural Authority," chapter 1, this volume.

2 It is not just patients who are dissatisfied and alienated. A number of recent books by physicians chronicle deep disillusionment. See, for example, Sandeep Jauhar, *Doctored: The Disillusionment of an American Physician* (New York: Farrar, Straus & Giroux, 2014) and Danielle Ofri, *What Doctors Feel: How Emotions Affect the Practice of Medicine* (Boston: Beacon Press, 2013).

3 Paul A. Cantor, *The Invisible Hand in Popular Culture* (Lexington: University Press of Kentucky, 2012), chapter 10.

4 Christopher Lawrence and George Weisz, "Medical Holism: The Context," in Lawrence and Weisz, eds., *Greater than the Parts: Holism in Biomedicine, 1920–1950* (Oxford: Oxford University Press, 1998), 1–22, at 2.

5 See, for example, Matthew Schneirov and Jonathan David Geczik, *A Diagnosis for Our Times: Alternative Health, from Lifeworld to Politics* (Albany: SUNY Press, 2003).

6 Lawrence and Weisz, "Medical Holism"; Charles E. Rosenberg, "Holism in Twentieth-Century Medicine," in *Greater than the Parts,* 335–55. Further historical

treatments are identified in the notes that follow. *The Oxford Companion to Medicine* (Third Edition), edited by Stephen Lock, John M. Last, and George Dunea (New York: Oxford University Press, 2001), offers this definition of "holistic medicine": "a doctrine of preventive and therapeutic medicine which emphasizes the importance of regarding the individual as a whole being integral with his social, cultural, and environmental context rather than as a patient with isolated malfunction of a particular system or organ." Online at: http://www.oxfordreference.com/view/10.1093/acref/9780192629500.001.0001/acref-9780192629500.

7 See, among a large literature, Elliot G. Mishler, "Viewpoint: Critical Perspectives on the Biomedical Model," in Elliot G. Mishler, et al., eds., *Social Contexts of Health, Illness, and Patient Care* (Cambridge: Cambridge University Press, 1981), 1–23; Margaret Lock and Deborah R. Gordon, eds., *Biomedicine Examined* (Dordrecht: Kluwer Academic Publishers, 1988); Nancy Krieger, *Epidemiology and the People's Health: Theory and Context* (Oxford: Oxford University Press, 2011), chapter 5; Regula Valérie Burri and Joseph Dumit, *Biomedicine as Culture: Instrumental Practices, Technoscientific Knowledge, and New Modes of Life* (New York: Routledge, 2007); and George L. Engel, "The Need for a New Medical Model: A Challenge for Biomedicine," *Science* 196 (1977): 129–36.

8 Charles E. Rosenberg, *Our Present Complaint: American Medicine, Then and Now* (Baltimore: Johns Hopkins University Press, 2007), 49.

9 Rudolf Karl Virchow, "Report on the Typhus Epidemic in Upper Silesia," *American Journal of Public Health* 96, 12 (December 2006): 2102–105. Excerpted from Virchow, *Archiv für pathologische Anatomie und Physiologie und für klinische Medicin*, Volume 2 (Berlin: George Reimer, 1848), 143–332. On nineteenth-century holism, see R. Taylor and A. Rieger, "Medicine as Social Science: Rudolf Virchow on the Typhus Epidemic in Upper Silesia," *International Journal of Health Services* 15, 4 (1985): 547–59; Ian F. McNeely, *"Medicine on a Grand Scale": Rudolf Virchow, Liberalism, and the Public Health* (London: Wellcome Trust Centre, 2002).

10 Lawrence and Weisz, "Medical Holism," 2.

11 See Jack D. Pressman, "Human Understanding: Psychosomatic Medicine and the Mission of the Rockefeller Foundation," in Lawrence and Weisz, eds., *Greater than the Parts*, 189–208; and Elin L. Wolfe, A. Clifford Barger, and Saul Benison, *Walter B. Cannon, Science and Society* (Cambridge, Mass.: Harvard University Press, 2000).

12 Allan Young, "Walter Cannon and the Psychophysiology of Fear," in Lawrence and Weisz, eds., *Greater than the Parts*, 234–56. Also see Russell Viner, "Putting Stress in Life: Hans Selye and the Making of Stress Theory," *Social Studies of Science* 29, 3 (June 1999): 391–410; and Rhodri Hayward, "The Invention of the Psychosocial: An Introduction," *History of the Human Sciences* 25, 5 (2012), 3–12.

13 George L. Engel, "The Need for a New Medical Model: A Challenge for Biomedicine," *Science* 196: 4286 (April 8, 1977), 133. Also see his further elaboration in George L. Engel, "The Clinical Application of the Biopsychosocial Model," *American Journal of Psychiatry* (1980) 137: 535–44.

14 Engel had already been writing in this general vein for twenty years. But something new was clearly in the air, for he suddenly got a hearing. His 1977 paper "The

Need for a New Medical Model" was widely discussed across many medical special-
ties, particularly psychiatry, and cited in the literature thousands of times. According
to the historian Edward Shorter, "It placed the biopsychosocial model firmly on the
undergraduate teaching agenda of the world's medical schools and on the educational
programme of residency training in psychiatry in many places" (Edward Shorter,
"The History of the Biopsychosocial Approach in Medicine: Before and After Engel,"
in Peter White, ed., *Biopsychosocial Medicine: An Integrated Approach to Understanding Illness* [New York: Oxford University Press, 2005], 1–19, at 6). Further, it inspired
humanities programs in medical schools and has been important in bioethics, nursing,
and other disciplines. It has been criticized for an overly expansionist view of medicine. See Jeffrey P. Bishop, "The Dominion of Medicine: Bioethics, the Human Sciences, and the Humanities," chapter 10, this volume.

15 According to two prominent psychiatrists, for example, "*DSM-III* was a landmark in the development of psychiatric classification, drawing on the best available
research from the preceding decades and placing psychiatry firmly back in the medical
model of basing treatment decisions on diagnosis." Deborah Blacker and Ming T. Tsu-
ang, "Classification and DSM-IV," in Armand M. Nicholi Jr., ed., *The Harvard Guide
to Psychiatry*, Third Edition (Cambridge, Mass.: Belknap Press of Harvard University
Press, 1999), 65–73, at 70.

16 Steven S. Sharfstein, "Big Pharma and American Psychiatry: The Good, the Bad,
and the Ugly," *Psychiatric News* (August 19, 2005), 3.

17 Michael Marmot, *The Status Syndrome: How Social Standing Affects Our
Health and Longevity* (New York: Times Books/Henry Holt, 2004). Also see Richard
G. Wilkinson, *The Impact of Inequality: How to Make Sick Societies Healthier* (New
York: New Press, 2005). On the sociology of stress, especially research building on the
pioneering work of Leonard Pearlin, see William R. Avison and Stephanie S. Thomas,
"Stress," in William C. Cockerham, ed., *The New Blackwell Companion to Medical
Sociology* (Malden, Mass.: Blackwell, 2010), 242–67.

18 Quoted in Henry Ernest Sigerist, *Medicine and Human Welfare* (New Haven,
Conn.: Yale University Press, 1941), 93. For accounts of social medicine in its proponents' own words, see Edgar Sydenstricker, *Health and the Environment* (New York:
McGraw-Hill, 1933); George Rosen, "What Is Social Medicine? A Genetic Analysis
of the Concept," *Bulletin of the History of Medicine* 21, 5 (1947): 674–733; and Iago
Galdston, ed., *Social Medicine: Its Derivations and Objectives* (New York: Common-
wealth Fund, 1949).

19 Indeed, smoking in 1962 was more a population-wide than an individual problem, and "Smoking and Health" proposed *political* solutions to the problem: increased
taxes on tobacco products, restriction of sales, and a nationwide education campaign.

20 See Jerry Morris, *Uses of Epidemiology* (Edinburgh: Livingston, 1957); George
Davey Smith, "The Uses of 'Uses of Epidemiology,'" *The International Journal of Epidemiology* (2001) 30 (5): 1146–155.

21 Krieger, *Epidemiology and the People's Health*, 169.

22 See Davis, chapter 1, this volume; Lawrence and Weisz, "Medical Holism," 17.

23 Allan M. Brandt and Martha Gardner, "Antagonism and Accommodation: Interpreting the Relationship Between Public Health and Medicine in the United States During the 20th Century," *American Journal of Public Health* 90 (2000): 707–15.

24 Thomas McKeown, *The Role of Medicine: Dream, Mirage or Nemesis?* (London: Nuffield Provincial Hospitals Trust, 1976). For an earlier and influential treatment in this vein, see René and Jean Dubos, *The White Plague: Tuberculosis, Man and Society* (Boston: Little, Brown, 1952); and René Dubos, *Mirage of Health: Utopias, Progress, and Biological Change* (New York: Harper & Brothers, 1959). For challenges to McKeown's use of data, see Johan P. Mackenbach, "The Contribution of Medical Care to Mortality Decline: McKeown Revisited," *Journal of Clinical Epidemiology* 49 (1996): 1207–213; and John P. Bunker, "The Role of Medical Care in Contributing to Health Improvements within Societies," *International Journal of Epidemiology* 30 (2001): 1260–63.

25 See, for example, Ivan Illich, *Medical Nemesis: The Expropriation of Health* (New York: Pantheon, 1976); Irving K. Zola, "Medicine as an Institution of Social Control," *Sociological Review* 20 (1972): 487–504; and Michel Foucault, *The Birth of the Clinic: An Archaeology of Medical Perception* (New York: Pantheon, 1973). For an overview, see Joseph E. Davis, "Ivan Illich and Irving Kenneth Zola: Disabling Medicalization," in Fran Collyer, ed., *The Palgrave Handbook of Social Theory in Health, Illness and Medicine* (New York: Palgrave Macmillan, 2015), 306–23.

26 For example, Barbara Ehrenreich and Deirdre English, *Complaints and Disorders: The Sexual Politics of Sickness* (New York: Feminist Press, 1973); and Ellen Frankfort, *Vaginal Politics* (New York: Quadrangle, 1972).

27 See, for example, Stanley J. Reiser, *Medicine and the Reign of Technology* (New York: Cambridge University Press, 1978); Paul Ramsey, *The Patient as Person* (New Haven, Conn.: Yale University Press, 1970); and Eric J. Cassell, *The Healer's Art* (New York: Penguin, 1976).

28 See, for example, Lesley Doyal, with Imogen Pennell, *The Political Economy of Health* (London: Pluto Press, 1979); Vicente Navarro, *Medicine Under Capitalism* (New York: Prodist, 1976); Howard Waitzkin and Barbara Waterman, *Exploitation of Illness in Capitalist Society* (Indianapolis: Bobbs-Merrill, 1974); and Deborah Lupton, chapter 6, this volume.

29 Krieger, *Epidemiology and the People's Health*, 172.

30 See the discussion of this transition in Anne Hardy, chapter 5, this volume.

31 Robert A. Aronowitz, *Making Sense of Illness: Science, Society, and Disease* (Cambridge: Cambridge University Press, 1999), 112.

32 Ibid., 18.

33 Ibid., 127.

34 Aronowitz, *Making Sense of Illness*; Krieger, *Epidemiology and the People's Health*; and William G. Rothstein, *Public Health and the Risk Factor: A History of an Uneven Medical Revolution* (Rochester, N.Y.: University of Rochester Press, 2003).

35 Other related frameworks include the population health perspective and the "fundamental-cause theory of health inequalities." See, respectively, Robert G. Evans, Morris L. Barer, and Theodore R. Marmor, eds., *Why Are Some People Healthy and*

Others Not? The Determinants of Health of Populations (New York: Aldine de Gruyter, 1994); and Bruce Link and Jo Phelan, "Social Conditions as Fundamental Causes of Health Inequalities," 3–17 in *Handbook of Medical Sociology*, Sixth Edition, edited by Chloe E. Bird et al. (Nashville: Vanderbilt University Press, 2010).

36 World Health Organization, World Conference on Social Determinants of Health, "Rio Political Declaration on Social Determinants of Health" (Rio de Janeiro, October 2011), 2. http://www.who.int/entity/sdhconference/declaration/Rio_political_declaration.pdf?ua=1 (accessed May 13, 2014).

37 Richard Wilkinson and Michael Marmot, eds., *Social Determinants of Health: The Solid Facts*, Second Edition (Geneva: World Health Organization, 2003).

38 See Krieger, *Epidemiology and the People's Health*, 180–84. For more on the social determinants of health, see Harold J. Cook, Sanjoy Bhattacharya, and Anne Hardy, eds., *History of the Social Determinants of Health: Global Histories, Contemporary Debates* (Hyderabad, India: Orient Black Swan, 2008); Mel Bartley, *Health Inequality: An Introduction to Concepts, Theories and Methods* (Cambridge: Polity Press, 2004); and Ichiro Kawachi and Bruce Kennedy, *The Health of Nations: Why Inequality Is Harmful to Your Health* (New York: New Press, 2002).

39 For further reading on the history of medical holism in the twentieth century, see generally Dorothy Porter and Roy Porter, eds., *Doctors, Politics and Society: Historical Essays* (Amsterdam: Editions Rodopi, 1993); Dorothy Porter, ed., *Social Medicine and Medical Sociology in the Twentieth Century* (Amsterdam: Editions Rodopi, 1997); and Dorothy Porter, ed., *The History of Public Health and the Modern State* (Amsterdam: Editions Rodopi, 1994).

40 See, for example, Mary Jane West-Eberhard, *Developmental Plasticity and Evolution* (New York: Oxford University Press, 2003); and Evelyn Fox Keller, *The Century of the Gene* (Cambridge, Mass.: Harvard University Press, 2000).

41 Brandt and Gardner, "Antagonism and Accommodation," 713.

42 See, for example, Wylie Burke and Bruce M. Psaty, "Personalized Medicine in the Era of Genomics," *Journal of the American Medical Association* 298, 14 (2007): 1682–84; and Mark D. Neuman and Charles L. Bosk, "Medicine and the Radiant City," *The Lancet* 381 (2013): 1176–77.

43 For instance, Simko found that the pursuit of meaning and purpose in the memoirists' experience introduces their own agency and decisions, and one of the messages of their books is how they sought professional help and embraced the arduous task of self-reconstruction, a task that even very positive responses to medication did not eliminate.

44 See, generally, Peter Conrad, *The Medicalization of Society: On the Transformation of Human Conditions into Treatable Disorders* (Baltimore: Johns Hopkins University Press, 2007); Joseph E. Davis, "Medicalization, Social Control, and the Relief of Suffering," in William C. Cockerham, ed., *The New Blackwell Companion to Medical Sociology* (Malden, Mass.: Blackwell, 2010), 211–41.

45 See, for example, Aronowitz, *Making Sense of Illness*, chapter 1; Conrad, *The Medicalization of Society*, chapter 3; and Paul Rabinow, *French DNA: Trouble in Purgatory* (Chicago: University of Chicago Press, 1999).

46 Various concepts have been used to describe new subjectivities characterized by greater reflexivity, activism, and expertise, and by changed relations to the body, health, and medical authorities. See, for example, Nikolas Rose and Carlos Novas, "Biological Citizenship," in Aihwa Ong and Stephen J. Collier, eds., *Global Assemblages: Technology, Politics, and Ethics as Anthropological Problems* (Malden, Mass.: Blackwell, 2005), 439–63; Nick Fox and Katie Ward, "Health Identities: From Expert Patient to Resisting Consumer," *Health* 10 (2006): 461–79; and Deborah Lupton, *The Imperative of Health: Public Health and the Regulated Body* (London: Sage, 1995).

47 On bioethics, generally, see Jennifer K. Walter and Eran P. Klein, eds., *The Story of Bioethics: From Seminal Works to Contemporary Explorations* (Washington: Georgetown University Press, 2003). More critically, see Raymond DeVries and Janardan Subedi, eds., *Bioethics and Society: Constructing the Ethical Enterprise* (Upper Saddle River, N.J.: Prentice Hall, 1998); and Anne Maclean, *The Elimination of Morality: Reflections on Utilitarianism and Bioethics* (New York: Routledge, 1993). Also see John H. Evans, chapter 9, this volume; and Jeffrey P. Bishop, chapter 10, this volume.

48 Barbara Wootton, *Social Science and Social Pathology* (London: Allen and Unwin, 1959), 329.

PART I

Reductionist Medicine in Cultural Context

1

Reductionist Medicine and Its Cultural Authority

JOSEPH E. DAVIS

Criticism of medicine as centered in molecular biology and technology, and prone to neglect the personal and social dimensions of health and illness, has a long history. Already in the 1880s, at the very epoch-making moment in which medicine was being reconstituted by discoveries from laboratory science, there was pushback. In early 1886, just weeks after the public announcement of a breakthrough with regard to a vaccine for rabies, *Puck*, the famous American magazine of humor and political satire, ran a panel of cartoons about medicine. One has the caption "No Time for Common Sick Folks." The drawing (see figure 1.1) shows a doctor in a lab coat leaving the bedside of a patient, hat in hand and rabbit in pocket, with the apology, "Excuse me, but I have an experiment to make."[1] In an 1899 address to the Massachusetts Medical Society, James J. Putnam observed that a concern to treat "not the disease only, but also the man" was a "familiar sentiment" among older members of the profession.[2] On and off ever since, medicine has been hailed for its extraordinary explanatory and technical successes while at the same time generating considerable discontent. Against a narrow biologism and procedure-orientation, critics have argued for more socially oriented and humanistic approaches. These holistic approaches have always run counter to the mainstream and they have seldom sustained much traction.

Why not? Why have socially oriented and integrative approaches, despite their long and continuous appeal, remained marginal? Why, to turn the question around, does medicine continue on a course characterized by reductionism, mechanism-based explanations for clinical syndromes, and heavy reliance on technological solutions, despite important reasons to change? No answer can be remotely complete, but I want to frame a general explanation by considering the powerful appeal of two enduring legacies, one from the seventeenth century and one from the nineteenth.

No Time for Common Sick Folks.
DOCTOR.—"Excuse me, but I have an experiment to make."

Figure 1.1. "No Time for Common Sick Folks. Doctor.—'Excuse me, but I have an experiment to make.'" A scene from "The Profession Gone Mad," illustration by G. E. Ciani; *Puck* 18:462 (January 13, 1886), 314 (New York: Puck Publishing Co., 1877–1918). Courtesy of the Bert Hansen Collection, New York, New York.

Each is familiar enough. Philosophers and theologians have often reflected on the implications of seventeenth-century natural philosophy, particularly the works of Francis Bacon and René Descartes, to understand the commitments of modern science and medicine. Historians more commonly concentrate on the nineteenth-century changes that joined medicine with the physical and life sciences and gave birth to a particular constellation of ideal-types—the "biomedical model"—that have structured and constrained thinking about disease and treatment ever since. The problem for integrative, holistic approaches, I hope to show, arises from these two legacies together. As interwoven with central contemporary values, these legacies have given reductionist medicine a distinct cultural authority.

This authority—the authority to "name the world"—is rooted in biological science and therapeutic optimism. Optimism is grounded, in part, in past technological success, but it is also rooted in particular modern preoccupations: the valuation of health, which has increasingly become an end in itself; the "war against all suffering," to use Ivan Illich's phrase; and the project of self-determination.[3] These preoccupations lay down powerful moral imperatives and hopes that carry over into medicine and, paradoxically, imbue medicine with an image of objectivity and moral neutrality. These imperatives, I want to suggest, help to account for both the continued assertion of the reductionist biomedical model, despite reasons to move in a more holistic direction, and for its extension over more and more areas of our lives, an extension held back only by the available technologies.

The Baconian Legacy

The story of biomedicine begins with the birth of modern science in the seventeenth century. That birth was complex and included new discoveries, such as Kepler's and Galileo's observations of the solar system; the growing sophistication of the mechanical arts and workings of complex mechanisms, such as clocks and pumps; rapid advances in mathematics; and new ideas about man and nature. The ideas, the philosophical part of the story, are particularly relevant here. Seventeenth-century natural philosophy (the precursor of natural science) articulated a revolutionary new stance toward the world, elaborated with particular clarity and influence by Frances Bacon, René Descartes, and Isaac Newton. The new stance begins from a rejection of traditional understandings of final causes, and of the universe as a hierarchy of meaningful order. It affirms an objectified conception of nature, wherein the world is no longer a locus of meaning—the reflection of the divine plan or the embodiment of the Ideas[4]—but a neutral domain capable of mechanistic explanation and, most important, prediction and instrumental manipulation.

In what might be called, following the historian Stephen Gaukroger, "Bacon's project," true knowledge is not abstract and speculative, as it was for the ancients and scholastics, but practical and useful.[5] It is painstakingly acquired through the application of systematic and disciplined analysis. This analysis is based on experiment and observation, moves from effects to causes, and seeks to discover the fundamental mechanisms and general laws by which all of nature is ordered. Its method is logical, reductionist, and rigorously empirical. Its reasoning is inductive but in a very controlled, machine-like way. As Bacon expressed the idea in a famous passage in his *New Organon*:

> Now my method, though hard to practice, is easy to explain; and it is this. I propose to establish progressive stages of certainty. The evidence of the sense, helped and guarded by a certain process of correction, I retain. But the mental operation which follows the act of sense I for the most part reject; and instead of it I open and lay out a new and certain path for the mind to proceed in, starting directly from the simple sensuous perception. . . . There remains but one course for the recovery of a sound and healthy condition [of understanding]—namely, that the entire work of the understanding be commenced afresh, and the mind itself be from the very outset not left to take its own course, but guided at every step; and the business be done as if by machinery.[6]

For Bacon, as for Descartes, the new natural philosophy begins with skepticism—the setting aside of preconceived notions—and brings knowledge of and power over nature. And for both it originates in a deep moral imperative to serve human well-being and better the human condition.

Philosophers have interpreted this moral imperative in somewhat different ways, but it includes at least two principal directives. The first is an injunction to relieve suffering and conserve health, and the second is an injunction to extend emancipation—from fate, from social constraint, from the authority of tradition—and self-determination.[7] These goals are particularly clear in the writings of Bacon and Descartes, who formulate their projects not in terms of the domination of nature but from a theological conviction that an instrumental approach to nature is required for the sake of God's glory and human benefit.[8] But even as these theological beliefs are slowly stripped away in the succeeding years, the humanitarian imperative remains, and in a sense expands, as the relief of suffering and freedom from necessity become ends in themselves and the yardstick by which every conception of order is subsequently measured.[9]

The cure of disease is integral to this enterprise from the beginning. The remediation of illness, the conserving of health, and the prolongation of life are central concerns of Bacon, especially in his later works, including *New Atlantis* (1620).[10] So too for Descartes, who in the *Discourse on the Method* (1637) observes, "It is true that the medicine currently practiced contains few things whose usefulness is so noteworthy" and that "everything known in medicine is practically nothing in comparison with what remains to be known." But he is confident that science will begin to determine the causes and uncover "all the remedies that nature has provided us" such that "one could rid oneself of an infinity of maladies, as much of the body as of the mind, and even perhaps also the frailty of old age. . . ."[11] Despite the state of actual medical practice at the time, these heady ambitions, infused with the same moral purpose, decisively shaped the emerging scientific revolution. They are, in an important sense, what made the whole effort worthwhile.

The drivers of the revolution were the societies dedicated to scientific research that began to appear in the mid–seventeenth century. The society that emerged in England, the Royal Society, was directly animated by Bacon's thinking. It grew out of informal meetings of educated men in London and Oxford in the mid-1640s who recognized, with Bacon, that the new science would be a public and collective endeavor. They called themselves an "invisible college" and met to discuss the new approach to investigating the natural world through experiment and observation. In 1660, the group, which included such leading figures as Christopher Wren and Robert Boyle, formally organized and was chartered in 1662 by Charles II as "The Royal Society of London for Improving Natural Knowledge." Its motto was "*Nullius in verba*," roughly "take nobody's word for it," a clear indicator of the break with traditional authority.[12]

Over the next century and more, the Royal Society and its journal the *Philosophical Transactions*, were the foremost institutions of experimental science in England. At its founding, most of the members were interested laymen (there were no female members until 1945), only a fraction of whom devoted themselves mainly to science.[13] Over time, the Society helped to institutionalize the scientific enterprise, and many notable British scientists (and some early American ones; Benjamin Franklin was a member) were Fellows of the Royal Society, including Newton, who was president for more than twenty years. Similar organizations, inspired by the Royal Society, sprang up subsequently in France, Germany, and elsewhere. Collectively, they had a hand in most of the inventions that produced the Industrial Revolution. Later, Fellows of the Royal Society would be instrumental in two of the first great medical breakthroughs: Edward Jenner with the smallpox vaccine (1798) and Joseph Lister with antiseptic surgery (1860s).

Shortly after the founding of the Society, one of its members, Thomas Sprat, wrote a *History of the Royal Society*. In the book, published in 1667, Sprat provides the details of the Society's founding, explains its scientific purposes, and describes some of the progress in experimental work. Heavily influenced by Bacon, whose image appears on the frontispiece, Sprat's *History* provides a good window on Baconian assumptions at work with respect to medicine. Sprat also shares Bacon's zeal for the immense and epoch-changing promise of the new natural philosophy, and his book is a bold apologia for the Society and all that it represents.

Sprat began his writing in 1664 but had to break it off because of the outbreak of the Great Plague in 1665, which was followed and partly stopped (the blaze consumed many infected rats) by the Great Fire of 1666. The Plague, an outbreak of bubonic plague, killed some 20 percent of the population of London, while the Fire destroyed as much as 80 percent of the city proper. When Sprat resumes his writing he comments on the disasters and how they have spurred him to complete his book, "because it seems to me," he writes, "that from the sad effects of these disasters, there may a new, and a powerful Argument be rais'd, to move us to double our labours, about the Secrets of Nature." He notes that the Royal Society had already been working on the improving of building materials and that the disasters should enliven "our Industry . . . to use more diligence about preventing them for the future." Although medicine had no remedies for The Plague, he is confident that with "much Inquiry" we may yet find a cure. And he concludes with a moral point that is absolutely central to the Baconian outlook: "If in such cases we only accuse the Anger of Providence, or the Cruelty of Nature: we lay the blame, where it is not justly to be laid. It ought rather to be attributed to the negligence of men themselves, that such difficult Cures are without [i.e., outside] the bounds of their reason's power."[14]

The call to action is powerful and unqualified. Sprat was a clergyman, incidentally, and the future bishop of Rochester; his comment about

Providence does not reflect any irreligion.[15] Rather, he is affirming a fervent belief in our God-given power to free ourselves from subjection to fate or necessity by gaining technological mastery over nature: No disease is necessarily incurable; no suffering or misfortune is necessarily unpreventable. At the same time, Sprat is asserting our complete and urgent responsibility to develop and use that power for human good. Passively accepting our limitations and not exercising "reason's power" to overcome them is a form of negligence. It is our positive moral obligation to engage in "much Inquiry"—the rigorous application of the scientific method—and so unlock nature's secrets and discover the means to relieve suffering and ease the burdens of finitude.

In this discussion of the disasters, Sprat asserts that because of human diligence in the past there has been some progress in medicine and "every first success of this kind, should alwayes strengthen our assurance of farther conquests," even over The Plague. Of what these successes consist, he does not say, but his optimism is clearly not fueled by past achievements. As Descartes noted, little had yet been accomplished in medicine. The optimism, rather, is grounded in the notion that all of nature is regulated by common basic mechanisms, and as these are understood so technological control will inevitably follow. Sprat argues:

> There is nothing of all the works of Nature, so inconsiderable, so remote, or so fully known; but, by being made to reflect on other things, it will at once enligten them, and shew itself the clearer. Such is the dependance amongst all the orders of creatures; the inanimate, the sensitive, the rational, the natural, the artificial: that the apprehension of one of them, is a good step towards the understanding of the rest: And this is the highest pitch of humane reason; to follow all the links of this chain, till all their secrets are open to our minds; and their works advanc'd or imitated by our hands.[16]

For Sprat, as for Bacon, Descartes, Newton, and the others, this yields a boundless ambition for a new age: "This is truly to command the world; to rank all the varieties, and degrees of things, so orderly one upon another; that standing on the top of them, we may perfectly behold all that are below, and make them all serviceable to the quiet, and peace, and plenty of Man's life."[17] Sprat is keenly aware of the scope of this ambition. With a reference to the Tower of Babel, he contrasts that disastrous affair with the ends of the new science. Here again he echoes a powerful moral idea that runs through Bacon's writings. In *New Atlantis*, for example, Bacon joins technological progress with moral progress. For the Bensalemites, the residents of his model society, great virtue is a fruit of natural philosophy (carried out according to rigorous Baconian methods).[18] That is why for Sprat the ambitions of the new science are not a repeat of Babel. The "ambition" of Babel, he says, "was manag'd with impiety, and insolence." The new project of science, on the other hand, because it is the way we serve God in creation, "is carried on by that humility and innocence, which can never be separated from true knowledg. . . ." Given this connection of true knowledge and virtue, the ambition of science is no affront to the Creator but "it must needs be the utmost perfection of humane Nature."[19]

Finally, Sprat, in delineating which matters the Society saw as its proper province, anticipates that the new science can and will extend beyond the body to the soul: the "Reason, the Understanding, the Tempers, the Will, the Passions of Men."[20] While the study of the human body comes within its purview, the Society does not discuss religion, politics, or the "Actions of the Soul." It omits these aspects of human life in part because it does not wish to encroach on other fields of study—"Politicks, Morality, and Oratory"—which are concerned with these domains, but even more so because human thoughts and actions "are so hard to be reduc'd to any certain observation of the senses, and afford so much room to the observers to falsifie or counterfeit. . . ." Dealing with such subjects at the present time would leave the Society "in danger of falling into talking, instead of working, which they carefully avoid." "But yet," Sprat continues, "when they shall have made more progress, in material things, they will be in a condition, of pronouncing more boldly on them [questions of soul and society] too."[21]

Sprat distances himself from the fully reductive, mechanistic account of human being that others of his time were already beginning to propose. He believes the human person is a "Spiritual and Immortal Being." Still, his empiricism resists limits, and though human reason and will and emotion are hard to reduce to "any certain observation of the senses," he seems to think it is possible, and that as experimental and other scientific work progresses it will get easier to study the soul empirically. Two incipient ideas are at work here that less religious minds would subsequently embrace with fewer reservations. First, the objectification and mechanization of nature includes human nature. Questions of meaning will (in time) yield to questions of how things *work*. And, second, what is *real*—what leaves no room to "falsifie or counterfeit"—is what can be apprehended by the senses. It has a position in physical space and thus, in principle, can be measured. These ideas too have been an important part of the Baconian legacy.

Sprat's exposition, then, outlines some key features of Bacon's project and their implications for medicine. Many of the ideas, of course, have influenced all of science and so medicine to the degree that it has drawn on the techniques and orientation of science. The foremost idea is the disenchantment of nature and the new criteria for conducting and appraising inquiry: a neutral world of facts, ordered hierarchically and reducible to objective, physical processes obeying mechanistic and predictable laws.[22] Human values or goods are treated as inherently subjective, mere projections onto this world that can (and must) be banned as much as possible from the reasoning process by methodical disengagement. At the same time, however, the very adoption of this naturalistic outlook is infused with humanitarian goals and moral valuations. The whole point is to foster human emancipation and relieve suffering, bringing technological control over all of nature, and making it, in Sprat's quaint phrase, "serviceable to the quiet, and peace, and plenty of Man's life."

Bacon's project lays a new and heavy burden of responsibility on the human race, a duty that we have an unbounded moral obligation to fulfill and for which medicine is a critical tool. In carrying out this endeavor, we can be confident that its larger moral purpose will not be lost or distorted: The pursuit of true knowledge, that knowledge provided by the instrumental, disengaged approach, has a prescriptive cognitive value and cannot lead us astray. So in an important sense the Baconian outlook, despite its apparently instrumental and value-neutral approach, itself becomes a basis for social and moral judgments. Its open-ended commitment to relieve suffering trumps other ways of thinking about the limits of medicine or bodily intervention.[23]

Further, by mechanizing human nature and materializing reality, the new science takes upon itself the power to recode human experience. Nature for Bacon and the others is neutral and indifferent to human purposes, a world of objects that is contrasted with subjects and subjective meaning. Dealing with the physical, the concrete, the real avoids the "danger of falling into talking," as Sprat puts it, and guarantees perforce that one is outside the subjective domains of morality, religion, and politics. The corollary is that when "Actions of the Soul" are reduced to their physical mechanisms, they are removed from the subjective to the objective, neutral, and indifferent world of nature. And if the real has a location in physical space, then whatever cannot be shown to occupy such a space is less real if not unreal. The materialist reduction, then, is imbued with the power to establish a kind of neutrality with respect to questions of the good—what is *not* divine intervention or moral or cultural or political—and objective reality.

To this general outlook and epistemology that medicine inherits from the scientific revolution we must add another more specific legacy, one that emerged in the historical moment when that revolution finally reached medicine.

The Specific Disease, Specific Treatment (Biomedical Model) Legacy

Despite the great hope for medical progress at the very heart of the scientific revolution, the fruits of the revolution came late to medicine. This is surprising and testifies against the popular notion that the triumphs of science and the growth of scientific authority have been on a more or less linear trajectory since the seventeenth century. They have not. What we regard as modern medicine begins to come into its own only in the late nineteenth century. Its development is in part a story of breaking free from humoral theory, the tradition of medicine going back to Galen (c. 130–200 C.E.), which offered a comprehensive and holistic account of health and disease. While in physics and astronomy Renaissance-era discoveries led to the replacement of theories tracing back to the Greeks, in medicine such seventeenth-century discoveries as William Harvey's work on the circulation of blood and Thomas Willis's on the autonomic nervous system were simply incorporated into revised versions of Galen's model. Even after Edward Jenner's vaccination for smallpox (1798) had become widely accepted, it was still situated within a therapeutic regime that related it back to the economy of the whole body.

Holism was the genius of the Galenist system. In this system, illness is idiosyncratic and unique to each individual; it is a disharmony, imbalance, or abnormal mixture of the four humors, which each individual has in some innate ("natural") and harmonious personal ratio. The humoral balance can be disturbed by any number of factors, including exposure to "noxious air" (or "miasma"; this theory arose to explain the etiology of contagious diseases), doing the wrong thing, experiencing strong emotions, inappropriate bodily discharges (e.g., those resulting from masturbation), and so on. In this system, there is no practical distinction between morality and mechanism, as personal habits are important to vulnerability; and there is no sharp distinction between mind and body as both are in simultaneous interaction. General prevention emphasized the value of prudently managing what Galen called the "nonnaturals," including environmental factors of air, food, and drink, and bodily functions such as exercise, rest, evacuation, and emotion. Medical treatment was geared to a readjustment of the balance, with bloodletting, enemas, and emetics among the physician's common tools. Ordinary people, who turned to the doctor as a last resort, took a Galenist approach to self-treatment. From the seventeenth century on, a growing number of what would later be called "patent" medicines were being sold that had tonic, purgative, stimulant, or sedative properties.[24]

Two general developments brought the 1,500-year-old Galenist tradition to an end in mainstream medicine. The first was the idea of disease specificity. Rather than disruptions of the whole body, diseases came to be understood as specific entities with separate and universally identifiable causes and characteristic physiological effects. This more ontological notion of disease, which in one form had been in circulation since the time of Paracelsus in the sixteenth century, was medical convention by the end of the nineteenth century. Various discoveries—for example, the postmortem studies of Giovanni Morgagni (1761) and Xavier Bichat (1800) on pathogens specific to particular organs—had been slowly fixing the notion of specific disease throughout the nineteenth century, but the decisive change came in the 1880s with the establishment of bacteriology. The idea that communicable diseases are caused by living organisms (the germ theory) had been in circulation for centuries, but resistance to it finally yielded with a string of breakthroughs from 1860 onward. Louis Pasteur, for instance, showed how sterilization can kill microbes ("pasteurization," 1862) and later developed a series of vaccines, including one for rabies (1885). In 1867, Joseph Lister published a series of papers on antiseptic surgery techniques that would slowly transform practice. In rapid order, beginning with the anthrax bacillus in 1876, Robert Koch isolated the tuberculosis bacillus (1882) and the cholera bacillus (1884) and demonstrated that they are contagious. Further, in 1883, Edwin Klebs, working in Koch's laboratory, isolated the bacterium responsible for diphtheria.

Germ theory revolutionized the theory and practice of medicine and the very conception of disease. The essential idiosyncrasy of disease is gone; the afflicted individual is the "host" for impersonal physiological processes. The historian Charles Rosenberg observes: "[G]erm theories constituted a powerful argument for a reductionist, mechanism-oriented way of thinking about the body and its felt malfunctions. These theories communicated metaphorically the notion of disease entity as ideal type, abstracted from its particular manifestations. A legitimate disease had both a characteristic clinical course and a mechanism, in other words, a natural history that—from both the physician's and the patient's perspective—formed a narrative. The act of diagnosis inevitably placed the patient at a point on the trajectory of that predetermined narrative."[25] In other words, the disease, not the patient, now tells the story. Additionally, the development of a whole range of new tools, from the thermometer to X-rays, made it increasingly possible to describe specific disease entities with new and standardized precision. The patient's own report of signs and symptoms counted for less and less, as did social and environmental determinants of disease.[26]

But another idea, more implicit and still little realized at the end of the nineteenth century, was also critical to the overthrow of humoral theory and the establishment of scientific medicine. This is the idea of treatment specificity. The newly identified bacteria suggested not only that each was associated with its own disease but that each might require specific management.[27] The diphtheria antitoxin came in 1894 and was followed by new immunizations at the turn of the century. The precise specificity of these treatments became an ideal type for medicine, the counterpart to the mechanism-based, specific-disease explanatory framework. In fact, they are two halves of a single explanatory framework, as *mechanism* implies manipulability and a predictable treatment response implies a valid underlying pathological mechanism. A contemporary of Pasteur and Koch, the chemist and founder of chemotherapy, Paul Ehrlich, famously labeled the treatment ideal type a "magic bullet." Magic bullets are medicines that go straight to and effectively attack the pathogens in the targeted cell structure while remaining harmless in healthy tissues.

Successful specific treatments also captured the public imagination and drastically changed public expectations of medicine and doctors. While many developments during the nineteenth century were connecting chemistry, biology, and medicine and were producing fruitful results (morphine, quinine, aspirin), few drew much public notice or enthusiasm. Neither medicine in general nor doctors, the majority of whom had low levels of education, were highly regarded. In a study of popular views of medical progress in America since Pasteur, the historian Bert Hansen identifies Pasteur's 1885 discovery of a vaccine for rabies as a seminal moment in which a medical breakthrough really engaged the public imagination. An incident in late 1885, involving five young boys bitten by a rabid dog, provided the galvanizing event. A doctor, who knew of Pasteur's vaccine, wrote the newspaper that reported the incident urging that the children be sent to Paris to be treated and that donations be solicited if necessary. The newspaper cabled Pasteur, who agreed, donations flowed in, the children were vaccinated in Paris, and none contracted rabies. The story became a *cause célèbre* all over the United States. Subsequent cases of rabies bites met similar demands to go to France, and within a year, domestic clinics known as "Pasteur Institutes" sprang up to administer the shots.[28] A threshold was crossed. A few years later when Robert Koch announced a cure for tuberculosis, the discovery was breathlessly reported for months. Though Koch was later proved mistaken, what is striking, as Hansen observes, is the speed and enthusiasm with which everyone—professionals and public alike—embraced the possibility of cures for disease.[29] In 1894, the diphtheria antitoxin was greeted with immediate and widespread publicity.

While "new developments in curative medicine were slow in coming," as the historian Anne Hardy has argued, they began in earnest after 1920.[30] By World War II, a tuberculosis vaccine, insulin, and the antibiotics (sulphonamides, penicillin) were available, among other new drugs, and working a powerful impact on public consciousness. A 1942 article in *Popular Science*, reflecting on the sulfa drugs, expresses some of the rising expectations: "The nature of these drugs, and the manner of their application, suggests that the biological revolution is beginning— only beginning—to catch up with the industrial revolution. Heretofore most of the human effort that has been invested in the development of the exact sciences has been devoted to improvements in machinery. Progress in the biological arts and sciences, although extensive, has nevertheless tended to lag behind mechanical progress in precision and certainty. . . . More and more, medicine is turning from cut-and-dry [*sic*] methods to exact measurement and to techniques based on physics and chemistry."[31] More new drugs followed in the postwar period: cortisone, chlorpromazine (the first successful antipsychotic), the polio vaccine, and others.

Meanwhile, accumulating critiques, along with new studies beginning in the 1940s, brought a shift away from "germ theory" (monocausal) accounts toward "multiple cause" approaches to noncommunicable diseases. The famous Framingham Heart Study, launched in 1948, one of the first longitudinal epidemiological studies of multifactorial etiology, showed strong correlations between elevated levels of such factors as serum cholesterol and blood pressure and the development of coronary heart disease.[32] This ongoing study and others, including research on the correlation of cigarette smoking with heart disease and cancer, were instrumental in framing multiple causation in terms of what came to be called in the early 1960s "risk factors"—specific exposures that increase the probability of disease but are not in themselves necessary or sufficient to cause it. The subsequent regime of disease prevention concentrated almost exclusively on individual-level "lifestyle" behaviors and consumption patterns, such as smoking, diet, exercise, and so on. This approach did not challenge the existing biomedical model of physiological disease mechanisms but enlarged it.[33] The introduction of a drug for hypertension, increasingly discussed as a disease in its own right, in 1958, and later for other risk factors, helped solidify risk-factor and

Slow but Sure

Figure 1.2. Bruce Shanks, "Slow but Sure," *Buffalo Evening News*, April 13, 1955. Editorial page cartoon. © 1955.

lifestyle approaches and fuel new medical hope for the prevention and successful management of, if not cure for, chronic conditions.

A 1955 editorial cartoon by Bruce Shanks, a Pulitzer Prize winner, titled "Slow but Sure" (see figure 1.2) perfectly captures the widespread perception among both lay people and physicians that medical history is an inexorable progression of conquests over disease. With the "Salk vaccine report," polio has been crossed off the dread disease list after smallpox, diphtheria, and pneumonia; cancer and heart disease lie ahead on the next page of history.

More than half a century later, the great killers, heart disease and cancer, are still on the list. But the remarkable therapeutic optimism expressed by Shanks, Baconian in its belief in disease eradication and cure, is, if less triumphantly, still very much alive. Of course, the prestige and achievements of science continue to feed the hopes for medical progress. After World War II, not only a flood of new pharmaceuticals but the scope and sophistication of medical technology grew at an exponential rate. Over the past two decades, gene therapy and stem cell research have been the leading repositories of popular and professional enthusiasm for breakthrough cures. In his 2010 book *The Language of Life*, Francis Collins, Director of the U.S. National Institutes of Health and former head of the international Human Genome Project, sees a "growing ocean of potential new treatments for diseases that are flowing in from the world's laboratories, thanks to our new ability to read the secrets of the language of life." With a Shanks-like image, he recounts the chorus of a song that he once sang to the annual North American Cystic Fibrosis Conference:

> Dare to dream, dare to dream,
> All our brothers and sisters breathing free.
> Unafraid, our hopes unswayed,
> 'Til the story of CF is history.[34]

If initial expectations for applications of the new genomic knowledge were naïve, Collins avers, those expectations were not misplaced. With a sustained commitment to vast outlays for research, cures will inevitably follow. The mechanisms can and will be found.

Popular optimism and expectations remain high, if less nourished by any precise sense of historical development. Without too much exaggeration, one might say that medical optimism has been industrialized in recent decades, ceaselessly produced by health groups and media. The sites of this production have proliferated exponentially in the past generation. Private medical foundations, patient advocacy and medical identity groups, pharmaceutical and medical device companies, research universities, television news segments, newspaper health sections, health magazines, Internet health sites, and more all generally speak a buoyant message of unceasing "life-changing advances," progress toward prevention and cures, and routine "miracles." Even the producers of scientific research have media relations departments that help popularize the latest studies. Medical hope has become a big business.

In part because of past successes, the specific disease and treatment models, with their mechanism-oriented reductionism—the biomedical model—remain dominant. Here, for example, is how two researchers describe the direction for the treatment of cancer, now viewed as a multifactorial disease: "We foresee the design of magic bullets," they write, "developing into a logical science, where the experimental and clinical complexity of cancer can be reduced to a limited number of underlying principles and crucial targets." The new paradigm, they argue, "is the development of 'personalized and tailored drugs' that precisely target the specific molecular defects of a cancer patient."[35] Throughout *The Language of Life*, Collins describes the promise of genetic medicine in identical and euphoric terms: molecules, targets, and personalized treatments. The debate over the fifth revision of psychiatry's *Diagnostic and Statistical Manual of Mental Disorders*, to give another example, featured a strong call by many in the field to move beyond heuristic categories toward a "hard medical model" of psychiatric illness "based on etiological mechanisms."[36] These mechanisms would be identified through neuroscience and molecular genetics, have validated laboratory or imaging biomarkers, and be subject to manipulation by specific treatment interventions. According to the first chapter of a leading psychiatry textbook, the goal is a "brain-based diagnostic system."[37]

The promise of specific treatment is a crucial element of the enduring appeal of disease specificity and reductionism. But it is not the only one. Precise and specific disease categories are now woven into every feature of medicine, from structuring professional specialization, to doctor-patient interaction, to research and clinical trials, to all aspects of the centralized and bureaucratic delivery and regulation of health care. The former director of the U.S. National Institute of Mental Health, though speaking in the context of psychiatry, provides a concise list, most of which is applicable to all of medicine:

Reliable and widely shared disease definitions are a necessary antecedent for rational treatment decisions. Diagnosis guides a clinician's thinking about treatment, about other symptoms that might be present, about likely impairments, and about prognosis. Shared and reliable diagnoses are the cornerstone of communication between the clinician and the patient and, where appropriate, with families, other caregivers, and institutions. Diagnosis is also central to translational and clinical research: Without clear diagnostic guideposts, idiosyncratic groupings confound clinical trials, epidemiology, genetics, imaging, and other laboratory studies. In their absence, academia and industry lack indications for which to develop new treatments, and regulatory agencies cannot judge efficacy. Diagnosis also plays an important role outside the clinic and laboratory, influencing, for example, insurance reimbursement, determinations of disability, school-based interventions for symptomatic children, and diverse legal proceedings.[38]

To all this could be added a long list of administrative and bureaucratic functions of specific diagnostic categories. The day-to-day management of hospitals, for example, is organized around these categories, and all the readings and statistics and codes and protocols and lab tests and thresholds and charts take their meaning from these categories and, not inconsequently, reaffirm their ontology.[39] Contemporary rationalized medicine depends on the specific disease model.

The Cultural Authority of Reductionist Medicine

Therapeutic promise and bureaucratic need, while important, do not capture the grip that reductionism, mechanism-based explanations, and the reliance on technology hold on contemporary society. More is at work. This type of medicine also bears a distinct cultural authority. Cultural authority, following Paul Starr, involves conceptions of reality and judgments of meaning and value that are taken to be valid and true.[40] At stake are not narrow questions of utility or effectiveness, or of the relative social power of physicians. Rather, the issue is legitimacy and the power to pronounce and enforce agreement on definitions of the nature of the world and the status of particular facts and values in the world. Reductionist medicine has such power to an important, but not absolute, degree. No single feature can account for this power, but one critical element lies in the nexus between medicine and liberal society, between the deep-seated meanings carried by the twin legacies—Baconian and biomedical model—and core cultural ideals.

Modern Western societies, and perhaps most strongly the United States, recognize two unequivocal goods: personal freedom and health. Both have become ends in themselves, rather than conditions or components of a well-lived life. Neither has much actual content; both are effectively defined in terms of what they are not and what they move away from, namely constraint and suffering. As such, both are open-ended, their concrete form depending on particular and mutable circumstances that can only partially be specified in advance (against certain conditions of exploitation, for example, or disease). Personal freedom is the hallmark of liberalism, which centers on a picture of an "unencumbered self," in Michael Sandel's felicitous phrase,[41] able to act on its own inhibited by only the barest necessity of social interference or external authority, and bearing rights to equal treatment and opportunities for social participation and personal expression. The reciprocal responsibility centers on respecting the rights and dignity of others and working out one's self-definition and lifestyle in a personally fulfilling and generative fashion.

Since at least the nineteenth century, health has contended with freedom for pride of place as the preeminent value in Western societies. The preoccupation with health has only intensified in recent decades. Some speak of the emergence of the "health society" wherein "health is everywhere" and has become central to the telos of living.[42] In the health society the languages of medicine have taken on new existential functions; in the words of the anthropologist Jean Comaroff, "Biomedical metaphors have . . . become increasingly central to our world-view, to our self-perception and our interpretations of everyday experience."[43] Matters of health, joined to the obligations of liberal selfhood, come increasingly within the ambit of individual responsibility, calculation, and optimization. The active citizens of the health society are informed and positive, exercise independent judgment and will, and engage experts as partners in a kind of alliance relationship. The ideal is to live a "healthy lifestyle," which prioritizes the avoidance of behaviors correlated with increased risk of disease, such as smoking, and the cultivation of a wide

range of "wellness activities," including a carefully crafted diet and a vigorous exercise regimen. The concern with health is more than a matter
of avoiding illness, though it certainly includes that. It is also a means
of moral action, a way to take responsibility for oneself and one's future and confirm one's solidarity with the values of a good society. The
mass production of medical optimism, as well as the dissemination of
research findings and how-to advice, serves as an important and necessary backdrop, urging individuals to place their hope in professional expertise and self-consciously reorder their daily lives in light of the latest
information and findings. Fatalistic explanations, explanations in terms
of mortality, are no longer permissible; individuals can and *should* exert
control over their health through risk management.[44]

Medicine is deeply implicated in the cultural priorities of autonomous
selfhood and optimized health. Both priorities have a central concern
with the body and its active shaping and control. Of course, the link between medicine and illness—disease processes or distinctive anatomical
or molecular abnormalities—represents the most obvious connection
to the body. But that is only the beginning. The body has also become a
crucial site for projects of emancipation and the construction and elaboration of selfhood and lifestyle. "Biology is not destiny" was a rallying
cry for the unmaking of gender roles a generation ago, part of a broader
challenge to bodily boundaries and limitations once regarded as simply
given or natural but increasingly seen as oppressive and inconsistent
with free self-determination. Destiny was overcome by technological interventions that severed "fateful" connections (such as between sexuality
and reproduction) and that opened up an increasing range of bodily
matters to choices and options—the shape of one's nose, a tendency to
blush, baldness, wrinkles, infertility. Not all cultivation and manipulation of the body is medical. Bodily regimes and many lifestyle products,
from cosmetics to body art, are available to modify the body's "outer
layer." Yet through medicine and the technologies it controls, the ability
to intervene and alter the body for emancipatory and lifestyle purposes
has been radically enlarged.

These enhancement uses of medical technology are only one way in
which medicine is now interwoven with cultural ideals of self and health.
The Baconian legacy established the background assumptions that situate medicine in service to self-determination, emancipation from fate,

and relief of suffering; and reductionist, mechanism-oriented medicine offers powerful means to achieve these goals. These humanitarian commitments are open-ended. While it is tempting to think that the boundaries of disease itself (or anatomical or molecular abnormalities) would constitute a limit, they do not. In the examples from reproductive and cosmetic medicine alluded to earlier, the medical technologies are deployed not for the treatment of disease but for enhancement purposes. Many routine medical interventions are performed merely to ease the discomforts of everyday life, life processes, and aging and have little to do with disease.[45] And many prescription-only medications play another role as "lifestyle drugs." Disease, as such, does not set limits.

If not disease, then surely bodily interventions constitute the limits of medicine's Baconian commitments? Already in the seventeenth century, as we have seen, the idea of a biological reductionism was gaining a hearing, and it became increasingly solidified in the nineteenth and twentieth centuries. Psychiatry would seem to offer the clearest exception. Virtually none of its hundreds of specific disease categories has any known etiology or pathophysiology. But as Sprat predicted, the soul has entered the scientific agenda. Nineteenth-century neurologists, like George Beard with his diagnosis of neurasthenia ("tired nerves") or the young Sigmund Freud, saw themselves as dealing with biological phenomena. Contemporary neuroscience resolves the mind–body problem by treating mind as an emergent property of the hierarchical organization of the nervous system. So, as noted earlier, the lack of known mechanisms, the *de facto* deviation from the biomedical model, is viewed by many in psychiatry as a temporary situation, a sign that the science is still in its "early stages" and that with the "advance of science" the neurological and genetic mechanisms that underlie psychiatric disorders will be discovered.[46] It's only a matter of time.

The body, then, does represent something of a conceptual limit, but as the example of psychiatry suggests, it is not a practical limit. Intervention need not wait for biology. A great many drug discoveries have been serendipitous; that they work for some desired purpose is far more important than why they work, and their use in medicine has proceeded despite the failure to understand them. Further, by the specific treatment rationale—wherein predictable treatment response implies an underlying mechanism—the clinical effects of drugs are often taken as evidence that something is awry in the body. This, for example, is what the psychiatrist Peter Kramer meant by the title of his bestselling book *Listening to Prozac*. The intervention may supply the evidence for the biology.[47]

In the absence of actual limits, medicine's open-ended commitment to foster self-determination and relieve suffering, as woven together with cultural priorities of self and health, draws it into treating an ever-wider range of concerns and complaints. As autonomy has become more of a cultural ideal, so limitations on, say, autonomy of movement are felt to be a burden, and medicine is called upon to provide whatever technological means it controls to relieve this burden. It is similar with virtually any attribute that an individual might regard as inhibiting to them or their life plans: short stature, anxiousness, shyness, perfectionism, low task-specific energy or concentration, insufficient libido, and much more. So too with troublesome emotions, and with various role conflicts or inadequacies, such as in parent, spouse, student, or employee roles. Intervention in these matters is legitimate medicine in the Baconian sense because it addresses burdens for the patient, the modification or reduction of which is regarded as a good, one enabling or enhancing her or his pattern of life.

Furthermore, medicine is called upon to address many issues of difference and deviance in society. While it may be that some of this type of medicalization is the result of an aggressive expansionism on the part of medicine or the "medical-industrial complex," there is no question that medicine has been and continues to be drawn in where other cultural institutions have already largely disappeared. Case in point: the elimination in the fifth edition of the *Diagnostic and Statistical Manual of Mental Disorders* of the "bereavement exclusion" from the diagnostic criteria for depression. Previously, depression was not to be diagnosed if an individual had lost a loved one within the previous two months, because grief and depression are not phenomenologically distinct and grief is not a mental disorder. The Mood Disorder Work Group for the *DSM 5*, which originally proposed the change, argued that some of what looks like normal bereavement is actually depression, and a failure to diagnose would to be to deny needed treatment.[48] Critics, on the other hand, contended that removing the exception would be pathologizing normal behavior.[49] But my point is that it is very unlikely that this discussion would even be taking place if the larger communal system of customs and rituals that once defined and guided mourning had not already collapsed. Experiencing grief as a primarily private burden, individuals seek out antidepressants; psychiatrists, being "clinically proactive," want to make the diagnosis and provide the treatment. The issue here is not so much that psychiatry seeks this role as it is that when people seek clinical help, it is exceedingly difficult to refuse. Doing so can seem insensitive, even cruel, a failure to discharge medicine's Baconian mandate.

Besides relieving suffering and enhancing self-determination, there is another reason why medicine has come increasingly to manage issues of difference and deviance. Medicine, it hardly needs saying, has no answers to existential questions or social problems. What it offers is something different; indeed, something better, from the point of view of a liberal order in which the dominant idea is that each person's good is a question of her own convictions or preferences. Medicine offers (seemingly) objective, value-free modes of discourse that can bypass conflicting conceptions of the good, offer plausible "accounts" for behavior and emotion (diagnostic categories) that also emplot persons within a positive narrative trajectory, legitimate intervention and some sick role exemptions (e.g., relief from social responsibilities), and decrease stigma by qualifying, though not eliminating, thorny questions of responsibility.[50]

This is a powerful discourse built on the reductionist, mechanism-oriented, specific treatment approach. It includes both appropriations and dispossessions. On the one hand, a reduction to biological malfunction recodes bodily states, behaviors, or emotions as morally neutral: ontologically real objects, distinct from the patient's self and causal agency. The language of the body is not a moral language, and the language of health needs no justification; it is by definition in the patient's own and best interest. Qualitative, evaluative distinctions—about what deviance is considered an illness, about what will be extracted from a moral or social or cultural nexus, about what constitutes appropriate intervention, about what features of individual "lifestyles" will constitute risks, and so on—are in fact made, but they take place in bureaucratic and professional contexts far upstream of the clinic. In the actual clinical interactions, the language is not of judging but of diagnosing, not of moral failures but of disorder mechanisms, not of social problems or exploitative structures but of individual illnesses. All moral, social, or other normative evaluations, all affronts to the patient's autonomy and self-image, appear to have been excluded, all questioning of legitimacy put off the table. Meanwhile, social norms are enforced, and some needs for meaning and certainty are met.

On the other hand, the key to this clinical truth and cultural authority is the reduction to the body. So the biomedical model speaks only that truth about illness, behavior, and emotion which can be naturalized by being linked to the body, and the tighter the linkage (physical measurements are the gold standard), the more legitimate the illness. Without a clear biology, questions of culpability and malingering and social influences may be and often are reasserted. This is another reason why psychiatry so doggedly pursues neurology and genetics to the exclusion of other explanatory approaches. It is why in the many domains in which medicine enforces norms in matters of difference and deviance its interventions are often controversial and sometimes contested. Medicine's role in dealing with the dual imperatives of the school—behavior/physical docility and performance—through the Attention Deficit Hyperactivity Disorder (ADHD) entity and psychostimulant treatment is a prominent example. The debate over classifying obesity as a disease is another. The reduction to the body is why patient advocacy, medical specialty, and social movement groups have to lobby for certain categories, like post-traumatic stress disorder or chronic fatigue syndrome, and why they can lobby against others, such as homosexuality or masochistic personality disorder.[51] It is why psychosomatic disorders have a low status and why there seems to be a constant need to repeat that depression or social phobia or most any psychiatric disorder is a "real disease" and "not a flaw in character." The biomedical model leaves some things out, thereby consigning them to the not quite legitimate, the imaginary, the ambiguous, the subjective, and the culpable.[52] The power to dispose is also part of its cultural authority.

Conclusion

I began with the question of why socially oriented and integrative approaches to medicine, despite attentiveness to crucial realities, never seem to get very much traction, and with the question of why we invite the extension of medicine over more and more areas of our lives. The foregoing remarks about the appropriations and dispossessions of the biomedical model will, I hope, suggest why holistic models, which challenge the dispossessions, are attractive—but also why they fail to take hold. Charles Rosenberg, considering the question of the failure of integrative approaches in both the recent and more distant past, argues: "The laboratory's cumulative triumphs have made this holistic point of view seem not so much wrong as marginal, elusive, and difficult to study in a systematic way."[53] But that is only part of the story. A comprehensive theoretical model that could integrate biological and psychological, as well as social and environmental, underpinnings of disease would still run up against serious problems. The cultural priorities of autonomous selfhood and optimized health are deeply individualistic, and the reductionist biomedical model and lifestyle approach do important moral and ontological work that a holistic model would be hard-pressed to perform. To make judgments transparent is to make them controversial. Even bioethics largely avoids this terrain.

For much the same reasons, we can see why we invite medicalization. On the individual level, a specific diagnosis provides a "predetermined narrative" that can decrease the burden of responsibility, account for problematical experience, legitimate exemptions from social expectations, and offer a positive prognosis and access to treatment, all within a seemingly value-neutral framework. Access to medical technologies for emancipatory and lifestyle issues is another incentive, one that in the liberal health society can become an obligation. The relentless yearning for control, coupled to the optimism industry, makes even the contemplation of therapeutic limits difficult to accept.

We can also see why, with respect to socially problematic behaviors or emotions, postulating a specific disease and biological mechanism and formulating new indications for medications have a powerful appeal[54] and might even be regarded as a matter of justice. Granted, the lack of a clear biological etiology will tend to qualify the acceptance of a postulated entity as a legitimate, value-free disease. But, as noted previously, the biological can be finessed, and the cultural authority at work here is such that once a useful disease category is created, it takes on a life of its own. Skepticism and contestation may not be entirely silenced, but effective resistance is far less likely. ADHD, with no known etiology or pathophysiology and a long history of public controversy and skepticism, yet skyrocketing rates of diagnosis and treatment, is a case in point.[55]

In tracing some of the origins of reductionist medicine's cultural authority and drawing out implications, I have sought to offer reasons for certain obdurate patterns in the relation of medicine and society. I have focused primarily on ideas and on cultural authority and have said relatively little about the role of commercial forces and political institutions in promoting a reductionist/lifestyle perspective. My point was not to deny their importance. Reductionist medical and lifestyle orientations to personal and social problems deflect attention from the larger social and physical environment to the individual and, combined with their ostensible grounding in scientific fact, are attractive in policy matters and synergistic with consumerism. But I have stressed the moral/cultural power of reductionist medicine to bring into relief a critical feature that is typically relegated to an afterthought. The appeal of reductionism has longer and deeper roots than any specific government policy or commercial strategy. And it remains strong despite widespread technological and diagnostic skepticism, sharp critiques of the "medical-industrial complex," persuasive demonstrations of the social determinants of health and illness, and a decline in the social power of the medical profession. If we are to make progress in a more holistic direction—and strong crosswinds are certainly blowing—the question of cultural authority, ultimately an ethical question, will have to be addressed.

NOTES

1 See Bert Hansen, *Picturing Medical Progress from Pasteur to Polio: A History of Mass Media Images and Popular Attitudes in America* (New Brunswick, N.J.: Rutgers University Press, 2009), 70–71.

2 James J. Putnam, "Not the Disease Only, But Also the Man," *Boston Medical and Surgical Journal* 141 [July 20, 1899]: 53–57.

3 Ivan Illich, *Medical Nemesis: The Expropriation of Health* (New York: Pantheon, 1976), 127.

4 Charles Taylor, *Human Agency and Language* (Cambridge: Cambridge University Press, 1985), chapter 9.

5 Stephen Gaukroger, *Francis Bacon and the Transformation of Early-Modern Philosophy* (Cambridge: Cambridge University Press, 2001), 6.

6 Francis Bacon, *Novum Organum Scientiarum*, in James Spedding, Robert Leslie Ellis, and Dennis Denon Heath, eds., *The Collected Works of Francis Bacon* (London: Longmans, 14 vols., 1857–74), Preface.

7 See the exposition of these points in Gerald P. McKenny, *To Relieve the Human Condition: Bioethics, Technology, and the Body* (Albany: SUNY Press, 1997).

8 Charles Taylor, *Sources of the Self: The Making of the Modern Identity* (Cambridge, Mass.: Harvard University Press, 1989), chapter 13.

9 Ibid., chapter 19. Also see McKenny, *To Relieve the Human Condition.*

10 Richard Serjeantson, "Natural Knowledge in the *New Atlantis*," in Bronwen Price, ed., *Francis Bacon's* New Atlantis: *New Interdisciplinary Essays* (Manchester: Manchester University Press, 2002), 90.

11 René Descartes, *Discourse on Method and Meditations on First Philosophy*, Fourth Edition, trans. Donald A. Cress (Indianapolis: Hackett, 1998), 35.

12 For a short history of the Society, see its website at http://royalsociety.org/about-us/history/.

13 Lewis A. Coser, *Men of Ideas: A Sociologist's View* (New York: Free Press, 1997), 5.

14 All quotations in this paragraph are from Thomas Sprat, *History of the Royal Society*, ed. Jackson I. Cope and Harold Whitmore Jones (St. Louis: Washington University Studies, 1958), 122–23 (spellings and capitalization in the original).

15 Sprat was not a natural philosopher himself but a preacher and a poet. He was an advocate of "physico-theology," which was an effort to establish a convergence between natural philosophy and theology so that they had a shared focus. See Stephen Gaukroger, *The Collapse of Mechanism and the Rise of Sensibility* (New York: Oxford University Press, 2010), 30–40.

16 Sprat, *History of the Royal Society*, 110.

17 Ibid.

18 In *New Atlantis*, Bacon takes great care to explain how the Bensalemites have gained their technological knowledge, but he does not explain how they have come by their great virtue. He offers no account of their political or economic arrangements, nor does he outline any ethical system. Rather, according to one commentator, "The islanders exist in a vaguely outlined but allegedly desirable state of peace, political contentment, and Christian-Hebraic virtue, which fosters or is fostered by the natural philosophical researches of Salomon's House." David Colclough, "Ethics and Politics in *New Atlantis*," in Bronwen Price, ed., *Francis Bacon's* New Atlantis, 62.

19 Sprat, *History of the Royal Society*, 111.

20 Ibid., 83. There was nothing unusual about Sprat's raising the question of the soul in this context. The study of the soul, following in the tradition of Aristotle's *De anima*, had long been the province of the field of natural philosophy, though by the mid–seventeenth century this study was increasingly being questioned. See Richard W. Serjeantson, "The Soul," in Desmond M. Clarke and Catherine Wilson, eds., *The Oxford Handbook of Philosophy in Early Modern Europe* (Oxford: Oxford University Press, 2011), 119–41.

21 Sprat, *History of the Royal Society*, 82.

22 Simple and inert notions of "mechanism," which had guided in different ways Bacon and Descartes, and which underlay the grander idea that a single, unified, and comprehensive account might be given of all natural phenomena, did not hold. The

challenge to the explanatory power of mechanics was already launched by the late seventeenth century, and studies in chemistry, electricity, physiology, and other fields finally dislodged it. See Gaukroger, *The Collapse of Mechanism*.

23 Gerald McKenny illustrates the contrast with more traditional ways of life: ". . . moral convictions about the place of illness and health in a morally worthy life are replaced by moral convictions about the relief of suffering and the expansion of choice, concepts of nature as ordered by a telos or governed by providence are replaced by concepts of nature as a neutral instrument that is brought into the realm of human ends by technology, and the body as object of spiritual and moral practices is replaced by the body as object of practices of technological control." McKenny, *To Relieve the Human Condition*, 21.

24 David Healy, *The Antidepressant Era* (Cambridge, Mass.: Harvard University Press, 1997), 16.

25 Charles E. Rosenberg, *Our Present Complaint: American Medicine, Then and Now* (Baltimore: Johns Hopkins University Press, 2007), 19.

26 This shift was not limited to clinical medicine. Paul Starr writes that
with the development of bacteriology in the late 1800s, the theory
and practice of public health and its relation to medicine greatly
changed. Public health authorities gradually developed a more
precise conception of the sources and modes of transmission of
infectious disease . . . Shifting attention from the environment to the
individual, they increasingly relied on the techniques of medicine
and personal hygiene. This development was partly a response to
the discovery that a number of diseases were transmitted by human
carriers. For if the sick are the source of infection, one way to prevent
the spread of disease (a recognized function of public health) is to
diagnose and cure the people who are ill.
Paul Starr, *The Social Transformation of American Medicine* (New York: Basic Books, 1982), 181.

27 David Healy, *The Antidepressant Era*, 12.

28 Hansen, *Picturing Medical Progress*, 46–47.

29 Ibid., 85–91.

30 Anne Hardy, "After the Therapeutic Revolution: The Return to Prevention in Medical Policy and Practice," chapter 5, this volume.

31 *Popular Science*, June 1942, 212.

32 See the discussions in William G. Rothstein, *Public Health and the Risk Factor: A History of an Uneven Medical Revolution* (Rochester, N.Y.: University of Rochester Press, 2003), Part 4; and Robert A. Aronowitz, *Making Sense of Illness: Science, Society, and Disease* (Cambridge: Cambridge University Press, 1999), chapter 5.

33 Aronowitz, *Making Sense*, 125. See also Nancy Krieger, *Epidemiology and the People's Health: Theory and Context* (New York: Oxford University Press, 2011), chapter 5.

34 Francis S. Collins, *The Language of Life: DNA and the Revolution in Personalized Medicine* (New York: HarperCollins, 2010), 37.

35 Klaus Strebhardt and Axel Ullrich, "Paul Ehrlich's Magic Bullet Concept: 100 Years of Progress," *Nature Reviews Cancer* 8 (June 2008), 478, 473.

36 K. S. Kendler, "Levels of Explanation in Psychiatric and Substance Use Disorders: Implications for the Development of an Etiologically Based Nosology," *Molecular Psychiatry* 17 (2012): 18.

37 Jack A. Grebb and Arvid Carlsson, "Introduction and Considerations for a Brain-Based Diagnostic System in Psychiatry," in Benjamin J. Sadock, Virginia A. Sadock, and Pedro Ruiz, eds., *Kaplan and Sadock's Comprehensive Textbook of Psychiatry*, Ninth Edition (Philadelphia: Wolters Kluwer Health/Lippincott Williams and Wilkins, 2009), Vol. 1, 1–5.

38 Steven E. Hyman, "The Diagnosis of Mental Disorders: The Problem of Reification," *Annual Review of Clinical Psychology* 6 (2010): 159.

39 Rosenberg, *Our Present Complaint*, chapter 2.

40 Starr, *Social Transformation*, 13.

41 Michael J. Sandel, *Democracy's Discontent: America in Search of a Public Philosophy* (Cambridge, Mass.: Harvard University Press, 1996).

42 Ilona Kickbusch, "Health Governance: The Health Society," in David V. McQueen and Ilona Kickbusch, eds., *Health and Modernity: The Role of Theory in Health Promotion* (New York: Springer, 2007), 151. See, more generally, Irving Kenneth Zola, "Medicine as an Institution of Social Control," *Sociological Review* 20 (1972): 487–504; and Illich, *Medical Nemesis*.

43 Jean Comaroff, "Medicine: Symbol and Ideology," in Peter Wright and Andrew Treacher, eds., *The Problem of Medical Knowledge: Examining the Social Construction of Medicine* (Edinburgh: Edinburgh University Press, 1982), 49–68, at 55.

44 Nikolas Rose, *The Politics of Life Itself: Biomedicine, Power, and Subjectivity in the Twenty-First Century* (Princeton, N.J.: Princeton University Press, 2007).

45 Arthur J. Barsky and Jonathan F. Boros, "Somatization and Medicalization in the Era of Managed Care," *Journal of the American Medical Association* 274, 24 (1995): 1931–34.

46 Steven E. Hyman, "Diagnosis," 171, 157.

47 For further examples, see Jeremy A. Greene, *Prescribing by Numbers: Drugs and the Definition of Disease* (Baltimore: Johns Hopkins University Press, 2007).

48 Jerome C. Wakefield and Michael B. First, "Validity of the Bereavement Exclusion to Major Depression: Does the Empirical Evidence Support the Proposal to Eliminate the Exclusion in DSM-5?" *World Psychiatry* 11 (2012): 3–10.

49 See, for example, Allen Frances, *Saving Normal* (New York: Morrow, 2013).

50 On the personal and social functions of "accounts" and their similarities to and differences from "illness narratives," see Joseph E. Davis, *Accounts of Innocence: Sexual Abuse, Trauma, and the Self* (Chicago: University of Chicago Press, 2005), chapter 1.

51 Masochistic personality disorder, the "need to be disappointed or humiliated," was included in the third edition (1980) of the *Diagnostic and Statistical Manual of Mental Disorders* (*DSM*). After a strong campaign by feminist psychologists, who rejected the scientific validity of the category and sounded alarms about potential misapplication, the category was renamed "self-defeating personality disorder" and rel-

egated to an appendix of "proposed diagnostic categories needing further study" in the third edition, revised in 1987. After more controversy, the category was deleted entirely from the fourth edition of 1994. See Thomas A. Widiger, "Deletion of Self-Defeating and Sadistic Personality Disorders," in W. John Livesley, ed., *The DSM-IV Personality Disorders* (New York: Guilford Press, 1995), 359–73.

52 Laurence J. Kirmayer, "Mind and Body as Metaphors: Hidden Values in Biomedicine," in Margaret Lock and Deborah R. Gordon, eds., *Biomedicine Examined* (Dordrecht: Kluwer Academic Publishers, 1988), 57–93.

53 Rosenberg, *Our Present Complaint*, 9.

54 Of course, for the same reason, it can also be seen as a political, legal, or commercial imperative.

55 See Joseph E. Davis and Benjamin Snyder, "Drawing the Line on ADHD: Medicalization, Public Opinion, and the Imperatives of Biocitizenship," paper presented at the Eastern Sociological Society meeting, Boston, March 20, 2010.

2

The Problem of Suffering in the Age of Prozac

A Case Study of the Depression Memoir

CHRISTINA SIMKO

It seemed that suddenly, some time in 1990, I ceased to be this freakishly depressed person who had scared the hell out of people for most of my life with my mood swings and tantrums and crying spells, and I instead became downright trendy. This private world of loony bins and weird people that I had always felt I occupied and hid in had suddenly been turned inside out so that it seemed like this was one big Prozac Nation, one big mess of malaise.

—Elizabeth Wurtzel, *Prozac Nation*

Introduction

In 1990, the novelist William Styron published *Darkness Visible*, a brief, unrelentingly intense memoir describing his plunge into the depths of suicidal depression. His personal story gripped the public: It hit the number one spot on the *New York Times* bestseller list and reinvigorated interest in Styron's other work.[1] Since the appearance of *Darkness Visible*, the depression memoir has become a veritable genre in its own right. Elizabeth Wurtzel's 1994 account of her illness, *Prozac Nation*, also soared to bestseller status, eventually inspiring a motion picture with the same title. The stream has continued, with scholars (Sharon O'Brien, Eric Wilson), journalists (Tracey Thompson, John Falk, David Awbrey), and therapists (Martha Manning) getting in on the act. As Wurtzel reflected in *Prozac Nation*, personal stories about depression—and perhaps more specifically, *antidepressants*—have become a ubiquitous facet of American public culture.

Arthur Frank argues that illness memoirs are—at heart—responses to the "narrative wreckage" that serious illnesses bring about.[2] Illness creates a "complication"—or, in Frank's terms,[3] an "interruption"—in one's personal narrative: The future that one anticipated may no longer be tenable in light of present circumstances, requiring extensive self-reconstruction. This "narrative wreckage" may be especially devastating in a cultural and historical moment in which individuals face intense social pressure to tell a unique and compelling personal narrative. As Anthony Giddens puts it, in our late modern moment "[a] person's identity is to be found not in behaviour, nor—important though this is—in the reactions of others, but in the *capacity to keep a particular narrative going* . . . . It must continually integrate events which occur in the external world, and sort them into the ongoing 'story' about the self."[4]

While the "restitution narrative"—a plot structure that takes the protagonist from health, through illness, to cure—is "culturally preferred,"[5] people whose illnesses are chronic, recurrent, or fatal may find themselves grasping for narrative resources to make sense of these grave experiences. As Arthur Kleinman and Stanley Hauerwas suggest, illnesses bring people face-to-face with the age-old "problem of suffering."[6] Although the problem of suffering is frequently perceived as an esoteric theological conundrum, the sociologist Peter Berger—following and extending the classical theorist Max Weber—argues that it is an inevitable facet of human existence.[7] We may respond in religious or secular terms, lay or technical terms, but the question confronts us nonetheless. In our own moment, illness memoirs—and confessional genres generally, including essays, blogs, and television talk shows[8]—represent a crucial forum for grappling with this quintessential human question.

How, then, do people suffering from depression construct or reconstruct their self-narratives in light of severe psychological suffering? What narrative templates do people possess in the face of depression? Memoirs provide a crucial window onto these questions because they represent an intermediary cultural form: They are simultaneously personal stories and—at least potentially—narrative templates.

Medicine and the Problem of Suffering

The epigraph from Wurtzel with which I began this chapter expresses in colloquial terms a critique with a long history in medical sociology and adjacent disciplines: the medicalization critique.[9] Beginning in the 1950s and 1960s with Thomas Szasz and Michel Foucault and continuing into the 1970s with Irving Zola and Ivan Illich, scholars and cultural critics have examined the ever-expanding jurisdiction of medicine—an institution that increasingly addresses deviance and criminality, natural life processes such as pregnancy, and circumstantial emotions such as grief. One of the most salient concerns in this literature of late is the expanding boundaries around mental illness[10]: changes in diagnostic criteria and clinical practice which redefine sadness as depression,[11] shyness as social anxiety disorder,[12] and distraction as attention deficit disorder.[13] Central to this expansion has been the advent of selective serotonin reuptake inhibitors (SSRIs) such as Prozac and Zoloft, released in the late 1980s and prescribed ever more frequently—as Wurtzel observed—for depression and anxiety.

In the case of mental illnesses such as depression, a crucial underlying concern in the medicalization literature is the ramifications of illness frameworks for self-identity. David Karp explores how people taking antidepressants distinguish their own stable sense of self from the effects of mood-altering drugs in his aptly titled *Is It Me or My Meds?*,[14] while Allan Horwitz and Jerome Wakefield explain the social process through which normal sorrow was transformed into clinical depression in modern psychiatry.[15] Direct-to-consumer advertisements have intensified scholars' concerns regarding the narratives that such advertisements make available. The sociologist Jeffrey Stepnisky argues that advertisements for SSRIs such as Zoloft and Prozac emphasize a "narrative magic" that eliminates the need "to incorporate incomprehensible and disturbing experiences into the ongoing story of self," allowing people to "perform feats of self-completion that in other contexts"—including both therapeutic and religious settings—"would require exhaustive and challenging self-examination and narrative reconstruction."[16]

An interdisciplinary literature on illness narratives approaches the same cultural development—the increasing salience, even hegemony, of biomedical frameworks—from a different standpoint.[17] Rather than interrogate and critique the shifting boundaries between normality and pathology, this literature considers the ways in which ill people seek meaning in experiences that are now defined predominantly in medicine's technical-rational terms. The drive underlying contemporary medicine is—to borrow from Zygmunt Bauman—the modern project of "deconstructing mortality": the effort "to dissolve the issue of the struggle against death in an ever growing and never exhausted set of battles against particular diseases and other threats to life," breaking it down into discrete "problems of health" that are "in principle 'soluble.'"[18] But in the midst of the "health society,"[19] wherein optimistic restitution narratives have become a cultural imperative even in the face of devastating diagnoses,[20] how do people respond when there is no narrative template, no cultural trope, for coming to terms with chronic suffering? Do they accept the "narrative magic" of the biomedical restitution narrative, or do they turn to alternative archetypes? While scholars have examined the ways in which memoirs of physical illness grapple with these questions, they have not yet examined the growing number of mental illness memoirs.

In one such study, Anne Hunsaker Hawkins argues that one way of interpreting "the popularity of pathography today is to see it as a reaction to our contemporary biomedical model, one so dominated by a physical understanding of illness that its experiential aspects are virtually ignored."[21] On the surface, at least, it seems that mental illness memoirs are indeed bound up with the increasing cultural salience of biomedical models for human suffering. For one, the outpouring of depression memoirs coincided almost precisely with the release of SSRIs and the shift toward a biochemical understanding of the condition. The first such memoir published by a mainstream press and listed in the Library of Congress catalog is Styron's.[22] Furthermore, even some of their titles—*Prozac Nation*; *Prozac Diary*; *Hello to All That: A Memoir of War, Zoloft, and Peace*—indicate that the ascendancy of SSRI medications often forms the crux of the narratives. What role do biomedical frameworks play in these stories? Do they perform the "narrative magic" that Stepnisky describes?[23] Do authors engage with the biomedical model one way when their medication succeeds and a different way when it fails? To what extent do biomedical frameworks *colonize* authors' language of suffering?[24] I analyze nineteen depression memoirs, published by mainstream U.S. presses between 1990 and 2011 and identified using subject headings from the Library of Congress and the bookseller Amazon. I limit my sample to the memoirs published by mainstream presses—excluding self-published memoirs and memoirs published by religious presses—because such works best represent personal stories and narrative templates simultaneously.[25] Their liminality makes them an especially compelling site for analysis. Unlike interviews, they are public narratives that may—like *Prozac Nation*—be a springboard for public dialogue and a wellspring for cultural tropes; unlike advertisements, they are personal narratives that may or may not draw upon dominant cultural frames. It is important to note, though, that sampling decisions were made on the basis of publisher rather than on the basis of substantive content. As I argue in what follows, religious and spiritual narratives are a core component of several memoirs in the sample.

Though each narrative is personal, with its own nuances in both interpretation and style, there are a few clear templates for the ways in which memoirists reconcile biomedical accounts with larger projects of self-reconstruction. Together, they speak not only to the increasing salience of the biomedical model for depression but also to the various ways in which it is co-opted into the project of recasting the self in light of mental illness. Among authors who embrace the biomedical model—and a majority do so, although to varying extents—I argue, similar to Joseph Davis,[26] that it provides an *account* rather than a narrative.[27] Accounts, in a sociological sense, serve as excuses, justifications, or explanations for breaches of social norms or "failure events" more generally—including, I argue, the narrative "complication" of mental illness: They provide a ready-made response to "imposing problems or stressful life events" that can be deployed in order to keep a larger self-narrative moving in the face of an interruption.[28] These accounts serve as devices within larger narratives: cultural "tools" used primarily to explain the origins of suffering and to alleviate the social stigma and moral burdens often associated with mental illness.[29]

Crucially, I find that the biomedical account may be decoupled from the use of medication itself: It is not necessary to experience a medical "cure" or even relief deriving from medications to adopt the biomedical explanation for suffering or embrace the relief of social stigma and moral burdens that the account offers. The obverse is also true: Finding relief from medication does not necessitate the adoption of a biomedical account. Yet the biomedical model is not merely one option among many. Instead, it forms a nearly ubiquitous backdrop to narratives with very different orientations and goals. In the pages that follow, I describe three broad types: (1) memoirs that report positive benefits from medication and accept the biomedical account but integrate it with a larger narrative of quest or journey, (2) memoirs that report little benefit from medication but still accept the biomedical account, and (3) memoirs that reject both medicine and the biomedical account. Only one of the memoirs ignores the biomedical model entirely.[30]

Quest Narratives, Biomedical Accounts

For most authors, the biomedical account exists in an uneasy relationship with a larger "quest" narrative. Quest narratives imbue the interruption of illness with meaning by framing it as "the occasion of a journey that becomes a quest . . . defined by the ill person's belief that something is to be gained through the experience."[31] These memoirs suggest that adopting a biomedical account does not necessarily lead to a reductionist view of suffering: The impulse to address the existential questions posed by serious illness remains. As authors grapple with these existential questions, they integrate biomedical accounts into broader narratives that conceptualize illness in more holistic terms. Even if they define depression as—at least in part—an illness with a somatic etiology, then, these memoirs go on to describe spiritual and/or therapeutic journeys through which authors re-narrativize their pasts and recast their identities in light of their experience with depression. Yet the biomedical account provides a crucial narrative device in these memoirs: It resolves the narrative "complication" that debilitating psychological suffering produces by alleviating the moral weight that might otherwise be associated with it.

These authors often reflect explicitly on the extensive self-revision that illness—and its cure—requires. Emblematic is Lauren Slater's *Prozac Diary*, one of the earliest memoirs to explore the experience of drug-taking in detail. Slater recalls her "remission" from depression and obsessive-compulsive disorder—brought about by Prozac shortly after it hit the market—as "redemption, both bright and blinding, heaven opening up, letting me in."[32] Prozac worked marvelously—as Slater puts it, even *miraculously*. Yet despite Prozac's efficacy, Slater grapples mightily with the implications of a drug that affects a profound transformation in her own identity. She recalls: "I was concerned that Prozac, and the health it spawned, could take away not only my creativity but my very identity. And the answer to that—although there had been 'no studies'— was a certain yes. I was a different person now, both more and less like me, fulfilling one possibility while swerving from another. There is loss in that swerving. And my experience on Prozac showed me how few there are who understand that loss or are prepared for its expression."[33]

Slater's concern is not merely that Prozac erodes valuable *qualities* or *characteristics*—her creativity, for instance—but that it transforms something deeper and more enduring. "Cure," she suggests, is "disorienting,"[34] and she longs for more time to inhabit the liminal space between illness and health—to transition to a new-found and indeed radically different identity:

> My experience with Prozac and the kind of rushing recovery it spawned has caused me, at the risk of nostalgia, to look with favor upon the old sanatoriums and convalescent homes of the late-eighteenth and early-nineteenth centuries, halfway houses where the chronically ill, now recovering, hovered in their newfound health, tentatively trying it out, buttoning and unbuttoning, resewing the seams, until at last the new outfit seemed right. The old-fashioned convalescent home, chairs stretched out by the salty sea, isolated from the world and yet close to the cusp of it, acknowledged the need for a supportive transition, moving the patient incrementally from an illness-based identity to a health-based identity, out of the hospital, and not yet home, hovering, stuttering, slowly learning to speak the sanguine alphabet again.[35]

When medication works "magically" or "miraculously," it may obliterate a lengthy transition at an emotional and physiological level: The patient may feel cured, even transformed. Yet Slater suggests that healing also has an existential dimension that medicine does not address: a transition in self-identity that unfolds only over a longer temporal horizon.

Indeed, several other memoirs narrate this transition in detail, seeking to reconcile the efficacy of medication with a larger story of spiritual or personal transformation. Most commonly, these transformations unfold through religious exploration, therapeutic self-discovery, or both.

For Tim Farrington (*A Hell of Mercy*), the journey is spiritual, and the biomedical account is embedded within a larger existential quest. Invoking the Catholic Saint John of the Cross, Farrington refers to depression as "the dark night of the soul" and argues that deep psychological suffering has a powerful spiritual purpose:

> We can treat the life-disrupting realities of depression, darkness, terror, and despair when they come (and they will) as speed bumps on the road to the usual and devote our efforts to get back up to speed as soon as possible; or we can take the car wreck of the dark night as a grace, as what Joan Halifax calls "a sacred catastrophe" and a "holy failure." Led by suffering into the mapless country of faith, silence, and darkness, perhaps we will even glimpse the truth of what the sages and saints have been saying for ages when they talk about the necessary death of the ego and the mystery of divine life.[36]

The "dark night," Farrington suggests, yields spiritual wisdom, and his memoir strings together insights from his own journey through it. The insights come from a veritable pastiche of traditions and communities: Zen Buddhism, existentialist philosophy, Western psychology, yoga and meditation, the *Bhagavad Gita*, Christian mysticism. His tenure with depression takes him into ashrams, academic institutions, and churches. Along the way, he explains, both John of the Cross's *Dark Night of the Soul* and the *Diagnostic and Statistical Manual of Mental Disorders* are his "faithful companions" as he attempts to discern "whether I was making my blind way to God through the cloud of unknowing or was just clinically fucked-up."[37] Ultimately, Farrington understands his "depression . . . as a gift of God—a hell of mercy . . . and not of wrath"[38]: Indeed, he concludes his memoir with reflections on the divine gift of suffering. Yet the biomedical account never disappears from view entirely: Farrington treats his suffering with medication, which—he reports—works magnificently.

How, then, does Farrington reconcile the concept of the "dark night" as a divine gift that promotes wisdom through suffering with a medical intervention that alleviates suffering? Farrington's prescription, he explains, was sent by God at the right moment, the moment when his suffering had ceased yielding wisdom and become divorced from the larger spiritual purpose for which it was sent: "I think God sent the indomitable woman with the prescription pad and that by God's grace I was desperate enough by then to grab the lifeline. I think the Kmart pharmacy is an outpost of heaven. The dark night is not about suffering for suffering's sake; it is about a certain work of soul being accomplished. When the work is done, it is time to move on."[39] Medication, then, is to be used in alleviating depression after one has emerged from the "dark night," equipped with the insights it yields.

Similarly, Eric Wilson (*The Mercy of Eternity*) literally describes the moment when he embraced the biomedical account using the language of religious enlightenment. In a group therapy session, Wilson—who reluctantly attends the group at his wife's urging—confesses that he has been using alcohol to cope with suicidal thoughts, and that depression has left him disengaged from his young daughter. Anticipating sympathy from the group, Wilson is instead chastised by a young woman who recalls her own alcoholic father's neglect. The encounter, he writes, was "an undeniable epiphany,"[40] a crucial turning point at which he takes initiative in pursuing treatment.

> I read once, maybe in Joseph Campbell, that a man is ready to seek spiritual liberation from his prideful ego only when his desire for salvation is as urgent as a burning man's is for water. I felt that night something akin to that desperate need for living currents and decided right then that I would do whatever it took, no matter how difficult, to wash away my sins. The first thing I had to do, I realized, was once more to see a psychiatrist, this time in earnest, on my own initiative. I'd take any pill imaginable, forever if need be, or undergo any therapeutic exercise, no matter how radical, if it would help me recognize and accept those rare invitations to love.[41]

Taking on the biomedical account is, for Wilson, an *epiphany*, a stroke of divine wisdom: The first thing he must do to "wash away" his "sins" is to "see a psychiatrist," to "take any pill imaginable." Working with his new psychiatrist—who diagnoses him with bipolar II—he comes to see psychopharmaceuticals as *protective*: While "bipolar disorder can destroy the brain's gray matter," he explains, "[t]he proper drugs can counteract the destruction," working "*with* the brain's chemistry, not against it." This new framework enables him to embrace the biomedical account, ameliorating his concern that drugs were "assaults on identity."[42] Armed with medication and the account his psychiatrist offers, Wilson describes an experience of spiritual "rebirth" as he embraces Christian faith and learns to engage fully in a loving relationship with his young daughter. His journey toward rebirth thus begins with the decision to pursue medical treatment, and he recasts his suffering in biomedical terms. Yet Wilson places the biomedical account within the context of a more holistic narrative that addresses the existential challenges of illness and plays a critical role in his healing process.

The quest, of course, is not always religious or spiritual. Sociologists from Philip Rieff[43] to Eva Illouz[44] have pointed to the ways in which therapeutic discourses function as a surrogate for religion in secular culture by addressing the problem of suffering. As Illouz argues, the therapeutic narrative conceptualizes present suffering as the product of past trauma and encourages adherents to re-emplot their pasts— especially early childhood—in light of the present. Danny Evans (*Rage Against the Meshugenah*) juxtaposes the biomedical account with this project of therapeutic self-reconstruction. Depression, Evans writes, is a "mental illness," a "disease."[45] He wishes he could stop taking antidepressant medication but says he is "reminded on days when I skip my meds that the distance between contentment and depression is quite short."[46] But ultimately, the etiology Evans provides locates depression's causes in his relationship with his father. Evans's father was severely neglected throughout his childhood: "unnoticed" and "disregarded" by his parents, even moved around to live with other family members. Evans reports that, because his father grew up "perpetually vulnerable," he ultimately became "the kind of man who would not allow himself to be in that position ever again": He became "[h]ard," "[i]mpenetrable," and "[i]naccessible." Evans reflects: "I believe this was the root of my depression, and I now know that without his knowledge or intention, my dad passed down to me a sense of powerlessness over my own course in life. Like him, I went where I was told to go. I marched down that path until my mind decided it couldn't take any more and broke down in the fall of 2001."[47] Therapy enabled Evans to reconstruct the origins of his depression and to revise his sense of self-identity in ways that promote healing. Evans is clear that it was a lengthy and painstaking process of re-*construction*—far from the instantaneous transformation medical advertisements promise: "With the hard work of therapy, I found ways to close the holes in my life where the harsh, blinding light of vulnerability could shine through and burn me. I took myself apart like a busted carburetor, examined the pieces, retrofitted where necessary, and rebuilt myself to be stronger—new and improved."[48] "Recovery," he analogizes, "is a marathon."[49]

Evans reflects explicitly on the importance of the biomedical account in alleviating the moral weight that depression brought about in earlier eras. Much as he faults his grandmother for his father's suffering—a legacy passed on to Evans in the form of depression—he also recognizes how difficult it must have been for her to cope with "nervous breakdowns" in a time when the stigma they carried was immense. "Despite the collateral damage that altered my father's youth," Evans writes, "I feel a tinge of empathy for my grandmother because the collective ignorance about her ailment at the time it occurred must have exponentially worsened the ordeal."[50] Even if Evans's journey toward recovery is rooted in therapeutic self-reconstruction, then, the biomedical account plays a crucial role in enabling him to seek treatment (both medical and therapeutic) and to embrace an illness identity rather than perceive his experience as a moral failure. Indeed, his memoir is subtitled *Why It Takes Balls to Go Nuts*, a glorification—albeit comedic—of his condition.

Medicine without Medication

While the majority of authors find at least partial relief in medication, if not a full-fledged alleviation of symptoms, not all find that their suffering responds to drug treatment. The stories these authors tell, even more than those described earlier, illustrate the cultural power of the biomedical account: Authors need not experience a medical cure in order to interpret their suffering in biomedical terms. In these memoirs, medication and the biomedical account are *decoupled*: The biomedical *account* may still serve as a crucial cultural tool even though medication itself is ineffective.

William Styron's memoir—perhaps the founding moment of the genre—is exemplary here. Medications do nothing to alleviate Styron's symptoms, yet the biomedical understanding of depression provides the narrative foundation for his memoir. Depression, Styron explains, is a disease, but it is a disease that remains—at least in many cases, including his own—incurable. He writes:

> [D]epression, in its extreme form, is madness. The madness results from an aberrant biochemical process. It has been established with reasonable certainty (after strong resistance from many psychiatrists, and not all that long ago) that such madness is chemically induced amid the neurotransmitters of the brain, probably as a result of systemic stress, which for unknown reasons causes a depletion of the chemicals norepinephrine and serotonin, and the increase of a hormone, cortisol. With all of this upheaval in the brain tissues, the alternate drenching and deprivation, it is no wonder that the mind begins to feel aggravated, stricken, and the muddied thought processes register the distress of an organ in convulsion.[51]

Styron draws an analogy between the failure of antidepressants and "the failure of nearly all drugs to stem massive bacterial infections in the years before antibiotics became a specific remedy."[52] Medication never cures Styron—though he did recover after hospitalization—but it does give him an account for aberrant behaviors. His memoir opens with a description of his trip to Paris to accept the *Prix Mondial Cino Del Duca*, an international literary prize. He was, at the time, "at a critical stage in the development of the disease [depression]"[53] and refused to attend the formal luncheon that followed the award ceremony. The decision, he reflects, "was outrageous; it had been announced months before to me and everyone else concerned that a luncheon—moreover, a luncheon in my honor—was part of the day's pageantry. But my behavior was really a result of the illness, which had progressed far enough to produce some of its most famous and sinister hallmarks: confusion, failure of mental focus and lapse of memory." Recognizing the impropriety of his decision in retrospect, he reversed it with a mea culpa invoking illness: "'I'm sick,'" he said, "*un problème psychiatrique*," quite literally "accounting" for his faux pas with biomedical language.[54]

Sharon O'Brien (*The Family Silver*)—an English professor at Dickinson College—also invokes the biomedical account even though her own depression has not responded to drug treatment. She recalls the relief she felt when she received the initial diagnosis, which imposed order and clarity upon suffering that had been incomprehensible: "Being told I was in a 'clinical depression' actually felt good. I was relieved to know I *had* something, a condition, an illness, as in childhood when the family doctor said 'You have the measles.' 'Clinical depression' . . . sounded like a category that other people had occupied, and so instead of feeling erased by the classification I felt consoled. I was part of a community of sufferers."[55]

Despite the relief that the diagnosis provides, antidepressants ultimately fail to relieve her suffering—leading O'Brien to search for a narrative that transcends the biochemical model. This search forms the basis for a larger quest narrative. Recognizing that her own father—now deceased—suffered similarly, O'Brien delves into her family's history. She grasps for the connections between her father's depression and her own and comes to believe that both "were linked up with American culture: with success and failure, education and academia, the pressure to achieve and produce."[56] In the end, O'Brien states quite clearly that she cannot tell a restitution story. Instead, she reflects, she must learn to incorporate depression into her broader self-identity, using a narrative template that is "more complex" than "the recovery story of illness and cure."[57]

Yet at the same time, O'Brien's concluding reflections suggest that she is nonetheless working consciously to adopt a biomedical account. During a sabbatical in Cambridge, Massachusetts, she began attending a self-help group for people with depression and manic depression. Group members, she says, have "all internalized the belief that our illnesses are our own individual fault: you can't grow up in American society without doing that. But we're all fighting against that, and the group helps me to make progress." For instance, she explains, the group's "drop-in center is filled with buttons saying 'Depression: It's Nobody's Fault' and bumper stickers asking you to 'Honk If You're on Lithium.'"[58] The biomedical account—reinforced in this group context—helps to relieve the moral weight with which depression once burdened O'Brien, even as she weaves it into a more holistic narrative that identifies multiple and intersecting causes of illness. Indeed, she counts herself fortunate to have access to the account even if the treatments associated with it have failed. Her father—like Danny Evans's grandmother—had no such benefit:

> In contrast to my father's time . . . by the 1990s there was a much clearer understanding of the biochemical and genetic components of the illness; I was lucky to be living in a time of such medical progress. It had become clear that people could inherit a biochemical predisposition toward depression, as my father likely did, as I and my siblings surely did. Neurotransmitters in the brain, like serotonin, had been linked with depression, and antidepressants seemed to increase the amount of serotonin and other neurotransmitters and so alleviate, or even erase, depression.[59]

Even when medications fail, then, the biomedical account offers powerful moral reassurance along with an explanation that both Styron and O'Brien embrace: a clear illustration of its cultural power.

Rejecting Medicine in the "Prozac Nation"

As the preceding examples illustrate, none of the authors—even those for whom traditional SSRIs are both welcome and effective—straightforwardly reproduce the narrative presented in pharmaceutical advertisements. Authors' efforts to re-envision their self-narratives frequently draw upon medical metaphors as accounts. But the struggle to deal with the "complication" of depression ultimately generates more holistic narratives that engage in the very efforts at "self-reconstruction" that pharmaceutical advertisements—which often feature deeply reductionist images of illness—invite viewers to omit.[60] However, there are two authors whose books represent thoroughgoing rejections of the biomedical model: not efforts to complicate it—such as O'Brien's—but critiques of its very premises.

Yet ironically, these memoirs—perhaps even more than the others—also illustrate the cultural power of the biomedical account. It cannot be ignored, but—if it is not adopted—it must be grappled with, overtly rejected, and even polemicized against. In short, as Hawkins argues, oppositional narratives illustrate the durability and salience of the biomedical model: "That this myth can generate complaints of its ineffectiveness or unhelpfulness is actually a sign of its vitality. The mark of a living myth is not so much its veracity, nor even its utility . . . but its authority and power, the degree to which people feel compelled to believe in it."[61] Rejecting it requires an explicit justification.

David Awbrey's memoir illustrates the second way in which medicine and the biomedical account may be decoupled: Prozac improves his level of functioning—the medication "works"—and yet he ultimately rejects the biomedical account and ceases taking the medication itself. His self-conscious rejection is prompted not by the failure of psychotropic drugs but by the conviction that the causes of his malaise are cultural rather than biochemical and by a critique of the reductionism he perceives in biomedical models of depression. Prozac, Awbrey reports, helped him to "function smoothly," but it did so "mainly by dulling rather than relieving my inner psychic tensions."[62] His suffering originates, he believes, not from faulty brain chemistry but from a deficit of meaning endemic to "postmodern" times. Ultimately, he refers to his suffering as "melancholy" and—like Farrington and Wilson—reconceptualizes it as a source of wisdom: "[M]elancholy," he suggests, "can be a sublime discontent. Through despair, people can clarify what is important in life, connect themselves to timeless reality, and create a cherishing society."[63]

Yet for Awbrey, depression is not just the impetus for a personal and/or spiritual transformation, but a sign that something is awry in the culture at large: "Perhaps . . . human consciousness uses melancholy as a warning that something is disastrously wrong in society."[64] Noting the rise in diagnoses of depression, he suggests: "Much of the psychological depression of the 1990s is due to a personal disconnection from a larger vision of life. There is no consensus, no clear direction to the future."[65] Depression, for many of his contemporaries, is "primarily moral and spiritual rather than medical or circumstantial,"[66] a "corrosive" effect of "moral relativism"—a relativism Awbrey traces to postmodern philosophy and culture.[67] Ironically, Awbrey's overarching narrative is perhaps best classified as a postmodern variant of the archetypal "quest" narrative: In the end—much like Farrington—he finds meaning in a pastiche that juxtaposes Christianity with Zen Buddhism and other traditions. Yet his narrative is structured as a foil to the biomedical account that he encountered first, an account he explicitly condemns as reductionistic: "[P]sychotropic drugs," he argues, "threaten to reduce character and self-identity to biotechnology," and Awbrey "wanted [his] life to have moral consequence"[68]—an end that he felt he could not achieve while taking Prozac.

Jeffrey Smith (*Where the Roots Reach for Water*)—like authors such as Styron and O'Brien—found that antidepressants did not restore him to health: He briefly had success with Zoloft, but its effects fizzled, and he subsequently experienced an adverse reaction to trazodone. In contrast to that of other authors who had little success with pharmaceuticals, however, Smith's experience prompted him to reject not only pharmaceutical treatments but also the biomedical account for his suffering. In so doing, he rejects a fundamental premise of the "health society": the assumption, as Smith puts it, "that happiness is the natural state of our species." He finds an alternative in the notion of an inborn temperament. At first blush, the notion of inborn temperament might seem akin to biochemical accounts of depression. Yet it differs fundamentally: It *normalizes* suffering that, in the biomedical framework, is considered pathological. Smith writes: "[O]ur science explains not only the melancholic temperaments ('dysthymia' and 'cyclothymia') and clinical depression, but also more explicable and transient states of sadness, such as mourning the loss of a loved one, not as age-old natural life experiences, painful but necessary, but as biochemical defects to be readily vanquished with a pill." In direct contrast to Styron, who classifies depression as an as-yet-incurable disease, Smith suggests that medicine's inability to cure many cases of depression is evidence that depression is not a "disease" but a state within the normal range of human experience: "Biological psychiatry is fond of likening clinical depression to juvenile diabetes: neurotransmitter deficiencies, its advocates assert, are no different from the lack of pancreatic insulin suffered by juvenile (or Type I) diabetics. Just as those diabetics require insulin to go on living, those with neurotransmitter deficiencies require anti-depressants." While medical metaphors or analogies do the important work of alleviating stigma, "[b]eyond that, the analogy's usefulness dissipates rather quickly." While "you will find very few diabetics for whom insulin has failed," antidepressants frequently fail to alleviate sufferers' pain—suggesting, for Smith, that the pain reflects not a breakdown of health but a natural state to be incorporated into one's self-narrative.[69]

In the end, Smith's narrative allows him to live *with* his suffering: "to coexist with depression."[70] He seeks ways to "live faithful to [his] native constitution,"[71] seeing "melancholia as a kind of spiritual mentor" and developing "creative way[s] to respond to it"—with "'creative' used here to indicate the antonym of 'passive.'"[72] Unlike "depression" (the illness), Smith's "melancholia" (the temperament) is not an enemy to be eliminated at all costs but a partner that teaches Smith how to live in harmony with his constitution. But his melancholic narrative is always woven in direct opposition to—and direct contrast with—the culturally predominant biomedical account. Thus biomedical language forms a ubiquitous backbone to his memoir precisely because he must reject it so vehemently.

Conclusion

Depression memoirs embody the complexity people face in addressing the problem of suffering in our cultural and historical moment. Authors almost inevitably engage with the biomedical model, whether they adopt it, complicate it, or rail against it. Yet much as biomedical language—references to illnesses and disease, medication, and biochemical imbalances—runs throughout the pages of these memoirs, so, too, do more holistic narrative templates: spiritual discovery and rebirth, therapeutic self-reconstruction, even oppositional models rooted in alternate etiologies. Sometimes these broader templates exist in an uneasy tension with, or even seemingly overt contradiction to, the biomedical account. And yet a number of authors—among them Farrington and Wilson—manage to sustain the juxtaposition in ways that appear, at least, to render their own experiences more comprehensible than they once were.

O'Brien's case is emblematic of both the possibilities and liabilities associated with the biomedical model's rise as a framework for depression. The biomedical account alleviates stigma and encourages her to shed moral burdens that have plagued her for quite some time. Indeed, its power as a social psychological account is so great that it can be decoupled from medications: O'Brien incorporates biomedical language not because antidepressants are effective for her but because the account accompanying them does important moral and narrative work. And yet the "recovery plot"—as O'Brien calls it—is inadequate to her lived experience. Depression, for O'Brien, is not a fleeting interruption resolved with medical intervention but a source of ongoing suffering. The unfulfilled promises of the recovery plot leave her grasping for a narrative which captures that suffering. If biomedical language is indeed colonizing languages of emotional suffering—and depression memoirs certainly indicate that it is—it seems that this process is a double-edged sword.

On its own, each memoir communicates the contours of a particular life with depression. Collectively, however, these narratives represent an enduring effort to find sense in suffering: to work with, through, and around the biomedical model so prevalent in the current age in order to find a place for depression in a meaningful self-narrative. In so doing, the authors offer templates to fellow sufferers after depression has intruded on their own stories.

NOTES

1 Daniel William Ross, *The Critical Response to William Styron* (Westport, Conn.: Greenwood Press, 1995).

2 Arthur W. Frank, *The Wounded Storyteller: Body, Illness, and Ethics* (Chicago: University of Chicago Press, 1995), 54.

3 Ibid., 56.

4 Anthony Giddens, *Modernity and Self-Identity: Self and Society in the Late Modern Age* (Stanford, Calif.: Stanford University Press, 1991), 54.

5 Frank, *The Wounded Storyteller*, 83.

6 See Arthur Kleinman, *The Illness Narratives: Suffering, Healing, and the Human Condition* (New York: Basic Books, 1988); and Stanley Hauerwas, *Naming the Silences* (London: T & T Clark International, 2004).

7 See Peter L. Berger, *The Sacred Canopy: Elements of a Sociological Theory of Religion* (Garden City, N.Y.: Doubleday, 1967); Max Weber, *The Sociology of Religion* (Boston: Beacon Press, 1922); and Weber, "The Social Psychology of the World Religions," 267–302 in *From Max Weber: Essays in Sociology* (New York: Oxford University Press, 1946).

8 See Eva Illouz, *Oprah Winfrey and the Glamour of Misery: An Essay on Popular Culture* (New York: Columbia University Press, 2003).

9 See Joseph E. Davis, "Medicalization, Social Control, and the Relief of Suffering," 211–41 in *The New Blackwell Companion to Medical Sociology*, ed. William C. Cockerham (Malden, Mass.: Blackwell, 2010).

10 See, for example, Peter D. Kramer, *Listening to Prozac: A Psychiatrist Explains Antidepressant Drugs and the Remaking of the Self* (New York: Penguin, 1993); and Davis, "Medicalization."

11 Allan V. Horwitz and Jerome C. Wakefield, *The Loss of Sadness: How Psychiatry Transformed Normal Sorrow into Depressive Disorder* (New York: Oxford University Press, 2007).

12 Christopher Lane, *Shyness: How Normal Behavior Became a Sickness* (New Haven, Conn.: Yale University Press, 2007).

13 Peter Conrad, *Identifying Hyperactive Children: The Medicalization of Deviant Behavior*, Expanded Edition (Aldershot, UK: Ashgate, 2006).

14 David A. Karp, *Is It Me or My Meds? Living with Antidepressants* (Cambridge, Mass.: Harvard University Press, 2006).

15 Horwitz and Wakefield, *The Loss of Sadness*.

16 Jeffrey N. Stepnisky, "Narrative Magic and the Construction of Selfhood in Antidepressant Advertising," *Bulletin of Science, Technology & Society* 27(1) (2007): 24–36, at 26.

17 See Kleinman, *The Illness Narratives*; Frank, *The Wounded Storyteller*; and Cheryl Mattingly, *The Paradox of Hope: Journeys Through a Clinical Borderland* (Berkeley: University of California Press, 2010).

18 Zygmunt Bauman, *Mortality, Immortality and Other Life Strategies* (Stanford, Calif.: Stanford University Press, 1992), 10.

19 Ilona Kickbusch, "Health Governance: The Health Society," 144–61 in *Health and Modernity: The Role of Theory in Health Promotion*, ed. David V. McQueen and Ilona Kickbusch (New York: Springer, 2007). See also Joseph E. Davis, chapter 1, this volume.

20 Barbara Ehrenreich, *Bright-Sided: How the Relentless Promotion of Positive Thinking Has Undermined America* (New York: Macmillan, 2009).

21 Anne Hunsaker Hawkins, *Reconstructing Illness: Studies in Pathography*, Second Edition (West Lafayette, Ind.: Purdue University Press, 1999), 11.

22 There are also four memoirs published by Christian presses listed in the Library of Congress for the years 1983–89, prior to Styron's book.

23 Stepnisky, "Narrative Magic."

24 Davis, chapter 1, this volume.

25 The sample includes books written by people with depression and bipolar II. It does not include books written by those with bipolar I (e.g., Kay Redfield Jamison, *An Unquiet Mind* [New York: Picador, 1997]). Bipolar II is more similar to major depression, and the authors in my sample suffering from bipolar II were initially diagnosed with—and continue to describe themselves as suffering from—depression.

26 Joseph E. Davis, *Accounts of Innocence: Sexual Abuse, Trauma, and the Self* (Chicago: University of Chicago Press, 2005), chapter 1.

27 Marvin B. Scott and Stanford M. Lyman, "Accounts," *American Sociological Review* 33(1) (1968): 46–62.

28 Terri L. Orbuch, "People's Accounts Count: The Sociology of Accounts," *Annual Review of Sociology* 23 (1997): 455–78, at 467–68.

29 Ann Swidler, "Culture in Action: Symbols and Strategies," *American Sociological Review* 51(2) (1986): 273–86.

30 This memoir is Emily Fox Gordon's *Mockingbird Years: A Life in and out of Therapy* (New York: Basic Books, 2000). It is primarily a retrospective reflection on her experience in psychoanalysis and psychotherapy before the advent of SSRIs.

31 Frank, *The Wounded Storyteller*, 115.

32 Lauren Slater, *Prozac Diary* (New York: Random House, 1998), 34.

33 Ibid., 49.

34 Ibid., 9.

35 Ibid., 36–37.

36 Tim Farrington, *A Hell of Mercy: A Meditation on Depression and the Dark Night of the Soul* (New York: HarperCollins, 2009), 115–16.

37 Ibid., 37.

38 Ibid., 116.

39 Ibid., 100–1.

40 Eric Wilson, *The Mercy of Eternity: A Memoir of Depression and Grace* (Evanston, Ill.: Northwestern University Press, 2010), 74.

41 Ibid., 75.

42 Ibid., 79.

43 Philip Rieff, *The Triumph of the Therapeutic: Uses of Faith After Freud* (Chicago: University of Chicago Press, 1966).

44 Illouz, *Oprah*; and Illouz, *Saving the Modern Soul* (Berkeley: University of California Press, 2008).

45 Danny Evans, *Rage Against the Meshugenah: Why It Takes Balls to Go Nuts* (New York: Penguin, 2009), 302.

46 Ibid., 328.

47 Ibid., 319.

48 Ibid., 319–20.

49 Ibid., 196.

50 Ibid., 185.

51 William Styron, *Darkness Visible: A Memoir of Madness* (New York: Vintage, 1990), 47.

52 Ibid., 55.

53 Ibid., 8.

54 Ibid., 14–15.

55 Sharon O'Brien, *The Family Silver: A Memoir of Depression and Inheritance* (Chicago: University of Chicago Press, 2004), 277.

56 Ibid., 152.

57 Ibid., 271, 270.

58 Ibid., 261.

59 Ibid., 264.

60 See Stepnisky, "Narrative Magic."

61 Hawkins, *Reconstructing Illness*, 33–34.

62 David S. Awbrey, *Finding Hope in the Age of Melancholy* (Boston: Little, Brown, 1999), 46.

63 Ibid., 28.

64 Ibid., 66.

65 Ibid., 97.

66 Ibid., 138.

67 Ibid., 247.

68 Ibid., 151, 152.

69 Jeffery Smith, *Where the Roots Reach for Water: A Personal and Natural History of Melancholia* (New York: Macmillan, 1999) 111–12.

70 Ibid., 30.

71 Ibid., 154.

72 Ibid., 221.

3

After Medicine

The Cosmetic Pull of Neuroscience

LUIS E. ECHARTE

Writing in the *Hastings Center Report* in 2002, Paul Wolpe drew the attention of bioethicists to the "neuroscience revolution," a major transformation being driven by advances in neuroimaging, the new generation of psychotropic drugs, neural-technological interfaces, cerebral stimulation technology, and more.[1] Although the revolution has far-reaching ethical and social implications, from challenging the "proper limits of technology" to "redefining our sense of selfhood and brain-body relations," the neuroscientists, Wolpe argued, are proceeding without "waiting for the ethical groundwork to be laid."[2] And, in fact, in the intervening years, empirical researchers have confidently pressed these implications in debates over enhancing human traits, human nature and morality, and other fundamental philosophical questions: Am I my brain? Is it possible to reduce the good, the true, and the beautiful to neuronal phenomena? Is God in my head?

This discussion has not been confined to scientific journals. Quantitative studies of the social impact of neuroscience in the media, such as those conducted by Judy Illes's group, show how deeply the sciences of the nervous system have affected popular understandings of the world.[3] In a study published in 2010, for example, Illes and her colleagues identified three forms of neurocentric discussion in mass-media representations: "neuro-essentialism," defined as a combination of biological reductionism and unfounded enthusiasm for neuroscience; "neuro-realism," the belief that the method and discourse of neuroscience are sufficient to enable us to know what is real; and "neuro-policies," referring to the popular use of neuroscience by governments to modify the lifestyles of citizens.

Many already believe sufficient evidence exists to show that neuroscience, bridging the psychological and the physical, can now answer fundamental and age-old questions about our aesthetic, moral, religious, and other human experiences. These reductionist claims, however, are controversial, and in my judgment unpersuasive.[4] So too is the suggestion that the warm reception neurocentric explanations get in society is a natural result of scientific progress. It is not scientific progress, I argue in this chapter, but social factors that are at work. Much of the enthusiasm for neurocentric claims is attributable to two sociomedical factors: first, the increasing medicalization of everyday experience under the auspices of a reductionist biomedicine (as defined by Joseph E. Davis in the Introduction to this book); and, second, the joining of medicine with cultural preoccupations of enhancement and, ultimately, cosmetic alteration. If neurocentric claims are becoming part of our social imagination, I argue, that is because of new psychopharmacological practices, not new scientific discoveries. These practices emerge, in turn, from the general social atmosphere of what authors like Philip Rieff, Eva Illouz, and Frank Furedi, among others, call "therapeutic culture."[5] Further, as I will show, bioethics has played an important role through its strong assertion of autonomy in matters of health and illness.

Before discussing the origins of medicalization, I need to clarify what I mean by this term. One of the most commonly used contemporary formulations is that of the sociologist Peter Conrad: "a process by which nonmedical problems become defined and treated as medical problems, usually in terms of illnesses or disorders."[6] It strikes me that Conrad is somewhat ambiguous regarding the essential characteristic of medicalization: Under his definition, is medicalization the medical treatment of a given subject, or the exclusion of other approaches in addressing that subject? The first interpretation is redundant because medical knowledge has long been used in all kinds of different activities: education, gastronomy, painting, sports, and much more. We know that Galen himself helped train the gladiators.[7] To differentiate an "inclusive" medicalization of this sort from an "exclusive" medicalization, which claims exclusive jurisdiction over the subject, the ethicist Erik Parens distinguishes between good and bad kinds of medicalization, with the first, inclusive type being "good."[8] I believe, however, that speaking of "good medicalization" confuses more than it clarifies, because it refers only to the medical approach that can have a part in any aspect of human life. The same inclusive notion could be applied to any other approach: the artistic approach, for example. Few people would think that promoting the aesthetic dimensions of gastronomy, or engineering, is a process of redefinition that deserves to be called the "aestheticalization" of the human condition. I therefore prefer to define medicalization in terms that make it clear I am referring to the second kind of medicalization, Parens's "bad" kind: the *exclusion* of nonmedical approaches from widening areas of human existence. In other words, I will use a harder definition of medicalization, replacing "defined as" with "reduced to" in the Conrad definition.

Medicalization

The process of medicalization, thus defined, began two decades before the formal emergence of neuroscience. The psychiatrist Philip A. Berger points to the decade of the 1950s as the time when a new era in prescription psychopharmaceuticals got under way. What was new about this era was not simply the large increase in social demand for these products but the reasons for that increase. It was not caused by the appearance of new mental diseases, or by new medical categorizations of existing pathologies. Rather, the main cause, Berger argues, was the appearance of a new type of *patient*. This patient was characterized by a desire to resolve by chemical means every kind of suffering. People sought remedies classically found in friendship, literature, art, philosophy, or religion in drugs that modified the emotions and conduct.[9] The philosopher Antonio Escohotado agrees with Berger that the post–World War II period was the watershed moment, the time when amphetamine and barbiturate use became acceptable, across different classes, for "elderly people, housewives and students; parts of society harassed by boredom and the lack of motivation, and by the need to pass their exams."[10]

There were a number of reasons for the popular enthusiasm for psychopharmaceuticals. Unlike cocaine and opium, for instance, amphetamines and barbiturates had been discovered in the context of medical research and had been classified as medicines from the outset. As a result, they had legitimacy and a reputation for safety that promoted casual prescription and use. Another reason these drugs became so popular was their instant and evident effect. Within minutes, amphetamines— besides curbing the desire for food and sleep—can revive the user to face a full day's work or a full night's partying. Already in the 1960s, according to Escohotado, surveys conducted in Spain showed that many family doctors prescribed amphetamine-type stimulants to boost students' alertness during exam periods. Barbiturates, for their part, can induce a state of daze and disinhibition very similar to that caused by opium. The big difference is that the barbiturates are legal. Given the vast reserve of everyday emotional problems and anxieties, and the misplaced faith in their safety, these drugs attracted a lot of enthusiastic attention.[11]

We must also recognize that the prevailing social environment of the twentieth century contributed to the phenomenon of medicalization. For instance, it is significant that during the 1960s and 1970s the "counterculture," which emerged mainly in Western countries, delineated and campaigned for a personal right to manipulate one's own body. Two of the main consequences of this social campaign were the sexual revolution and the growing role of patient autonomy in the field of medicine. I would especially like to emphasize the second of the two, because the idea of patient autonomy created, as the ethicists Edmund Pellegrino and David Thomasma argue, a growing distrust of physicians, who were now perceived as obstacles that patients had to get around in order to achieve the treatment they desired.[12] This individualistic emphasis on autonomy was largely adopted within bioethics and made it easier for the psychopharmaceutical craze to continue even after mental health professionals began to realize the associated dangers.[13]

Another catalyst of medicalization, and more specifically of psychiatrization, was the social establishment of therapeutic culture. Part of the reason for this turn to subjectivity was, as Alasdair MacIntyre says, a disillusionment with Enlightenment ideals, owing to the failure of efforts "to provide rational foundations for an objective morality"—a failure most recently and dramatically illustrated by the two world wars.[14] Another cause was the growing influence of psychoanalysis in the arts and the general mainstreaming of the "philosophies of suspicion" in the radical guise of postmodern relativist approaches. The characteristic aspect of the new therapeutic culture (which began as a subculture, a neo-romantic crusade) was the self-referencing interpretation of affectivity: an interpretation in which the emotions were no longer valued as a manifestation or consequence of a particular way of living but as an end in themselves, pursued for their own sake. In other words, the emotions had been elevated to the place formerly accorded to objective knowledge: the ultimate end of action. In such a social environment, psychopharmaceuticals that can act directly on emotion and mood were seen as a promising and legitimate tool for better living.[15]

In conclusion, the currently widespread belief that the medicalization process was a necessary effect of scientific development has little empirical foundation. Tellingly, the first and strongest critique of medicalization came from the medical community, as doctors began to realize the danger of the drugs they were prescribing. Not new science, but a new fashion in the management of emotions, was the starting point of medicalization.[16] Moreover, as I will show, emotional management was also the reason doctors' resistance to medicalization gradually began to dissolve—a process, involving a loss of medicine's commitment to objectivity, that could undermine the entire scientific enterprise.

Biological Reductionism: The Scientific Acceptance of Medicalization

In the 1990s, the process of medicalization reached medical institutions themselves and became institutional and rationalized. The publication in 1994 of the fourth edition of the *Diagnostic and Statistical Manual of Mental Disorders* (*DSM-IV*) was a crucial step in this direction. For the first time, "subclinical problems" were included in what was, and still is, one of the principal diagnostic tools for psychiatrists and psychologists throughout the world. Various sub-optimal psychological tendencies that people show in adapting to their environment were given ambiguous, unspecific diagnostic classifications. Although *DSM-IV* did propose a rich multi-axial nosography, another problem was that the final criteria used to evaluate the effectiveness of adaptations had a strong touch of biological reductionism. In its framework, the concept of "health" came to be understood as a measurement of the successful adaptation of a given organism; as such, the content of "health" was extremely context-dependent.[17] An individual could be considered gravely sick in certain habitats, but not in other, more favorable ones.

The context-dependent approach to mental health used in the *DSM-IV* has practically erased the line between an unhealthy human being and an unhealthy environment.[18] In the fourth edition, "health" delimits a whole spectrum of possible interactions, but it hardly recognizes any intrinsic attributes of individual human beings. Unfortunately, the fact that the paradigm of mental diagnosis had changed was not appreciated by the broader society, which (to its astonishment) discovered overnight that it suffered from innumerable mental ailments. According to Paul Chodoff, 33 million Americans have come to believe they suffer from pathological shyness or some other limiting personality disorder, as a result of their taking *DSM-IV* at its word.[19] This number increases tremendously if the number of patients diagnosed with "generalized anxiety disorder" is included. The majority of these people, unaware of the paradigm under which they were diagnosed, believe that the diagnosis refers to their very identity. The lack of understanding between the scientific community and sick people is reflected in the fact that these new patients, the "worried well," carry the heavy social burden of mental illness. And as Chodoff points out, this same confusion is also reflected in the often fruitless crowding of psychiatric offices—subclinical patients are by definition never truly ill, and one cannot be cured of a disease one does not have.

The *DSM-IV* pathologizes behaviors and emotional states once considered adequate affective responses if they are not biologically effective. A typical example of this is the reduction that has been applied to the "grieving process." Before the fourth edition of the *DSM*, a manifestation of the grieving process was considered a positive thing for two reasons. First, it helped the subject psychologically overcome the loss of the loved one; second, it was considered a natural response. However, in *DSM-IV*, references to natural and existential factors practically disappear. The only two things that seem to be important are resolving the emotional tensions and promoting adaptation to the environment, no matter what.

However, even today most people believe it is both proper and natural to grieve over the death of a loved one, even if the tears and anguish do not bring any beneficial physiological consequences. For the same reason, most people would disapprove if the medical community informed us that bursting into laughter was the best method for dealing with the death of a loved one. The natural dimension of the concept of mental health is what has been left aside, reduced to a mere cultural factor for measuring one's environmental adaptation. As I noted earlier, references to the intrinsic attributes of human beings, to the difference between the organism and its environment, have been replaced by balances and coping.[20] As a result, psychiatry has opened the doors to medicalization. Within the *DSM-IV* framework, there are no objective reasons *not* to change one's personality or conduct if it becomes emotionally bothersome or afunctional.[21] If there is no line dividing the subject and the environment, why insist that a patient change her living situation—for example, by quitting an oppressive, monotonous job—if a pill enables her to adapt more quickly and effectively?[22]

This second, *DSM-IV*–induced phase in the process of medicalization (the introduction of prescription psychopharmaceuticals in the 1950s marking the onset of the first) had decisive consequences in the social establishment of medicalization. It is not a coincidence that during the 1990s practices in administering drugs to children began changing. Indeed, there is no better proof of the consolidation of medicalization than the fact that it began affecting the population that society most tries to protect. Methylphenidate, one of the most frequently used pediatric psychotropic drugs, is a particularly well-studied case.

Although most published studies on the widespread use of behavior-modifying drugs have focused on the United States and Canada, there are already some indications that Europe is headed in the same direction.[23] For example, the health ministry of Spain reported that during 2007 more than 41 million anti-anxiety agents and almost 24 million antidepressants were prescribed.[24]

In short, the psychopharmaceutical boom that began in the 1990s is not very different from the boom of the 1950s. The difference this time is that while doctors are better informed about the adverse effects, they are also more inclined to satisfy patients' requests.

The category of subclinical disorders makes us feel that we are neither healthy nor normal. And the rise of biological reductionism has increasingly justified the use of psychiatry for such "disorders."[25] These two developments have combined to foster the habits of psychopharmaceutical consumption that have become so widespread. The same developments are now provoking a debate about the enhancement of the human condition.

Between Medical Therapy and Medical Enhancement

Writers, painters, philosophers, visionaries—over the centuries, many have addressed themselves to the perfection of the human body, questioning the limits of human potential, the mutability of human nature, the correspondence (or lack thereof) between scientific advance and social progress, even the limits of rationality itself. The medical community, however, has generally treated bodily perfection as a side issue, and for several reasons. First, the very foundation of medicine is bodily weakness and suffering. Medicine finds its purpose in the need to cure, tend to, prevent, and alleviate our diseases and disabilities. A second (and closely related) reason is that the doctor–patient relationship is grounded in this purpose: The trust of the sick is based on the ends of medicine. The sick, as the Spanish medical research scientist Pedro Laín Entralgo said so well, wait in hope. For healthy people to go to the doctor's office to improve their bodies is a situation fundamentally foreign to medicine, strange to doctors and patients alike.[26]

Third, "health," meaning a normal physiological condition, has not fulfilled a merely regulatory role for medicine. It has been a reference point based on more than just the standards of the time. As Leon Kass points out, the ideal of health has always appealed to certain characteristics, especially to a particular organic harmony.[27] But this harmony is more intentional than real, an aspiration more than a normal human state. Throughout human history, medical knowledge has been used to improve living conditions in pursuit of this universal goal. In recent times, greater understanding of factors such as hygiene, nutrition, and sleep have enabled our bodies to attain a state of health few of our ancestors could have enjoyed.[28] However, such improvements have been perceived not as an attempt to overcome human limits but rather as the development of human potential within those limits. The doctor's job has consisted of taking people toward a state of better health, not into some place beyond it. At least until now. Now, the concept of "enhancement" is emerging to refer to the redefining of health, the modification of human ends themselves.

What is meant by medical "enhancement" today is not the improvement of general living conditions—which has long been an end of medicine and public health—but the achievement of particular *super-optimal* goals: Patients want to run faster, or see farther, or remember more. The role of enhancement medicine consists of redesigning the overall organic system to meet such particular ends, effectively subordinating the whole to one of its parts. It is logical that doctors' first reaction to this proposal should be one of caution: Change the harmony of the system just to meet a single specific goal? This road would take medicine to a strange and potentially dangerous place. And on this new road there are no points of reference, as there were in the old understanding of health, nothing that allows doctors to find their bearings—nothing even to measure the success of the venture once it is undertaken. It is thus unsurprising that, as Sheila and David Rothman show in *The Pursuit of Perfection*, the majority of enhancement doctors have been unscrupulous or outright deceitful, taking advantage of their medical authority to make a profit.[29]

If solving the puzzle of organic homeostasis in order to achieve the goal of general well-being is already a major challenge, the hope of modifying homeostasis to reach particular ends is a pipe dream. This fact is especially evident to those researchers—whatever their philosophical commitments—who study the central nervous system, one of the most complex systems in the known universe.[30] Yet, today, industry supports expensive neuro-enhancement research. And drugs that change the brain are being advertised for nontherapeutic purposes on the pharmaceutical market.[31] Why is it that enhancement is becoming a part of medicine? One key reason is the growing acceptance in recent decades of a certain picture of scientific and technological advances. While it is true that certain drugs and methods of electrical brain stimulation have been shown to improve the performance of some physiological functions, this is true only in the short term and for very specific tasks, and even these benefits cannot be explained. So when medical technologies are promoted for enhancement purposes, what is being sold?

This question affects more than the field of (supposed) medical enhancement, for the problem of neuro-technology is not limited to enhancement. Even the active mechanisms of antidepressants—probably the drugs most studied over the last three decades—are still a mystery to psychiatry. Steve Hyman, director of the Stanley Center for Psychiatric Research at the Broad Institute of MIT and Harvard, acknowledges this fact when he states that in pediatric psychopharmacology, "every kid is an uncontrolled experiment."[32] Our lack of scientific understanding is why, after five decades of research and development, the evolution of antidepressants remains so slow. The problem, as Thomas Insel of the U.S. National Institute of Mental Health has noted, is that a large part of the pharmaceutical industry tries to convince us otherwise: continually changing the commercial names of drugs whose active ingredients have scarcely been modified, and employing expensive ad campaigns to tout the extraordinary scientific advances of products that offer no real improvement over the ones that preceded them.[33] The most striking feature of these progress myths is that they are not directed primarily at patients but at the supposed experts in mental health. I will return to the question of persuading the medical community shortly.

It is undeniable that psychopharmacology was (albeit largely by accident) an area of significant scientific and, clinically, highly ameliorative discoveries during the twentieth century. As troubling as the issues of side effects, uncertainties, and dishonest marketing have been, at least those issues are balanced by genuine decreases in the mental suffering of psychiatric patients. The calculus, however, is completely different with respect to enhancement: There is a lot to lose—health—in order to gain who-knows-what.

The Myth of Medical Enhancement: The Pro-Enhancement Movement

In addition to a misleading picture of scientific progress, another key reason for the growing interest in medical enhancement arises from the process of medicalization itself. Of all the neuro-enhancers, methylphenidate and other stimulants have been the most heavily consumed drugs for nontherapeutic purposes and, consequently, the principal subject of enhancement-related arguments in the medical community. These drugs have been prescribed for decades, primarily to treat people with ADHD, but also to increase the attention span of children on the threshold of normal levels of attentiveness. In the context of the expanding medicalization of attentional problems, many parents and guardians of "normal" children began to ask whether the prescription of stimulant medications was essentially arbitrary, and to defend its consumption by those who, though they did not want to participate in the medicalization comedy and receive a diagnosis, seemed in most respects similar to their peers who had. If the drug was so safe and useful for improving attention in children with "academic difficulties," why not also prescribe it for those who were pursuing academic excellence? Given extensive medicalization, there are no easy answers to this question.

Another decisive factor in legitimizing medical enhancement has been the recent enshrinement of patient autonomy in bioethics. This elevation is most central to the libertarian and principlist bioethical frameworks but can be seen in other areas of contemporary bioethics as well.[34] As such, it is ultimately unsurprising that influential figures in bioethics like Arthur Caplan, Henry Greely, and Jonathan Moreno and, in the recently emerged subfield of neuroethics, Martha Farah and Judy Illes, now openly defend the nontherapeutic use of biotechnology. For these ethicists, the autonomy of the individual is the main criterion for determining what should and what should not be addressed or enhanced through biotechnology.

The pro-enhancement arguments of Caplan and these other authors have two rhetorical similarities. First, they usually downplay any meaningful distinction between the objectives of therapy and those of enhancement, thereby encouraging doctors not to resist the latter as beyond the proper scope of medicine. They may recognize the right of medical professionals to refuse to participate in nontherapeutic activities but contend that social demand is going to force the issue whether they like it or not.[35] The second common feature is that most pro-enhancement bioethicists give only passing attention to the problem of safety. Their writing typically begins by affirming the importance of achieving enhancement with minimal risks and adverse effects, but little else is said on the matter. They assume that everyone involved—patients, doctors, laboratories, and politicians—knows and agrees on the relative risks of each technology. But this attitude does not faithfully reflect the current situation: In reality very little is known about many of the drugs consumed for enhancement purposes or their long-term effects. Bioethical talk of neurocognitive enhancement often floats free of the actual limits of neuroscientific research and pays short shrift to its dangers.

Bioethicists do discuss some of the controversies surrounding the question of enhancement. In an article published in 2004, jointly signed by Farah and other prominent neuroscientists and bioethicists, for example, there is, besides the token remarks about safety, discussion of three other ethical issues: coercion, distributive justice, and "personhood and intangible values."[36] It is revealing that in discussing this last topic, Farah and her colleagues acknowledge that enhancement trends might be connected to a social process of medicalization. In my opinion, they are correct in saying this: If there is an abyss between therapeutic and nontherapeutic activity, there is only a small step between medicalization and enhancement. But what is more important than the fact that the authors recognize this connection is the conclusion they reach regarding it: that the process of medicalization "has accompanied many improvements in human life."[37] Yes, there are trade-offs with neurocognitive enhancements, they argue, but many of our "lifestyle decisions" are like that: They "end up on the right side of one value and the wrong side of another, but this does not necessarily mean that these decisions are wrong."[38] Medicalization and enhancement, in this view, are simply matters of lifestyle and, in the end, a matter of the cultural values and particular beliefs of the individual.

In "Personhood and Neuroscience: Naturalizing or Nihilating?" Farah and the psychologist Andrea Heberlein explain more clearly and explicitly the grounds for such an autonomy-oriented (autonomist) approach.[39] Their argument for autonomy is based on the premise that neuroscience findings are undermining theories of human nature and "personhood." Our perception of personhood, according to Farah and Heberlein, is simply an evolved brain mechanism of recognition between members of the same species. "Personhood" is a "kind of illusion," a psychological projection that corresponds to no other reality than a function of the organism for better adaptation.[40] So it cannot be considered, in and of itself, a constraint on human freedom or a guide to ethical thinking. That leaves us with a "more utilitarian approach." The questions that should guide our ethics are matters of individual capacities and interests: "[R]ather than ask whether someone or something is a person, we should ask how much capacity exists for enjoying the kinds of psychological traits previously discussed (e.g., intelligence, self-awareness) and what are the consequent interests of that being."[41]

Farah is representative of the scientists and bioethicists who interpret neuroscientific findings to naturalize autonomism and then draw unwarranted ethical inferences in support of practices of enhancement. They are not alone; the pro-enhancement movement includes many other philosophers, writers, artists, and more who argue the case for enhancement on other grounds. One example is the philosopher Allen Buchanan, whose medical and political influence is attributable to his roles as staff philosopher for the President's Commission on Medical Ethics and consultant to the Presidential Commission for the Study of Bioethical Issues. Buchanan has written articles, as well as a book, in defense of the benefits of enhancement. His main argument is a historical one: "The agricultural revolution that began in England around 1760 had dramatic positive effects on human physical well-being through better nutrition, which in turn meant greater resistance to disease and greater longevity."[42] If no one dares criticize the technological advances of the agricultural revolution, Buchanan says, how can we reject medical enhancement simply and solely because it drives us toward new human horizons?[43] According to Buchanan, we must put all our effort into evaluating how technology can promote more prosperous societies, instead of arguing about where it should be applied—in the habitat or in the subject. He goes so far as to state that the human species has some "design flaws" that we could try to remedy in the future. Would we stop being human beings as a result? He does not think so; even if that were the case, what would be so bad about becoming "better than human"?[44]

Taking the "better than human" idea a step further are the enhancement visions of transhumanism. This philosophical and literary movement, launched in the 1970s, has more recently achieved significant popularity and funding thanks to its forays into the realm of bioethics.[45] For its followers, the evolutionary process does not always work to the benefit of our species. Humankind must therefore take control of its evolution, with perfection and lifestyle freedom as the primary ethical imperatives. This quest is not new, according to transhumanists: Humans have always sought to push back limits, and human nature and rationality, completely open and unlimited, do not constitute restrictions. Further, our corporeality has always been inextricably intertwined with our technologies and techniques. We are not a body, according to advocate Andy Miah, director of the Creative Futures Institute, a university-based research center in Scotland, but a "somatechnics." We are not even a body that makes use of instruments but a crystallization of these uses.[46] If the quest is old, what is new for the transhumanists is our current and emerging technological capacities. These capacities give us much greater powers to overcome our alleged design flaws and enhance our abilities, which through biological modification open up new possibilities for remaking and enriching our lives. In the transhumanist vision, enhancement is critical to the ongoing work-in-progress of our species—and, for some, to the enhanced species that may come to replace us.

For all its peculiarities, three ideas of the pro-enhancement movement must be granted: first, the view of science and technology as inherent goods to persons; second, the undeniable cultural changes that humanity has undergone over the course of history; and, third, the right of all individuals to pursue happiness and to improve their lives. However, these three truths do not necessarily lead to autonomist conclusions or to the view that there is nothing permanent and inalterable in human beings—or, in more transhumanist thinking, that the only essential characteristic of the human is our instrumental rationality. While there have been a number of trenchant critiques of the pro-enhancement arguments, one of the least noticed but most important in the past decade is the philosopher Jürgen Habermas's *The Future of Human Nature.*[47] Habermas rescues a conception of human nature that is very similar to the one classically used by medicine (and today, by some holistic models of medicine) and that attacks the Achilles' heel of the pro-enhancement arguments.

For Habermas, the basis of our self-understanding is the "intersubjective habitat" we share as human beings.[48] The pro-enhancement desire to manipulate this basis, which is the very *condition of satisfaction* for our goals, makes no sense. It is like changing the rules of chess so that we can beat our opponent. Once the rules are modified, the game and its value are also modified. The problem is even more elementary when the object of change is also the subject. In what sense, Habermas asks, can we be said to achieve victory if we stop being ourselves? And will the "new man" we have become even value this victory? The closest real-world analogy to this hypothetical experience is not an encouraging one: Parents who hope to fulfill their own dreams in their children's lives often cause their children significant harm.

Habermas's idea that the *natural* gives not only content but meaning to any human goal is very close to the classical interpretation of nature—though not identical. In the classical interpretation, nature does not merely make possible and limit the ends of rational animals but is itself the source of those ends. In other words, in the classical approach, human reason does not *create* so much as *infer* ends from the dynamism of reality. In both understandings of nature (and, by extension, of health), it is clear which environmental or bodily improvements transgress human limits and, with them, the limits of reason. The criterion is simple: A natural change is one that an external observer would recognize as part of his or her own horizons of life. This criterion allows us to see the misstep in Buchanan's analogy: Agrarian improvements are not alien to people in this day and age, nor would they have been for people in the age of Caligula. On the other hand, an unnatural change (one that disregards the natural limits of the individual) is not accompanied by human recognition. For example, the pleasure taken in killing for pure fun attributed to Caligula was considered inhuman then, as it is now, despite the frequency with which that action has been repeated throughout history.

At first it might seem that Habermas would endorse an incremental approach to enhancement, tolerating small changes but resisting large ones. But that would be wrong. In fact, he recognizes that seemingly minor enhancement practices, normalized in everyday medicine, greatly complicate ethical reflection. It is just these "accidental precedents and inconspicuous practices" that are "retrospectively exploited . . . in order to shrug off moral misgivings as 'too late.'"[49] Precisely for this reason, ethical reflection has to begin prior to such changes and consider not only the small changes at hand but also those larger changes that might be on the horizon. Further, bodily modifications themselves are not his sole or even main concern. He is also disturbed by the change in attitude toward the body that those who defend enhancement modifications must adopt: They must accept the interference (whether great or small) of human will in humanity's own nature.[50] For Habermas, this new attitude is itself a more radical and unnatural modification than any given change to the body.

Habermas uses the example of choosing the sex of one's children to explain how a single, apparently trivial instance of such interference can put the balance of the whole at risk—even to the point of affecting our nature, how we view ourselves as human beings.[51] To summarize, Habermas claims that parents are equal to their children in that they teach their children to critically take control of their lives, as they were earlier taught by their parents. But the changes effected by biotechnology—the ability of one generation to irreversibly shape the next—break this mutual and symmetric intergenerational recognition. The irreversibility of "enhancements" makes them different from other interventions: Making a choice for other people that they cannot unmake not only violates the democratic principle of equality but, worse, may prevent succeeding generations from even understanding that principle. No one actually intends this change of worldview, but very few people recognize that they may already be living it, by the mere practice of conceiving children à la carte.

Cosmetic Medicine: The Triumph of Subjectivism

The projects of medicalization and human enhancement are utopian, dangerous, and, as Habermas points out, finally irrational. Even so, bioethics is promoting these projects, whether knowingly or merely by effect. It has popularized the belief that the patient's judgment should be the last word in using biotechnology. And in the past half-century the medical community has begun to wash its hands of such matters. Everything seems to be valid as long as there is an informed-consent form. What has brought about this change of attitude?

One should keep in mind the medicalizing environment in which doctors are immersed: pressure to treat imaginary ailments from patients who want medications for enhancement purposes; a *DSM* that trivializes mental disorder and leads to millions of people feeling they are mentally ill; long days of nonstop appointments that greatly inhibit real communication with patients; tendentious promotional campaigns by the pharmaceutical industry. Moreover, medicine is excessively specialized. This division of labor spurs many doctors, far from the world of research and accustomed to the more practical side of medical activity, to lose sight of the brain's complexity, and therefore of the potential consequences of their prescribing actions. It is significant in this respect that patients in search of psychopharmaceuticals typically go first to their primary care physicians, not psychiatrists. But even mental health professionals are falling into the enhancement trap. Increasingly, they naïvely let other experts—often directly or indirectly under the influence of the pharmaceutical industry—shape essential patient care. In this instance, medical trust is subverting good medicine.

Another factor promoting the growth of subjectivism in the medical world involves the increasing acceptance of the biological reductionist and autonomist paradigms, an alliance that is breeding a new cosmetic medicine. I will end this section with an exposition of the concepts underlying these paradigms.

No one could expect advocates of the biological reductionist paradigm to resist the assertion that, in therapeutic decision making, the will of the patient should always take precedence. After all, from this standpoint, the doctor's job consists merely of giving the patient objective information about the best strategies for adapting to his or her environment. But within this framework, the doctor can say little about the normative character of this goal: She cannot even say whether or not the organism's adaptation and survival are beneficial. It is thus no coincidence that subjective factors have become so important to medicine over the past two decades, especially when it comes to questions regarding the beginning and end of life. This tendency has begun to affect even formerly objective diagnostic criteria. One need only compare successive editions of the *DSM* to see the relativization of concepts like "adequate affective response." In fact, in the fifth edition, many of the common clinical standards that helped define the appropriateness of emotional reactions have been reduced to the most minimal explanations. In practical terms, mental patients are not people who *feel* sick but who think they have some kind of pathology. One sign of how psychiatry is replacing the functionalist paradigm with the autonomist paradigm is that the *DSM-5* has eliminated the exception for bereavement from the definition of depression. The consequence is that psychiatrists are able to diagnose depressive disorder even among those who have just lost a loved one. This is one of the reasons, among many, why the National Institute of Mental Health is re-orienting its research away from *DSM* categories.[52]

Should it continue on its current course, psychiatry will become ever more dependent on cultural standards, popular trends, and, especially, as Farah sees, on the emotions and preferences of those who decide to medicalize their lives. These states of dependency are producing what I call *cosmetic medicine*: the application of medical and biotechnological knowledge for subjective ends.[53] At present, there are still barriers obstructing this tendency. For example, it is still socially unimaginable that mental health experts would prescribe psychoactive drugs for recreational use, even if their opposition owes much to the practical problems of expense and potential public disorder. Such impediments, however, are not permanent and could someday be overcome. In fact, medicalization is already changing the ways in which we think about narcotics users, who are, as a group, much more socially integrated now than in the past.[54]

The cosmetic approach affects not only psychiatry. For some time now, the doctor's office has been the place to go to increase or reduce breast size, eliminate fat through liposuction, even choose the sex of one's children. Many of these interventions fulfill essentially arbitrary desires and do not have even (objectively) enhancing ends. The majority of those interested in these treatments, as well as their doctors, are aware that they are following fashion or indulging a fancy they may later regret.[55] Most patients are also aware of the risks of surgery. But these deterrents are not enough to counteract the strong emotions that lead people to biotechnology. In regard to this issue of motivation, we may wonder at what point the use of supposedly enhancing drugs, such as methylphenidate, is actually driven by cosmetic considerations. The fact that many patients seek such drugs, even against the advice of their doctors—who too frequently just give in and write a prescription—is certainly suggestive.[56]

The alliance of therapeutic culture with the reductionist paradigm is undermining medicine's commitment to objectivity. Again, leading the way is work at the intersection of neuroscience and ethics, where many key thinkers have adopted the philosophical stance known as eliminative materialism, or eliminativism, as it is called for short. Eliminativism is the position that mental events are identical to and coextensive with the physical events that correspond to them in the brain.[57] So, for instance, statements about pain and about C-fiber neural firing are responses to descriptions of the same reality. In this view, many or all of our commonsense mental states have no place in science, and all references to such popular or "folk" psychology should be abandoned. Mental states such as beliefs and desires that we employ in our everyday psychological explanations simply do not exist.[58] According to the philosopher Paul Churchland, one of the principal advocates of eliminativism, such states are merely mythical, illusory ways of referring to reality—rudimentary stratagems for surviving. As the neurosciences progress and folk concepts are no longer necessary to manipulate reality, he argues, it becomes reasonable and convenient to drop them.[59]

Churchland is not alone. Others in the field of neuroethics—the ambassador between bioethics and neuroscience—have also embraced eliminativism and its critique of commonsense psychology. This statement by Martha Farah clearly shows the eliminativist influence: "The problem with neuroscience accounts of behavior is that everything we do is like a knee-jerk in the following important way: it results from a chain of purely physical events that are as impossible to resist as the laws of physics. . . . Neuroscience has begun to challenge [dualism], by showing that not only perception and motor control, but also character, consciousness and sense of spirituality may all be features of the machine. If they are, then why think there's a ghost in there at all?"[60]

Farah is aware of the serious moral implications of this deterministic theory for our ideas about freedom, will, responsibility, self-determination, and much more.[61] She cannot even say that human beings act for reasons. In the final analysis, in her view, science will one day show that human conduct is caused by our particular, determining, neurophysiological state.

Farah's solution to the ethical conundrum posed by determinism, also embraced by Churchland and for the same reason, is to separate ethical theory from everyday practice. After asserting that personhood is an illusion, Farah writes, "for ethics, the only alternative we can see is the shift to a more utilitarian approach. . . ." But, "as individuals . . . it matters little whether personhood is illusion or reality."[62] The reason it matters little, Farah believes, is that we will continue to perceive ourselves as the authors of our decisions, no matter what science says.

The net effect of the biological reductionism in this case, then, is to open a chasm between science and the human life world (*lebenswelt*). Aside from Churchland and Farah, other noted thinkers defend the separation of ethical theory and everyday practice, including Richard

Dawkins, Daniel Dennett, Antonio Damasio, and Steven Pinker. In his book *Breaking the Spell*, Dennett uses the figure of Santa Claus as an example of this necessary bifurcation.[63] Only little children do not know that Santa isn't real, that their parents are the ones who supply the gifts on Christmas. But the traditional dinner, the gifts and well-wishing, continue year after year. There is no reason to take away our delight and happiness. The key, according to Dennett, is in not asking too many questions and going with the flow; we suspend our disbelief in Santa Claus, like the audience in a movie theater. Curiously, his analogies presuppose a sort of folk psychology of their own, one in which people can regard their understanding of the world and of themselves as useful fictions yet carry on in the conduct of their affairs as though they were true.[64] In any event, the ethics that derives from these reductive speculations is one in which an autonomous will reigns supreme.

Yet another step may follow if the medicalizing trend continues. The confident determinism of eliminativism—perhaps the most reductionist of all biomedical models—is seemingly not so far from an epistemological relativism. The course followed by Richard Rorty, considered the father of eliminativism and a convert to what he called neopragmatism, is suggestive. Much earlier than Churchland, Rorty contemplated a future in which science would abandon mentalist terms to use a language based on neural states. In the middle of his career, however, he came to the conclusion that the human mind does not act, nor can it act, as the *mirror of nature*.[65] According to Rorty, no matter how complex neurosystems may be, it is impossible to prove the veracity of a statement based solely on the study of efficient causes. After the failure of his epistemological project—and with it, as far as he was concerned, all of science—Rorty dedicated the rest of his life to studying and defending the substitution of "truth" with "fiction." Putting the different human fictions—those of science, literature, religion, and so on—on the same level, he argued that all can be equally useful for building realities (medical or nonmedical) that are, on the one hand, emotionally lovable and, on the other, sufficiently persuasive to gain social consensus. In this way, humankind is freed from the limits imposed by metaphysics, and from the inhumanity of positivist reductionism.[66] And because Rorty was well aware of the human need for coherence, he finished by identifying unity as one of the principal characteristics of a good discourse—that is, a persuasive discourse.

Medicalization, enhancement, and cosmetic tendencies represent the very last developments one would expect from a medicine that privileges scientific knowledge and objectivity. Yet that is exactly what is happening. And it is illusory to think that eliminativism and related forms of neuroscientific determinism will not change lifestyles, especially when many people have been putting these ideas into practice for some time. Technological trivialization and neo-romanticism have led to new psychopharmaceutical practices, and those practices, in turn, have been teaching people to think of themselves as machines. The new cosmetic medicine will only further encourage these developments.

Unfortunately, the change does not promise to be a good one. There are many problems associated with the new psychopharmaceutical habits, and it is notable that they are precisely the ones that characterize addiction disorders: diminished experience of agency, life narrative incoherence, and the loss of social ties, all following when the concept of truth is abandoned.[67] Further, addicts generally try to solve their problems with the same things that caused them. Nowadays, people take psychopharmaceuticals not just to feel better but also to forget and compensate for the distress of an increasingly contradictory world. And might they also be seeking to silence the inherent longings for reality and agency that go unfulfilled? If so, then the end of cosmetic medicine may consist of further alienating people from themselves and undermining their capacity for effective resistance.

NOTES

1 Paul R. Wolpe, "The Neuroscience Revolution," *Hasting Center Report* 32, no. 4 (2002): 8.

2 Ibid.

3 Eric Racine et al., "Contemporary Neuroscience in the Media," *Social Science and Medicine* 71 (2010): 725–33. Also see Racine et al., "FMRI in the Public Eye," *Nature Reviews Neuroscience* 6, no. 2 (2005): 159–64.

4 Raymond Tallis describes this sort of scientific rhetoric as "neuromania" and writes:

Let us begin by giving all proper respect to what neuroscience can tell us about ourselves: it reveals some of the most important conditions that are necessary for behavior and awareness. What neuroscience does not do, however, is provide a satisfactory account of the conditions that are sufficient for behavior and awareness. . . . The pervasive yet mistaken idea that neuroscience does fully account for awareness and behavior is neuroscientism, an exercise in science-based

faith. . . . This confusion between necessary and sufficient conditions lies behind the encroachment of "neuroscientistic" discourse on academic work in the humanities.
Raymond Tallis, "What Neuroscience Cannot Tell Us About Ourselves," *The New Atlantis* 29 (2010): 3–25.

5 Philip Rieff, *The Triumph of the Therapeutic* (New York: Harper & Row, 1966); Eva Illouz, *Saving the Modern Soul* (Berkeley: University of California Press, 2008); and Frank Furedi, *Therapy Culture: Cultivating Vulnerability in an Uncertain Age* (London: Routledge, 2004).

6 Peter Conrad, "Medicalization and Social Control," *Annual Review of Sociology* 18 (1992), 209.

7 George A. Snook, "The History of Sports Medicine, Part I," *American Journal of Sports Medicine* 12, no. 4: 252–54.

8 Erik Parens, "On Good and Bad Forms of Medicalization," *Bioethics* 27, no. 1 (2013): 28–35. doi:10.1111/j.1467-8519.2011.01885.x.

9 Philip A. Berger, "Medical Treatment of Mental Illness," *Science* 200 (1978): 974–81.

10 Antonio Escohotado, *Historia general de las drogas* [General History of Drugs] (Madrid: Espasa Calpe, 1983), 577.

11 See, for example, Andrea Tone, *The Age of Anxiety: A History of America's Turbulent Affair with Tranquilizers* (New York: Basic Books, 2008).

12 Edmund D. Pellegrino and David C. Thomasma, "The Conflict between Autonomy and Beneficence in Medical Ethics: Proposal for a Resolution," *Journal of Contemporary Health Law and Policy* 3 (1987): 23–46.

13 David Cohen et al., "Medications as Social Phenomenon," *Health* (London) 5 (2001): 441–69.

14 Alasdair MacIntyre, *Tras la Virtud* (Barcelona: Crítica, 1987), 35. (Originally published as *After Virtue*, Notre Dame, Ind.: University of Notre Dame Press, 1981.)

15 Carl Elliott, *Better than Well: American Medicine Meets the American Dream* (New York: Norton, 2003).

16 This is what Aldous Huxley was referring to when he compared the new horizons (those of therapeutic culture) and the old and romantic "artificial paradises" of the nineteenth century. He found many similarities between them but also saw an important difference. The current paradises on sale are guarded not only by the "demons of the mind"—as Huxley called the fear that reason instills toward the new and irrational—but also by the "demons of objectivity," which prevent human beings from making unreal decisions (cf. Huxley, *The Devils of Loudun* [New York: Harper, 1952], and *The Island* [New York: Harper & Row, 1962]).

17 David J. Buller, *Adapting Minds: Evolutionary Psychology and the Persistent Quest for Human Nature* (Cambridge, Mass.: MIT Press, 2005).

18 John Z. Sadler and George J. Agich, "Diseases, Functions, Values, and Psychiatric Classification," *Philosophy, Psychiatry, and Psychology* 2, no. 3 (1995): 219–31.

19 Paul Chodoff, "The Medicalization of the Human Condition," *Psychiatric Services* 53 (2002): 627–28.

20 Christopher Megone, "Aristotle's Function Argument and the Concept of Mental Illness," *Philosophy, Psychiatry, and Psychology* 5, no. 3 (1998): 187–201.

21 K. L. Armstrong, N. Previtera, and R. N. McCallum, "Medicalizing Normality? Management of Irritability in Babies," *Journal of Paediatrics and Child Health* 36 (2000): 301–5.

22 Peter Conrad, *The Medicalization of Society: On the Transformation of Human Conditions into Treatable Disorders* (Baltimore: Johns Hopkins University Press, 2007).

23 Cohen, "Medications as Social Phenomenon."

24 María Antonia Sánchez-Vallejo, "Los fármacos ganan a la psicoterapia" (Pharmaceuticals are surpassing psychotherapy), *El País* (Madrid), January 5, 2009, http://elpais.com/diario/2009/01/05/sociedad/1231110001_850215.html.

25 Indeed, the subclinical category makes it easier than before to get psychopharmacological prescriptions, especially in situations, not uncommon today, in which psychiatrists hardly have enough time to do a proper anamnesis and diagnosis. Patients who self-diagnose and want medication need only know how to simulate a bit of stress or sadness.

26 Leon Kass, "Ageless Bodies, Happy Souls: Biotechnology and the Pursuit of Perfection," *The New Atlantis*, Spring 2003, 9–28.

27 Recognition between human beings is possible, Kass says, because the human body possesses an intrinsic order, an internal law by which it is governed, but also, thanks to our rational intelligence, with which we are capable of inferring facts as well as ends.

28 Leon Kass, *Toward a More Natural Science: Biology and Human Affairs* (New York: Free Press, 1985), 246.

29 Sheila Rothman and David Rothman, *The Pursuit of Perfection: The Promise and Perils of Medical Enhancement* (New York: Random House, 2003).

30 Two characteristics of the central nervous system make its study especially complicated. First, it works as a whole. The brain is a network that is very difficult to understand merely from the various parts of which it is composed. But this is all that neuroscience can know: parts of the brain (and few of them). Second, the nervous system is a plastic organ: Its development and maturity depend on the stimuli it receives from the environment. This property provokes enormous variability among the healthy brains of adult human beings and, as a result, innumerable problems for establishing generalizations. Unfortunately, the immense complexity of the brain is normally de-emphasized in the presentation of scientific results and entirely left out in the commercialization of neuro-technology. For instance, known short-term risks are indeed listed in patient information leaflets for psychopharmaceuticals, but our near–total ignorance about middle- and long-term effects is hardly mentioned. This significant omission can usually be attributed to the simple fact that there are no long-term studies.

31 Andreas Heinz et al., "Cognitive Neuroenhancement: False Assumptions in the Ethical Debate," *Journal of Medical Ethics* 38, no. 6: 372–75. doi:10.1136/medethics-2011-100041.

32 Steven Hyman, "Ethical Issues in Psychopharmacology: Research and Practice," in *Neuroethics: Mapping the Field*, ed. Steven J. Marcus (San Francisco: Dana Press, 2002): 135–43.

33 Thomas Insel, "Grand Challenges in Global Mental Health" (talk presented at the annual meeting of the Neuroethics Society, San Diego, Calif., November 12, 2010).

34 "Principlism" is currently the dominant system of ethics in the medical field. Although in theory this system asserts four irreducible and inalienable ethical principles (nonmaleficence, beneficence, autonomy, and justice), the principle of autonomy has come to outweigh the rest in practice: that is, in decision making, in most hospital ethics committees that use this method. See Evans, chapter 9, and Bishop, chapter 10, this volume.

35 Erik Parens, "Is Better Always Good? The Enhancement Project," *Hastings Center Report*, 28, no. 1 (1998): S1–S17.

36 Martha J. Farah et al., "Neurocognitive Enhancement: What Can We Do and What Should We Do?," *Nature Reviews Neuroscience* 5 (2004): 421–25.

37 Ibid., 424.

38 Ibid.

39 Martha J. Farah and Andrea S. Heberlein, "Personhood and Neuroscience: Naturalizing or Nihilating?" *American Journal of Bioethics* 7 (2007): 37–48.

40 Ibid., 45.

41 Ibid., 46.

42 Allen E. Buchanan, *Beyond Humanity? The Ethics of Biomedical Enhancement* (New York: Oxford University Press, 2011), 38.

43 Allen E. Buchanan, "Enhancement and the Ethics of Development," *Kennedy Institute of Ethics Journal* 18, no. 1 (2008): 1–34.

44 Allen E. Buchanan, *Better than Human: The Promise and Perils of Enhancing Ourselves* (New York: Oxford University Press, 2011).

45 A sign of the current importance of transhumanism in bioethics was the creation in 2009 of the Oxford Centre for Neuroethics by Julian Savulescu, one of the principal figures in the transhumanist movement. Another Centre investigator is Nick Bostrom, co-founder of the World Transhumanist Association and the Institute for Ethics and Emerging Technologies. Savulescu is also a member of the executive committee of the International Neuroethics Society, and Bostrom actively participates in the Center for Neuroscience and Society.

46 Miah presented a conference on somatechnics that can be accessed at http://www.andymiah.net/2006/12/21/somatechnics/.

47 Jürgen Habermas, *The Future of Human Nature* (Cambridge: Polity Press, 2003).

48 Ibid., 15.

49 Ibid., 19.

50 Something similar can be said from a teleological perspective on nature: the principal problem of enhancement has to do with believing it is legitimate to substitute ends chosen by the subject for ends inherent to the body.

51 See, for example, Habermas, *The Future of Human Nature*, chapter 5.

52 Talking about why NIMH will not fund experimental studies based on the *DSM-5*, Thomas Insel wrote:

> The strength of each of the editions of DSM has been "reliability"—each edition has ensured that clinicians use the same terms in the same ways. The weakness is its lack of validity. Unlike our definitions of ischemic heart disease, lymphoma, or AIDS, the DSM diagnoses are based on a consensus about clusters of clinical symptoms, not any objective laboratory measure. In the rest of medicine, this would be equivalent to creating diagnostic systems based on the nature of chest pain or the quality of fever. Indeed, symptom-based diagnosis, once common in other areas of medicine, has been largely replaced in the past half-century as we have understood that symptoms alone rarely indicate the best choice of treatment.

NIMH Director's Blog: Transforming Diagnosis. April 29, 2013. See http://www.nimh.nih.gov/about/director/2013/transforming-diagnosis.shtml.

53 Compare my definition with that of Anjan Chatterjee in "Cosmetic Neurology and Cosmetic Surgery: Parallels, Predictions, and Challenges," *Cambridge Quarterly of Healthcare Ethics*, 16 (2007): 129–37. Chatterjee points out the link between *cosmetic medicine* and autonomism. However, he describes cosmetic decisions primarily as a patient's rational choices.

54 In this context we can frame the increasingly well-understood role of medicine in the ongoing legislation of recreational uses of marijuana. See Robin Room, "Legalizing a Market for Cannabis for Pleasure: Colorado, Washington, Uruguay and Beyond," *Addiction* 109, 3 (March 2014): 345–51; Bettina Friese and Joel W. Grube, "Legalization of Medical Marijuana and Marijuana Use Among Youths," *Drugs* 20, 1 (Feb. 1, 2013): 33–39; and J. Michael Bostwick, "Blurred Boundaries: The Therapeutics and Politics of Medical Marijuana," *Mayo Clinic Proceedings* 87, 2 (Feb. 2012): 172–86.

55 Franklin G. Miller, Howard Brody, and Kevin C. Chung, "Cosmetic Surgery and the Internal Morality of Medicine," *Cambridge Quarterly of Healthcare Ethics* 9 (2000): 353–64.

56 Jayne C. Lucke et al., "Deflating the Neuroenhancement Bubble," *AJOB Neuroscience* 2, no. 4 (2011): 38–43.

57 Paul M. Churchland, *The Engine of Reason, the Seat of the Soul: A Philosophical Journey into the Brain* (Cambridge, Mass.: MIT Press, 1999), 322.

58 William Ramsey, "Eliminative Materialism," *The Stanford Encyclopedia of Philosophy* (Summer 2013 Edition), ed. Edward N. Zalta, http://plato.stanford.edu/archives/sum2013/entries/materialism-eliminative/.

59 Paul M. Churchland, "Eliminative Materialism and the Propositional Attitudes," *Journal of Philosophy* 78, no. 2 (1981): 67–90.

60 Martha Farah, "Neuroethics: The Practical and the Philosophical," *Trends in Cognitive Sciences* 9, no. 1 (2005): 34–40.

61 Farah repeats the mistake Churchland is making. Combating dualism does not necessarily imply the belief that the human body can be understood as merely an organic machine.

62 Farah and Heberlein, "Personhood and Neuroscience," 46.

63 Daniel Dennett, *Breaking the Spell: Religions as a Natural Phenomenon* (London: Penguin, 2006).

64 Surely, Christmas is itself a good example of how practice changes when the theory, in this case the holiday's original meaning, is removed.

65 Richard Rorty, *Philosophy and the Mirror of Nature* (Princeton, N.J.: Princeton University Press, 1980).

66 Richard Rorty, "Pragmatism as Romantic Polytheism," in *The Revival of Pragmatism: New Essays on Social Thought, Law, and Culture*, ed. Morris Dickstein (Durham, N.C.: Duke University Press, 1998), 21–36.

67 One interesting work in which truth and addiction are related is Bruce K. Alexander, *The Globalization of Addiction: A Study in Poverty of the Spirit* (Oxford: Oxford University Press, 2008). Also see Alexander, "Replacing the Official View of Addiction," chapter 8, this volume.

4

Reductionism, Holism, and Consumerism

The Patient in Contemporary Medicine

ROBERT DINGWALL

In trying to understand the cultural authority of medicine, an examination of the claims made about the nature and extent of medicine's influence must be balanced by an assessment of the demands that it faces.[1] What do the people who receive the attention of medicine require from it? What do the people who pay for medicine—not necessarily the same as those who receive it—expect that it will do?

This chapter investigates the changing place of the sick person within the historical shift from the welfarist provision of health care by various public or private forms of collective action to a consumerist form of provision that treats the utilization of care as a matter of individual preferences and judgments. It explores the problems and contradictions that emerge from the attempts to maintain collective payment for the costs of personal choices without a corresponding obligation on the part of individuals toward the collective. The discussion counterposes two visions of the patient within the cosmology of medicine. On the one hand, there is the half-forgotten legacy of Talcott Parsons's analysis of the sick role, wherein the patient is a deviant to be humanely managed and contained so that he or she may be restored to productive citizenship. On the other, there is the more recent model of the patient as the active consumer of a luxury good, picking and choosing in the market for medical interventions in much the same way as the eighteenth-century aristocrats described by Jewson, but without the corresponding means fully to fund these choices.[2] Reductionist medicine appeals to a consumerist age because it seems to strip out the moral and collective elements associated with the sick role. The physician need fix only the body, not the environments and life choices that have done the damage.

Consumer preferences go unchallenged. Arguably, however, the moral and collective elements are simply relocated because the problems of dependency identified by Parsons do not disappear. The costs of fixing the body remain to be paid. If the bill is to be picked up by a third party, that party will inevitably be concerned with the costs and the causes of the problems that are being repaired.

The Sick Role

Talcott Parsons's analysis of the sick role was introduced in *The Social System*.[3] He was not the first sociologist to write about health and medicine—Harriet Martineau, Frederick Engels, Herbert Spencer, and Robert S. Lynd, among others, had all explored aspects of this topic.[4] Applied studies, particularly in the field of mental health, had been developing since the 1920s.[5] However, Parsons's use of medicine as a case study in the general theory of social order that he developed in *The Social System* formulated sickness and its societal management as core problems for sociology. This analysis is the beginning of the sociology *of* medicine.

The sick role remained a central concept in medical sociology until the 1970s, attracting respectful treatments even from scholars who are conventionally contrasted with Parsons, like Erving Goffman and Eliot Freidson.[6] However, since that time, this approach has been increasingly marginalized, despite recent efforts at revival from U.K. scholars like Chris Shilling and Simon Williams.[7] When a special issue of the *Journal of Health and Social Behavior* commemorated fifty years of the Medical Sociology section of the American Sociological Association in 2010, it contained only one reference to the sick role, dismissing it as a historical curiosity rendered irrelevant by social change.[8] Properly understood, however, the sick role still speaks to fundamental issues of social organization. It provokes important questions about the implications of the drift toward consumerist medicine, and about the future of welfare more generally.

The Sick Role and the Management of Deviance

The Social System begins by exploring the challenges that face all social groups: What are the fundamental problems—reproduction, sustenance, succession, and so on—that any society, or smaller group, must resolve, if it is to survive and persist for any length of time? These potentially disruptive challenges are handled by institutions that have evolved to manage them in ways that establish a sufficient degree of order for individuals to carry out their personal projects. As Shilling notes, Parsons saw himself as an analytic realist, inducing general features of social organization from specific empirical observations.[9] What are the possible institutional solutions to these fundamental problems? How do those solutions interlock at different scales? When Parsons and Renée Fox wrote about illness and the contemporary American family, then, they were not *advocating* the gendered arrangements that they describe but *exploring* how these worked to create a relatively stable microsystem consistent with the society in which it was embedded, albeit under considerable stress from wider social changes.[10] Order is always temporary and fragile, constantly undermined by the passage of time and a changing environment: "[T]he evidence generally points to the conclusion that the main occupational pattern is upheld as well as it is by a rather precarious balance of social forces, and that any at all considerable change in this balance may have far-reaching consequences."[11]

In Chapter VII of *The Social System*, Parsons examines the problems of deviance and social control. Conformity and deviance both exist in the same society as the result of the same processes. Deviance is a judgment on behavior from a particular point of view in a particular social context. As Shilling observes, Parsons stresses the maintenance of an orientation to this-worldly instrumental activism as a basis for social order.[12] This does not make Parsons an apologist for capitalism so much as express his recognition that productive capacity is basic to all societies. A society that does not produce enough to sustain its members will become extinct. Disengagement from the commitment to productive activity is a particularly challenging form of deviance. Judgments will invariably need to be made about the balance of demands on resources from members who are considered to be currently active and productive and those who are not.[13]

Stabilization is attempted in social systems through control institutions that try to prevent deviance from occurring in the first place or, if this is not possible, to minimize the deviant actor's commitment to it. "Deviant motivational factors are always operating . . . . [T]he mechanisms of social control account not for their elimination but for the limitation of their consequences, and for preventing their spread to others."[14] The coercion of potential deviants is one possible solution. Parsons follows Durkheim's analysis of the way in which the ceremonial exclusion of the criminal can be an occasion to display the values treated as legitimate within a society.[15] This process is, however, costly in terms of the need for specialized enforcement agencies, the risks of corruption and subversion, the loss of the criminal's productive contributions, and the effort required to prevent the emergence of countervailing definitions of legitimacy. Parsons, then, is more concerned with how force is avoided: "It is through their relation to the subtler types of control mechanism that the problems of greatest sociological interest arise."[16]

Medicine is Parsons's paradigm case of a "subtler type of control mechanism." His radical insight is to see that sickness can be considered within the framework of deviance and social control. In effect, Parsons prises apart the identification of the biological and the social that marked earlier sociological writings: Even if sickness is a biological phenomenon, this fact cannot simply be read across into social action. From the perspective of social systems, sickness is a form of deviance that compromises productive capacity. As such, the analysis of sickness, and the way in which it is managed through the institution of the sick role, has wider significance for understanding the attempt to stabilize social order: "[T]he bearing of the therapeutic process on the problems of deviance and social control has implications reaching far beyond the particular field."[17] Medicine becomes a critical case study for the themes of *The Social System*: "It will perhaps help the reader to appreciate the empirical relevance of the abstract analysis we have developed, if . . . we attempt to bring together many if not most of the threads of the foregoing discussion in a more extensive analysis of some strategic features of an important sub-system of modern Western society."[18]

The most important of these strategic features is "support," a mechanism that retains the deviant within the social group while refusing to treat the deviant's behavior or motivations as legitimate. Medicine is the most important institution that administers this type of control. The effect of such interventions is, on the one hand, to *insulate* deviants, preventing them from coming into conflict with "normals" and their "mainstream" understandings of legitimacy, and, on the other hand, to *isolate* deviants, preventing the formation of groups to challenge those understandings. All troubles are made personal and without any claim to wider legitimacy. The sick role is the exemplar, albeit one that "can be used for the observation of balancing processes within the social system which have generalized significance."[19] While the criminal is written off, the sick person is offered "a *relative* legitimacy, that is so long as there is an implied 'agreement' to 'pay the price' in accepting certain disabilities and the obligation to get well."[20] This is often characterized as a matrix of rights and obligations, although this is not consistently Parsons's own language.[21] Occupants of the sick role are exempted from their normal role expectations and offered support rather than sanctions, provided that they accept the undesirability of their condition and cooperate with technically competent help to get well. The subtlety of this control strategy lies in the way that the sick person is embedded in a group of non-sick persons and exposed to reintegrative pressures. A sick person who has to enter a control institution, the hospital, is isolated from other sick persons in a single bed or single room, with restricted access to the wider community. Opportunities to form "solidary communities of the sick," resisting their deviance, are limited.[22]

Much of Parsons's analysis assumes some level of motivation to claim the sick role and to derive the benefits of dependency.[23] Loss of capacity is not explored in such detail. From a strict functionalist perspective, however, these are not distinguishable: Both are breakdowns in productive commitment, either voluntarily or involuntarily.

The Criminal and the Sick

Vilhelm Aubert and Sheldon Messinger, writing in the late 1950s, suggest a more helpful distinction. They argue that the key demarcation is between deviance considered by observers to be motivated and deviance considered by observers to be unmotivated.[24] Crime is the archetype of the first, sickness of the second. The investigation and ascription of motivation is critical in determining whether to respond to the deviance by means of overt sanctions or by support and reintegration. The conditional exemption represented by the sick role is a claim rather than a right. It is valid only insofar as, and for as long as, the suspicion of motivation, of seeking dependency so as to benefit from other people's productive contribution, can be dispelled. Goffman discusses how this requires the sick, particularly those whose dependency is long-term, continually to demonstrate in interaction that they are doing everything possible to minimize the degree and duration of their claims: "He gives accounts, belittles his discomfort, and presents an apologetic air, as if to say that, in spite of appearances, he is, deep in his social soul, someone to be counted on to know his place, someone who appreciates what he ought to be as a normal person and who is this person in spirit, regardless of what has happened to his flesh."[25] The longer the duration of dependency, and the more difficult it is to treat the disorder as a fact of nature, the greater the challenge to the claimant. While medical sociology research in the 1950s and 1960s documented the empirical difficulties in using the sick role concept in the context of disability and mental illness,[26] this rather missed the point. These cases underlined the fragility of the claim and the difficulty of sustaining any long-term dependency on the tolerance, good will, or resources of others. Although this point was not made at the time, the fragility of the claim to the sick role also creates a potential for dispute and positions physicians as potential adjudicators on claims: Is this person really entitled to make this claim for this length of time?[27]

From this perspective, the sick role may be much better thought of as an exercise in mutual obligation rather than in terms of rights and duties. To the extent that sick people can be said to have rights, such rights are highly conditional on their own behavior and whether or not it attracts the endorsement of those with whom they interact. Those interaction partners are not *required* to honor the claim for support unless it is properly formulated. Any suspicion of malingering must be dispelled, and efforts to minimize the burden of the claim on those asked to honor it must be transparent. The claims to exemption may, however, enroll a much wider network of associations, particularly in complex modern societies. A number of audiences may be required to honor a claim to the sick role. Moreover, the support required may involve a scale of investment and level of technical competence beyond that of the ordinary primary group. This is much of the story behind the rise of the formally licensed medical profession as supplier of a standardized and indisputable authorization of the legitimacy of a claim to the sick role to all who may properly be concerned. It is also behind the rise of means for spreading the costs of support, whether through insurance or tax-funded health care. The capacity of the primary group to control its deviant members is sustained by this kind of burden sharing. At the same time, the burden sharing is justified by the general benefits of containing this deviance, of maximizing the productive capacity of the society, and of minimizing the challenges to the legitimacy of its social order.

Conceived in these terms, the sick are positioned as people who make claims on the well, which the well may or may not choose to accept and treat as legitimate. The resources allocated to the sick reflect the societal choices about where public or private funds should be invested. This distribution may allocate resources to health care at a level that is too low to meet all the claims of the sick or in ways that the sick would not choose for themselves. The sick, or their proxies, may challenge this allocation, but they do not have a *right* to everything that they might consider desirable. Their claims are constrained in two ways: by the balance between health care and other possible objects of public or private expenditure and by the ethics of taxation and insurance. To elaborate on the latter, the question is whether it is ethical to take money from A and spend it on B in ways that are not demonstrably efficient or effective.[28] If the test of efficiency and effectiveness is not satisfied, then we are looking at extortion rather than burden sharing between taxpayers or contributors to an insurance pool. The sick are not objects of charity because the well have an interest in their management. Investments in the restoration of productive capacity, or the minimization of care needs, may bring collective benefits. None of these are, however, driven by the choices or desires of the sick.

The Sick Role in Historical Context

The sick role was conceived in an era of welfarism. Parsons himself was a New Deal Democrat,[29] but the model is generalizable to most of the tax-funded or social insurance–based welfare states that developed after World War II. Philip Strong has characterized this as a time of "bureaucratic medicine," wherein citizenship established an entitlement to treatment that was administered in an impersonal and morally neutral fashion by disinterested professionals. He contrasted this system with "charity medicine," wherein treatment is provided in the context of explicit, and sometimes aggressive, moralizing, and with "private medicine," wherein the wealth of the purchaser buffers the dimensions of social control. The patient is commissioning a professional to provide a service of his or her choice, as a consumer of medicine rather than as an object of medical discipline.[30]

In a series of recent papers, Alex Mold has outlined the revival of patient consumerism in the U.K.[31] Before the foundation of the National Health Service (NHS) in 1948, there was a medical market, with a variety of consumer statuses, from fee-for-service clients through participants in local mutual insurance schemes, often linked to trade unions, run by member-directors, to recipients of services from local governments under the supervision of elected councilors.[32] U.S. health care in the 1940s did not look radically different.[33] With the creation of the NHS, however, most of these institutions were displaced by the assumption of parliamentary accountability: As the founding minister, Aneurin Bevan, is reported to have declared, "[I]f a bedpan is dropped on a hospital floor in Tredegar [his constituency], its noise should resound in the Palace of Westminster." While local governance structures were created, they were oriented to implementing central plans rather than representing patients or communities.

Although Mold does not make this point, the pre-1948 market did not necessarily create sovereign consumers. The member-directors of mutual insurance schemes and local councilors on health committees balanced the interests of both those paying for care and those receiving it. This is reflected in the *Beveridge Report on Social Insurance and Allied Services*, which laid the foundations of the postwar welfare state, including the NHS: "The insured persons should not feel that income for idleness, however caused, can come from a bottomless purse. . . . The making of insurance benefit without means test unlimited in duration involves of itself that conditions must be imposed at some stage or another as to how men in receipt of benefit shall use their time, so as to fit themselves or to keep themselves fit for service; imposition of any condition means that the condition may not be fulfilled and that a case of assistance may arise."[34] The beneficiary of the proposed scheme of national insurance who failed to meet the obligations that legitimated this status would risk being downgraded to the lower tier of recipients of state assistance, whose treatment would be closer to that of an object of charity, intended merely to prevent complete destitution. In this spirit, as Mold notes, the founding statute of the NHS created a duty on the state to provide health care, rather than a right of patients to receive it. That statement of principle has survived successive modifications of the legislative framework.

Consumerist Medicine

By the 1960s, however, there were growing concerns that bureaucratic medicine had become too unresponsive to the concerns of patients. Mold identifies two currents in the thinking of the time. The first was triggered by the evidence of abusive treatment of patients in medical research, documented in the work of a concerned physician, Maurice Pappworth, and expressed in a movement for patient autonomy and self-determination.[35] This was complemented by other social movement campaigns of the 1960s, particularly in relation to the treatment of women in childbirth, of children in hospitals, and of mental health service users. The second reflected more general thinking about the position of the consumer within a society dominated by an increasing scale of both production and service delivery. Consumers needed to organize themselves to check the power of large corporations, including those in public ownership. The individual purchaser or user envisioned by neo-classical economics could not be sufficiently well informed or have sufficient impact to assess product or service quality or to ensure provider responsiveness. If these consumers could act collectively, however, they might exercise greater influence. Both of these have parallels in the U.S. context.

In contrast to the Parsonian model, the patient activist movements can be seen to promote "solidary communities of the sick" capable of challenging the obligations associated with the sick role. The extent of this challenge varied from those who asserted that treatment should be considered as a right rather than as a conditional entitlement to those who questioned the applicability of the sick role altogether. The latter response was particularly associated with mental health and disability rights groups—their disadvantages resulted from discriminatory social organization rather than being intrinsic to their condition. On occasion, this led to questioning of the very basis of instrumental activism: that people qualified for social recognition only by virtue of their productive contributions. All had an unconditional and indefinite right to support as and when they might call upon it without the matching obligations envisaged in the Parsonian model. The impact of these demands has been mixed, in both the United States and the U.K. Where they have allied with other stakeholder interests, as in the closure of the large nineteenth-century hospitals for people with mental health problems or learning disabilities, radical change has occurred. Where they have collided with liability concerns, for example, as in the case of childbirth, these voices have had less influence.

This kind of activism must, however, be distinguished from the new forms of consumerism that have been associated with the increasing domination of neo-classical economic thinking about the most appropriate structures for the provision of medical services. In effect, all are to be forced to be *homo economicus* (or *femina economica*) whether they like it or not. The search for cost containment and efficiency in health care provision will be advanced by creating competitive markets, within which patients will act as rational and informed choice-makers to drive up standards and attack provider monopolies, whether in professional work or in the organizational forms of service delivery. The process involved has been examined in a number of U.K. studies, which note how the consumer rhetoric of the 1960s has gradually been adopted in the service of marketization in the English NHS by successive governments from Margaret Thatcher through New Labour,[36] and continuing under the present Coalition.[37] While this began with the introduction of quasi-markets, wherein physicians would act as proxy consumers for their patients, it has developed into a much more individualized model, driven by individual patient choice on the basis of patient-oriented information. The state has invested heavily in IT projects intended to compile and deliver this information impartially, but it is facing increasing competition from pharmaceutical and other supplier companies. Although direct-to-consumer advertising is severely restricted in the U.K. and Europe, suppliers have been able to form collaborations with activist groups to avoid some of this regulation.[38] In effect, the "solidary communities of the sick" have been recruited as ancillary sales and marketing forces. Recent Coalition reforms envisage that primary and secondary care provider organizations will also compete for patient choices by providing information about the quality and effectiveness of their services. Competition regulators have been introduced to challenge local monopolies that might interfere with this market.

Margaret Stacey, a sociologist who had been prominent in some of the consumer and activist movements of the 1960s, identified the limitations of this model of patient behavior at a very early point.[39] As she noted, patients typically lacked information, or the technical knowledge to evaluate such information, and mostly had episodic contacts with health services, thus giving them limited influence over provider behavior. To borrow from a different field, they were "one-shotters" rather than "repeat players."[40] Some patients, of course, do have a longer-term engagement with providers—but the result of this is typically that each party develops specialized knowledge of the other that makes the relationship hard to break. Information technologies do not adequately substitute for this because their data still require evaluation and interpretation. Moreover, as even Adam Smith recognized, professional services rest on a basis of trust that is quite different from that of other market actors.[41] A transactional model of the provider–patient relationship may actually introduce inefficiencies if it requires each treatment episode to begin anew with no reference to previous encounters. Given the inherent asymmetry in knowledge between professionals and patients, it is also likely that patients will evaluate provision by reference to aspects that do not necessarily relate to its technical quality. A family practitioner may have a loyal group of patients who share his taste for a glass of whiskey with the first consultation of the day—and most consultations thereafter!

Consumerism and the Hegemony of Reductionist Medicine

In chapter 1 of this book, Joseph E. Davis explored the foundations of the cultural authority of reductionist medicine. Two dimensions that might be added to this are that it grew up in an era of medical consumerism and of limited government, from the sixteenth century to the nineteenth. The authority of reductionism is part of the same story as the rise of individualism, particularly in the Anglophone world, reflected throughout its cultural forms.[42] For a relatively brief historical period, individualism was significantly challenged by collectivism. This is a complex story, but some part in it is played by the spread of infectious diseases in more industrial and urbanized societies and by the concern for the health of the working class required by mass warfare.[43] The rich could not insulate themselves from the illnesses of the poor and nations could not defend themselves without a population fit to be soldiers or the mothers of soldiers.[44] To varying degrees, European states enlarged the role of government in the interests of national efficiency and reformed their medieval guilds of physicians to create modern medical professions and health systems. This process was more limited in the United States, where the medical guilds were seen to be incompatible with the new democracy: Many states repealed their medical licensing laws during the 1830s and opened the medical market to a variety of healing systems.[45] While many of these systems were distinctly holistic in character, the European model established an alliance between medicine and natural science that rapidly achieved significant pragmatic successes, as Davis notes.

Nevertheless, the introduction of this model into the United States was as much a political and an epistemic contest as a pragmatic one.[46] U.S. states were reluctant to re-establish professional monopolies just as they were dismantling the commercial and industrial trusts that had formed in the second half of the nineteenth century. American medicine was profoundly influenced by the antipathy between doctors and state legislatures, and by the emphasis that both parties placed on the market freedom of patient consumers. The place of values in the reluctance of the United States to introduce some form of nationalized health insurance system is somewhat disputed and should probably not be exaggerated.[47] Even so, the United States remained attached to a model of consumerist medicine that went into eclipse in most of Europe from the second half of the nineteenth century until late in the twentieth century.

European governments developed welfare states that incorporated sections of the working class and that are epitomized by the conception of the sick role. The respectable worker could expect that transient problems resulting in periods of dependency, whether due to fluctuations in the labor market, ill health, or old age, would be met with conditional but reasonably generous support, in precisely the terms defined by Parsons. This was distinguished from the situation of the idle poor, who might be prevented from total destitution at the cost of a greater measure of discipline. A New Deal Democrat like Parsons, especially given his familiarity with Europe—he had lived in both Germany and England for periods of time in the 1920s and maintained contacts in Germany until the outbreak of World War II—may well have expected more convergence in U.S. social policy than actually existed. In the confrontation with communism, European states looked to improve on their prewar welfare provisions, often by developing the collectivist approaches that had characterized wartime societal management. While this continuation of central planning was bitterly criticized by some libertarians,[48] it reflected a broad social consensus that survived until the economic crises of the 1970s.

These crises challenged the confidence that the Keynesian economic policies of the postwar period could deliver more or less continuous growth through the activities of a generally benevolent state. The assumption of state benevolence had already come into question from the activist movements of the 1960s, which argued that developed societies did not work well for women or for various ethnic and cultural minorities. Now it was challenged further by other kinds of libertarians, who claimed that the problem was the state itself. In the postwar period, it had expanded its functions and reach in ways that were harmful to individuals and society. This had been concealed by the long post–World War II economic boom, which had allowed individuals to enjoy rising standards of living without questioning the efficiency and effectiveness with which the state used its share of this increased wealth. During the 1970s, the claims of individuals and the state came into a conflict that was generally resolved by a retreat of the state. Rather than be a provider or guarantor of welfare, the state now adopted a more limited role of regulating the conditions under which individuals were expected to make their own choices. These would, by definition, be better than those made on their behalf by the state, not least because individuals would become responsible for the consequences. At best, the state would provide only a basic safety net.

In the context of health care, this has tended to mean the introduction of greater elements of competition between providers and more limited coverage for their services. The former is intended to bring about price competition and reduce costs, while the latter is expected to focus patient attention on their personal cost benefit equation, through co-payments, charges for supplementary cover, or invest-ments in health maintenance.

> The often-concealed side of health consumerism is that patients are po-sitioned not only as conscious choosers of possible treatment, but also as choosers of their lifestyle, and that they must therefore take greater responsibility for making healthy choices of food and exercise. . . . Health consumerism gives patients the right to demand what they wish from health services, but also requires them to take greater responsibil-ity for their choices. If patient choice is taken to an extreme, patients could request treatments that have unproven efficacy, but have to take the responsibility for those choices should they prove to be deleterious to their health.[49]

The practical problems identified by Margaret Stacey have not disap-peared, but they have been assumed away. A bad outcome is evidence of a personal failure to behave as an active and responsible consumer, researching treatment options, appraising provider credentials, and selecting a "best buy." No one else is responsible for this. At best, the victim can seek redress for misinformation or product defects, but these are difficult to establish in the health field because of the variability of individual needs and responses to interventions. Maybe poor results are just the lottery of nature rather than the result of professional or corpo-rate failings.

Reductionist medicine sits happily within this context. The welfarism associated with the sick role called for a comprehensive mode of medical interventions that would represent both a technical and a moral fix. This was not the thoroughgoing moral makeover described by Philip Strong in his discussion of charity medicine, wherein the treatment of patients was designed to remind them of their failure as members of society. Bu-reaucratic medicine, in national health, national insurance, or managed care organizations, respected the citizenship of patients and affirmed their entitlements. As these entitlements came to be seen to be unafford-able, bureaucratic medicine took on a dimension of rationing that was deeply uncomfortable for both parties. Physicians were disinclined to tell patients that they were being denied certain treatments from which they might derive some benefit that third-party payers considered to be uncertain or inefficient. At least some patients became very angry that their supposed entitlements were being withheld. Consumerism seemed to square this circle. If the consumer could not afford the treatment or had chosen an insurance plan that would not pay for it, then such was not a problem for the physician. If the consumer wanted treatment that was unproven or drew on unorthodox theories, and could pay, then that was his or her choice.

While consumers could choose holistic interventions, often from sources other than the socially licensed providers of medical treatment, reductionism has many attractions for them. In effect, it reduces the body to a machine to be fixed. The machine's owner has a free choice of service agents who will sort out the defective parts or settings. If the owner wants advice on his or her personal maintenance program, this will be available on request, but it is unlikely to be initiated unless the owner has purchased a service plan and the agent has an interest in reducing the number of fixes required. Reductionism strips out the moral and the collective dimensions that are associated with the holistic program in medicine. It does not require the owner of the machine to examine his or her own behavior: Auto mechanics replace the parts in your car without critiquing your driving standards. The drivers for reductionism, however, are not all located on the supply side, in medicine and industry: Consumerism helps to explain the demand for this model of provision and practice. An analysis in terms of the sick role demonstrates the instability of this outcome when the costs of provision are borne by third parties, whether publicly or privately. The sovereign consumer cannot escape more scrutiny, and the third parties are entitled to set boundaries on their commitment to funding the claims being made.

Conclusion

This chapter has explored the shifting cosmology of medicine and, by extension, medical sociology over the past 150 years or so. At the beginning of this period, consumerism dominated, particularly for the rich, although the poor could never wholly escape the concern of their immediate caregivers about the validity of their claims for support. As a result of various social, economic, and technical changes, developed countries came to assume more collective responsibility for the costs of health care, whether through private or social insurance or direct state action. In the process, questions of entitlement came to the fore and were addressed by the sick role: Patients were agents required to display their moral worth and commitment to minimizing their claims on the well. Although investigations into the motivation of the sick were not pursued aggressively in the era of citizen patients and bureaucratic medicine, they remained in the background, particularly for those whose dependency seemed to be long-term or less than self-evident. Beginning in the 1960s, the limitations of this model, from the perspective of both patients and states, led, by different routes, to the reconstruction of the patient as a consumer. Reductionist medicine was a natural fit, given its apparent indifference to the possible responsibility of patients for their own condition or to the collective implications of the individual problems that it addressed.

However, both the moral and the collective dimensions of medicine seem to be genuinely inescapable. The dilemmas of the sick role cannot simply be legislated away. The withdrawal of the state does not eliminate the problems of dependency as much as relocate them. Other providers of support still face the challenge of identifying secondary gain. Clearly, all deviants could be treated as motivated and the sick as objects of charity. However, as Parsons saw, this is socially inefficient and difficult to reconcile with the idea that people may simply have drawn different tickets in the lottery of natural endowment. While any measure of burden sharing in times of sickness and dependency remains, the function of adjudicating on claims and determining which are and are not legitimate is unlikely to disappear. That function requires an inspection of both the physical and the social condition of the sick person: If there is genuine damage or disturbance to the structures or processes of the body, how did this occur and with what motivational implications? Moreover, if there is an aggregation of individuals with similar problems, is it really an efficient use of societal resources not to investigate possible environmental causes rather than just patch up the victims? Clearly, a variety of institutional answers to these questions are possible. If, however, we are looking for an economically and socially sustainable health care system, it is likely to be one that incorporates an understanding of mutual obligation rather than one that is based purely on individual choice: The expectations of the sick must necessarily be constrained by the willingness of the well to fund them. Part of this willingness may be triggered by self-interest—that paying for someone else today will encourage others to pay for us when we are in need. Much of it, however, necessarily involves looking both at the responsibility for the conditions of the sick—in the holistic terms of lifestyles, environments, and efforts at self-maintenance—and at their commitment to change those things that are within their power. This might present a new set of questions to medical sociology: What can we learn about the people who succeed in the face of health challenges, and how can we disseminate this experience to others in the same position?

NOTES

1 An earlier version of this chapter was presented as a Medical Sociology stream plenary at the British Sociological Association Annual Conference, London, April 2013. I am grateful to the participants on that occasion for their comments and feedback.

2 See N. D. Jewson, "Medical Knowledge and the Patronage System in 18th Century England," *Sociology* 8, 3 (1974): 369–85; and Jewson, "The Disappearance of the Sick-Man from Medical Cosmology, 1770–1870," *Sociology* 10, 2 (1976): 225–44.

3 Talcott Parsons, *The Social System* (London: Routledge and Kegan Paul, 1951).

4 See Harriet Martineau, *Life in the Sick-Room* (Boston: Crosby, 1845); Martineau, *The Sickness and Health of the People of Bleaburn* (Boston: Crosby, 1853); Martineau, *Health, Husbandry, and Handicraft* (London: Bradbury and Evans, 1861); Frederick Engels, *The Condition of the Working-Class in England in 1844 with a Preface Written in 1892* (London: George Allen and Unwin, 1892); Herbert Spencer, *The Principles of Sociology* (London: Williams and Norgate, 1882); and Robert S. Lynd and Helen Merrell Lynd, *Middletown in Transition: A Study in Cultural Conflicts* (New York: Harcourt, Brace and Company, 1937).

5 Samuel W. Bloom, *The Word as Scalpel: A History of Medical Sociology* (New York: Oxford University Press, 2002).

6 Erving Goffman, "The Insanity of Place," *Psychiatry* 32 (1969): 357–87; Eliot Freidson, "Disability as Social Deviance," 71–99 in *Sociology and Rehabilitation*, Marvin B. Sussman, ed. (Washington: American Sociological Association, 1966); Freidson, *Profession of Medicine: A Study of the Sociology of Applied Knowledge* (New York: Dodd, Mead, 1970).

7 Chris Shilling, "Culture, the 'Sick Role' and the Consumption of Health," *The British Journal of Sociology* 53, 4 (2002): 621–38; and Simon J. Williams, "Parsons Revisited: From the Sick Role To . . . ?" *Health* 9, 2 (2005): 123–44.

8 Carol A. Boyer and Karen E. Lutfey, "Examining Critical Health Policy Issues within and beyond the Clinical Encounter: Patient-Provider Relationships and Help-Seeking Behaviors," *Journal of Health and Social Behavior* 51 (1 suppl) (2010): S80–S93. See S81.

9 Shilling, "Culture," 622.

10 See Talcott Parsons and Renée C. Fox, "Illness, Therapy and the Modern American Family," *Journal of Social Issues* 13 (1952): 31–44.

11 Talcott Parsons, "The Professions and Social Structure," in Parsons, *Essays in Sociological Theory* (New York: Free Press, 1954), 48.

12 Shilling, "Culture," 623–24.

13 This is not to say, for example, that the claims of the young on the support of others may not be considered a legitimate investment in the future or that the claims of the old may not be considered a legitimate return on their earlier contributions to the sustenance of others. It is simply to recognize that these are claims whose legitimacy must be established.

14 Parsons, *The Social System*, 208.

15 Ibid., 310.

16 Ibid., 311.

17 Ibid., 429.

18 Ibid., 428.

19 Ibid., 479.

20 Ibid., 312.

21 When Parsons introduces the sick role, he describes this as a conditional entitlement (*The Social System*, 441), although he later uses the language of rights ("Illness, Therapy, and the Modern American Family").

22 See Parsons and Fox, "Illness, Therapy, and the Modern American Family." If this all sounds rather Foucauldian, it is—but a decade before the first publication of *Folie et déraison: Histoire de la folie à l'âge classique* (Paris: Plon, 1961). Equally it anticipates Erving Goffman's discussion of total institutions in *Asylums: Essays on the Social Situation of Mental Patients and Other Inmates* (New York: Anchor, 1961).

23 As Williams (2005, 130), following Gerhardt (1979), notes, Parsons sometimes refers to illness as a simple unmotivated breakdown in role capacity and sometimes as motivated deviance. In the latter respect, he is drawing on the Freudian thinking that was central to U.S. intellectual life in the late 1940s and that is reflected throughout the discussions of personality in *The Social System*. This perspective suggests that illness can be seen as a possibly unconscious response to intolerable pressures and failure to meet dependency needs.

24 Vilhelm Aubert and Sheldon L. Messinger, "The Criminal and the Sick." *Inquiry* 1, 1–4 (1958): 137–60.

25 Goffman, "The Insanity of Place," 366.

26 Sol Levine and Martin A. Kozloff, "The Sick Role: Assessment and Overview," *Annual Review of Sociology* 4 (January 1978): 317–43.

27 Robert Dingwall, "Professions and Social Order in a Global Society," *International Review of Sociology* 9, 1 (1999): 131–40.

28 Murray N. Rothbard, *The Ethics of Liberty* (New York: New York University Press, 1998).

29 Charles Camic, *Talcott Parsons: The Early Essays* (Chicago: University of Chicago Press, 1991).

30 Philip Strong, *Ceremonial Order of the Clinic: Parents, Doctors and Medical Bureaucracies* (London: Routledge and Kegan Paul, 1979).

31 Alex Mold, "Patient Groups and the Construction of the Patient-Consumer in Britain: An Historical Overview," *Journal of Social Policy* 39, 4 (2010): 505–21; Mold, "Making the Patient-Consumer in Margaret Thatcher's Britain," *Historical Journal* 54 (2011): 509–28; and Mold, "Patients' Rights and the National Health Service in Britain, 1960s–1980s," *American Journal of Public Health* 102, 11 (2012): 2030–38.

32 Although Mold does not add this point, the system also contained residual charity elements, particularly in the emergency rooms of the major teaching hospitals where the poor received free care in exchange for serving the training or research interests of physicians.

33 Jill S. Quadagno, *One Nation, Uninsured: Why the U.S. Has No National Health Insurance* (New York: Oxford University Press, 2006).

34 Sir William Beveridge, *Social Insurance and Allied Services* (Cmd 6404), (London: His Majesty's Stationery Office, 1942), 12.

35 See Maurice H. Pappworth, "Human Guinea Pigs: A Warning," *Twentieth Century* (1962): 66–75; and Pappworth, *Human Guinea Pigs: Experimentation on Man* (London: Routledge, 1967).

36 Janet Newman and Elizabeth Vidler, "Discriminating Customers, Responsible Patients, Empowered Users: Consumerism and the Modernisation of Health Care," *Journal of Social Policy* 35, 2 (2006): 193–209; and Ian Greener, "Towards a History of Choice in U.K. Health Policy," *Sociology of Health and Illness*, 31, 3 (2009): 309–24.

37 It is important to recognize that health care in the U.K. is a devolved responsibility and that the governments of Scotland, Wales, and Northern Ireland have declined to follow the same path as England. See Scott L. Greer and David Rowland, eds., *Devolving Policy, Diverging Values? The Values of the United Kingdom's National Health Services* (London: Nuffield Trust, 2008); David Hughes and Peter Vincent-Jones, "Schisms in the Church: National Health Service Systems and Institutional Divergence in England and Wales," *Journal of Health and Social Behavior* 49, 4 (2008): 400–16.

38 See Hans Lofgren, "Pharmaceuticals and the Consumer Movement: The Ambivalences of 'Patient Power,'" *Australian Health Review* 28, 2 (2004): 228–37; Orla O'Donovan, "Corporate Colonization of Health Activism? Irish Health Advocacy Organizations' Modes of Engagement with Pharmaceutical Corporations," *International Journal of Health Services* 37, 4 (2007): 711–33; Elina Hemminki et al., "Co-Operation between Patient Organisations and the Drug Industry in Finland," *Social Science and Medicine* 70, 8 (2010): 1171–75.

39 Margaret Stacey, "The Health Service Consumer: A Sociological Misconception," *Sociological Review Mongraph*, no. 22 (March 1976): 194–200.

40 Marc Galanter, "Why the 'Haves' Come out Ahead: Speculations on the Limits of Legal Change," *Law and Society Review* 9 (1975): 95–160.

41 See Dingwall, "Professions and Social Order."

42 Alan Macfarlane, *The Origins of English Individualism* (Oxford: Blackwell, 1978).

43 Richard M. Titmuss, *Commitment to Welfare* (London: Unwin, 1968).

44 Robert Dingwall, "Collectivism, Regionalism and Feminism: Health Visiting and British Social Policy 1850–1975," *Journal of Social Policy* 6, 3 (1977): 291–315.

45 Owen Whooley, *Knowledge in the Time of Cholera: The Struggle over American Medicine in the Nineteenth Century* (Chicago: University of Chicago Press, 2013).

46 Ibid.

47 See Quadagno, *One Nation*.

48 See F. A. Hayek, *The Road to Serfdom*, Second Edition (London: Routledge, 2001).

49 Greener, "Towards a History of Choice," 322.

PART II

Reductionist Medicine and the Disease Burden

5

After the Therapeutic Revolution

The Return to Prevention in Medical Policy and Practice

ANNE HARDY

For most of human history, medicine of some kind has been practiced, and for most of human history it has been all but powerless to prevent or cure disease. It was only at the very end of the nineteenth century that medicine began to acquire real powers over disease, and it was only during the second half of the twentieth century that those powers achieved a degree that bestowed authority on medical science and gave popular currency to the belief that there was, or could be—or should be—a cure for all the ills of humankind.[1] For more than thirty years after 1950, curative medicine became a political and scientific priority in the West and was widely viewed as highly desirable for and by the developing world.[2] Yet by the end of the twentieth century, despite major advances in medical competence, the political and medical emphasis was turning away from cure to prevention.[3] As Joseph E. Davis notes in the Introduction to this book, all medicine was holistic before 1850, and even as a new scientific ethos took hold after that date, prominent scientists and physicians continued to emphasize the importance of the older concept of medicine. For much of its history since the mid–nineteenth century, public health (preventive medicine) continued in this tradition, perceiving the health and welfare of the wider environment, the household, and the individual to be interconnected within one system of well- or ill-being. Even as the miasmatic theory of disease was displaced by the science of bacteriology, the interconnection between environment and human health remained clear for diseases such as typhoid and tuberculosis.[4] It was perhaps only from the identification of tobacco smoking with lung cancer and heart disease in the 1940s that the reductionist "lifestyle" element that Davis and the social epidemiologist Nancy

Krieger have identified as aligning prevention with biomedicine in the twenty-first century entered the preventive ethos.[5]

Individual human beings have, from time immemorial, practiced both preventive and curative behaviors in the face of illness, injury, and disease and have on occasion sought expert attention from recognized medical authorities, whether wise women, witch doctors, shamans, so-called orthodox practitioners, or other type of healer. Historically, health had been a private concern to individuals and family; only in times of widespread crisis, as with plague epidemics, did disease become a matter for community or state. In early modern England, for example, families stricken by plague would be immured in their homes, both well and sick, until all illness was past and the survivors were allowed out; threatened with plague imported from abroad, European states developed quarantine protocols.[6] It is only in very recent history that the concerns of the modern state brought health and medicine into the arena of state policy and national concerns.[7] It was first in the eighteenth century that European nation-states began to interest themselves in population health, and until the mid-1940s the predominant political approach to health improvement was prevention.

Several formulations of a preventive approach to health and disease appeared in the years prior to 1850. The concept of medical police, for example, developed by Johann Peter Frank between 1779 and 1827 in his multivolume tome *A Complete System of Medical Police*, although little implemented in practice, remained influential into the nineteenth century.[8] Eighteenth-century mercantilism fostered state interest in population health, and France, Austria, and Sweden were among the countries initiating public health measures in the late eighteenth and early nineteenth century, although most failed to establish systematic state policies of disease prevention.[9] Rather it was the English practice of "public health," developed between 1840 and 1870, that became the model for preventive action throughout Europe in the later decades of the century, and in America after 1900.[10] The English preventive model was essentially an environmental one, based in miasma theory—the idea that the vapors given off by rotting organic matter were the cause of disease—and it was developed in the context of the massive and unregulated urban growth that saw half of England's population concentrated into cities within the space of fifty years. Prevention in these terms meant cleaning the streets, installing the water carriage of human wastes, providing supplies of clean water for domestic use, reducing domestic overcrowding, disposing hygienically of organic refuse, and controlling offensive trades in urban areas. It was a comprehensive environmental program—what the historian Charles Rosenberg has identified as "ecological holism."[11] The administrative measures necessary to achieve these ends became the responsibility of local government, and medically qualified professionals were appointed to initiate and manage local measures of disease control.[12] From the 1870s onward, the hygienic management of the environment was supplemented by the introduction of isolation hospitals for cases of infectious disease, where victims of typhoid, scarlet fever, and smallpox could be treated but also removed as foci of further infection in the community.[13]

The English preventive model was widely looked to by other European states after 1850, as they too began to interest themselves in population health. New features began to be added to the English model, in particular an emphasis on personal hygiene, and on veterinary public health—the hygienic management of meat and milk supplies. In Sweden, for example, schools were provided with modern and adequate toilet and hand-washing facilities, while Denmark introduced pasteurized milk supplies and Germany pioneered new methods of meat inspection.[14] The development of national health insurance schemes, again pioneered by Germany, from the 1880s, was also intended preventively: Valuable workers were to have their health safeguarded. Similarly in Britain, the object in introducing health insurance in 1911 was to support breadwinners during illness and so prevent the pauperization of families.[15] A growing political emphasis on infant and child health in the last decades of the century reflected economic but also military concerns, as the shadows of Darwinian survival theory, colonial competition, and international conflict began to drift over Europe.[16] Edwin Chadwick, the pioneer of the English public health movement, had been motivated by economic considerations to take action, and to develop the specific environmental forms of action that he did.[17] Economic concerns with population health drove concerns about alcohol consumption in Scandinavia and France.[18] Economic and later military concerns were the principal political forces driving preventive medical action by European states. Individual medical men might have been driven by humanitarian motives, but states operated according to national interest.

Toward the end of the nineteenth century, therefore, the environmentalist English model of preventive medicine was being incorporated into, or overlaid by, a more direct concern with the welfare of individual human bodies. While this shift of perspective came about for political reasons, it also took place against a background of greatly improved sanitary provision and the emergence of new and effective medical treatments and techniques, many of which combined a direct benefit to the individual with a wider significance for population health. The one specific medical measure of prevention, available since 1796, was vaccination against smallpox, widely used and sometimes enforced by European states.[19] Until the mid-1890s, smallpox vaccination remained the only effective specific intervention against an infectious disease. Although advances in surgery—anesthesia, the artery clamp, antisepsis and asepsis—had extended the range of practicable operations to include the "cure" of such common and economically disabling conditions as hernias, it was not until the development of the antitoxin serum for diphtheria in the mid-1890s that the new disciplines of bacteriology and immunology began to extend the range of curative medicine.[20] New immunizations began to become available around 1900, against typhoid, cholera, plague, and diphtheria, but in general—and contrary to longstanding myths about the bacteriological "revolution"—new developments in curative medicine were slow in coming. Paul Ehrlich's discovery in 1909 of the arsenical compound later named Salvarsan, the first successful treatment for the universal scourge of syphilis, provided the first indication that chemotherapy might offer another route through to the actual cure of disease.[21]

New preventive technologies made World War I the first war in history in which deaths from infectious disease represented only a small fraction of the total dead—at least on the Western Front. The immunization of troops against smallpox, typhoid, and paratyphoid, and the availability of anti-tetanus serum, all but removed three potent natural killers from the theaters of war. Prevention played a large part in this war: The British and Austrian armies, for example, enlisted mobile bacteriological units in an effort to combat infections such as meningitis, bacillary dysentery, and malaria, as well as new afflictions arising from this war, such as trench fever and trench foot.[22] The knowledge that the human body louse transmits typhus effected maintenance of the best achievable standards of cleanliness of person and clothing and confined the depredations of the disease to a swath of territory on Europe's Eastern Front. Bitter experience in India and South Africa had taught the British Army that the successful management of human wastes and the education of the ordinary soldier in personal hygiene were vital to maintaining the gastric health of troops in the field.[23] Everything was done that could be done to limit collateral damage to fighting power by disease. Curative medicine, although increasingly able to mend shattered bodies, was very effectively partnered with prevention in the preservation of military strength.

The preventive ethos continued to dominate during the interwar period, although new advances were being made in treatment, for example with radium therapy for cancer.[24] The infectious diseases which had been the major killers in the nineteenth century were now largely under control and rapidly decreasing in fatality. Death rates for the sanitary marker disease, typhoid fever, for example, fell markedly in America, England, and France between 1912 and 1920.[25] Public health administrations began to turn to other issues, such as maternal and child care, cancer, and venereal disease.[26] Health education, as communicated through posters, exhibitions, and reading matter in doctors' surgeries, became a new concern, and one in which the Americans were held to be notably successful.[27] In the home, too, preventive activities were inscribed in domestic practices. A recent study of working-class lives in three Lancashire towns argues that working families were engaged in a constant endeavor to deflect ill health and infection using domestic remedies, foodstuffs, clothing, and social behaviors to that end.[28] Medical attention remained an expensive luxury for working-class folk excluded from national insurance provisions. In Britain during this period, these included most women, children, the elderly, and the self-employed, while in most of Europe orthodox medical practitioners were a rarity outside urban areas. Domestic wisdom was as yet unchallenged by the authority of modernizing medicine.[29]

By the 1920s, however, intensive medical research and experiment was beginning to yield new and effective treatments for a number of hitherto intractable conditions. Three contributions stand out: insulin treatment for diabetes, vitamin B therapy for pernicious anemia, and the introduction of the sulphonamide drugs around 1935, which proved effective against an array of unpleasant infections, including childbed fever, gonorrhea, and bacterial pneumonias.[30] New preventive tools were also being developed, notably the BCG (Bacillus Calmette Guerin) vaccine against tuberculosis, the one major infectious killer still persisting in Western societies. Serious questions were raised about this vaccine following the Lubeck disaster of 1930, in which seventy-three infants died as a result of immunization with contaminated vaccine. Nonetheless, the operation was eventually adopted by many states, although national attitudes varied.[31] Denmark, for example, ran a trial tuberculosis eradication program using the vaccine on the island of Bornholm in the 1930s, which set a pattern for subsequent eradication programs.[32] In Britain, by contrast, where a vigorous nineteenth-century anti-smallpox immunization campaign had sensitized government to problems with immunization programs, such an eradication program was only reluctantly entered into after 1952. Similar suspicions also delayed the introduction of polio vaccine in the mid-1950s.[33]

The sulphonamide drugs were widely regarded as a revolutionary breakthrough by contemporary medical practitioners, although the impact of their initial introduction has been overshadowed by the popular mythology surrounding the later introduction of penicillin.[34] Research into the curative properties of chemical products had resulted in just two new therapeutics, Salvarsan and the suphonamides, in forty-odd years. During World War II, however, research based in natural substances—molds, to be precise—delivered two curative drugs in the space of five years: penicillin, of course, but also streptomycin, the first effective therapy against the ancient scourge of tuberculosis. There followed with the return of peace a positive feeding frenzy of research into the therapeutic potential of natural and chemical substances and the development of an astonishing array of new therapies, curative or ameliorative, for everything from tuberculosis to depression.[35] Viewed through the contemporary medical lens, the accumulation of new therapies between 1920 and 1970 appeared to constitute a "therapeutic revolution." As has recently been observed, that half-century saw a "radical shift in medical practice, with major improvements in patient care" as a result of the introduction of whole new classes of drugs: Whether taming microbes, exorcising madness, or mobilizing the body's own hormonal mediators for therapeutic ends, these molecular innovations seemed to fulfill the promise of "miracle cures."[36]

It was with this "therapeutic revolution" that the ethos of prevention finally began to take a back seat in the post-1945 era. Prevention remained applicable to the communicable diseases, with vaccines for polio, whooping cough, measles, German measles, mumps, meningitis, hepatitis, and human papilloma virus arriving in the decades that followed. By 1960, the infections that had been the big killers a century earlier had all but disappeared as such from human consciousness, at least in the developed world. Their disappearance as mortal threats to human life took place against an unprecedented shift in human demographics. On the one hand, barriers to human population increase seemed to have fallen; on the other hand, the span of human life lengthened dramatically. In 1900, life expectancy at birth in England and Wales had been forty-six years; by 1940 it had reached sixty-one years, and by 2000 it stood at seventy-eight.[37] In 1900, just 4.5 percent of the population was aged over sixty-five years; by 1970 that percentage had risen to 12.5. Similar increases were observed in other Western societies, although the United States lagged behind England and Wales as well as France and Sweden in this respect.[38] Moreover, the postwar years also saw the democratic extension of medical benefits to European populations generally, in Britain and Scandinavia through tax-funded national health services, elsewhere in Europe through the insurance model. The almost universal acquisition of access to medical treatment ensured that the new therapeutics were made available to those who needed them. In Britain, for example, the medical demand for pharmaceutical products rapidly exceeded expectations by an enormous margin. The cost of general practitioner–prescribed drugs, for example, soared from £35 million to £53 million a year between 1949 and 1953.[39] If access to medical treatment improved the lives and productivity of national populations to the benefit of national economies, those improvements came at a price.

The post–World War II world thus saw a transformation in the medical landscape of the West. First, the threat of sudden death from lethal infections had all but disappeared; second, medicine was beginning to deliver alleviation or cure for a host of afflictions, major and minor, that had previously shortened life or made it irksome; and, finally, the new democratic health systems made these treatments available and affordable to most of the population, except in the United States, where in the late 1990s some 37 million Americans had no health insurance.[40]

Increasingly, the search for "cure" became the goal of the pharmaceutical companies, while patients came to expect relief or cure by visiting the doctor.[41] These developments to some extent masked the emergence of a new disease regime, which had already been becoming evident in the years around 1900. As the great infections declined, so the proportionate mortality from diseases of aging and degeneration rose. Heart disease, cancers, and diabetes became increasingly prominent as killers of older age groups.[42] The postwar years also saw an explosion in medical research, generously funded by governments and charities, as well as within pharmaceutical companies. In particular, the emergence of new epidemiological techniques, such as cohort studies, was to have long-term consequences in relation to state medical policies and population health. Medical concern over the dramatic twentieth-century rise in deaths from lung cancer proved the occasion for key epidemiological studies on the causation of the disease, published almost simultaneously in England and the United States. Both demonstrated a significant link between cigarette smoking and lung cancer.[43] Because cigarette smoking was now almost universal among adult males in the West and was also being taken up by increasing numbers of women, these findings were something in the nature of a medical landmark: They revealed that a significant proportion of adult populations throughout the West were at risk of a debilitating, fatal, and self-inflicted medical condition. By the mid-1980s, cigarette-related illness was estimated to be costing the British National Health Service £165 million a year.[44] Yet the medical and political climate of the 1950s and 1960s was not propitious to preventive action. Austin Bradford Hill, senior author of the English study, refused to indicate policies for limiting the health damage caused by tobacco when interviewed in 1954: He did not think it appropriate for doctors to dictate government policy.[45] Governments, indeed, proved singularly reluctant to endanger tax revenues from tobacco, or to endanger the complex economic relationships that lay behind its production, marketing, and consumption.[46] While government policy remained in abeyance, popular responses to the rising toll of deaths from cancer were telling: Charitable funding was increasingly directed to finding "a cure for cancer."

The story of tobacco usage in the late twentieth century is one of cultural, social, political, and above all economic networks which initially encouraged the idea of "cure" and downplayed the possibilities of prevention. Yet the tobacco story also illustrates the rise of a popular association between health and lifestyle that began to emerge in the 1970s, and which by the twenty-first century had been adopted as a central tenet of government health policies and medical politics. The "social determinants of health" were big epidemiological business by 2010, both in the developing and in the developed world.[47] The preventive crusade against tobacco was not, however, initiated and conducted by governments but by private individuals. Government responses were slow, often seemingly confined to steadily rising but not prohibitive taxes on tobacco. Tobacco advertising was gradually banned; but it was only with the emergence of dedicated anti-smoking groups like the British organization ASH (Action on Smoking and Health) that popular tobacco dependence began to be whittled away. The years between 1970 and 2000 saw a staggering transformation in public attitudes toward tobacco use, from unquestioning general acceptance to widespread public aversion and locational, if not political, control.[48]

The rise of lifestyle as a private preventive measure against potential health problems emerged gradually in the years after 1970 in Britain and the United States, if less so elsewhere in the West. In part this was a popular movement, possible in populations that had achieved a higher health standard than had ever previously been reached, and which actively feared any decline from that standard. But it was also encouraged and fueled by the new epidemiology, which increasingly interested itself in the environmental and social factors operating on the dominant pathologies of the later twentieth century. Despite the initially limited impact of the epidemiological studies on lung cancer, those studies initiated a new trajectory in epidemiology. In the first place, they established methodological tools for new types of investigation—cohort studies, prospective and retrospective studies—and second they legitimated the principle of investigating the impact of lifestyle factors on morbidity and mortality. From the 1960s onward, epidemiologists investigated a vast range of environmental, occupational, and dietary factors and personal behaviors in the search for clues to disease prevalence, with outcomes that were not always reliable and that were, indeed, sometimes misleading.[49]

Lifestyle epidemiology came at a time when Western governments were becoming increasingly concerned about the rising costs of health care. Expenditure on health as a percentage of Gross National Product (GNP) rose in all Westernized countries from 1960.[50] In 1960, the United States, the largest spender, spent 5.3 percent of GNP on health, rising to 7.4 by 1971.[51] Lifestyle studies provided an information background that permitted a gradual accommodation between the fact of rising health care costs on the one hand and the development of political strategies for its control on the other. Epidemiological findings suggested preventive strategies for reducing the toll of heart disease, certain cancers, and Type 2 diabetes. Falling death rates from heart disease and lung cancer among educated Western males from the 1980s, as they cut back on or stopped smoking cigarettes, helped to demonstrate the power of individual preventive action.[52] If the findings of the epidemiologists could be successfully communicated to national populations, it might prove possible to reduce levels of expensive illness and improve health and productivity. While health education had proved a problematic area since its introduction in the interwar period, by the 1970s increasingly well-educated and affluent Western populations, distanced from the experience of serious illness in youth and middle age, began to listen to health messages.[53] An emphasis on the importance of exercise led to a vast increase in running, swimming, and the use of gymnasia, while the new dietary gurus enjoined the avoidance of animal fats, hydrogenated vegetable oils, refined flour and sugar, and so on. In England, where full cream milk had been the only type generally available, a revolution took place in the 1980s so that skimmed and semi-skimmed milk, reduced-fat creams, and low-fat yogurts were widely available by the end of the decade.

Yet if some components of Western populations were adapting their lifestyles according to the new health orthodoxies, others were not. Obesity, first identified as a medical problem in the 1930s, did not begin to attract serious medical concern until the 1980s but had become a very general concern by the end of the twentieth century.[54] The arrival of home entertainments, initially the television, but from the mid-1990s also computer games and other sedentary amusements, and the exponential growth in consumption of attractive high-fat, high-salt "convenience foods" created new types of high-risk behavior. By the first decade of the twenty-first century, Type 2 diabetes, previously a disease found only in adults, was being identified in children under the age of ten. This phenomenon was regarded as a deeply ominous marker of the health problems in store for future generations.

The emergence of the "new public health" in the 1970s constituted a further facet in the gradual re-emergence of preventive approaches to health. The publication of the LaLonde Report, *A New Perspective on the Health of Canadians*, in 1974 is thought to have triggered this movement. Although the movement's aims were never clearly defined, they did include the expectation that individuals as responsible citizens would take responsibility for their own health. In Britain at least, this expectation emerged as a significant political theme in the following decades.[55] The Labor Party adopted this perspective in the late 1970s and continued to stress the significance of lifestyle issues for health after achieving political power in 1998. This emphasis was still apparent in, for example, the Department of Health's 2004 publication, *Choosing Health*, and was further endorsed by Prime Minister Tony Blair when, in a major speech on public health in 2006, he declared, "Our public health problems are not, strictly speaking, public health questions at all. They are questions of individual lifestyle." Similarly individualistic rhetoric was also to be found in other government pronouncements on health, such as the European Code against Cancer and the American Institute of Public Medicine's Ten New Year Commandments.[56] While the impact of such rhetoric is difficult to judge, there are indications that some population groups and food manufacturers are responding to such messages. The food chain branch of the British company Marks and Spencer, for example, ran an advertising campaign in spring 2010 boasting of its low-salt and no-hydrogenated-oils policy with respect to its manufactured ready meals.

Seen in historical perspective, therefore, the modern emphasis on disease prevention, although aimed at a very different group of diseases, has a clear affinity with nineteenth-century preventive medicine in its underlying economic imperatives. When Edwin Chadwick developed the idea of sanitary reform in the 1830s, it was through his observation of the costs of premature death to the British taxpayer. In the late twentieth and the twenty-first centuries, it is the costs to the British National Health Service of treating heart disease, cancer, AIDS, obesity, and other major conditions that drive the emphasis on individual responsibility for healthy living. Obesity alone currently costs the NHS some £5 billion a year; this is projected to double by 2050, with the wider costs to society as a whole estimated at five times that.[57]

The differences between prevention in the era of an infectious disease regime, and that in the era of a chronic disease regime, dictates significant differences in public health approaches between the nineteenth and twenty-first centuries. The great infections were manageable by state intervention—by sanitary improvements, enforced isolation, disinfection, population surveillance, and vaccination. The chronic and degenerative diseases of the modern era are not similarly amenable to interventionist state management; indeed, in modern democratic societies in which the concept of "human rights" is firmly established, it may be suggested that it would be politically unacceptable to intervene on the nineteenth-century model. Thus it appears that the only way to approach disease in the modern era is by the attempted manipulation of individual lifestyle choices according to the findings of epidemiological research. State intervention appears potentially to be permissible only in the face of renewed, dire, external epidemic threat, as in the case of SARS, or bubonic plague, virulent influenza, and imminently, perhaps, Ebola fever.

The period between 1945 and c. 1980, that of the "therapeutic revolution," was an exceptional, and possibly unique, interval in the history of health and disease prevention in the West. In those years the killer infections were in abeyance and the full consequences of affluent Western lifestyles not yet realized. The enchantment of "cure" that came to dominate medicine in those years was delusory, perhaps a manifestation of the modern belief in ineluctable "progress." Medical "realities" can be constructed by illusion and delusion as much as by observed fact and actual experience. Already in the 1940s, it was becoming evident that the new treatments were not unproblematic: The first penicillin-resistant strain of *Staphylococcus aureus* was isolated in 1942, and the numbers of antibiotic-resistant bacteria increased rapidly thereafter.[58] By the twenty-first century, antibiotic-resistant bacteria were threatening to outstrip the capabilities of biomedicine.[59]

The era of promise in modern medicine was short: In the 1960s, voices critical of modern medical approaches began to be raised and the adequacy of modern medical discourse and practice questioned. In 1961, Thomas Szasz first critiqued the motives of the psychiatric profession;

in 1972, Archibald Cochrane questioned the effectiveness of most therapeutic interventions; and in 1976, Thomas McKeown argued that rising standards of living rather than therapeutic advances were responsible for the modern rise of life expectancy, while Ivan Illich contended that modern medicine made people ill.[60] Against a social background that now included the thalidomide crisis of the earlier 1960s, the emergence of modern feminism with its antagonism to male medical attitudes toward women, the rise of modern investigative journalism, and rising health costs, such critiques of the technocratic and individualistic biomedical model found a ready audience.[61] As reports began to come in of new or resurgent, frightening, and often untreatable epidemic diseases, beginning with outbreaks of Marburg virus, yellow fever, and meningitis in the late 1960s, and achieving global awareness with the arrival of AIDS in the early 1980s, there came a growing recognition that the microbial world is not static but continually evolving.[62] The merits of preventive strategies began to assume an increasing relevance, although nowhere was any firm stance taken to develop such strategies even in the face of such immediately unsettling developments as the emergence of multi-drug-resistant (MDR) tuberculosis in the wake of the AIDS epidemic.[63] At the time of writing, the advance of epidemic Ebola fever in West Africa, and incursions of the virus into Spain and the United States, demonstrates both the real and continuing threat to humankind presented by infectious diseases, and humanity's inefficiency in responding to such threats.[64]

In light of such developments as MDR infections and the current Ebola epidemic, it may appear that the "therapeutic revolution" might have been no more than an irregularity in the pattern of human mortality, a moment of stability as the tectonic plates shifted from one disease regime to another, because human attempts to prevent infections such as HIV may also open windows for opportunistic, resistant bacteria.[65] The claim that the therapeutic revolution was perhaps a delusory moment of security in human history does not seek to deny the real advances made in the treatment of human disease since 1940 but rather to suggest the inevitability of challenges to human health and the necessity of remaining alert to the relevance of strategies of prevention. Prevention, not cure, has been the dominant strategy against disease for most of history, but recognition of that reality depends on the prevalence of intractable diseases, on economic pressures, and on medical and political acceptance of the limitations of therapeutic intervention.

The emergence of the modern "lifestyle" model of chronic disease prevention does not represent a return to the holism of the past, however. Rather, as Davis and Krieger suggest, it is yet another manifestation of the reductionist philosophy of modern curative medicine. Whereas nineteenth-century prevention embraced environment plus person, from the later twentieth century the approach to such major problems in public health as high blood pressure, heart disease, diabetes, and obesity increasingly focused on the remodeling of individual lifestyles.[66] The model of cure remained attractive, however, notably to the pharmaceutical industry, which had been created around the post-1945 therapeutic ideal. Achieving the objective of prevention through education and changed lifestyle choices proved difficult,[67] and alternative population-based medical strategies—the preemptive drug-based treatment of asymptomatic disease—became increasingly attractive.[68] By the twenty-first century the "subjectively healthy but highly medicated individual" had become a common phenomenon in America,[69] although perhaps less so elsewhere. In the 2010s, however, battle lines were being drawn; in Great Britain, for example, over a 2013 Cochrane Review recommending the wholesale prescription of statins for all persons aged over fifty.[70] If the idea of holism in public health persists in the lifestyle choices of individuals who choose to eat healthily, exercise, limit indulgence in alcohol or recreational drugs, or even opt for a rural or small-town habitation over the big city, powerful drivers within the worlds of medicine and pharmacy continue to advocate the path of reductionism.

NOTES

1 For a survey of the history of medicine since Antiquity, see William F. Bynum et al., *The Western Medical Tradition to 1800* (Cambridge: Cambridge University Press, 1995); and William F. Bynum et al., *The Western Medical Tradition 1800 to 2000* (Cambridge: Cambridge University Press, 2006).

2 Anne Hardy and E. M. Tansey, "Medical Enterprise and Global Response 1945–2000," in Bynum, *Tradition 1800–2000*, 405–533. On the therapeutic revolution, see Stephen Lock, "Medicine in the Second Half of the Twentieth Century," in Irvine London, ed., *The Oxford Illustrated History of Western Medicine* (Oxford: Oxford University Press, 1997), 126–28.

3 Charles E. Rosenberg, "Holism in Twentieth Century Biomedicine," in Christopher Lawrence and George Weisz, eds., *Greater than the Parts: Holism in Biomedicine 1920–1950* (Oxford: Oxford University Press, 1998), 347.

4 Anne Hardy, *The Epidemic Streets: Infectious Disease and the Rise of Preventive Medicine 1856–1900* (Oxford: Oxford University Press, 1993), 181–90, 264–66.

5 Nancy Krieger, *Epidemiology and the People's Health: Theory and Context* (Oxford: Oxford University Press, 2011).

6 Arnold Zuckerman, "Plague and Contagionism in Eighteenth-Century England: The Role of Richard Mead," *Bulletin of the History of Medicine*, 78 (2004): 288–92.

7 Dorothy Porter, *Health, Civilization and the State* (Abingdon: Routledge, 1999), 97 et seq.

8 Patrick Carroll, "Medical Police and the History of Public Health," *Medical History* 46 (2002): 461–94; Porter, "Introduction," in Dorothy Porter, ed., *The History of Public Health and the Modern State* (Amsterdam: Rodopi, 1994), 6–8; for other approaches, see also James C. Riley, *The Eighteenth-Century Campaign to Avoid Disease* (Basingstoke: Macmillan, 1987).

9 Matthew Ramsey, "Public Health in France," in Porter, ed., *The History of Public Health*; Paul Weindling, "Public Health in Germany," in ibid.; Karin Johannisson, "The People's Health: Public Health Policies in Sweden," in ibid. See also Porter, *Health, Civilization*, 97–110.

10 For the development of the English model, see Christopher Hamlin, *Public Health and Social Justice in the Age of Chadwick: Britain 1831–1854* (Cambridge: Cambridge University Press, 1998); and Royston Lambert, *Sir John Simon (1816–1904) and English Social Administration* (Bristol: McGibbon and Kee, 1965).

11 Rosenberg, "Holism," 341.

12 Anthony Wohl, *Endangered Lives: Public Health in Victorian Britain* (London: Methuen, 1983). See also Hardy, *The Epidemic Streets*.

13 Gwendolen Ayers, *England's First State Hospitals* (London: Wellcome Trust, 1985); John Pickstone, *Medicine and Industrial Society: A History of Hospital Development in Manchester and Its Region, 1752–1946* (Manchester: Manchester University Press, 1985).

14 For the Swedish Hygienic Code for schools, see Albert Palmberg, *A Treatise on Public Health and Its Applications in Different European Countries* (London: Swann Sonnenschein, 1893), 470–73; on milk pasteurization and meat controls, see T. Morrison Legge, *Public Health in European Capitals* (London: Swann Sonnenschein, 1896), 183–92, 104–12.

15 Bentley Gilbert, *The Evolution of National Insurance in Great Britain: The Origins of the Welfare State* (London: Michael Joseph, 1966), 230–32, 314–15. See also Bernard Harris, *The Origins of the British Welfare State: Society, State and Social Welfare in England and Wales, 1800–1945* (Basingstoke: Palgrave Macmillan, 2003).

16 Anna Davin, "Imperialism and Motherhood," *History Workshop Journal* 5 (1978): 9–66; Deborah Dwork, *War Is Good for Babies and Other Young Children* (London: Tavistock, 1987).

17 Hamlin, *Public Health and Social Justice*.

18 Johannisson, "The People's Health," 175–76; Jack D. Ellis, *The Physician-Legislators of France: Medicine and Politics in the Early Third Republic 1970–1914* (Cambridge: Cambridge University Press, 1990), 208–14.

19 Peter Baldwin, *Contagion and the State in Europe 1830–1930* (Cambridge: Cambridge University Press, 1999), chapter 4.

20 William F. Bynum, "The Rise of Science in Medicine," in Bynum, ed., *Western Medical Tradition 1800–2000*, 155–59, 123–36. The best general account of developments in nineteenth-century surgery remains Frederick F. Cartwright, *The Development of Modern Surgery* (London: Arthur Barker, 1967).

21 George Stopford-Taylor and Robert W. MacKenna, *The Salvarsan Treatment of Syphilis in Private Practice: With Some Account of the Modern Methods of Diagnosis* (London: William Heinemann, 1914).

22 Major A. H. C. Grey, "Mobile Laboratories," *Guy's Hospital Reports* 70 (1922): 259–60, 262–65.

23 Mark Harrison, *The Medical War: British Military Medicine in the First World War* (Oxford: Oxford University Press, 2010), chapter 1.

24 Patrice Pinel, "Cancer," in Roger Cooter and John Pickstone, eds., *Medicine in the 20th Century* (Amsterdam: Harwood Academic, 2000), 677–80.

25 Martin Melosi, *The Sanitary City: Urban Infrastructure in America from Colonial Times to the Present* (Baltimore: Johns Hopkins University Press, 2000), Table 7.9, 148.

26 See Notes and Comments, "Cancer," *The Medical Officer*, 22 (1919, 173); and Charles D. Bolduan, "The All-America V.D. Conference," Ibid., 25 (1921), 27.

27 Editorial, "Health Teaching in the United States," *The Medical Officer*, 24 (1920): 115.

28 Lucinda McCray Beier, *For Their Own Good: The Transformation of English Working Class Health Culture, 1880–1970* (Columbus: Ohio State University Press, 2008), 145–207.

29 On this transformation see Beier, *For Their Own Good*, 310–46, 347–64; idem, "Expertise and Control: Childbearing in Three Twentieth-Century Working-Class Lancashire Communities," *Bulletin of the History of Medicine*, 78 (2004): 379–409.

30 On insulin see Michael Bliss, *The Discovery of Insulin* (Edinburgh: Edinburgh University Press, 1983); for vitamin B therapy, see M. W. Wintrobe, *Hematology: The Blossoming of a Science* (Philadelphia: Lean & Febiger, 1985); on the sulphonamides, see John E. Lesch, *The First Miracle Drugs: How the Sulfa Drugs Transformed Medicine* (Oxford: Oxford University Press, 2007).

31 Linda Bryder, "'We Shall not Find Salvation in Inoculation': BCG Vaccination in Scandinavia, Britain and the USA, 1921–1960," *Social Science and Medicine* 49 (1999): 1157–68.

32 Johannes Holm, "BCG Vaccination in Denmark," *Public Health Reports (Washington)* 61.2 (1946): 1309–10.

33 Anne Hardy, "Poliomyelitis and the Neurologists: The View from England, 1896–1966," *Bulletin of the History of Medicine* 71 (1997): 270, n. 83.

34 Irvine Loudon, personal information, 14 October 1998.

35 Christopher M. Callahan and German E. Berrios, *Reinventing Depression: A History of the Treatment of Depression in Primary Care, 1940–2004* (Oxford: Oxford University Press, 2005).

36 Christian Bonah et al., *Harmonising Drugs: Standards in the 20th Century Pharmaceutical Industry* (Paris: Editions Glyphe, 2009), 19.

37 Hardy and Tansey, "Medical Enterprise," Table 4.1, 422.

38 J. Rogers Hollingsworth et al., *State Intervention in Medical Care: Consequences for Britain, France, Sweden and the United States, 1890–1970* (Ithaca, N.Y.: Cornell University Press, 1990), 47.

39 Charles Webster, "Doctors, Public Service and Profit: General Practitioners and the National Health Service," *Transactions of the Royal Historical Society* 40 (1970): 216.

40 Rosemary Stevens, *In Sickness and in Wealth: American Hospitals in the Twentieth Century* (Baltimore: Johns Hopkins University Press, 1999), 346.

41 Lucinda McCray Beier, *Health and Culture in the Heartland 1880–1980: An Oral History* (Urbana: University of Illinois Press, 2009), 136–78.

42 Richard Doll, "Major Epidemics of the 20th Century: From Coronary Thrombosis to AIDS," *Journal of the Royal Statistical Society*, Series A, 150 (1987): 373–95.

43 Richard Doll and A. Bradford Hill, "Smoking and Carcinoma of the Lung," *British Medical Journal*, 2.4682 (1950): 739–48; E. L. Wynder and E. A. Graham, "Tobacco Smoking as a Possible Etiologic Factor in Bronchiogenic Carcinoma: A Study of 684 Proved Cases," *Journal of the American Medical Association*, 143.4 (1950): 329–36.

44 Peter Taylor, *Smoke Ring: The Politics of Tobacco* (London: Bodley Head, 1984), xix.

45 Austin Bradford Hill, personal communication to Lise Wilkinson, 1985.

46 Taylor, *Smoke Ring*, xix.

47 Michel Marmot and Richard G. Wilkinson, eds., *Social Determinants of Health* (Oxford: Oxford University Press, 1999); Johannes Siegrist and Michael Marmot, eds., *Social Inequalities in Health: New Evidence and Policy Implications* (Oxford: Oxford University Press, 2006); Michael Marmot et al., *Fair Society, Healthy Lives: The Marmot Review* (London: Marmot Review, 2010).

48 See Matthew Hilton, *Smoking in British Popular Culture, 1800–2000* (Manchester: Manchester University Press, 2000); Sander L. Gilman and Zhou Xun, eds., *Smoke: A Global History of Smoking* (London: Reaktion Books, 2004).

49 James Le Fanu, *The Rise and Fall of Modern Medicine* (London: Little, Brown, 1999).

50 Peter Yuen, *OHE Compendium of Health Statistics* (London: Office of Health Economics, 2001), Table 2.24.

51 Ibid.

52 Peter Townsend, Nick Davidson, and Margaret Whitehead, eds., *Inequalities in Health: The Black Report and the Health Divide* (Harmondsworth: Penguin, 1988), 290–92.

53 Porter, *Health, Civilization*, 296–303.

54 Robert Pool, *Fat: Fighting the Obesity Epidemic* (New York: Oxford University Press, 2001), 7, 15–37.

55 Martin Powell, "Neo-Republican Citizenship in the British NHS since 1979," in Frank Huisman and Harry Oosterhuis, eds., *Health and Citizenship* (London: Chatto and Pickering, 2013), 188.

56 Ibid., 189.

57 Ibid., 190.

58 Milton Wainwright, *Miracle Cure: The Story of Penicillin and the Golden Age of Antibiotics* (Cambridge, Mass.: Blackwell, 1990), 85.

59 National Health Council, *Antibiotic Resistance: A Serious Public Health Threat: Symposium Proceedings* (Washington: National Health Council, 2000).

60 Thomas Szasz, *The Myth of Mental Illness: Foundation of a Theory of Personal Conduct* (New York: Dell, 1961); Archibald L. Cochrane, *Effectiveness and Efficiency: Random Reflections on the Health Services* (London: Nuffield Provincial Hospitals Trust, 1972); Thomas McKeown, *The Modern Rise of Population* (London: Edward Arnold, 1976); Ivan Illich, *Medical Nemesis: The Expropriation of Health* (London: Calder and Boyars, 1975), idem, *Limits to Medicine: Medical Nemesis: The Expropriation of Health* (London: M. Boyars, 1976).

61 On thalidomide see H. Sjøstrom and R. Nilsson, *Thalidomide and the Power of the Drug Companies* (Harmondsworth: Penguin, 1972); on the women's health movement see Boston Women's Health Book Collective, *Our Bodies, Ourselves: A Book by and for Women* (New York: Simon and Schuster, second edition, 1976); for investigative journalism, see *Sunday Times Weekly Review*, 10 May 1968, "The Thalidomide File" (London: Times Newspapers, 1968), 49–52; The Sunday Times Insight Team, *Suffer the Children: The Story of Thalidomide* (London: Andre Deutsch, 1979); health costs and post-1970s stringency are described for Europe in E. Mossialos and J. Le Grand, eds., *Health Care and Cost Containment in the European Union* (Aldershot: Ashgate, 1999); see also D. Wilsford, "States Facing Interests: Struggles over Health Care Policies in Advanced Democracies," *Journal of Health Politics, Policies and the Law*, 20 (1995), 571–61.

62 See Jon Arrizabalaga, "*The Global Threat of (Re)emerging Diseases*," chapter 7, this volume; and Laurie Garrett, *The Coming Plague: Newly Emerging Diseases in a World out of Balance* (New York: Farrar, Straus & Giroux, 1994).

63 For MDR tuberculosis, see Leigh Phillips, "Infectious Diseases: TB's Revenge," www.nature.com/news/infectious-disease-tb-s-revenge-1.12115, accessed 10 October 2014.

64 Reuters, "United Nations $1bln Ebola appeal severely underfunded," https// uk.finance-yahoo-com/news/united-nations-1-bln-ebola-184347190.html, posted 10 October 2014, accessed 13 October 2014.

65 C. K. Okoro et al., "Intracontinental Spread of Human Invasive *Salmonella* Typhimurium Pathovariants in sub-Saharan Africa," *Nature Genetics*, 44 (2012): 1215–21, published online 30 September 2012.

66 William G. Rothstein, *Public Health and the Risk Factor: A History of an Uneven Medical Revolution* (Rochester, N.Y.: Rochester University Press, 2003), 362–67.

67 Ibid., 365.

68 Jeremy A. Greene, *Prescribing by Numbers: Drugs and the Definition of Disease* (Baltimore: Johns Hopkins University Press, 2007).

69 Ibid., viii.

70 Editorial, "Statins for the Over 50s? No," BMJ 2013.347.f6412 at www.bmj.com/content/347/bmj.f6412.

6

Digitized Health Promotion

Risk and Personal Responsibility for Health and Illness in the Web 2.0 Era

DEBORAH LUPTON

Since the first years of the twenty-first century, governments in many countries have been faced with harsh economic challenges. One way in which they have sought to meet these challenges is by introducing into the health care and public health arenas the use of the new digital technologies facilitated by Web 2.0. The new apparatus of what is often termed "digital health" (also "Health 2.0," "Medicine 2.0," "eHealth," or "mHealth"), a conglomeration of new technologies addressed at delivering health care, preventive medicine, and health promotion, has facilitated a focus on measuring and monitoring the functions and activities of laypeople's bodies and encouraging self-care among patients with chronic diseases. Digital health technologies are coming into use across a range of contexts, including telemedicine/telehealth, or the use of digital devices to monitor patients' health status and treatment remotely and to promote self-care; the employment of digital media and tools to track and respond to disease outbreaks; electronic medical records; and health promotion activities provided through technologies such as text messaging, self-tracking tools, and health apps.

There are strong and clear overlaps between the discourses and practices of digital health initiatives in the health care arena and those of public health. As applied to health and disease, many of these initiatives focus on the importance of members of the lay public "engaging" in their own health care or preventive health efforts. They represent digital technologies as offering the answers to significant fiscal and health-related problems. Discourses on digital health also emphasize the importance of the "big data" generated from digital technology use, representing this new type of data as offering the opportunity to improve most areas of health care and public health.

This chapter focuses in particular on the digital health phenomenon as it has been taken up in health promotion endeavors, or what I will refer to here as "digitized health promotion." The discussion identifies digitized health promotion as the latest stage in the trajectory of health promotion ideology and practice over the past four decades in wealthy Anglophone nations such as the United States, the United Kingdom, Canada, Australia, and New Zealand. I argue that over this period the individualistic approach to preserving and maintaining good health that was commonly espoused in medicine and public health was challenged by advocates arguing for a greater focus on social justice and social epidemiology, as expressed in ideals of "the new public health." The individualistic approach to health promotion never fully disappeared, however, and has gathered momentum in the current economic and neoliberal political climate. While many health promotion workers still champion the ideals of "the new public health" and "health for all," public health policy in the context of digitized health promotion has begun to return to emphasizing personal responsibility for health. Straitened economic circumstances and the possibilities generated by the emergence of new technologies have converged to advance digitized health promotion.

Health Promotion Discourses and Practices

In the mid–twentieth century, policy approaches to health promotion in wealthy Anglophone countries largely took an individualistic, reductionistic, and paternalistic approach. Particularly in the United States, in response to what was viewed as a growing health care crisis, laypeople were urged to take personal responsibility for their health so as to avoid imposing additional costs on the health care system. The concept of "lifestyle" began to be employed in policy documents and health promotion materials to emphasize the contribution individual choices made to people's health, diverting attention from the environmental and socioeconomic aspects that structured health outcomes.[1] This approach adopted the "cause-and-effect" individualistic biomedical model of disease causation. Members of the lay public were encouraged to look to medical and public health experts for advice on how best to care for their bodies.[2] Illness was represented as a "moral failing,"[3] evidence of an individual's ignorance and apathy or the inability or refusal to make the appropriate "lifestyle choices."[4] People were accused of courting health risks and inviting illness into their bodies by not acting on health promotion advice.[5]

In the 1970s, as part of a newly politicized approach to health and health care underpinned by Marxist and other political economy critiques of social inequality and injustice, various movements and activist endeavors emerged in response to what was viewed as "healthist" and "victim-blaming" discourses in health care and health promotion policies in wealthy countries.[6] Instead of emphasizing personal responsibility for protecting and maintaining good health and placing priority on good health above other priorities, as was then common in government policy and practice, advocates argued for redirecting attention to "the social determinants of health": the social, cultural, and economic underpinnings that influenced patterns of illness and disease throughout the community.[7] In its focus on the broader contexts, this approach actively sought to avoid the reductionist position that underpinned the notion that people should be made personally responsible for achieving and maintaining good health and avoiding disease, preferring a holistic perspective that was overtly political (the "holism of the environment" or "social medicine" positions discussed by Joseph E. Davis in chapter 1).

During this period, perspectives on and policies related to health promotion and public health began to change in line with the new social movements that were highlighting social justice and inequality issues. Writers concerned with public health policy directed their attention to identifying the social determinants of health and attempted to develop policies that would move away from victim blaming and healthism to a focus on mitigating the structural socioeconomic disadvantages that contributed to poor health outcomes, such as belonging to a marginalized social group, working in a hazardous occupation, living in poor housing and general conditions of poverty, and earning a low income.[8] The "new public health" emerged as a means of focusing attention on the social-structural causes of ill health and disease and engaging members of the community in participating in preventive health endeavors.[9]

In *Health for All by the Year 2000*, a declaration at the Alma-Ata Conference of 1978, the World Health Organization called for social justice to be an integral part of public health policy and action.[10]

The term *social epidemiology* began to be used in the early 1990s in health promotion policy and practice to denote research directed at the health of populations, as opposed to the health of individuals. The social epidemiology perspective also drew on a Marxist political economy approach in challenging mainstream approaches to health promotion. This change in focus highlighted the notion that social groups, taken as a whole, could be considered "healthy" or "unhealthy" as a result of social determinants of health.[11] Although these foci were evident in health promotion policies at the time, personal responsibility for achieving and maintaining good health continued to constitute a major plank. Despite the rhetoric of "the new public health," concepts of "the healthy citizen" in health promotion policies often left unexamined the power relations and social inequalities that detracted from efforts to achieve "health for all." Citizens were represented as having the obligation to achieve a "healthy environment," positioned as responsible, therefore, not only for their own health status but that of the immediate community in which they lived as well as the natural or urban environment.[12]

In the twenty-first century, influential organizations such as the World Health Organization have continued to champion a focus on social justice and the alleviation of social and economic inequalities in their policies on public health.[13] In the neoliberal political systems that currently dominate in wealthy countries, however, and particularly in Anglophone countries, the more reformist and politically activist approach to *public* health tends to be neglected in favor of a focus on individuals' personal responsibility for managing their behavior, regardless of their life circumstances.[14] The role that governments are able to play in ameliorating the living conditions of those "at risk" of ill health and disease tends to be diverted to funding public health campaigns exhorting people to change their behavior[15] or to seeking medical solutions to public health problems.[16] Health promotion programs have been subjected to cuts or downsizing in an economic context in which other public health approaches have been prioritized, particularly those that appear to offer short-term savings to governments.[17]

It may be contended, therefore, that while the rhetoric of public health policy has continually focused on the importance of identifying the social and economic determinants of health and alleviating those that are inequitable, in practice these inequalities have hardly been redressed.[18] This has led to a paradoxical stance taken by many departments of health and those who work in them in wealthy countries, in which public acknowledgment of the strong link between socioeconomic disadvantage and ill health and disease is combined with a renewed emphasis on lifestyle change and a continued victim-blaming approach.[19] As I demonstrate below, the discourses and practices related to digital health technologies have even further distanced health promotion from maintenance of a broader, less individualistic social justice perspective. Instead of concentrating on the holistic "healing" or "preventive" approaches that were central to the "new public health," there is evidence of a return to biomedical reductionism, in which an individual's willingness and skills to take up and actively use digital technological devices become the focal point.

The Rise of Digital Health Technologies

In the context of the austerity measures introduced in many wealthy countries in response to the global financial crisis, the focus of governments on managing and governing health through the individual actions of their citizens has intensified even further.[20] It is partly in response to these conditions that the governmental apparatus of digital health has been generated. The twin incentives of "better health outcomes" and "lower health costs"[21] are driving the current enthusiasm for laypeople to engage with digital technologies as part of taking responsibility for their health status and health care,[22] particularly in relation to aging populations.[23]

Enthusiastic statements are constantly made in the medical and public health literature about the potential of the new digital technologies to "engage" or "activate" laypeople with a view to having them manage their own health and learn more about their body's functions and activities or, as I have termed it, to become the ideal "digitally engaged patients."[24] The terms *disruptive* and *destructive* are employed by some writers to suggest that a new paradigm of medical care, preventive medicine, and health promotion is emerging as a result of digital health initiatives.[25]

Digital devices such as smartphones, iPods, and tablet computers now allow for ubiquitous computing and are increasingly connected to one another as part of the "Internet-of-Things,"[26] whose capabilities are regarded as key features of the digital health phenomenon. These include the devices' portability and ability to connect to the Internet almost anywhere, and the opportunity to connect them wirelessly to technologies embedded with sensors that can constantly monitor bodily functions and activities, as well as their ability to converge with one another and readily exchange data. In addition, sophisticated algorithms can be used to process and interpret the data that are collected.[27] The affordances of Web 2.0 technologies mark a major departure from Web 1.0 technologies such as websites, which encouraged far less participation, largely conveying information to passive recipients. Users of the newer digital technologies can contribute to or comment on blogs and online news items and upload data and images to social media sites such as Twitter, Facebook, YouTube, and Instagram. Such individuals are thus able to be both the consumers and the producers of digital content, as suggested by the word *prosumption*, which is now frequently used to describe this phenomenon of users' active engagement with digital media.[28]

These mobile digital devices and related software and the Web 2.0 platforms to which they connect offer not only ready access to or provision of medical and health information on the Internet but also new ways of monitoring and measuring the human body. They are able to produce detailed biometric data that may be collected by individuals and then easily shared with others. Thousands of health-related apps for mobile digital devices have been developed to assist users in tracking their bodily functions and activities. Because of the increasing trend of embedding tiny digital sensors and microprocessors into everyday objects that are then able to transmit wirelessly the data they collect to other digital devices, apps, and platforms, increasingly greater amounts of data on many aspects of the human body's movements, geographic location, and physical function may be collected and analyzed.[29] A range of digital products are currently on the market that can be worn on the body for the purpose of self-tracking biometric data. Body functions and indicators such as blood glucose level, body temperature, breathing rate, blood chemistry readings, and even brain activity can all be monitored with sensors embedded in devices that can be worn on the body, woven into clothing, or laminated onto ultra-thin patches and other skin interfaces.

Wearable devices that are currently available include a rubber wristband, the Jawbone Up, which is fitted with tiny motion sensors that can track how much the user is walking and sleeping and that work with an iOS app to upload the collected data. Together with other technologies, the Up app can keep a record of meals eaten (using photographs of the food), calories burned, and hours slept, as well as physical activities completed; for those who are competitive, the latter data can be graphed and compared with that of other users of the app. The bracelet can be programmed to vibrate at various times throughout the day to remind its wearer to move. The developers of the device note that it uses algorithms to "discover hidden connections and patterns in your day-to-day activities" that will "deliver insights that keep you moving forward."[30] Sports watches can be purchased that can be worn during walking or running to record heart rate, time, distance, pace, and calories burned, which data can then be uploaded to a computer. The Wakemate, another bracelet worn during sleep, uses sensors to monitor the wearer's sleep cycles and then chooses the best time to wake the wearer when she or he has entered a light sleep mode; it also provides detailed metrics on body movement during sleep to indicate how much deep, restful sleep was obtained.

People use many of these apps and devices voluntarily in an effort to track their health, exercise, and consumption habits.[31] However, as integral elements of digitized health promotion, digital health technologies are increasingly championed in the health promotion and preventive medicine literature as offering unprecedented opportunities to reach target groups with tailored messages, to encourage members of these groups to engage in self-monitoring of their health-related behaviors, and to both track individuals and collect mass data on these behaviors for use in monitoring populations. In the notion of "personalized preventive medicine," the concepts of medicine and health promotion meet. The "personalized" aspect of this approach focuses on collecting as much data as possible about individuals and their health states, everyday habits, and the social and geographic environments in which they live—their "personal health informatics," as one writer puts it.[32]

Many articles have recently appeared in the health promotion and preventive medicine literature discussing the possibilities of using digital technologies for health promotion.[33] Such strategies as tweeting or texting people with reminders to exercise, forgo smoking, wash their hands, limit their alcohol use, take a screening test, immunize their children, or practice safer sex, and apps and designated Facebook pages related to specific public health campaigns or health behaviors, have been proposed as ways of reaching target groups via mobile digital devices and social media platforms.

As such, digital technologies are presented as conduits for conveying health information that have the potential to far exceed the relatively blunt instrument of the social marketing campaign. What are sometimes described as "digital interventions" are represented as far more specifically targeted and individualized, serving as proxy health coaches by offering motivation, support, and feedback—reaching, in the process, ever further into people's everyday lives.[34] Instead of the "one-way" media traditionally used as part of social marketing health campaigns, such as advertisements and brochures, digital technologies such as social media are represented as facilitating "engagement" of and fostering "partnerships" with members of the public if used strategically.[35] Writers in health promotion now frequently make reference to linking health promotion strategies that use digital health devices with encouraging members of targeted "risk groups" to become responsible for promoting their own health.

Corporations, as well as government agencies, have entered the digital health market. The American retail giant Walmart now provides interactive self-service health kiosks where shoppers are encouraged to check their eyesight, weight, body mass index, and blood pressure and access health-related information (as well as view advertisements for relevant products stocked by Walmart that can be targeted to users based on their responses). In the United Kingdom, the National Health Service (NHS) has developed an initiative to fund libraries, community centers, and pubs to act as "digital health hubs." These are designed to provide training and support to enable people to access health and medical information online; the hubs feature websites such as NHS Choices, which offers free health-related apps that interested persons can use to download information and advice on medical conditions, online patient support communities, and health care services. As the website's title suggests, the focus is on supporting laypeople as they make "choices" about their health and health care, the idea being to "put you in control of your healthcare."[36]

Digitizing the Body

Medical technologies are playing a growing role in how individuals experience and think about their bodies. Human bodies now interact every day with a vast number of technologies that are designed to change, extend, or enhance their physical capacities and capabilities. In the era of digital health, these technologies are increasingly able to monitor and measure bodily capabilities, functions, and behaviors and to produce data that may be used to construct concepts of health, illness, self-care, and personal responsibility. Now that computers are not only wearable but can be inserted into the body or ingested as pills and are used as part of medical care and preventive health strategies, new possibilities and limitations have arisen in relation to the ways we think about and use these technologies.

Despite their representation as inert, neutral participants in the collection of data in the interests of health promotion and medical self-care, digital medical devices that function in or on one's person may be viewed as actively shaping the bodies of those who use them. Several writers in the sociology of science and technology have pointed to the mythology of control that underpins discourses on technology in medicine and in health care more generally. These writers highlight the messiness of technologies, their changing meanings, and their situated functions in time and place, as well as their contribution to concepts of selfhood and the body. This sociomaterial perspective views human bodies as assemblages of flesh, discourses, practices, others' bodies, material objects, and spatial location that are constantly open to reconfiguration, depending on the context. Scholars writing from this perspective emphasize that technologies are actors with agency. They discipline and order bodies in certain ways, just as bodies discipline and order technologies. They are not politically neutral but, rather, are implicated in a dense web of power relations.[37]

In the age of "informational medicine,"[38] both the human body and medicine tend to be represented in terms of information processing and mechanical systems.[39] The idea of using technology to peer inside the body is part of a mentality which assumes that more information about the body is always better. Testing and screening technologies offer the opportunity to identify health risks before they pose a serious threat. They have become more commonly used in preventive medicine as part of a wider move in medical care toward the use of technology.[40] Calculations of the risk associated with using these technologies appear to be scientific, and therefore reliable.[41]

Writing before the advent of sensor-embedded wearable digital devices, Marc Chrysanthou commented on the "fantasy of bodily perfection through information" that has become prominent in wealthy Western societies.[42] He argued that the medicalized information society had generated a new form of embodiment that represented the body as transparent and as controllable and perfectible through the gathering and judicious use of information. Chrysanthou referred to such technologies as self-screening devices and home-based diagnostic kits, available at pharmacies or by mail order, as examples of an increasing interest in self-monitoring for health purposes.[43]

A mere decade or so later, digital technologies provide a bewildering array of devices by which the body can be visualized, documented, tested, and monitored. The techno-utopianism that once pervaded medicine and health care has given way to digital utopianism across a range of governmental and commercial enterprises. Laypeople have been urged to use these technologies to "digitize their bodies" in the interests of achieving better knowledge of what lies within.[44] Discourses on "digitizing the body" as part of the project of self-monitoring take up the ideal of the transparent body. While people have been able to monitor and measure aspects of their bodies and selves using nondigital technologies for centuries, digital devices have facilitated the ever more detailed measurement and monitoring of the body and everyday life. As noted earlier, many self-tracking devices, particularly those that are wearable, such as adhesive skin patches, wristbands, and headbands, allow for tracking of the body throughout the day (and night).

This perspective on the body represents it as a series of digital codes, subject to algorithmic calculation and prediction. Failing to avoid disease becomes a problem of ignorance of the appropriate information.[45] It is here that "small data"—the conglomeration of data about themselves that people can bring together through interactions on and monitoring by digital devices—become represented as important. These small data are represented as providing unique insights into the self and the body,[46] including the identification of illness by means of biometrics and algorithms before the individual begins to feel ill. As one advocate of self-tracking bodily functions, Steven Dean, put it, "An advantage of putting numbers on aspects of our bodies is that we don't always know what's going on. We don't feel certain things—like the early onset of illnesses, for example—but there are metrics and biomarkers that can tell us they're happening. . . . I really do strongly believe that the more mystery we can take out of understanding the body the better."[47]

There is a dualism here between knowing our bodies "subjectively" from the inside, as in relying on self-awareness of one's physical well-being and state of health, and knowing them "objectively" from the outside, as can be made possible by medical or digital monitoring technologies.[48] The implication of statements such as Dean's is that the haptic sensations we feel from experiencing and living in our bodies are no longer reliable or detailed enough to provide adequate knowledge of our health. We require digital technologies to perform a monitoring function that our bodies are unable to achieve alone.

Surveillant Assemblages and Self-Monitoring

Digital surveillance technologies have proliferated in recent times. From the ubiquitous closed-circuit television camera to government agencies' databases, Internet cookies, and shopping loyalty cards, such technologies allow the continual and routine collection of data on such aspects as people's movements in public space, their use of government services, and their Internet browsing and purchasing habits.[49] Many of these surveillance technologies are "top-down" and hidden, often imposed on the bodies of the individuals they monitor without their knowledge or consent. The development of digital devices with embedded sensors able to detect bodily functions and movements has contributed to an innovative approach to the surveillance of bodies that works from inside the body outward. While surveillance cameras observe bodily movements in space, body sensor technologies monitor the body from the inside and transmit data to outside devices for interpretation and visualization. In the process, the transparent body becomes a "data double"[50] of the fleshly body, a collection of data that may be drawn from a variety of sources and reassembled in different ways to suit various purposes.

Drawing on Michel Foucault's work on biopolitics and the disciplinary and normalizing functions of the medical gaze, several sociologists have written about the surveillance strategies that operate in the context of the clinic and medical encounters.[51] Many critical scholars have also drawn on Foucault's writings on governmentality to identify the ways in which health-related behaviors are positioned as part of the government of the self in neoliberal political contexts.[52] This perspective continues to constitute a dominant critique of public health and its role in configuring concepts of bodies, health, and selves.[53]

However, the new practices of self-monitoring engendered by digital technologies go beyond the hierarchical panoptic approach developed in Foucauldian theories of disciplinary surveillance techniques in what has been termed a "post-panoptic" society.[54] Because technologies such as mobile self-tracking devices allow users to collect data on themselves in unprecedented quantity and detail, the potential for self-monitoring offered by mobile digital devices configures a different kind of surveillance that is voluntary rather than imposed, visible rather than hidden.[55]

Rather than a small number of hidden observers watching and monitoring a large number of others, as the Foucauldian metaphor of the panopticon has it, the new digital technologies directed at promoting health often depend on individuals' turning the gaze on themselves, and then inviting others to participate in their own surveillance by sharing the data they have collected on themselves.[56] This is a version of the *synopticon* model of surveillance, in which, instead of "the few watching the many," the "many are watching the few."[57] Indeed, people interacting with one another on social media are watching one another, as more and more personal information is uploaded and shared on these sites and comments (or "likes," or followers) are invited. It has been argued that participation in social media contributes to a "confessional society"[58] and a culture of sharing,[59] in which it is expected that intimate and mundane aspects of one's life are constantly shared with others, including those that may previously have been kept private.

Given the possibilities that are afforded by these new technologies, it has been argued that the concept of "surveillant assemblages" might be a better alternative to the panoptic gaze,[60] as it acknowledges the mutually constitutive nature of selves, bodies, data, and technologies; their constantly mutable form; and the participatory nature of surveillance.[61] In relation to digital health technologies, surveillant assemblages include those that are configured when people use technologies to engage in self-care or self-monitoring practices that involve wearing digital devices or inserting them into their bodies. As part of the neoliberal requirements of layperson/patient "engagement," these surveillant assemblages are ideally configured voluntarily, as laypeople judge their participation in self-surveillance as being in their own best interest. They are seeking to monitor their own bodies as part of their own choices about how to achieve good health and physical fitness and make their own decisions about who will be given access to the information they collect with these devices.[62]

Despite the rhetoric of participatory surveillance that tends to be expressed in discourses on digitized health promotion, users of digital devices do not always have full control over the data that are generated, or even free choice about whether to use these technologies. There are moves in some sectors to employ digital devices in a more imposed manner. In the United States, for example, some insurance companies have started attempts to "incentivize" clients who are designated as obese to lose weight by using sensor devices such as pedometers as part of "wellness programs." Such individuals are informed that unless they lose weight, they face significant increases in their insurance premiums. One weight-loss method they are offered is participation in a walking program in which the number of steps they take each day is counted by digital pedometers that upload this information to a website monitored by the health insurer. Not surprisingly, an evaluation of one such program found that while the financial "incentive" did result in most people walking the number of steps required to avoid higher payments, a significant proportion of participants (one-third) found the strategy coercive.[63]

Many employers in the United States pay at least a portion of their work force's health insurance premiums, so some have begun to use workplace wellness programs as a means of reducing their costs; some of these programs are mandatory. These programs often use financial incentives or disincentives to motivate employees to engage in health-promoting behaviors. Some companies have begun encouraging their employees to use mobile or wearable digital self-tracking devices to assess their sleep, diet, and exercise habits; the collected data are then uploaded to a company website.[64] Employees who have a high body mass index or high blood pressure, or cholesterol levels that are deemed "unhealthy," can be penalized by the company with higher premiums or deductibles or in other ways. These actions have provoked questions about privacy rights and discrimination against employees who are identified as insufficiently "responsible" in their preventive health efforts.[65]

Digitizing Risk: The Algorithm and Big Data

In discourses on digital health, much emphasis is placed on the role played by the big data accumulated from people's interactions with digital technologies in providing knowledge about health care services and providers. It is regularly contended that, whether accumulated as by-products of people's use of websites or apps, entered as part of electronic medical records, or more deliberately produced as part of laypeople's prosumption activities on social media sites, the reams of data that are generated across many thousands of users offer the potential for new ways of achieving health promotion objectives.[66]

Self-tracking digital devices produce data on everyday habits across their thousands of users when these data are uploaded to the associated websites. A growing number of patient experience and opinion platforms have been developed to "crowdsource" data about medical treatments and infectious disease outbreaks.[67] In the growing digital data economy, companies have emerged that profit from "scraping," or harvesting, data from Internet sites, including social media, for commercial purposes. This information includes data generated from self-tracking devices that are uploaded to the developer's website[68] and the comments people make about their habits and health-related activities on social media sites.[69]

Big data and algorithms are now becoming central to digitized health promotion, both in gathering relevant information and in generating predictive patterns. The terms *infodemiology* and *infoveillance* have been used in some quarters to describe the use of digital technologies to collect data about patterns of illness and disease from online sources such as social media and Internet search engine terms. Various social media tools have been employed in public health efforts to disseminate information about health risks and disease outbreaks and to collect data on the incidence of illness and disease. For example, researchers have used Google to develop systems to track outbreaks of infectious diseases such as influenza by monitoring online queries and search terms.[70]

Digital calculations of risk are central to these efforts. In any attempt to educate the population about health as part of encouraging people to avoid certain ("unhealthy") behaviors and take up ("healthy") others, the concept of risk is employed. Certain groups are singled out as being "at risk" and therefore requiring more intervention than others. Risk assessments that employ quantitative methodologies have been an integral feature of public health strategies for decades. Populations are ranked and ordered by means of data from various data sets such as national and local health surveys, with certain "risk groups" identified through this process. These risk groups are then targeted for special interventions in an attempt to persuade their members to change their behaviors to conform to expectations about preventive health and self-responsibility.[71]

The concepts of risk and "at-risk groups" and the problems related to their calculation are also central to digitized health promotion. In recent times, the big data sets generated from digital technologies have become a focal concern of authorities and policymakers in health care and public health. As I have already noted, such data sets, as well as the small data that are gathered from individuals using self-tracking digital devices to monitor their biometrics, are viewed as ways to calculate risk in ever finer detail and to pinpoint health problems before they even begin to show physical signs. Calculations of risk are part of the apparatus and promise of digital devices and the algorithms used to make sense of the data they produce. Many apps and self-tracking digital devices are also directed at measuring the bodily attributes and behaviors of their users and comparing these against a norm to generate risk calculations. For instance, Internet calculator sites have been instituted with online tools made available to members of the public to enter their own data and calculate their risk of developing diabetes or heart disease.[72] Another example is the Ovuline digital platform and associated app for pregnant women. Users are encouraged to measure and monitor a wide range of bodily indicators and activities using various digital devices (exercise and sleep-monitoring devices and digital scales, all of which can be purchased from the website), as well as to enter other data into the database. The women are asked to upload the data they have collected using their devices or to manually enter data on their diet, exercise patterns, blood pressure, weight, mood, health state, and sleep patterns. All of these data are combined to produce calculations (expressed with charts and an interactive timeline) that are used to advise on whether the pregnancy is conforming to norms in relation to diet and weight gain, to provide "customized plans" to ensure that "your unique pregnancy" is as healthy and as normal as possible, and to provide "immediate alerts for health risks."[73]

In the utopian discourse on the possibilities and potential of big data, metricization, and algorithmic calculation for health care, there is little room for acknowledgment that data themselves and the algorithms that interpret them and generate predictions based on them are social actors rather than neutral, objective sources of knowledge. As a growing number of social analyses of digital data have pointed out in the face of all the glorification of these data in both the popular media and expert forums, digital data, like any other source of information, whether "big" or "small," are social configurations that are partial, incomplete, and often inaccurate.[74] Indeed, the technologies that collect the data are themselves not as seamless and precise as suggested in many discourses championing their use. Just as telemedical technologies employed for patient self-care and self-monitoring are sometimes unreliable and difficult to use,[75] the types of self-tracking devices used for promoting health can be frustrating to operate and variable in their efficacy and precision.[76]

Conclusion

For many decades, medical technologies have been promoted as the means by which health care costs may be reduced and the productivity of service provision increased. Those who champion digitized health promotion are the latest contributors to this perspective, positioning digital technologies as providing the obvious solutions to social and economic problems. While the development of technologies that can focus ever more closely on the body and people's behaviors and "lifestyles" represents a new mode of health promotion, older, more established concepts underlie the application of these technologies. Notions that tout self-control, taking charge of one's own health, and warding off illness and disease through rational action are revived and intensified in contemporary discourses of digitized health promotion, as is the tendency toward healthism and blaming the victim for ill health. In a context in which digital data are considered a valuable form of knowledge, digital devices are available to help people learn about their health, and the detailed information these devices collect can be easily shared with others (or demanded by insurance companies or employers), there seem to be few excuses for people to refrain from personally managing their health. Digital devices and platforms represent a new technological "fix" for the ills that may befall people. At first glance, these technologies appear to offer a simple solution to the rising costs of health care. Once again, the emphasis in health promotion on recognizing and ameliorating the social inequalities that cause some social groups to suffer greater ill health than others has been lost. Digitized health promotion discourses hold out the promise of control not only over the vagaries of the body by engendering greater knowledge of what lies inside[77] but also over unruly members of the population who are viewed as making ever greater demands on health system and government budgets.

Where once health promotion was a relatively low-tech endeavor, the new digital health technologies have introduced tools and devices that have significant implications for both health promotion professionals and the "at risk" groups they identify as requiring their interventions.[78] The new digital technologies may now be combined with concepts of self-responsibility for health and encourage people to engage in self-surveillance and the surveillance of others in ways that were unimaginable in the past. Social marketing approaches intended to change behavior may now be complemented by methods that are able to reach into the most detailed and intimate aspects of people's bodies and relationships, monitoring and measuring them in many different dimensions. Where once laypeople targeted as part of "at risk" groups for health promotion interventions could simply choose to ignore or discount the messages disseminated in health-related social marketing campaigns, they can now be reached individually via the digital devices they carry or wear on their bodies. Where once health promoters relied on individuals' self-reports of their activities and behaviors, digital devices are now able to monitor multitudes of people simultaneously at any hour of the day or night and report the data that are collected.

The algorithms configured through the use of digital media create new assemblages as part of the operation of "soft biopower" and "soft biopolitics."[79] By bringing together heterogeneous elements in new ways, ontological categories created by digitally generated algorithms have a profound impact on how individuals view themselves and the world. These categories form new objects of knowledge and new bodies of information that exert a normalizing power, suggesting defined possibilities for action and for relations with others.[80] When directions for behavior emerge from an algorithm, the operations of power and surveillance are diffused and indirect. The digital device issues the directive or advice: "Answer this question." "Take these medications." "Increase your physical activity." "Upload your data." Just as telemedicine requires patients to discipline their bodies in certain ways to meet the demands of medical technologies,[81] the imperatives of self-monitoring and self-knowledge inherent in digitized health promotion oblige their target groups to accede to the expectations these imperatives generate.

Digital health technologies as they are used for health promotion, therefore, represent another dimension of the government of the self that citizens in neoliberal political systems are incited to achieve. Digital health discourses assume that laypeople are willing and able to take up the technologies espoused in these discourses. They privilege a rational, "activated" consumer who, in turn, privileges health over other priorities, is familiar with and confident about using digital technologies, and is willing to take responsibility for self-care and preventive health efforts.[82] But the dominant discourse of digital health fails to acknowledge that the members of some social groups lack access to the new digital technologies[83] or would simply rather not use them, for a variety of reasons.[84] Just as some patients using digital telemedical devices resent these devices' intrusion into their everyday lives and domestic spaces,[85] so too the targets of digitized health promotion may respond with ambivalence, indifference, or outright hostility to the directives issued from their devices.

Because of the assumption that digital technologies and the data they generate are neutral, objective, and powerful tools that lead to greater self-knowledge and greater efficiency of health services and health promotion, little attention has been paid to the moral, political, and ethical implications of these technologies. Yet, as I have shown in the present chapter, there is great potential for deeper entrenchment of socioeconomic disadvantage and a failure to confront the underpinnings of this disadvantage when digitized health promotion is embraced.

NOTES

1 Robert Crawford, "You Are Dangerous to Your Health: The Ideology and Politics of Victim Blaming," *International Journal of Health Services* 7, no. 4 (1977): 663–80; Deborah Lupton, *The Imperative of Health: Public Health and the Regulated Body* (London: Sage, 1995).

2 Lupton, *The Imperative of Health*; Deborah Lupton, *Medicine as Culture: Illness, Disease and the Body*, Third Edition (London: Sage, 2012).

3 Crawford, "You Are Dangerous to Your Health," 672.

4 Ibid.; Lupton, *The Imperative of Health*.

5 Deborah Lupton, "Risk as Moral Danger: The Social and Political Functions of Risk Discourse in Public Health," *International Journal of Health Care Services* 23, no. 3 (1993): 425–35; Lupton, *The Imperative of Health*.

6 Robert Crawford, "Healthism and the Medicalization of Everyday Life," *International Journal of Health Care Services* 10, no. 3 (1980): 365–88; Crawford, "You Are Dangerous to Your Health."

7 Michael Marmot and Richard Wilkinson, eds., *Social Determinants of Health*, Second Edition (Oxford: Oxford University Press, 2006).

8 Ibid.; Dennis Raphael, "A Discourse Analysis of the Social Determinants of Health," *Critical Public Health* 21, no. 2 (2011): 221–36; Raphael, "Grasping at Straws: A Recent History of Health Promotion in Canada," *Critical Public Health* 18, no. 4 (2008): 483–95.

9 Fran Baum, *The New Public Health*, Second Edition (South Melbourne, Australia: Oxford University Press, 2002).

10 Fran Baum, "The Commission on the Social Determinants of Health: Reinventing Health Promotion for the Twenty-First Century?," *Critical Public Health* 18, no. 4 (2008): 457–66.

11 Ichiro Kawachi, "Social Epidemiology," *Social Science and Medicine* 54, no. 12 (2002): 1739–41; Nancy Krieger, "A Glossary for Social Epidemiology," *Journal of*

Epidemiology and Community Health 55, no. 10 (2001): 693–700; "Why Epidemiologists Cannot Afford to Ignore Poverty," *Epidemiology* 18, no. 6 (2007): 658–63.

12 Alan Petersen and Deborah Lupton, *The New Public Health: Health and Self in the Age of Risk* (London: Sage, 1996).

13 Baum, "The Commission on the Social Determinants of Health."

14 Nike Ayo, "Understanding Health Promotion in a Neoliberal Climate and the Making of Health-Conscious Citizens," *Critical Public Health* 22, no. 1 (2011); Dennis Raphael, "The Political Economy of Health Promotion: Part 1, National Commitments to Provision of the Prerequisites of Health," *Health Promotion International* 28, no. 1 (2013): 95–111.

15 Paul Crawshaw, "Governing at a Distance: Social Marketing and the (Bio) Politics of Responsibility," *Social Science and Medicine* 74, no. 1 (2012): 200–7; Marilou Gagnon, Jean Daniel Jacob, and Dave Holmes, "Governing through (in)Security: A Critical Analysis of a Fear-Based Public Health Campaign," *Critical Public Health* 20, no. 2 (2010): 245–56; Lupton, *The Imperative of Health*; Deborah Lupton, "'How Do You Measure Up?' Assumptions about 'Obesity' and Health-Related Behaviors and Beliefs in Two Australian 'Obesity' Prevention Campaigns," *Fat Studies* 3, no. 1 (2014): 32–44; Raphael, "A Discourse Analysis."

16 Baum, "The Commission on the Social Determinants of Health."

17 Michael Sparks, "The Changing Contexts of Health Promotion," *Health Promotion International* 28, no. 2 (2013): 153–56.

18 Raphael, "A Discourse Analysis"; Raphael, "The Political Economy of Health Promotion."

19 Ayo, "Understanding Health Promotion"; Crawshaw, "Governing at a Distance"; Daniel Goldberg, "Social Justice, Health Inequalities and Methodological Individualism in U.S. Health Promotion," *Public Health Ethics* 5, no. 2 (2012): 104–15; Lupton, "'How Do You Measure Up?'"; Raphael, "The Political Economy of Health Promotion."

20 Roberto De Vogli, "Neoliberal Globalisation and Health in a Time of Economic Crisis," *Social Theory and Health* 9, no. 4 (2011): 311–25.

21 Susan Dentzer, "Rx for the 'Blockbuster Drug' of Patient Engagement," *Health Affairs* 32, no. 2 (2013), 202.

22 Maggie Mort, Tracy Finch, and Carl May, "Making and Unmaking Telepatients: Identity and Governance in New Health Technologies," *Science, Technology, and Human Values* 34, no. 1 (2009): 9–33; Nelly Oudshoorn, *Telecare Technologies and the Transformation of Healthcare* (Houndmills, England: Palgrave Macmillan, 2011).

23 Maggie Mort, Celia Roberts, and Blanca Callén, "Ageing with Telecare: Care or Coercion in Austerity?" *Sociology of Health and Illness* 35, no. 6 (2013): 799–812.

24 Deborah Lupton, "The Digitally Engaged Patient: Self-Monitoring and Self-Care in the Digital Health Era," *Social Theory and Health* 11, no. 3 (2013): 256–70. See also, for example, Jessica Greene and Judith Hibbard, "Why Does Patient Activation Matter? An Examination of the Relationships between Patient Activation and Health-Related Outcomes," *Journal of General Internal Medicine* 27, no. 5 (2012): 520–26.

25 See, for example, Eric Topol, *The Creative Destruction of Medicine: How the Digital Revolution Will Create Better Health Care* (New York: Basic Books, 2012); Melanie Swan, "Health 2050: The Realization of Personalized Medicine through Crowdsourcing, the Quantified Self, and the Participatory Biocitizen," *Journal of Personalized Medicine* 2, no. 3 (2012): 93–118.

26 Daniele Miorandi et al., "Internet of Things: Vision, Applications and Research Challenges," *Ad Hoc Networks* 10, no. 7 (2012): 1497–516. In the abstract to this article, the authors write that "the term 'Internet-of-Things' is used as an umbrella keyword for covering various aspects related to the extension of the Internet and the Web into the physical realm, by means of the widespread deployment of spatially distributed devices with embedded identification, sensing and/or actuation capabilities" (p. 1497).

27 Melanie Swan, "Emerging Patient-Driven Health Care Models: An Examination of Health Social Networks, Consumer Personalized Medicine and Quantified Self-Tracking," *International Journal of Environmental Research and Public Health* 6, no. 2 (2009): 492–525; Swan, "Sensor Mania! The Internet of Things, Wearable Computing, Objective Metrics, and the Quantified Self 2.0," *Journal of Sensor and Actuator Networks* 1, no. 3 (2012): 217–53; Topol, *The Creative Destruction of Medicine*.

28 David Beer and Roger Burrows, "Consumption, Prosumption and Participatory Web Cultures: An Introduction," *Journal of Consumer Culture* 10, no. 1 (2010): 3–12; George Ritzer, Paul Dean, and Nathan Jurgenson, "The Coming of Age of the Prosumer," *American Behavioral Scientist* 56, no. 4 (2012): 379–98.

29 Swan, "Sensor Mania!"

30 "Introducing UP24 Now for Android and iOS," Up by Jawbone, accessed May 12, 2013, https://jawbone.com/up.

31 Deborah Lupton, "M-Health and Health Promotion: The Digital Cyborg and Surveillance Society," *Social Theory and Health* 10, no. 3 (2012): 229–44; "Quantifying the Body: Monitoring, Performing and Configuring Health in the Age of mHealth Technologies," *Critical Public Health* 23, no. 4 (2013): 393–403.

32 Swan, "Health 2050."

33 See, for example, Lorien Abroms et al., "iPhone Apps for Smoking Cessation," *American Journal of Preventive Medicine* 40, no. 3 (2011): 279–85; Robert Kaplan and Arthur Stone, "Bringing the Laboratory and Clinic to the Community: Mobile Technologies for Health Promotion and Disease Prevention," *Annual Review of Psychology* 64, no. 1 (2013): 471–98; Holly Korda and Zena Itani, "Harnessing Social Media for Health Promotion and Behavior Change," *Health Promotion Practice* 14, no. 1 (2013): 15–23; Craig Lefebvre, "Integrating Cell Phones and Mobile Technologies into Public Health Practice: A Social Marketing Perspective," *Health Promotion Practice* 10, no. 4 (2009): 490–94; Courtney Stevens and Angela Bryan, "Rebranding Exercise: There's an App for That," *American Journal of Health Promotion* 27, no. 2 (2012): 69–70; Swan, "Emerging Patient-Driven Health Care Models"; Swan, "Health 2050."

34 Wen-Ying Sylvia Chou et al., "Web 2.0 for Health Promotion: Reviewing the Current Evidence," *American Journal of Public Health* 103, no. 1 (2013): e9–e18, http://

ajph.aphapublications.org/doi/abs/10.2105/AJPH.2012.301071?prevSearch=web+2.0&se archHistoryKey=.

35 Enrico Coiera, "Social Networks, Social Media, and Social Diseases," *British Medical Journal* 346, f3007 (2013), doi: http://dx.doi.org/10.1136/bmj.f3007.

36 "About NHS Choices," National Health Service, accessed March 20, 2014, http://www.nhs.uk/aboutNHSChoices/aboutnhschoices/Aboutus/Pages/Introduction.aspx.

37 See, for example, Monica Casper and Daniel Morrison, "Medical Sociology and Technology: Critical Engagements," supplement, *Journal of Health and Social Behavior* 51 (2010): S120–32; Donna Haraway, *Simians, Cyborgs and Women: The Reinvention of Nature* (London: Free Association, 1991); Annemarie Mol, *The Body Multiple: Ontology in Medical Practice* (Durham, N.C.: Duke University Press, 2002); Maggie Mort and Andrew Smith, "Beyond Information: Intimate Relations in Sociotechnical Practice," *Sociology* 43, no. 2 (2009): 215–31; Mort, Finch, and May, "Making and Unmaking Telepatients"; Mort, Roberts, and Callén, "Ageing with Telecare"; Oudshoorn, *Telecare Technologies*.

38 Sarah Nettleton, "The Emergence of E-Scaped Medicine?" *Sociology* 38, no. 4 (2004): 661–79.

39 Marc Chrysanthou, "Transparency and Selfhood: Utopia and the Informed Body," *Social Science and Medicine* 54, no. 3 (2002): 469–79; Haraway, *Simians, Cyborgs and Women*.

40 Rory Coughlan, "The Socio-Politics of Technology and Innovation: Problematizing the 'Caring' in Healthcare?" *Social Theory and Health* 4, no. 4 (2006): 334–52.

41 Lupton, *The Imperative of Health*.

42 Chrysanthou, "Transparency and Selfhood," 470.

43 Ibid., 469–79.

44 Topol, *The Creative Destruction of Medicine*.

45 Deborah Lupton, "Understanding the Human Machine," *IEEE Technology and Society Magazine* (Winter 2013): 25–30; Lupton, "Quantifying the Body."

46 Ki Mae Heussner, "It's Not Just About Big Data: Here's Why Small Data Matters to Your Health," *Gigaom*, April 17, 2013, http://gigaom.com/2013/04/17/its-not-just-about-big-data-heres-why-small-data-matters-to-your-health.

47 Lauren Christensen, "Big Brother Health or Mindful Living? Quantified Self Organizer Steve Dean on the Difference between Self-Tracking and Surveillance," *Vanity Fair Online* (January 8, 2013), http://www.vanityfair.com/online/daily/2013/01/quantified-self-organizer-steven-dean-interview-surveillance.

48 Lupton, "M-Health and Health Promotion"; Lupton, "Quantifying the Body"; Lupton, "Understanding the Human Machine"; Annemarie Mol and John Law, "Embodied Action, Enacted Bodies: The Example of Hypoglycaemia," *Body and Society* 10, nos. 2–3 (2004): 43–62.

49 Kirsty Best, "Living in the Control Society: Surveillance, Users and Digital Screen Technologies," *International Journal of Cultural Studies* 13, no. 1 (2010): 5–24; Evelyn Ruppert, "The Governmental Topologies of Database Devices," *Theory, Culture*

and Society 29, nos. 4–5 (2012): 116–36; Beer and Burrows, "Consumption, Prosumption and Participatory Web Cultures."

50 Greg Elmer, "A Diagram of Panoptic Surveillance," *New Media and Society* 5, no. 2 (2003): 231–47.

51 For example, David Armstrong, "The Rise of Surveillance Medicine," *Sociology of Health and Illness* 17, no. 3 (1995): 393–404; Lupton, *Medicine as Culture*.

52 See, for example, John Coveney, "The Government and Ethics of Health Promotion: The Importance of Michel Foucault," *Health Education Research* 13, no. 3 (1998): 459–68; Lupton, *The Imperative of Health*; Petersen and Lupton, *The New Public Health*.

53 For example, Ayo, "Understanding Health Promotion"; Crawshaw, "Governing at a Distance"; Gagnon et al., "Governing through (in)Security."

54 Samantha Adams, "Post-Panoptic Surveillance through Healthcare Rating Sites," *Information, Communication and Society* 16, no. 2 (2012): 215–35.

55 Lupton, "M-Health and Health Promotion"; Emma Rich and Andy Miah, "Prosthetic Surveillance: The Medical Governance of Healthy Bodies in Cyberspace," *Surveillance and Society* 6, no. 2 (2009): 163–77.

56 Adams, "Post-Panoptic Surveillance"; Lupton, "M-Health and Health Promotion."

57 Aaron Doyle, "Revisiting the Synopticon: Reconsidering Mathiesen's 'The Viewer Society' in the Age of Web 2.0," *Theoretical Criminology* 15, no. 3 (2011): 283–99.

58 David Beer, "Researching a Confessional Society," *International Journal of Market Research* 50, no. 5 (2008): 619–29.

59 Nicholas John, "Sharing and Web 2.0: The Emergence of a Keyword," *New Media and Society* 15, no. 2 (2013): 167–82.

60 Kevin Haggery and Richard Ericson, "The Surveillant Assemblage," *British Journal of Sociology* 51, no. 4 (2000): 605–22.

61 Best, "Living in the Control Society."

62 Lupton, "M-Health and Health Promotion"; Lupton, "Quantifying the Body"; Lupton, "The Human Machine."

63 Donna Zulman et al., "Implementation and Evaluation of an Incentivized Internet-Mediated Walking Program for Obese Adults," *Translational Behavioral Medicine* 3, no. 4 (2013): 357–69.

64 Klint Finley, "What If Your Boss Tracked Your Sleep, Diet, and Exercise?" *Wired* (April 17, 2013), http://www.wired.com/wiredenterprise/2013/04/quantified-work-citizen.

65 Ann Hendrix and Josh Buck, "Employer-Sponsored Wellness Programs: Should Your Employer Be the Boss of More than Your Work?" *Southwestern Law Review* 38, no. 3 (2009): 465–78.

66 Coiera, "Social Networks"; Travis Murdoch and Allan Detsky, "The Inevitable Application of Big Data to Health Care," *Journal of the American Medical Association* 309, no. 13 (2013): 1351–52; Swan, "Health 2050."

67 Deborah Lupton, "The Commodification of Patient Opinion: The Digital Patient Experience Economy in the Age of Big Data," *Sociology of Health and Illness* (published online ahead of print January 21, 2014), doi:10.1111/1467-9566.12109.

68 Aarti Shahani Shahani, "Who Could Be Watching You Watching Your Figure? Your Boss," *All Tech Considered*, December 26, 2012, http://www.npr.org/blogs/alltech-considered/2012/12/26/167970303/who-could-be-watching-you-watching-your-figure-your-boss.

69 Lupton, "The Commodification of Patient Opinion."

70 Fahad Pervaiz et al., "Flubreaks: Early Epidemic Detection from Google Flu Trends," *Journal of Medical Internet Research* 14, no. 5 (2012): e125, http://www.jmir.org/2012/5/e125/.

71 Lupton, *The Imperative of Health*; Petersen and Lupton, *The New Public Health*.

72 Christine Holmberg, Christine Bischof, and Susanne Bauer, "Making Predictions: Computing Populations," *Science, Technology and Human Values* 38, no. 3 (2012): 398–420.

73 "Ovia Pregnancy," Ovuline, Inc., accessed April 3, 2013, http://www.ovuline.com/smart-pregnancy.

74 David Beer, "Power through the Algorithm? Participatory Web Cultures and the Technological Unconscious," *New Media and Society* 11, no. 6 (2009): 985–1002; Danah Boyd and Kate Crawford, "Critical Questions for Big Data: Provocations for a Cultural, Technological, and Scholarly Phenomenon," *Information, Communication and Society* 15, no. 5 (2012): 662–79; John Cheney-Lippold, "A New Algorithmic Identity: Soft Biopolitics and the Modulation of Control," *Theory, Culture and Society* 28, no. 6 (2011): 164–81; Mort and Smith, "Beyond Information"; Evelyn Ruppert, "Population Objects: Interpassive Subjects," *Sociology* 45, no. 2 (2011): 218–33.

75 Annemarie Mol, "Living with Diabetes: Care Beyond Choice and Control," *Lancet* 373, no. 9677 (2009): 1756–57; Oudshoorn, *Telecare Technologies*.

76 *This Sociological Life*, "Living the Quantified Self: The Realities of Self-Tracking for Health," blog entry by Deborah Lupton, January 11, 2013, http://simplysociology.wordpress.com/2013/01/11/living-the-quantified-self-the-realities-of-self-tracking-for-health/; Hans Van Remoortel et al., "Validity of Activity Monitors in Health and Chronic Disease: A Systematic Review," *International Journal of Behavioral Nutrition and Physical Activity* 9, no. 84 (2012), http://www.ijbnpa.org/content/9/1/84.

77 Lupton, "The Digitally Engaged Patient"; Lupton, "Quantifying the Body"; Lupton, "The Human Machine."

78 Lupton, "M-Health and Health Promotion."

79 Cheney-Lippold, "A New Algorithmic Identity."

80 Ibid.

81 Lupton, "The Digitally Engaged Patient"; Mort, Roberts, and Callén, "Ageing with Telecare"; Mol and Law, "Embodied Action, Enacted Bodies"; Oudshoorn, *Telecare Technologies*.

82 Lupton, "M-Health and Health Promotion"; Lupton, "The Digitally Engaged Patient"; Lupton, "Quantifying the Body."

83 Fran Baum, Lareen Newman, and Katherine Biedrzycki, "Vicious Cycles: Digital Technologies and Determinants of Health in Australia," *Health Promotion International* (published online ahead of print November 9, 2012), doi:10.1093/heapro/das062;

Frederico Cruz-Jesus, Tiago Oliveira, and Fernando Bação, "Digital Divide across the European Union," *Information and Management* 49, no. 6 (2012): 278–91.

84 Lupton, "The Digitally Engaged Patient"; Davide Nicolini, "Stretching Out and Expanding Work Practices in Time and Space: The Case of Telemedicine," *Human Relations* 60, no. 6 (2007): 889–920; Oudshoorn, *Telecare Technologies*; Mort, Roberts, and Callén, "Ageing with Telecare."

85 Lupton, "The Digitally Engaged Patient"; Oudshoorn, *Telecare Technologies*.

7

The Global Threat of (Re)emerging Diseases

Contesting the Adequacy of Biomedical Discourse and Practice

JON ARRIZABALAGA

Since the 1980s the world has witnessed the global emergence of new epidemic infections (HIV/AIDS having the most dramatic impact so far), as well as the reappearance of known infectious diseases, such as tuberculosis, malaria, and syphilis, that had seemed for some time to be under control. In the field of public health, these events have led to the designation of a new nosological category, emerging and re-emerging infectious diseases—hereafter referred to as *(re)emerging diseases*. The danger posed by these conditions constitutes a growing threat to the hegemony of biomedicine, raising many questions about the adequacy of biomedical discourse and practices to meet the global challenge of infectious diseases.

My objectives in this chapter are to analyze the construction of this new nosological category and to examine two of the most relevant questions concerning the implications of (re)emerging diseases for public health, food security, and human development on a worldwide scale. First, I will focus on the role that irresponsible use of biotechnological innovations by elements of the pharmaceutical, cosmetic, food, and agricultural industries has played, and is still playing, in triggering and spreading (re)emerging diseases. Then, by briefly looking back over the major "engagements" in the battle against the HIV/AIDS pandemic, I will emphasize a number of serious shortcomings, in terms of both focus and timing, in current global public health policies, as well as their disastrous implications with regard to the effects of the pandemic on sub-Saharan Africa.

The Construction of (Re)emerging Infectious Diseases

No illnesses have had a greater impact on humankind than infectious diseases; indeed, they persist in being the main public health concern in many communities. Over the course of the nineteenth century, the deadliest of the great epidemic diseases (plague, smallpox, yellow fever, cholera) took a gradually diminishing toll in the Western world. In terms of mortality, they lost prominence of place, first, to endemic infections (like tuberculosis, malaria, typhoid fever, and sexually transmitted diseases [STDs]), and later, starting around the beginning of the twentieth century, to nontransmissible chronic diseases (mostly malignant tumors and cardiovascular diseases) and traumatisms. Indeed, data for 2004 collected by the United Nations show that, in the world's "more developed regions," an overwhelming 86 percent of all deaths were attributable to chronic diseases, and 8 percent to traumatisms; only the remaining 6 percent were attributable to communicable, maternal, perinatal, and nutritional conditions.[1]

However, it cannot be overlooked that, according to a 2009 UN projection for the period 2005–10, of the annual average of 56.8 million deaths worldwide, more than 78 percent were expected to occur in "less developed regions." The UN also calculated that in 2004, nearly a third of all deaths, 31 percent, were attributable to communicable, maternal, perinatal, and nutritional conditions. The distribution of deaths due to these causes by region has been found to be extremely uneven: The proportion occurring in the "more developed" regions (6 percent) contrasted sharply with the 37 percent in "less developed regions," 63 percent in the "least developed regions," and 66 percent in sub-Saharan Africa.[2] According to the World Health Organization's estimates, in 2011 infectious diseases were second only to heart disease as the leading cause of death worldwide, with the four main "killers" being lower respiratory infections (3.46M, or 6.1 percent), diarrheal diseases (2.46M, or 4.3 percent), HIV/AIDS (1.78M, or 3.1 percent), and tuberculosis (1.34M, or 2.4 percent). In low-income countries the first three were the greatest "killers," accounting for 98, 70, and 69 deaths per 100,000 population, respectively, in contrast to high-income countries, where ischaemic heart disease, stroke, and lung cancers were the three greatest "killers," accounting for 119, 69, and 51 deaths per 100,000 population, respectively.[3]

Infections also continue to be responsible for a considerable proportion of infant deaths. The UN Inter-agency Group for Child Mortality Estimation has found that of the 6.9 million children who died in 2011 before reaching their fifth birthdays, "almost two thirds—4.4 million—died of infections, nearly all of which were preventable."[4]

The successes of biomedical campaigns in the first half of the twentieth century against a series of infectious diseases (poliomyelitis, tuberculosis, smallpox, malaria, and STDs), achieved with the help of immune serums, vaccines, sulfonamides, antibiotics, and pesticides, increased optimism in the decades after World War II that the technological power of biomedicine could control and even eradicate such illnesses. This euphoria pervaded institutions of public health in countries throughout the Western world, whether capitalist or communist, as well as the World Health Organization (WHO). Indeed, during the first thirty years of its life, this intergovernmental UN agency, which was to coordinate the fight against disease and the promotion of public health on a worldwide scale, accepted biomedical principles and methods enthusiastically and uncritically and implemented them on a markedly paternalistic and technocratic basis.[5]

By the late 1970s and early 1980s, the international community was exulting in the success of national and international vaccination programs and the availability of a growing number of antibiotic drugs. In 1977, smallpox was declared officially eradicated. In its declaration at the Alma-Ata Conference of 1978, *Health for All in the Year 2000*, WHO announced that, by means of extending primary health care on a worldwide scale, it aimed by the end of the century to immunize the whole of humankind against most infectious diseases and to guarantee basic health care for men, women, and children across the entire planet, regardless of their social class, race, religion, or place of birth. For a moment, the human race appeared to have come within reach of the dream of a definitive victory over infectious diseases. Anthony S. Fauci has recalled this heady atmosphere, referring to such authoritative sources from the 1960s as the physician and anthropologist T. Aidan Cockburn, who found it "reasonable to anticipate that within some measurable time . . . all the major infections will have disappeared."[6]

In these circumstances, the biomedical establishment tended to consider the new infectious diseases that had begun to be detected in the

1960s (e.g., the hemorrhagic fevers caused by infection with the Ma-chupo, Marburg, and Lassa viruses) as small, irrelevant anomalies that would by no means stop the race to liberate humankind from one of its most oppressive burdens. The outlook for the 1970s maintained by such qualified experts in infectious diseases as Sir Macfarlane Burnet and David O. White could not have been more clearly expressed:

> On the basis of what has happened in the last thirty years, can we fore-cast any likely developments for the '70s? If for the present we retain a basic optimism and assume no major catastrophes occur and that any wars are kept at the "brush fire" level, the most likely forecast about the future of infectious disease is that it will be very dull. There may be some wholly unexpected emergence of a new and dangerous infectious disease, but nothing of the sort has marked the last fifty years. There have been isolated outbreaks of fatal infections derived from exotic ani-mals as in the instance of the laboratory workers struck down with the Marburg virus from African monkeys and the cases of severe haemor-rhagic fever due to Lassa virus infection in Nigeria. Similar episodes will doubtless occur in the future but they will presumably be safely contained.[7]

Starting in the 1970s, however, these "isolated outbreaks" grew in both number and importance. In 1976 a pair of new, highly transmissible and lethal diseases, Ebola hemorrhagic fever and legionellosis, broke out for the first time in two entirely disparate places: the Ebola River valley in the Democratic Republic of the Congo and a hotel in Philadelphia host-ing the convention of a U.S. military veterans' organization, respectively. Since then, the impact of infectious diseases on global health, includ-ing that of high-income Western countries, has continued to increase, largely as a result of three groups of pathological events: first, the erup-tion of new diseases or pathogens (e.g., hantavirus pulmonary syndrome, HIV/AIDS, and hepatitis C virus infection); second, the identification of causal pathogens for previously known diseases and syndromes (e.g., the rotavirus responsible for infant diarrhea); and third, the increasing prevalence of long-present infectious diseases (such as tuberculosis, malaria, gonorrhea, and pneumonia) that have proved newly resistant to multiple antimicrobial drugs.[8]

The growing relevance of infectious diseases was reinforced following the isolation of the first pathogenic human retrovirus, HTLV-I, in 1978, by a research team led by Robert Gallo at the National Institutes of Health (NIH). A promising future was envisaged for new research lines in cancer, the so-called slow virus infections, and a series of more enigmatic conditions included in the immense hodgepodge of autoimmune diseases such as multiple sclerosis, Graves' disease, and Type 1 diabetes. During the 1980s and 1990s, a strong causal association began to become evident between specific microbiological pathogens and a number of chronic diseases and neoplasms with great impact on health and society—for example, *Helicobacter pylori* and gastroduodenal ulcer with gastric cancer, hepatitis B and C viruses with hepatic cirrhosis and hepatocellular carcinoma, and certain strains of human papillomavirus with cervical, vulvar, and anal carcinoma.[9]

However, it was only at the beginning of the 1990s that these disparate groups of increasingly relevant infectious diseases were finally jointly named "emerging infectious diseases" or "emerging and re-emerging infectious diseases." The sequence of events appears to have been as follows. In May 1989 Rockefeller University, the National Institute of Allergy and Infectious Diseases, and the Fogarty International Center jointly promoted a conference, "Emerging Viruses: The Evolution of Viruses and Viral Disease," the concern of which was broadened to include "the emergence and resurgence of all classes of infectious agents." The conference was chaired by Rockefeller University virologist Stephen Morse, to whom the creation of the concept of emerging diseases has been generally attributed.[10] In February 1991 the Institute of Medicine (IOM), a component of the prestigious U.S. National Academy of Sciences, convened a nineteen-member multidisciplinary committee to conduct an eighteen-month study of "emerging microbial threats to U.S. public health," although it was soon recognized that this issue "could not be adequately addressed without considering emerging threats globally."[11] In October 1992 this committee published a report, *Emerging Infections: Microbial Threats to Health in the United States*, in which these diseases were defined as "clinically distinct conditions whose incidence in humans has increased . . . in the United States within the past two decades." The report related "emergence" to "the introduction of a new agent, to the recognition of an existing disease that has gone undetected, or to a change in the environment that provides an epidemiologic 'bridge.'" It also referred to "re-emergence" as "the re-appearance of a known disease after a decline in incidence."[12]

In subsequent years, growing concern led to the convening in late 1994 of a U.S. government interagency working group to "consider the global threat of emerging and re-emerging infectious diseases." This working group was established under the aegis of the Committee on International Science, Engineering, and Technology Policy (CISET), part of the National Science and Technology Council (NSTC). It was chaired by the director of the Centers for Disease Control and Prevention (CDC), which earlier in 1994 had published a prevention plan for the United States against "emerging infectious disease threats," giving particular emphasis to the international component of this new health issue,[13] and which in 1995 began to publish a scholarly journal titled *Emerging Infectious Diseases*. The CISET report *Global Microbial Threats in the 1990s* served as the basis for a presidential directive by which President Bill Clinton established, in June 1996, "a national policy to address the threat of emerging infectious diseases through improved domestic and international surveillance, prevention, and response measures."[14] In 1998 and 2001, CDC released its second and third preventive plans on emerging diseases.[15] In the end, the U.S. public health campaign about emerging diseases associated them with globalization, so that "national self-interest" and "global humanitarianism" were equated. The solutions offered by the campaigners "had the advantage of immensely reducing the scale of intervention, from global political economy to laboratory investigation and information management. Whether the object was 'global health' or national security, interventions would involve 'passing through' American laboratories, biotechnology firms, pharmaceutical manufacturers, and information science experts."[16]

In April 1994, WHO decided to create a specific program of its own on "emerging infectious diseases" in the face of public awareness that "emerging and re-emerging diseases are an international problem, as pathogens do not respect geographical boundaries" and of the increasing number of demands it was receiving "for information both on specific diseases, and for guidance as to how best to address the problem of new and resurgent diseases." On the occasion of WHO's second meeting on emerging infectious diseases, held in January 1995, its executive board "endorsed a resolution calling for strengthening of international surveillance in order to recognize and respond to new, merging and re-emerging infectious diseases."[17] After WHO's governing forum, the World Health Assembly, considered this resolution in May 1995, WHO created a new Division of Emerging and Other Communicable Diseases Surveillance and Control. In 1996, it released its strategic plan.[18] In 1998, WHO replaced the division with a new Program on Communicable Diseases in order to "better integrate surveillance, prevention, control, and research over the whole spectrum of communicable diseases."[19]

Despite an increasingly proactive response to (re)emerging diseases by national and international health agencies, the relevance of these conditions and the questions they raise with regard to the suitability of the biomedical model in terms of both focus and practice have grown in the first two decades of the twenty-first century. The 1992 IOM report, *Emerging Infections*, had already identified six major factors thought crucial to the threat of (re)emerging diseases: human demographics and behavior, industry and technology, economic development and land use, international travel and commerce, microbial adaptation and change, and the breakdown of public health measures.[20] Yet in the subsequent decades, it has become clear that actions against (re)emerging diseases undertaken by national and international health institutions have been neither ambitious enough nor sufficiently expeditious to meet the huge global threat presented by these new diseases.

In the balance of this chapter, I will focus on two cases in which the shortcomings, both theoretical and practical, of the biomedical model in effecting global sanitary intervention against (re)emerging diseases appear especially disturbing: the severe impact on human health resulting from the mishandling of biotechnological innovations by the pharmaceutical, cosmetic, and food industries; and the disaster of the HIV/AIDS pandemic in sub-Saharan Africa—a result, to a great extent, of the slow pace and other inadequacies of global responses to the threat posed by this emerging disease.

(Re)emerging Diseases and Technological Innovations

In reference to the burgeoning AIDS crisis, the medical historian Mirko D. Grmek argued in 1990 that "a disastrous epidemic of this type could not have occurred before the mingling of peoples, the liberalization of sexual and social mores, and, above all, before progress in modern medicine had accomplished the control of the majority of serious infectious diseases and introduced intravenous injections and blood transfusion."[21]

To explain the outbreak of AIDS, Grmek referred to his concept of "pathocoenosis."[22] He had formulated it in the 1960s using an analogy with the nineteenth-century ecological concept of biocoenosis—later, "biotic community." Grmek defined pathocoenosis as a whole set of diseases, not only infectious but also hereditary, degenerative, or metabolic, that were characteristic of a specific population in a particular place and time. Regardless of several endogenous and ecological factors, the frequency and distribution of each condition in this disease set supposedly would depend on those of the remaining ones. The pathocoenosis would tend toward a state of balance, particularly if the ecological situation were stable. Yet the disappearance of one or more conditions defining the epidemiologic profile of a given population might imply that the ecological balance among the usual germs in that population had been disrupted. In these circumstances, the way could theoretically be opened for the emergence of new diseases, as other germs that had previously remained dormant in the ecosystem were then "promoted" to the status of pathogens.[23]

Grmek perceived AIDS as a devastating epidemic that had emerged from the immediate past in a discontinuous way, as a result of a breakdown in the ecological balance attributable to aggressive technological interventions—such as the generalization of blood transfusion and intravenous injections—that had opened new paths for the transmission of HIV during the previous decades. Doubtless, his point was emphasized by the shock experienced in France from 1982 to 1984 resulting from the infection of 1,000 people with hemophilia—that is, a quarter of French AIDS sufferers—by plasma contaminated with HIV.[24]

At the time, hypotheses like that of Grmek were criticized as unjustifiably feeding the end-of-the-millennium anxiety that was in the air in the 1990s.[25] Certainly, Grmek's emphasis on the impact of technologies on the ecosystem might be perceived as minimizing other causal factors (demographic, economic, political, cultural, and ideological) whose relevance to the outbreak and spread of HIV/AIDS has since become clear. Yet it would have been foolish not to pay attention to the role of technological innovations in the production and reproduction of HIV/AIDS and other (re)emerging diseases. Indeed, the number of (re)emerging diseases that are probably related to the introduction of new technologies in biomedicine, cosmetics, and food production has not stopped growing in recent decades.

For example, as is well known, the misuse of antibiotic drugs has promoted the pathogenicity of bacteria, viruses, and parasites that had long been dormant or scarcely problematic from a therapeutic point of view, causing them to become resistant to a growing number of medicines. Among the most outstanding instances of these "new" pathogens responsible for (re)emerging diseases are the so-called opportunistic germs that proliferate in hospital environments, and to which immune-depressed patients are particularly vulnerable. There is also the increasing variety of germs that have become resistant to many antimicrobial drugs used to combat diseases such as malaria, tuberculosis, and pneumonia.[26]

Additionally, the industrial exploitation of animal and human products for therapeutic or cosmetic purposes, as well as the marketing of these products on a worldwide scale, has not only fueled the global spread of pathogens within animals and humans but has also facilitated transfers between these two populations. The mass media continue to showcase examples of microbiological contamination of bioproducts used for therapeutic or preventive purposes, such as transplanted organs and blood derivatives used to produce serums and vaccines. Usually, there is viral contamination that goes unnoticed until these new pathogens are detected and the relevant indirect tests are developed. But contamination attributable to negligence resulting from incompetence or corruption is also notable. Particularly dramatic during the early years of the HIV/AIDS pandemic was the accidental HIV infection of a high proportion of the hemophilic population in high-income Western countries—I have already referred to the French case—from blood derivatives marketed by pharmaceutical companies, both local and transnational, for intravenous use by people with hemophilia to diminish their factor VIII deficiency.

Meanwhile, the most disturbing contribution of the food industry to (re)emerging diseases during the past decades derives from new technologies of animal production. This issue first hit the headlines in the 1990s, on the occasion of an outbreak of bovine spongiform encephalopathy (BSE)—the condition popularly known as mad cow disease—that affected a large proportion of British bovine livestock. This condition, a variant of Creutzfeldt–Jakob disease in humans, appears to be caused by a prion. A prion is a peculiar infectious agent that consists of a misfolded protein that causes normal proteins to misfold as well—thereby disrupting the cellular function of the brain or other neural tissues—and that may spread between different animal species. The original infection of bovine livestock appears to have derived from supplementation of the diets of these herbivores with animal proteins from meat industry residues—meat and bone meal—of sheep and cattle, presumably containing portions of BSE-infected nervous systems. The actual impact of BSE on human health is to a great extent still unknown, not least because of the extended period that BSE might remain clinically latent in humans. So far it appears to be much less than previously feared: Between 1995 and 2010, BSE caused the deaths of 168 individuals in the United Kingdom.[27] BSE also had a devastating impact on the beef industry in the United Kingdom, and its appearance "in cattle in other European countries further eroded the European public's trust that governments were able to assure the safety of food."[28]

Further, in the twenty-first century, new health threats revealing the impact that new—and not so new—technologies of animal production have on human health have continued to arise. I will refer briefly to three outstanding examples. First, it seems clear that consumption of meat from animals treated with antibiotics in a systematic and prophylactic way throughout their lives can encourage the spread of antibiotic-resistant pathogens from animal to human populations.[29]

Second, the 2002–3 outbreak in Hong Kong of an atypical Asian pneumonia, severe acute respiratory syndrome (SARS)—which, thanks to international epidemiologic surveillance, was limited to about 8,500 cases and 900 human deaths—has again reminded us of the threat that culinary habits, like the consumption of civet cats and other "exotic" animal species, might represent to human health, by transferring pathogenic viruses from animal species to humans.[30] Furthermore, SARS has exposed the vulnerabilities of global health security systems by demonstrating the profound repercussions on public health and economic security, on a national and international scale, that could derive from a new or uncommon, highly lethal pathogen capable of disseminating easily and rapidly through the air and being efficiently transmitted from person to person through respiratory droplets. The SARS episode demonstrated "the magnitude of damage that an emerging disease with the appropriate features can cause in a world where airlines carried an estimated 2.1 billion passengers in 2006, where financial markets and businesses are tightly intertwined, and where information is instantly accessible."[31] WHO, the source of this statement, taken from the *World Health Report 2007*, emphasizes the global dimensions of the threat represented by emerging diseases: "No country is automatically protected—by virtue of its wealth or its high levels of education, standards of living and health care, or equipment and personnel at border crossings—from either the arrival of a new disease on its territory or the subsequent disruption this can cause. SARS was, to a large extent, a disease of prosperous urban centers. Contrary to expectations, it spread most efficiently in sophisticated city hospitals."[32]

Finally, since the late 1990s the world has been vulnerable to the sustained threat of a lethal influenza pandemic caused by the type A virus, a product of the mutation or recombination of variants of the H5N1 virus. Global epidemiologic alarm bells first sounded in response to several outbreaks of avian influenza that between 2003 and 2006 killed 281 of the 476 infected individuals (lethality rate: 59.03 percent), mostly in Southeast Asia.[33] The alarms went off again in spring 2009, on the occasion of a new H1N1 virus influenza pandemic whose first outbreaks apparently occurred in Mexico and the United States. Most likely, both epidemics originally broke out at intensive animal production farms, of poultry in Mexico and pigs in the United States.[34] In his thought-provoking book on the global threat of avian flu, Mike Davis emphasizes the views of such qualified virologists as Richard Krause, who directed the National Institute of Allergy and Infectious Diseases in the early years of the AIDS epidemic, in reference to the new ecologies of disease resulting from globalization: "Microbes thrive in these 'undercurrents of opportunity' that arise through social and economic change, changes in human behavior, and catastrophic events such as war and famine. They may fan a minor outbreak into a widespread epidemic."[35]

More precisely, Davis has pointed to the urbanization of the Third World as one of these catastrophic events, because it "is shifting the burden of global poverty from the countryside to the slum peripheries of

new megacities," where 95 percent of the future increase in global population will occur, "with immense consequences for the ecology of disease."
Neither should it be forgotten that the relationship between population
density and viral evolution applies to human beings, just as it does to
beasts in animal production, and to the interactions between them.[36] It
was by no means by chance that the global flu pandemic of the H5N1
virus and SARS originated in the same small area—the Pearl River delta
of China's Guangdong Province, contiguous to Hong Kong—given that
"this is an ecozone where pigs, ducks, chickens, and miscellaneous other
livestock (including the now notorious civet cat) live cheek-by-jowl with
farmers—in one of the planet's most densely populated regions."[37]

Global epidemiologic surveillance systems have so far functioned
more or less efficiently, and the doomsayers' predictions have not come
true. This has given particular relief in regard to the most recent worldwide type A influenza pandemic, during the biennium 2009–10, briefly
feared to be a new iteration of the lethal 1918 pandemic. Ironically, its
mildness has become highly controversial, as critics have severely at-
tacked WHO for declaring a pandemic in the first place and have even
suggested that it made the decision to do so under the influence of the
pharmaceutical companies in charge of producing the antiviral drugs
and vaccines. Whether this accusation is confirmed or not, the experts'
concern that there is a real threat of a new lethal flu pandemic in the
coming years remains legitimate. As the historian John M. Barry has
stated, "Everything that happened in 2009 suggests that, if a severe outbreak comes again, failure to improve on our response will threaten
chaos and magnify the terror, the economic impact and the death toll."[38]

The alarm bells have been set off beyond the great factories of animal
production: There are increasing worries about the potential impact of
extensive transgenic monocultures, not only on biodiversity but also on
human health, including the re-emergence of infectious diseases. The
Argentinean case may be paradigmatic in this respect. In 2005, transgenic soybean cultures from seeds produced by Monsanto occupied
14 million hectares in Argentina (half of the country's entire cultivated
land), with an estimated production of 37 million tons. Ninety percent of
this production was destined for export. The business of exporting soy
(in the forms of grain, seed, oil, and flour) is Argentina's main source of
foreign currency. In 2004, for instance, it brought in $7.6 billion.[39] Ac-

cording to the testimony of Dario Gianfelici—a medical practitioner in a town of 5,000 inhabitants in the soy-producing province of Entre Ríos—reported in Marie-Monique Robin's noted book *The World According to Monsanto*, which has also been made into a documentary film, a variety of health problems have arisen in the province in recent times. Local practitioners have associated them with the toxicity of pesticides such as Roundup (glyphosate with ethoxylated amine surfactants), which is also produced by Monsanto:

> Several colleagues in the region and I have observed a very significant increase in reproductive anomalies such as miscarriages and premature fetal death; malfunctions of the thyroid, the respiratory system—such as pulmonary edemas—the kidneys, and the endocrine system; liver and skin diseases; and severe eye problems. We are also worried by the effects that might be caused by Roundup residues ingested by consumers of soybeans, because we know that some surfactants are endocrine disruptors. We have observed in the region a significant number of cases of cryptorchism and hypospadias* in boys, and hormonal malfunctions in girls, some of whom have their periods as young as three.
>
> *Cryptorchism is a birth defect characterized by undescended testicles; hypospadias is a malformation of the urethra [it does not reach the tip of the penis].[40]

Along with these health complaints there is a striking re-emergence of infectious diseases like dengue fever, yellow fever, and leishmaniasis, in concurrence with dramatically increasing levels of poverty and destitution in the wake of the 2001 Argentinean economic crisis. These various health problems—whose re-emergence and diffusion have been fueled by malnutrition, poverty, unemployment, and inequality—have seriously set back the public health agenda in northern Argentina, and even in regions of the more economically developed central part of the country, such as Santa Fe.[41] It has been demonstrated that the toxic effect of agrochemical products is boosted in populations with high levels of poverty; it is also evident that the persistence of serious problems of water supply in many rural areas facilitates water contamination with these toxic products.[42]

Finally, even the indirect effects of newly re-emergent infectious diseases on human health appear to be growing, through their negative impact on biodiversity. In this regard, there are increasing worries about the possible association between the pesticides used in the transgenic soy cultures and the dengue fever epidemic in Argentina in 2009, where this viral infection transmitted by the mosquito *Aëdes aegypti*—also the vector of yellow fever—has reappeared since the 1990s, having been eradicated in the 1960s. According to one plausible scientific hypothesis, there has been an invasion of the mosquito genera *Aëdes* and *Culex* in recent years "in unexpected areas of the country and out of season," with the map of these mosquitoes' areas of invasion coinciding with the boundaries of the "Soy United Republic"—a name given by the multinational agricultural products manufacturer Syngenta to a vast portion of South America, including large tracts of Bolivia, Paraguay, Argentina, Brazil, and Uruguay. Allegedly, this circumstance results from the exterminating effects of glyphosates on natural predators (fish and amphibians) of the dengue fever mosquito, as well as "deforestation of wooded and mountainous areas of north-eastern and north-western Argentina, which has destroyed their environmental balance, eliminating the refuge and natural habitat of other mosquitoes' predators, causing an uncontrolled increase in their population."[43]

The Disaster of HIV/AIDS in Sub-Saharan Africa: Failures in Fighting a Global Pandemic

In the midst of the euphoric atmosphere of the late 1970s and early 1980s, the discovery of a new pathological phenomenon that physicians and bioscientists eventually called "immune deficiency syndrome" came as a complete shock. The syndrome was detected in mid-1981, first in the United States and later in Europe and the rest of the world. Its infectious character was established two years later, in May 1983, after its causal pathogen was isolated by a team of virologists directed by Luc Montagnier at the Pasteur Institute in Paris. It was called "human immunodeficiency virus" (HIV)—a third pathologic human retrovirus, after the HTLV-I and HTLV-II viruses Robert Gallo had previously isolated at the NIH in Bethesda. The new disease was then officially named "HIV infection and AIDS," although the mass media ended up popularizing the latter acronym.

HIV/AIDS presented a number of peculiar epidemiologic and clinical features, such as persistence as a global pandemic, a strong likelihood of transmissibility through sexual activity and contact with an infected person's blood, and incurability, with disparate clinical symptoms and a high lethality rate. The disease consequently resurrected fears and stigmas that had seemingly vanished or at least been hidden in the West for the past half-century, if not longer. This might well explain the slow and insufficient response of international organizations and national health services in the face of a devastating pandemic whose scale and extent could have been foreseen. This dilatory approach cost millions of human lives. Yet more than thirty years after the earliest clinical cases of HIV/AIDS were diagnosed, we have yet to learn from mistakes in the face of this global pandemic, whose diffusion continues out of control in many areas of the world, and against which there is neither curative treatment (although an efficient therapy exists to suppress the virus) nor vaccine.

In 2007 there were 32.9 million people living with HIV/AIDS in the world, 2.7 million new infections, and 2 million fatalities caused by this disease. Twenty-two million people with HIV/AIDS (67 percent of the world total) were living in sub-Saharan Africa. That region was also the site of 70 percent of all new infections (1.9 million), and 75 percent of all AIDS deaths (1.5 million). Some distance behind, but gaining alarmingly quickly, Asia accounted for 15 percent of all people living with HIV/AIDS, 14 percent of new infections, and 19 percent of deaths. Most of these cases were occurring in Southeast Asia.[44]

The overwhelming number of people living with HIV/AIDS in sub-Saharan Africa, where the condition was already the leading cause of death in 1999, and in low-income countries, where HIV/AIDS was the third-ranking cause of death in 2002, should not lead us to think that this is a public health issue which has already been addressed in higher-income countries, regardless of its disappearance from the newspaper headlines. After all, HIV/AIDS was the fifth-ranking cause of death in middle-income countries in 2002.[45] That said, the impact of the pandemic in sub-Saharan Africa has been especially acute.

In 2008, the *World Disasters Report*—a highly regarded document published annually by the International Federation of Red Cross and Red Crescent Societies—was devoted to the HIV infection and AIDS, in view of the significance of the absolute "disaster" this pandemic represents for many countries, particularly in sub-Saharan Africa. The report took as a starting point the UN's definition of the word *disaster*: "a serious disruption of the functioning of a society, causing widespread human, material or environmental losses which exceed the ability of a society to cope using only its own resources."[46] Although it might seem strange to equate an epidemic infection with earthquake, drought, or war, the enormous impact of AIDS in many sub-Saharan countries requires just such a characterization. This is not only because of the number of human lives AIDS claims, or its particular incidence among the young people in these countries, or the way in which it is overwhelming the national health and social assistance services of these countries, but also because its stigma prevents many affected people from drawing upon those health and social services that could help them.[47]

Furthermore, the peculiar epidemiologic and clinical characteristics of the HIV infection mean that the impact of AIDS is not restricted to the present time but is projected to afflict future generations "by undermining the transfer of human capital from one generation to the next," as economists from the World Bank and International Monetary Fund have stated in a significant article on the long-term economic costs of the pandemic. According to the article's authors, Clive Bell and colleagues, the fact that

> AIDS is overwhelmingly a fatal disease of young adults, [making] it difficult for these young men and women to provide for the education of their children, not to mention offer them the love and care they need to complement their formal schooling. The result is possibly a whole generation of undereducated and hence underproductive youth, who in adulthood will find it difficult to provide for *their* children's education, and so on. In this way an otherwise growing economy could, when hit with an enduring and sufficiently severe AIDS epidemic, spiral downward into a low-level subsistence economy in three or four generations.[48]

As the International Federation of Red Cross and Red Crescent Societies has pointed out, in world regions like southern Africa, HIV/AIDS has become the cause of "a vast humanitarian emergency."[49] Its dimensions present a huge challenge to the entire transnational humanitarian community, as well as a major complication for the work that human-itarian organizations do on different fronts with the most vulnerable human populations in the world (e.g., poverty reduction, care of basic daily health and welfare, relief in the wake of natural or human-made disasters), not least because these populations' vulnerability as a result of poverty, inequality (including gender inequality), and environmental factors increases their risk of HIV infection: "The effects of disasters (whether acute or long-term, man-made or natural) are among the very factors that drive the epidemic—dislocation and disruption of people's lives, sexual exploitation and violence against women and children but also men, the disruption of health services including provision of anti-retroviral treatment (ART), psychosocial support and blood screening. Migration too is a growing challenge across the globe, as people travel in their millions to find work and escape poverty. Migrants and mobile workers may face an increased risk of HIV as they travel, and when they arrive."[50]

One of the most depressing aspects of the history of the fight against HIV/AIDS has been the slowness and insufficiency of reactions to the pandemic by leaders in politics, public and private organizations, trade unions, mass media, and other sectors around the world. It cannot be forgotten that during the first six years of the AIDS pandemic—from 1981, when the first cases were described in the United States, until 1987, when WHO launched its first program specifically targeting HIV/AIDS—the only sources of support for African people infected with HIV, apart from health workers and members of local communities, were a few nongovernmental organizations (NGOs) such as the Nor-wegian Red Cross and a number of Catholic religious orders.[51] Only in 1988 did WHO declare the new pandemic a global threat, by renaming its specific action plan the Global Program on AIDS.

Moreover, the limited resources the UN agencies did dedicate to the global fight against HIV/AIDS were gradually reduced in the course of the 1990s as a result of the implementation of neoliberal economic poli-cies all around the world. The richest countries, headed by the United States and Great Britain, imposed drastic cuts on the public funds as-signed to sustaining international organizations like WHO, the health programs of which were forced to develop a growing financial depen-dence on private sources. In the case of Africa, this situation became even worse as the continent lost its political relevance for the industrial-ized world with the end of the Cold War.

In 1994 WHO dissolved the Global Program on AIDS, which was replaced by UNAIDS, the United Nations Joint Programme on HIV/AIDS. The purpose of this program, which was initially constituted by six founding members and now consists of ten organizations,[52] is to co-ordinate the UN agencies' different activities in the global fight against HIV/AIDS. Despite its ambitious objectives, it was not until the end of the 1990s that UNAIDS was able to begin overcoming the restrictions imposed by the funding donors or by the recipient countries and to face the new challenges. The long period of latency (an average of ten years) from the initial HIV infection to the clinical appearance of AIDS, and the strong and persistent stigma associated with the condition, joined to reinforce denial of the true dimensions of the pandemic and the con-tinuing inaction in the area of health policy.[53]

Only at the turn of the twenty-first century was there a sea change in the attitude toward HIV/AIDS of many political and opinion leaders, as well as among public and private donor institutions.[54] In fact, WHO did not officially recognize that AIDS was the leading cause of death in Africa until its 1999 *World Health Report*.[55] In January 2000, the UN Security Council discussed the issue of AIDS in Africa as an essential concern for human security and a major obstacle to its development. This debate—the first ever on a health issue in the history of the Secu-rity Council—was followed in June 2001 by a special session of the UN General Assembly on AIDS. This session ended with the "Declaration of Commitment on HIV/AIDS." The declaration fixed a timetable for achieving objectives with regard to prevention and resource mobiliza-tion and established a clear and binding mandate on the governments of all countries to lead this response "with full and active participation of the United Nations, the entire multilateral system, civil society, the business community and private sector."[56]

Since then, the response to AIDS has been reinforced in the majority of the affected countries as a result of greater political commitment by their governments and of an enormous increase in funding. The new global strategy against AIDS is included in the Millennium Develop-ment Goals (MDGs) the UN is promoting on the basis of the resolution adopted by the General Assembly in September 2000.[57] This initiative includes eight goals, to be achieved by 2015: to eradicate extreme poverty and hunger; to achieve universal primary education; to promote gender equality and empower women; to reduce child mortality; to improve maternal health; to combat HIV/AIDS, malaria, and other diseases; to ensure environmental sustainability; and to develop global partnerships for development. Two of the three strategic targets of the sixth goal are specifically addressed to HIV/AIDS, namely to "have halted by 2015 and begun to reverse the spread of HIV/AIDS" and to "achieve, by 2010, universal access to treatment for HIV/AIDS for all those who needed it."[58] Moreover, an effective response to HIV/AIDS will also contribute to achievement of the other seven goals.[59]

Like the effort against malaria, the present fight against AIDS in Africa comes within the purview of the MDGs. It has some bright spots (a slowing and even a reduction in the rate of new infections in Cameroon, Kenya, Malawi, Rwanda, Tanzania, Togo, Zambia, and Zimbabwe) but still many, many shadows. The bright spots seem to indicate a change in young people's sexual behavior, while the persistent shadows derive from all kinds of limitations, not only in dealing with prevention and treatment but also in providing attention and support to those social groups particularly threatened by the pandemic. Especially relevant is the issue of elderly people's having to care for their sons and daughters with AIDS, and for orphaned grandchildren. There are also infected children, who, once they become adolescents, will require advice and support in managing their sexuality.[60]

In 1996, the first highly active antiretroviral therapy (HAART) was presented at the HIV/AIDS World Conference in Vancouver, Canada. This treatment could reduce the viral load of individuals infected with HIV in an efficient and sustainable way, although its then-prohibitive price made it accessible only to citizens of high-income countries who could afford to fund these therapies through their national health services, or to wealthy people in the rest of the world. Over the past few years, sustained pressure has been exerted on transnational pharmaceutical companies and national governments by alternative globalization activists and humanitarian agencies (NGOs and agencies of the UN), and this pressure has led to a reduction in the cost of the new antiretroviral therapy drugs, either adjustment of the terms of the patents applicable to their production and trade in the Third World, or by means of generic remedies mostly manufactured in India and Brazil. Thus, access has been substantially increased among the affected population. And the progressive simplification of HAART medication's dosage procedures has facilitated more effective distribution from preestablished health care centers.

However, it should not be forgotten that less than a third of those worldwide who require antiretroviral drugs (28 percent in 2006) are currently receiving this therapy in one form or another. Besides, these treatments need to be sustainably administered in order to be fully effective, as well as to prevent the emergence of viral resistance—already a severe problem for countries poor in resources. Otherwise, patients in these countries will have to resort to second-line drugs whose price, although somewhat less, would still be too high for use by those national populations most affected.[61]

The Declaration of Doha—adopted by the World Trade Organization (WTO) in November 2001—represented a crucial step toward favoring access to HAART by those who live with HIV/AIDS in middle- and low-income countries. This declaration supports those states' initiatives to protect their populations' health by taking advantage of loopholes in the WTO's agreement on "trade-related aspects of intellectual property rights" (TRIPS) in order to circumvent the barriers imposed by the patent system. Although it extended the patent-free transition period until 2016, the Doha Declaration is nevertheless being systematically undermined by bilateral trade agreements that impose levels of intellectual property protection much higher than those required by the WTO. Indeed, by virtue of these agreements, middle- or low-income countries like India, Brazil, and Thailand are patenting (or will patent) and will have the capacity to produce generic versions of second-line HAART, whose average cost is or will be four to ten times higher than that of first-line HAART. Furthermore, demand for these second-line versions will increase over the next few years as a result of the gradual appearance of resistance to first-line versions.[62]

In June 2031, fifty years will have elapsed since the first AIDS cases were detected. If neither a curative treatment nor an effective vaccine has been found by then, it is possible that 64.9 to 80.7 million individuals will be infected with HIV/AIDS, and 3.7 to 6.5 million will have died in 2030.[63] Meanwhile, the effective diffusion of fully verified prophylactic measures that prevent HIV from being transmitted in different ways (sexual relationships, intravenous injections, and vertical transmission during pregnancy, labor, and breastfeeding, all well known in general terms since the late 1980s) is a *sine qua non* of any effort to slow the unremitting progress of the pandemic.

Yet in contrast to traditional technocratic approaches to public health issues, which consist of applying the same biomedical template, with slight variations, to different health problems in the most disparate regions of the world, special emphasis has been put in recent years on the need to adapt public health programs as much as possible to the peculiarities of the issues targeted in each country, region, and social group— even more so with regard to health issues involving sexual behavior. Thus, it is claimed that health programs should be aimed at those targets previously identified as the most appropriate in each case, in order to ensure that donated resources reach the recipient population and are effectively used. Moreover, it seems essential that those living with HIV/AIDS, and their communities, become involved in the preventive programs, because only the local population knows its own community well enough to effectively and sustainably promote the changes in sexual behavior required to slow the spread of the infection. The work of donors, government authorities, and health agents external to these communities appears to be determinant in promptly detecting the need to act, but it is unlikely that any preventive program will be effective if it is implemented behind the targeted communities' backs or without their active involvement.[64]

In Conclusion: Some Lessons to Be Learned from (Re)emerging Diseases

As a growing threat to a globalized and interconnected world, "(re) emerging infectious diseases" can fruitfully be framed within the context of the "risk society"—which the German sociologist Ulrich Beck defines as "a systematic way of dealing with hazards and insecurities induced and introduced by modernization itself."[65] These are manufactured risks, risks whose production and mitigation are marked by a high level of human agency, and that are derived from modernity and have resulted from the development of human technology. The construction of the concept of "emerging infectious diseases" was instrumental in sensitizing experts as well as laypeople to the new health threats imposed by globalization. It also activated bureaucratic machinery to mobilize material and human resources to deal with these threats. Indeed, (re)emerging diseases have provoked significant organizational changes in the national and international agencies in charge of disease surveillance and control, which reflect efforts, both theoretical and practical, to adapt to these threats. However, as Paul Farmer has emphasized, the persistence of restricted and biased concepts like tropical medicine, health transitions, and national health profiles in the consideration of the health of populations continues to limit sharply the ways in which infectious diseases, whether emerging or long present, are confronted. There is, therefore, a compelling need for the "multifactorial nature of disease emergence" to be reassessed from a more dynamic, systemic, and critical perspective.[66]

For those who can set conceptual impediments aside, (re)emerging diseases provide the opportunity to learn eight important lessons.

1. Confidence in the Biomedical Model Has Been Unwarranted

The paramount lesson is that (re)emerging diseases have revealed that those who have put their faith in the technocratic biomedical model have been unduly confident of its capacity to control humankind's great infectious plagues. The fascination with every kind of technological achievement that was characteristic of the second half of the twentieth century should no longer fuel the illusion—against all evidence from disease ecology research since the 1950s—that we have escaped the constrictions and uncertainty of living in an environment of biological relationships that are neither entirely controllable nor predictable. As Charles E. Rosenberg emphasized two decades ago, HIV/AIDS, like plague and other epidemics, reminds us that human beings cannot "so easily escape the imminence of evil and the anxiety of indeterminacy" because "mortality is built into our bodies, into our modes of behavior, and into our place in the planet's ecology."[67]

2. Reductionist Approaches to Infectious Disease Have Failed

(Re)emerging diseases have dramatically shown that there is something essentially wrong in the reductionistic way biomedicine has usually operated in the face of infectious diseases. During the 1990s, experts began to claim that HIV/AIDS was not an exceptional and aberrant feature but rather a sign of the new health threats to humanity at the beginning of the third millennium, and that much greater attention should be paid to studying the ways in which micro-changes in the environment of any nation could end up affecting human life on a global scale. SARS and avian influenza have confirmed the same impression. In her splendid, popularizing synthesis of the new infectious threats to humankind, Laurie Garrett stressed that a renewed, audacious, transdisciplinary perspective was required in order to face the challenges of HIV/AIDS and other (re)emerging diseases. This new perspective would admit the existence of a "dynamic, nonlinear state of affairs between *Homo sapiens* and the microbial world, both inside and outside their [human] bodies," instead of insisting on seeing "humanity's relationship to the microbes as a historically linear one, tending over the centuries toward ever-decreasing risk to humans."[68]

3. The Biotechnological Perspective Needs to Be Replaced by a More Comprehensive View

(Re)emergent diseases have raised a recurrent issue, namely that the problem of their solution always goes beyond strictly scientific–medical parameters. Consequently, the reductionist biotechnological perspective, strictly focused on screening and treating these diseases in a way that placates the biomedical-pharmaceutical-technological complex, is in urgent need of being replaced by a comprehensive, integrative, and holistic analysis of infectious disease, one which plainly assumes that epidemics are social as much as biological events and which links "biotic and social domains in health and infectious disease research."[69] In this respect, Garrett's study called for multidisciplinary approaches to the whole range of infectious diseases, making it possible to integrate research from within the biomedical and social sciences, including such disparate fields as "medicine, environmentalism, public health, basic ecology, primate biology, human behavior, economic development, cultural anthropology, human rights law, entomology, parasitology, virology, bacteriology, evolutionary biology, and epidemiology."[70] Activities like the Special Program for Research and Training in Tropical Diseases—a coordinated effort by UNICEF, UNDP, the World Bank, and WHO that has been in existence since 1975—might be seen as pioneering efforts to develop an infectious disease research agenda at the interface of biomedical and social sciences in the area of "tropical medicine."[71] Yet despite these and other relevant steps taken in that direction since the mid-1990s, efforts to counter the new global threats continue to be overreactive and insufficiently integrative. Indeed, on the occasion of the 2009–10 influenza pandemic, WHO was heavily criticized for practicing an antipandemic policy of "viral counter-insurgence" based on a long-held "consoling faith . . . that pandemics can be contained by the rapid responses of medical bureaucracies, independent of the quality of local public health" with a "primitive, often nonexistent surveillance of the interface between human and animal diseases."[72] The current broad reorganization of CDC, including the creation of a "National Center for Emerging and Zoonotic Infectious Diseases," appears to be too closely related to the controversial handling of the last flu crisis by public health agencies worldwide to create expectations of any near-term paradigm changes in that U.S. government agency's approach to infectious diseases.[73]

4. Progress Does Not Go on Forever

(Re)emerging diseases, particularly HIV/AIDS, remind us that public health achievements can never be considered irreversible, and that the health of human populations can be subject to regression as well as progress over the course of time. More than any other epidemic in recent decades, the spread of AIDS has most emphatically raised questions about the validity of the linear and progressive models by which demographic and epidemiologic transitions heretofore have been explained. As UNAIDS's current executive director and two co-authors have written, AIDS is exceptional, not only because of the huge and lasting dimensions of its threat to humankind but also on account of the peculiar complexity of its relationship with poverty: The condition is not a classic disease of poverty (although poverty may increase individuals' vulnerability to HIV) but of the social inequality often associated with economic transitions.[74] Unsurprisingly, the features that Bruce K. Alexander has linked to his "dislocation theory" view of addiction also apply to AIDS in many ways.[75]

5. Standards and Solutions Are Closely Interdependent in Global Health

(Re)emergent diseases have demonstrated that health standards in different regions of the world are increasingly interdependent, so that, ultimately, solving health problems in specific regions, towns, or social groups, in isolation from the rest of humankind, is not possible. In the globalization era, socioeconomic and environmental changes are accelerating microbial evolutionary processes, as well as the transmission of new pathogens between different species, including *Homo sapiens*.[76] The biological mechanisms inherent in these processes are as old as life itself, and the incidence of anthropic effects has continued to grow since the Neolithic Revolution; but the dimensions of microbial evolution over the past 140 years—since the onset of the second Industrial Revolution (1870–1914)—have increased exponentially, to the point where their minimization is scientifically unacceptable and socially irresponsible. Thus, a holistic, transdisciplinary, and diachronic view of global health is required to better understand what is happening with infectious diseases on a worldwide scale, and what can be expected to happen in the future.

6. Community Involvement Is Critical

Public health policies must be adequately informed from a biomedical perspective and take into account the importance of economic, social, political, and cultural attributes. But it is also essential that the design and implementation of these policies be based on the active involvement of targeted communities and their leaders. In the field of global health, perhaps more than in any other, Western medicine should abandon its secular, paternalistic, technocratic model and recognize that its interventions in different parts of the globe would be more effective if a careful transcultural analysis of the communities concerned, one that did not ignore the radical historicity of human action, were undertaken. In *The Invisible Cure: Africa, the West, and the Fight against AIDS*, Helen Epstein magnificently illustrates this point through some new and essential things she says she has learned from her experience of HIV/AIDS in Africa:

I learnt, for example, that AIDS is a social problem as much as it is a medical one: that the virus is of recent origin, but that its spread has been worsened by an explosive combination of historically rooted patterns of sexual behavior, the vicissitudes of post-colonial development, and economic globalization that has left millions of African people adrift in an increasingly unequal world. Their poverty and social dislocation have generated an earthquake in their gender relations that has created wide-open channels for the spread of HIV. Most important, I came to understand that when it comes to saving lives, intangible things—the solidarity of ordinary people facing up to a shared calamity; the anger of activists, especially women; and new scientific ideas—can be just as important as medicine and technology.[77]

7. Short-Term Solutions Are Insufficient

Health care threats like HIV/AIDS force national, international, and transnational political institutions and humanitarian organizations to respond for much longer than is usual in other humanitarian emergencies, in order to guarantee the efficacy of their interventions. As the Red Cross Red Crescent's 2008 annual report on world disasters emphasized regarding AIDS, while there are no "short-term solutions to the underlying causes of vulnerability such as discrimination against marginalized groups and gender inequality," it may be possible to treat the humanitarian intervention as "an opportunity to strengthen those aspects of humanitarian work that build resilience and empower communities rather than merely to provide assistance when disaster has overwhelmed their capacity to cope."[78] The Social Drivers Working Group, which initiated the "aids2031" campaign in 2008, is working along these lines and claims that "a successful shift in emphasis [at the local, national, and international levels] from individualized approaches regarding prevention, care and treatment to approaches that take key structural determinants of vulnerability into account will be the critical 'game changer' that the AIDS response has been seeking."[79]

8. A More Critical Approach to Infectious Diseases Is Required

To better understand the emergence of infectious diseases, a critical approach is required, one that goes beyond the limits of customary academic politesse and attempts to answer, as Paul Farmer has suggested, less common and more complex questions.[80] We might begin by asking these:

- What measure of responsibility for the emergence and spread of infectious diseases lies with the neoliberal policies—economic liberalization, free trade, open markets, deregulation, privatization, and drastic reductions in the public budgets—that international financial and trade organizations, such as the World Bank, the International Monetary Fund, and the WTO, as well as the Western superpowers, have pursued since the 1980s?
- During this period, how much of the burden of (re)emerging diseases has derived from neocolonial policies of exploitation of natural resources (agriculture, livestock farming, and mining) and manufacturing industries in many world regions, mostly—albeit by no means exclusively—involving developing countries?
- To what extent are the lucrative profits from the industrial and commercial exploitation of biotechnological innovations in the pharmaceutical, cosmetic, agricultural, and livestock industries hampering an adequate and sufficient evaluation of collateral risks derived from these activities?

Finally, and most pressingly, we must wonder whether national, international, and transnational political elites are ready or able to undertake and further this task in the face of the power of big transnational biotechnology companies, and what roles citizens and social movements might play on the local and global scales to promote change.

NOTES

1 United Nations Department of Economic and Social Affairs, Population Division, *World Mortality 2009* (2009), http://www.un.org/esa/population/publications/worldmortality/WMR2009_wallchart.pdf.

2 Ibid.

3 World Health Organization, "The top causes of death," Fact sheet no. 310 (updated July 2013). http://www.who.int/mediacentre/factsheets/fs310/en/ .

4 UNICEF, *Levels & Trends in Child Mortality. Report 2012. Estimates Developed by the UN Inter-agency Group for Child Mortality Estimation* (New York: United Nations Children's Fund, 2012), 2. http://www.unicef.org/videoaudio/PDFs/UNICEF_2012_child_mortality_for_web_0904.pdf.

5 Sung Lee, "WHO and the Developing World: The Contest for Ideology," in *Western Medicine as Contested Knowledge*, ed. Andrew Cunningham and Bridie Andrews (Manchester: Manchester University Press, 1997): 24–45.

6 Anthony S. Fauci, "Infectious Diseases: Considerations for the Twenty-First Century," *Clinical Infectious Diseases* 32, no. 5 (2001), 675.

7 Macfarlane Burnet and David O. White, *Natural History of Infectious Disease*, Fourth Edition (Cambridge: Cambridge University Press, 1972), 263.

8 Joseph E. McDade and James M. Hughes, "New and Emerging Infectious Diseases," in *Principles and Practice of Infectious Diseases*, ed. Gerald L. Mandell, John E. Bennett, and Raphael Dolin (Philadelphia: Churchill Livingstone, 2000), 178–79.

9 Ibid., 180; Fauci, "Infectious Diseases," 678.

10 Nicholas B. King, "The Scale Politics of Emerging Diseases," *Osiris* 19 (2004), 64.

11 Joshua Lederberg, Robert E. Shoper, and Stanley C. Oaks Jr., eds., *Emerging Infections: Microbial Threats to Health in the United States* (Washington: National Academy Press, 1992), vi.

12 Ibid., 34.

13 Centers for Disease Control and Prevention, "Addressing Emerging Infectious Disease Threats: A Prevention Strategy for the United States (Executive Summary)," *Morbidity and Mortality Weekly Report* 43, no. RR-5 (1994), http://www.cdc.gov/mmwr/PDF/rr/rr4305.pdf.

14 Committee on International Science, Engineering, and Technology, *Report of the NSTC CISET Working Group on Emerging and Re-emerging Infectious Diseases* (Washington: National Science and Technology Council, 1995); White House, Office of Science and Technology Policy, *Fact Sheet: Addressing the Threat of Emerging Infectious Diseases* (Washington, D.C., June 12, 1996), http://www.fas.org/irp/offdocs/pdd_ntsc7.htm; McDade and Hughes, "New and Emerging Infectious Diseases," 181–82.

15 Centers for Disease Control and Prevention, *Preventing Emerging Infectious Diseases: A Strategy for the Twenty-First Century* (Atlanta: Author, 1998); Centers for Disease Control and Prevention, *Protecting the Nation's Health in an Era of Globalization: The CDC's Global Infectious Disease Strategy* (Atlanta: Author, 2001).

16 King, "The Scale Politics of Emerging Diseases," 69.

17 World Health Organization, *Report of the Second WHO Meeting on Emerging Infectious Diseases* (Geneva: Program on Bacterial, Viral Diseases, and Immunology, Division of Communicable Diseases, 1995), 12.

18 World Health Organization, *Emerging and Other Communicable Diseases: Strategic Plan 1996–2000* (Geneva: Author, 1996).

19 David Heymann and J. Dzenowagis, "Commentary: Emerging and Other Communicable Diseases," *Bulletin of the World Health Organization* 76, no. 6 (1998), 545–47.

20 Lederberg et al., *Emerging Infections*, 47–112.

21 Mirko D. Grmek, *History of AIDS: Emergence and Origin of a Modern Pandemic* (Princeton, N.J.: Princeton University Press, 1990), 109.

22 Ibid., 158–61.

23 Mirko D. Grmek, "Préliminaires d'une étude historique des maladies" (Preliminaries for a historical study of diseases), *Annales Économies, Sociétés, Civilisations* 24, no. 6 (1969): 1473–83. See also Jon Arrizabalaga, "History of Disease and the *Longue Durée*," *History and Philosophy of Life Sciences* 27, no. 1 (2005): 41–56.

24 Grmek, *History of AIDS*, 150–52.

25 Elisabeth Fee and Nancy Krieger, "The Emerging Histories of AIDS: Three Successive Paradigms," *History and Philosophy of Life Sciences* 15, no. 3 (1993), 463–64.

26 "Antimicrobial Resistance," *Essential Drugs Monitor*, nos. 28–29 (2000): 1, 7–19, http://apps.who.int/medicinedocs/pdf/s2248e/s2248e.pdf.

27 National Creutzfeldt–Jakob Disease Surveillance Unit, *CJD Statistics* (2010), http://www.cjd.ed.ac.uk/figures.htm.

28 Karen F. Greif and Jon F. Merz, *Current Controversies in the Biological Sciences: Case Studies of Policy Challenges from New Technologies* (Cambridge, Mass.: MIT Press, 2007): 289–97.

29 "Antimicrobial Resistance," 10–11.

30 WHO Regional Office for the Western Pacific, *SARS: How a Global Epidemic Was Stopped* (Manila: World Health Organization, 2006), 74. See also Megan Murray, "The Epidemiology of SARS," in *SARS in China: Prelude to Pandemic?*, ed. Arthur Kleinman and James L. Watson (Stanford, Calif.: Stanford University Press, 2006): 17–30.

31 World Health Organization, *The World Health Report 2007. A Safer Future: Global Public Health Security in the Twenty-First Century* (Geneva: Author, 2007), 38.

32 Ibid., 40.

33 WHO Regional Office for South-East Asia, *Avian Influenza Outbreaks in South-East Asia* (New Delhi: Author), 2010, http://www.searo.who.int/EN/Section10/Section1027.htm.

34 Mike Davis, "The Swine Flu Crisis Lays Bare the Meat Industry's Monstrous Power," *The Guardian*, April 27, 2009, http://www.theguardian.com/commentisfree/2009/apr/27/swine-flu-mexico-health.

35 Richard M. Krause, "Foreword," in *Emerging Viruses*, ed. Stephen S. Morse (New York: Oxford University Press, 1996), xvii–xix.

36 Mike Davis, *The Monster at Our Door: The Global Threat of Avian Flu* (New York: New Press, 2005), 55–57.

37 James L. Watson, "SARS and the Consequences for Globalization," in *SARS in China: Prelude to Pandemic?*, 202.

38 John M. Barry, "The Next Pandemic," *World Policy Journal* 27, no. 2 (2010), 12.

39 Marie-Monique Robin, *The World According to Monsanto: Pollution, Corruption, and the Control of Our Food Supply*, trans. George Holoch (New York: New Press, 2010), 256–72; María Alejandra Silva, "Poverty and Health in Argentina," *Medicina Social* 4, 2 (June 2009): 98–108.

40 Robin, *The World According to Monsanto*, 266.

41 Silva, "Pobreza y salud en Argentina," 106.

42 Ibid., 107.

43 Alejandro Rebossio, "Argentina sufre la peor epidemia de dengue de su historia" (Argentina suffers the worst dengue epidemic in its history), *El País*, April 9, 2009. See also Horacio Verbitsky, "Verano del '96: El escandaloso expediente de la soja transgénica" (Summer '96: The scandalous authorization of transgenic soy), *Página 12* (April 21, 2009), http://www.pagina12.com.ar/diario/elpais/1-123932-2009-04-26.html.

44 Joint United Nations Programme on HIV/AIDS (UNAIDS), *2008 Report on the Global AIDS Pandemic* (Geneva: Author, 2008): 29–62.

45 Ibid., 57–59.

46 UN Office for the Coordination of Humanitarian Affairs, *Model Agreement on Customs Facilitations in Humanitarian Assistance* (Geneva: Author, 1996). See also International Federation of Red Cross and Red Crescent Societies, *World Disasters Report: Focus on HIV and AIDS* (Geneva: Author, 2008), 39.

47 International Federation of Red Cross and Red Crescent Societies, *World Disasters Report*, 11.

48 Clive Bell, Devarajan Shantayanan, and Hans Gersbach, "Thinking about the Long-Run Economic Costs of AIDS," in *The Macroeconomics of HIV/AIDS*, ed. Marcus Haacker (Washington: International Monetary Fund, 2004), 128–29.

49 International Federation of Red Cross and Red Crescent Societies, *World Disasters Report*, 11.

50 Ibid., 16.

51 Ibid., 18.

52 International Labour Organization, Office of the United Nations High Commissioner for Refugees, United Nations Children's Fund, United Nations Development Programme, United Nations Office on Drugs and Crime, United Nations Population Fund, United Nations Scientific, Educational, and Cultural Organization, World Bank, World Food Programme, and World Health Organization.

53 International Federation of Red Cross and Red Crescent Societies, *World Disasters Report*, 20.

54 Ibid., 20–21.

55 World Health Organization, *The World Health Report 1999: Making a Difference* (Geneva: Author, 1999), 110.

56 United Nations General Assembly, *Declaration of Commitment on HIV/AIDS: Global Crisis, Global Action*, June 27, 2001, http://www.un.org/ga/aids/docs/aress262.pdf.

57 United Nations General Assembly, *United Nations Millennium Declaration*, September 18, 2000, http://www.un.org/millennium/declaration/ares552e.pdf.

58 United Nations, *We Can End Poverty. 2015 Millennium Development Goals: A Gateway to the UN System's Work on the MDGs*, accessed March 4, 2014, http://www.un.org/millenniumgoals/.

59 UNAIDS, *2008 Report*, 14–15.

60 International Federation of Red Cross and Red Crescent Societies, *World Disasters Report: Focus on HIV and AIDS* (Geneva: Author, 2008), 20–21.

61 International Federation of Red Cross and Red Crescent Societies, *World Disasters Report*, 24, 28.

62 Teresa Forcades i Vila, *Los crímenes de las grandes compañías farmacéuticas* (The crimes of the big pharmaceutical companies) (Barcelona: Cristianisme i Justícia, Monograph No. 141, July 2006), 8, http://mon.uvic.cat/tlc/files/2013/04/85787.pdf.

63 Faustin Barro, *Rapport de participation à la Conférènce Internationale sur le SIDA, Mexico 03–08 2008* (Report on participation in the AIDS World Conference, Mexico, 3 August 2008) (Ouagadougou, Burkina Faso: Ministry of Health, August 2008), 12; Colin D. Mathers and Dejan Loncar, "Projections of Global Mortality and Burden of Disease from 2002 to 2030," *PLOS Medicine* 3, no. 11 (2006): e442.

64 International Federation of Red Cross and Red Crescent Societies, *World Disasters Report*, 28–34.

65 Ulrich Beck, *Risk Society: Towards a New Modernity* (London: Sage, 1992), 21.

66 Paul Farmer, "Rethinking 'Emerging Infectious Diseases,'" in *Infections and Inequalities: The Modern Plagues* (Berkeley: University of California Press, 1999), 37–58.

67 Charles B. Rosenberg, "What Is an Epidemic? AIDS in Historical Perspective," *Daedalus* 118, no. 2 (1989), 14.

68 Laurie Garrett, *The Coming Plague: Newly Emerging Diseases in a World Out of Balance* (London: Virago Press, 1995), 10–11.

69 Johannes Sommerfeld, "Plagues and Peoples Revisited: Basic and Strategic Research for Infectious Disease Control at the Interface of the Life, Health, and Social Sciences," *EMBO Reports* 4, special issue (2003), S32–S34.

70 Garrett, *The Coming Plague*, 11.

71 Sommerfeld, "Plagues and Peoples Revisited."

72 Davis, "The Swine Flu Crisis Lays Bare."

73 "CDC Reorganization Creating Emerging and Zoonotic Disease Center," *JAVMA News* (February 1, 2010), https://www.avma.org/News/JAVMANews/Pages/100201h.aspx; Centers for Disease Control and Prevention [CDC organizational chart], accessed March 5, 2014, http://www.cdc.gov/maso/pdf/CDC_Chart_wNames.pdf.

74 Peter Piot, Robert Greener, and Sarah Russell, "Squaring the Circle: AIDS, Poverty, and Human Development," *PLOS Medicine* 4, no. 10 (2007): 1571–75.

75 Bruce K. Alexander, "Replacing the Official View of Addiction," chapter 8, this volume.

76 Davis, *The Monster at Our Door*, 55.

77 Helen Epstein, *The Invisible Cure: Africa, the West, and the Fight against AIDS* (New York: Farrar, Straus & Giroux, 2007), xiv.

78 International Federation of Red Cross and Red Crescent Societies, *World Disasters Report*, 35.

79 aids2031 Social Drivers Working Group, *Revolutionizing the AIDS Response: Building AIDS Resilient Communities* (Worcester, Mass.: Clark University; Washington: International Center for Research on Women, 2010), 4.

80 Farmer, "Rethinking 'Emerging Infectious Diseases,'" 44.

8

Replacing the Official View of Addiction

BRUCE K. ALEXANDER

This chapter is a historical critique of the dominant view of addiction in the United States, and a description of a perspective that I believe is steadily replacing it.

I begin with the observation that the centuries-old English word *addiction* originally had neither a medical nor a moral meaning. I then describe the nineteenth-century construction of a way of seeing addiction that was *both* medical and moral. The medical and moral redefinition of *addiction* evolved in the United States into what I call the "official view," a perspective that is held by most of today's policymakers, academics, and the major professional organizations that are concerned with drugs and addiction. This view has also been called the "official model"[1] and, more recently, the "NIDA brain disease paradigm"[2] or simply the "medical model."

To some extent, the official view is based on reductionist hi-tech neuroscience, but it also carries old assumptions and moralistic baggage that betray its deep cultural roots. I argue that this official view provides neither an adequate understanding of addiction nor a basis for effective intervention in the twenty-first century.

The final section of this chapter introduces a radically different perspective on addiction that I call the "dislocation theory" of addiction. Dislocation theory is holistic on both a personal and a social level. It is built on the historical meaning of *addiction* in the English language, rather than the nineteenth-century medical and moral redefinition. Although the basic ideas of dislocation theory have been worked out over decades, they may startle some readers because they repudiate major aspects of the official view that have come to seem unquestionable.

The Historical Meaning of the Word *Addiction*

Definition 1a in the latest edition of the *Oxford English Dictionary* (*OED*) encapsulates the historical meaning of *addiction* in the English language: "The state or condition of being dedicated or devoted *to* a thing, esp. an activity or occupation; adherence or attachment, esp. of an immoderate or compulsive kind."[3] This is how the word was used by Shakespeare, the translators of the King James Bible, David Hume, Jane Austen, Charles Dickens, and other masters of the English language, as well as everyday writers and speakers outside the field of drug addiction up to the present day.

Although this meaning of *addiction* is well established by centuries of English usage, it has a still longer history. Long before there was an English language—or even a country called England—this definition grew out of the Roman Empire's dismal practice of legally imposing slavery on people who could not pay their debts. The Latin term for such a slave is *servus addictus*, stemming from the Latin verb *addicere*. Like slaves everywhere, Roman slaves had to pay constant, intense attention to the demands of their masters, who could inflict immediate punishment if that attention faltered. Masters extracted as much work as possible from their slaves, leaving them little time or energy for anything else. In Rome, the meanings of the Latin word *addictus* and various forms of *addicere* eventually were broadened to include intense dedication or devotion to an activity or occupation that seemed voluntary or was at least not imposed with the chains and shackles of slavery. The English word *addiction* comes from the Latin, and definition 4 of the word in the current edition of the *OED* still refers to that history of legal slavery.[4]

The historical overtone of slavery may provide some insight into severe addiction, which can be tragically similar to enslavement. Nonetheless, the word *addiction* was used much more often over the centuries to describe involvements that were relatively minor, and often harmless or even beneficial. (This is easily confirmed by using the Google Ngram Viewer to search out instances of the words *addicted* and *addiction* since about 1600.) Throughout the history of the English language, people have understood that they could be addicted to any of a very large number of activities or occupations, but they usually did not worry too much about it.

The psychoactive properties of alcohol and drugs were well known from the beginnings of Western civilization, including the fact that some users became addicted to them. However, drug addiction was not a matter of unusual concern to either medical professionals or moralists before the nineteenth century.[5]

For example, opium use in England was not usually discussed in a medical and moral context until the mid–nineteenth century. Opium was legal, and large numbers of people from all social classes used it. Regular opium users were most often called "opium eaters." Most opium eaters were not regarded as dangerously addicted, although some were.[6] Even as late as 1821, when Thomas De Quincey described his own severe addiction to opium in *Confessions of an English Opium Eater*, the public reacted with literary excitement but without "fear or a desire for control."[7] No matter what word was used for it, opium addiction was not generally situated in a medical or moral context until later in the nineteenth century. Commenting on societal attitudes toward opium users in nineteenth-century England, Berridge and Edwards wrote that "regular opium users, 'opium eaters,' were acceptable in their communities and rarely the subject of medical attention at the beginning of the century; at its end they were classified as 'sick,' diseased or deviant in some way and fit subjects for professional treatment."[8]

The Medicalization and Moralization of Drug Addiction

Scientific medicine rose to prominence in the nineteenth and early twentieth centuries by conquering diseases that had long cursed the human race, including smallpox, cholera, typhoid, and rheumatic fever.[9] The nineteenth and twentieth centuries also witnessed an extended moral panic over increases in excessive drinking and, later, over excessive use of opium, morphine, chlorodyne, cocaine, heroin, and other drugs. New ways of speaking about alcohol and drug addiction in this rapidly changing cultural context eventually medicalized and moralized the word *addiction*.

Historians do not find it surprising that the word *addiction* was medicalized and moralized around the same time. Although doctors and moralists of the nineteenth century differed in some regards, they had much in common. Often the same people were members of medical associations, temperance societies, and anti-drug movements.[10] If the nineteenth century's approach to addiction could seem *exclusively* moral to some later addiction specialists, it was only because doctors' various approaches to excessive drinking and drug use, although numerous and often well funded,[11] were neither dramatic nor particularly successful and did not capture the imagination of the general public as early as the moral approach did.

The temperance movement, a powerful moral campaign in North America and Europe, proclaimed that liquor, characterized as "ardent spirits," "hard liquor," or "demon rum," was breaking down civilized society. Despite the movement's flamboyant hyperbole, the perception of widespread alcohol addiction was well founded. Although most Europeans and Americans drank prudently, a growing minority were adopting the drunken, socially abhorrent lifestyles the movement decried.[12] When speaking of excessive drinkers, temperance movement adherents first applied such labels as "inebriates," "drunkards," and "sots," but "addicts" gradually came into use as well.[13]

About the same time that the temperance movement was gradually appropriating the venerable word *addiction* as the name of a moral failure, the medical profession was appropriating it as the name of a disease. The most famous medical analysis of drunkards in the early nineteenth century was provided by an American physician, Benjamin Rush, who had earlier been one of the signers of the Declaration of Independence. However, there were many other medical theories, as well as numerous interventions and residential treatment facilities.[14]

The way in which temperance crusaders and medical doctors increasingly used the word *addiction* did not contradict its historical meaning but *narrowed* it. The formerly broad concept of addiction was being limited to people who were involved with distilled spirits to a degree that could be seen as indicative of a disease, a moral failure, or both.

By the end of the nineteenth century, the sensational images of the anti-alcohol temperance movement had become archetypes for new anti-drug movements, including the anti-opium movement of the late nineteenth century and, later, movements targeting other drugs.[15] Images of medically and morally ruined alcoholics and junkies were engraved in the public consciousness by the new photographic newspapers of the nineteenth century and the electronic media of the twentieth. In the twentieth century, these images were most widely associated with a succession of new drugs: morphine from the late nineteenth century until World War I, heroin from the 1920s until the 1970s, and "crack" cocaine in the 1980s. In the twenty-first century, the parade has continued with methamphetamine, popularly referred to as "crystal meth," "crystal," and "ice," and with oxycodone in the form of the prescription painkiller OxyContin.

When the emerging medical and moral definition of the word *addiction* made its way into the *OED* for the first time in its 1933 supplement, it was worded as follows: "2. b. The, or a, state of being addicted to a drug (see ADDICTED ppl a. 3b); a compulsion and need to continue taking a drug as a result of taking it in the past. Cf. drug-addiction s.v. DRUG sb.1 I b."

This new, narrowed definition encompassed overwhelming involvement with drugs (including alcohol[16]), but not with other activities or occupations. Moreover, the new definition made addiction both a medical and a moral issue. Unlike the historical definition, the new definition had the qualities of a reductionist *medical* diagnosis: Addiction was necessarily a "compulsion" that had a physical cause—taking a drug in the past—and was inevitably accompanied by "withdrawal symptoms." (The term *withdrawal symptoms* appeared in definition 3b of the word *addicted*, which was cross-referenced with the new definition of *addiction*.) The new definition was *moral* because there is no possibility that addiction, as re-defined, could be anything but an evil. No benign words like *dedicated* or *devoted* appeared in definition 2b, and the term *drug-addiction*, which was cross-referenced with this definition, was explained with a variety of moralistic terms, including *drug evil* and *drug fiend*.[17] Although the medical and moral definition descended from the historical definition of *addiction* logically, its medical and moral aspects gave it an altogether new character. This moral and medical definition appears in a longer (but not broader) form as definition 1b in the 2010 edition of the *OED*.

The new dictionary definition of *addiction* was a reflection of the increasingly popular medical/moral perspective on addiction, which was shaping public policy and inspiring many forms of treatment for drug-addicted people.[18] The balance between medical and moral language repeatedly shifted throughout the late nineteenth century and the twentieth century and tilted toward the medical after World War II. The most current form of the medical/moral way of looking at addiction can be called the "official view," for reasons that are explained below.

The Official View of Addiction

The medical/moral perspective on addiction gradually became the view of policymakers, academics, and professional organizations concerned with addiction. Today, it is most authoritatively promoted by the National Institute on Drug Abuse. An enormously influential branch of the U.S. National Institutes of Health, NIDA is said to fund 85 percent of all drug addiction research *in the world*.[19] The official view also now incorporates many of the key ideas and practices of the worldwide twelve-step movement. It is supported by the National Institute on Alcohol Abuse and Alcoholism, the American Society of Addiction Medicine, and the American Board of Addiction Medicine. All this support gives the official view a seemingly unassailable quality in the United States. Although it finds less support outside the United States, the official view has strong advocates in many countries.[20]

The official view was comprehensively and authoritatively summarized for the public in a 2007 American media package titled *Addiction: Why Can't They Just Stop?* This heavily promoted public information campaign included a book, a website, a series of broadcasts on the American television network HBO (among them a fourteen-part documentary series and four independent films), a series of DVDs offered to the public, and highly advertised public meetings in major American cities. The media package was based on interviews with twenty-two of the most highly placed American experts in addiction medicine and featured Nora Volkow, the director of NIDA. It also contained contributions from authors who were bestselling exponents of the twelve-step movement. The project was funded by HBO, NIDA, the National Institute on Alcohol Abuse and Alcoholism, and the Robert Wood Johnson Foundation.[21]

The official view, as summarized in this media package, can be distilled down to six foundational elements, some stated explicitly and some assumed:

1. Addiction is fundamentally a problem of drug or alcohol consumption. Even where other habits are described as addictions, they are recognized as such by what they can be shown to have in common with established drug addictions.
2. So-called addictive drugs have the power to transform the people who use them into drug addicts, overcoming their normal willpower. Drug-addicted people have fallen under control of an external power—a drug. This power is explained in the language of reductionist neuroscience.
3. Much of people's vulnerability to being overpowered by drugs comes from genetic or characterological predispositions to addiction.
4. People who become addicted suffer from a chronic, relapsing brain disease. The terms *chronic* and *relapsing* are taken to mean that there is no more possibility of a complete cure for this disease than would be expected for diabetes, asthma, or Alzheimer's disease.[22]
5. Although people cannot be cured of the disease of addiction, it can be successfully managed through professional treatment or participation in self-help groups.[23] If addicted people refuse treatment or enrollment in self-help groups, their addiction will continue unabated and they will damage themselves and society.[24]
6. Addiction is a problem of dysfunctional individuals. The possibility that addiction might be a general tendency of human beings trying to adapt to a dysfunctional society is not considered.

Beyond the six foundational elements, the official view is built on the great prestige of contemporary science and medicine: The belief that the official view is a product of reductionist neuroscience is taken as strong assurance that it is correct.[25] Generously funded medical research is expected to devise a more effective treatment for addiction that will probably be pharmacological.[26] Because the official view (schematized in Figure 8.1) has been continually reformulated, numerous forms of it have accumulated. A few of them are mentioned here.

The strong form of the official view holds that an "addictive drug" will quickly transform *every* drug user into an addict. This may sound like a relic of the nineteenth century, but it reappeared at full strength during the panics over crack cocaine in the 1980s and methamphetamine at the beginning of the twenty-first century. Both drugs were said for a time to

Figure 8.1. The official view of addiction.

be instantly and universally addicting. Today's official view takes a weaker form by acknowledging that many users will not become addicted to even the most feared drugs. In the genetic form of the official view, a drug user's addiction is said to occur in large part because of an individual genetic predisposition. Hundreds of individual genes have been associated with addiction, and it is now common to say that 50 percent of a person's vulnerability to the addictive power of drugs is genetic.[27]

Just as the drugs that have been in the spotlight of the medical/moral view have changed over time, so have the mechanisms by which any particular drug is said to cause addiction. For example, in the oldest versions of the medical/moral view of addiction as applied to heroin, individuals were said to be transformed into heroin addicts because of moral weakness (i.e., an inability to resist the euphoria or to endure the withdrawal symptoms). In the 1960s, the moral-weakness explanation was partly replaced by behavioristic conditioning theories, which held that all users were vulnerable to the unbearable withdrawal symptoms that could be produced by heroin, which, when they occurred, caused relapses as a form of conditioned response. In the 1970s, heroin was said to cause addiction in any user by crippling the brain's ability to produce endorphins and by providing a pharmaceutical substitute for the endorphin-producing mechanisms the drug had shut down. In today's official view, heroin (along with other "addictive drugs") is said to "flip a switch in the brain" of genetically predisposed people, most usually by augmenting the brain's normal release of the neurotransmitter dopamine. The augmented dopamine supply is said to transform the brain so that the affected individual is unable to experience the sense of well-being associated with dopamine's normal release. Moreover, heroin and the other "addictive drugs" are said to weaken those parts of the brain that function, under normal conditions, to inhibit destructive behaviors.[28]

Why the Official View Is Untenable

Although the official view receives the unswerving support of government, academics, and professional associations in the United States and other countries, continual reformulation is required to keep it from being undermined by the facts of addiction. Some problems that perplex the current form of the official view are briefly reviewed here.

1. Contrary to the official view, addiction is not primarily a problem of alcohol and drugs. In fact, alcohol and drug addiction is only a corner of the vast, doleful tapestry of addiction.

The official view of addiction grew from the erroneous belief that people could become addicted only to alcohol and certain drugs. But it is now clear that addictions to gambling, love, shopping, consumption, Internet games, and countless other habits and pursuits can be as prevalent, dangerous, and intractable as drug addictions.[29] The first element of the official view is thus no longer tenable.

Efforts are now being made to stretch the official view's explanations for alcohol and drug addiction to encompass some of the other habits and pursuits to which people can become addicted.[30] However, these efforts create new logical knots. For example:

- If all the habits and pursuits to which people can become addicted affect the brain's dopamine response in the way that cocaine and heroin do, how can there be anybody who is not addicted to something?
- If a person who shows all the behavioral signs of being addicted to a habit that does not affect dopamine response in the brain is considered not *really* addicted, then addiction as defined by the official view contradicts the historical meaning of the word *addiction* in the English language.
- Why are drug addicts not automatically addicted to sex, exercise, or any of the many other activities and experiences that might supply the dopamine their brains lack after they become addicted?

Fancy footwork is required to dance out of these logical entanglements.

2. Despite countless interventions carried out under the rubric of the official view, the prevalence of addiction has continued to grow throughout the twentieth century and into the twenty-first.

The dedication of the clinicians who have carried out the interventions sanctioned by the official view is unquestioned. However, their interventions, including prevention programs in the schools, twelve-step groups, conventional psychotherapy, cognitive behavioral therapy, pharmaceutical interventions, and methadone maintenance, among others, have had only limited success in individual cases and have failed to stem the rising flood of addiction around the world. Even treatment programs that are supported with unlimited funds succeed in only a minority of cases. No matter how wealthy you are, you can't buy your way out of addiction, even at the most expensive private treatment facilities.

It is because addiction has proven so resistant to treatment interventions that the official view has characterized it as essentially incurable (using the word *chronic* to imply that it is incurable yet treatable, in the way that diabetes, asthma, and Alzheimer's disease are). But this characterization is not tenable.

3. Natural recovery occurs frequently, contrary to the official view of addiction as a "chronic" disease.

Large-scale field studies show that about three-quarters of the people who become mildly or severely addicted to a drug in their youth recover, usually without receiving any addiction treatment. More than half recover by the time they are thirty years old. Moreover, the relapse rate for people who go through treatment is much higher than the relapse rate for those who overcome addiction without treatment.[31]

The basis of natural recovery without treatment is no mystery. It lies in establishing stronger relations with the community, or finding a strong sense of meaning in a new life.[32] Addicted people who do not recover on their own fill the treatment agencies and social service centers. A large number do not respond to treatment, creating the illusion of an incurable disease.

4. Contrary to its scientific appearance, the official view has drawn its principles more from moralistic social movements than from scientific discoveries.

Medieval European Christians spoke of consorting with demons as producing an irreversible loss of willpower, which they called "demon possession." The religious temperance movements of the nineteenth century spoke of "demon rum" as producing an irreversible and reprehensible change in people's behavior, turning them into "drunkards." Medical experts of the late nineteenth century held a similarly vehement view of alcohol and drug addicts, which they expressed in now-archaic technical language, including esoteric references to "malfunctioning brain structure," "failure of the higher ethical brain," inherited "degeneration," and "retrograde evolution."[33] Moralists of the early twentieth century thought heroin permanently changed people into "drug fiends." Mainstream biomedical researchers of the twenty-first century speak of "addictive drugs" as "flipping a switch in the brain" or putting people "beyond willpower" or "hijacking the brain," thereby causing a chronic, relapsing brain disease that has essentially the same behavioral effects as being possessed by a demon or becoming a drunkard, degenerate, drug fiend, or victim of failure of the higher ethical brain. What has really changed over this period?

Despite all the scientific razzle-dazzle, the idea that drugs cause the chronic disease of addiction by rewiring the brain is not essentially a new scientific paradigm, although the proponents of the official view claim that it is.[34] Rather, it is a restatement in neurological language of a folk theory that appeared and reappeared in Western literature for millennia before modern neuroscience existed.

Today, the official view is often illustrated with brilliantly colored brain images that people who are not neuroscientists cannot hope to understand or evaluate. It is important not to be overawed by these colorful displays, partly because some brain imaging technology, notably functional magnetic resonance imaging, has proved unusually vulnerable to error,[35] partly because hi-tech biomedical research is often shaped by the values of the scientists who carry it out and the institutions that fund them, and partly because science itself is no more capable of certainty than any other human endeavor.

People do not need a Ph.D. in neuroscience to make up their minds about the official view. It can be evaluated with a normal understanding of the rules of evidence and the facts of history and clinical experience. The official view of addiction, even when bolstered with the latest biomedical images, warrants no more uncritical faith than the academically and officially sanctioned models that provided apparently unassailable mathematical proof—until 2008—that the market for subprime securitized mortgages would not collapse.[36]

5. Contrary to the strong form of the official view, most people who use "addictive drugs" do not become addicted.

There are many cases of lifelong use of a supposedly "addictive drug" by eminent people whose lives were unblemished by the addictive problems that the official view regards as inevitably associated with use of these drugs. The evidence that "addictive drugs" can be used safely has not only been officially ignored, it has been actively suppressed. The *Guardian* newspaper reported on June 13, 2009, the rediscovery of a fourteen-year-old World Health Organization study on cocaine which showed that large numbers of people all over the world used cocaine and crack cocaine without becoming addicted, diseased, or antisocial. Although this was the largest study of cocaine use ever conducted, with data reported from twenty-two sites in nineteen countries, it has been officially ignored everywhere and its publication politically suppressed.[37] However, many smaller studies showing that people can use "addictive drugs" for very long periods without becoming addicted, including crack cocaine and methamphetamine, have been published.

6. Contrary to the weaker form of the official view, addiction cannot be understood simply as an affliction of certain individuals with predispositions to addiction in otherwise well-functioning societies.

Although addiction obviously manifests itself in individual cases, its prevalence differs dramatically between societies. For example, it can be quite rare in an individual society for centuries, then become common or almost universal among those same people when a tribal culture is crushed or a highly developed empire collapses. Whatever differences in individual predisposition exist are overridden by a cultural influence.

The classic illustration is the transformation of hundreds of aboriginal societies all over the world from highly integrated groups with negligible prevalence of addiction to fragmented societies with ruinously high addiction rates following their colonization by Western settlers.

When addiction becomes commonplace in a colonized society, people become addicted not only to alcohol and drug use but also to a thousand other destructive pursuits, such as gambling, dysfunctional love and sexual relationships, overeating, domestic violence, and accumulating wealth compulsively. It has been customary to attribute this tsunami of aboriginal addictions to the importation of alcohol and other drugs, for which indigenous people had no cultural or genetic defenses, but these explanations do not fit with existing anthropological evidence.[38] Thus, social factors that affect entire societies can completely overshadow differences in individual predisposition.

7. Contrary to the official view, people who become addicted to drugs have not lost their willpower.

Although it is sometimes convenient for street addicts to let police or other officials believe that they have lost their willpower or had their brains "hijacked," they are not drug zombies: They are human beings actively adapting to unfortunate life situations as they are best able. Clinicians and drug counselors who listen carefully know that in situations of trust many drug addicts, as well as people who are addicted to habits and pursuits other than drug use, can explain in great detail why they live the way they do, and why alternative lifestyles are so difficult for them to achieve.[39]

Some addicted people sincerely believe that they are out of control and are incapable of comprehending their own behavior, but these beliefs are readily understood psychologically in terms of attribution theory or Freudian defense mechanisms.[40] Furthermore, addicted people are unrelentingly *taught* to believe they are out of control by the powerful rhetoric of the official view and the practice of twelve-step groups.

8. Contrary to a version of the official view that stresses the etiological role of childhood abuse, such abuse is not a primary cause of the flood of addiction, although it is very important in some cases.

Quantitative research has verified a relationship between childhood abuse and later addiction to alcohol and drugs, especially for women. However, the relationship becomes much less evident when abused children are compared with children from families that are equally distressed but in which abuse has not occurred.[41] In general, sustained family and community dysfunction are far more powerful predictors of addiction than traumatic child abuse or any other individual dysfunction alone.

At the other end of the social spectrum, dedicated, non-abusive parents of drug addicts are often horrified to discover—in the context of dramatic presentations of the child-abuse version of the official view[42]— that many people automatically assume they must have abused their now-addicted child.

Horrific as it is, child abuse is simply one of many risk factors that predict addiction. It is neither a primary cause of the global flood of addiction nor more powerful than many other predictors, some dramatic and some subtle, that can be discerned within the families and communities of people who later become addicted.

9. Contrary to the claims of its advocates, the official view is intrinsically moralistic and punitive, most obviously in providing justification for some of the violent excesses of the "War on Drugs."

Most contemporary versions of the official view depict addicted people as sick rather than immoral, thus apparently absolving them of blame for being addicted. However, the official view designates drug traffickers and producers as more heinous criminals than addicted people were formerly taken to be. They are said to achieve obscene wealth by deliberately inducing a ruinous, incurable disease in their victims.[43] As the official view has gained acceptance, the punishments for drug-addicted people have become milder in many jurisdictions, while the punishments for traffickers and producers have become more severe. The official view, particularly the strong form, has been used to justify draconian punishments for drug traffickers in the United States as well as military attacks on drug-producing peasant farms in Latin America.

The most moralistic aspect of the official view is rarely recognized. Addicts are said to have had their brains "rewired" or "hijacked" by a drug. Therefore, they are not to be blamed for their actions because they are "beyond willpower."[44] But what does it mean to be *beyond willpower*? In the plainest language, it means that drug addicts are no more to be blamed for their reprehensible actions than is a cinematic zombie whose soul has been seized by monomaniacal lust to consume human flesh, or a person in medieval times whose soul is thought to be possessed by a demon. Addicted people are said to have permanently lost their critical judgment, which means that they are no longer fully human. Can a more extreme stigma than that be imposed on a human being? Of course, it can be said that the official view casts this judgment only on people who are addicted to drugs. But now that it is recognized that people can be addicted to a great many habits and pursuits other than drugs, the moral impact of this dehumanizing judgment becomes monumental and terrifying.

The fact that the official view medicalizes and moralizes addiction is not in itself a fatal flaw. Often people find it useful and comforting to think of addiction as a physical disease, and they should have this option. It is probable that addiction will ultimately be understood in reductionist as well as holistic terms. Moreover, addiction surely must be understood morally as well as logically. The downfall of the official view is that its *particular* medical-moral configuration is unstable, internally inconsistent, narrow, ineffectual, and incompatible with several basic facts about addiction. Both its origins and its current implications are dehumanizing and punitive. It exacerbates its problems by masquerading as pure, hi-tech science, when it is nothing of the kind.

Jon Arrizabalaga, a contributor to the present volume, has pointed out that simply labeling a condition as medical does not predetermine what kinds of measures will be taken to control it.[45] For example, bovine spongiform encephalopathy (BSE), popularly known as mad cow disease, quickly acquired the disease label when it appeared in human beings. Neither the disease label nor the now well-understood disease mechanism, however, enabled clinical physicians or pharmaceutical companies to cure BSE in animals or human beings. Mad cow disease cannot presently be controlled without a thorough analysis of modern agricultural practices and implementation of health measures that include rigidly controlling animal feed preparation, maintaining an intense system of feed surveillance on an international level, and eliminating potentially infected cattle. Nothing about being labeled a disease interfered with the holistic analysis and the effective preventative measures that have been undertaken to control BSE.

In the case of addiction, the problem is that the official view *has* interfered with the holistic analysis of addiction, which I describe in the remainder of the present chapter. Furthermore, the moralistic aspects of the official view allow it to coexist comfortably with the cruel and futile War on Drugs.[46]

The Dislocation Theory of Addiction: Neither Reductionistic, Medical, Moralistic, nor Drug-Oriented

An alternate view of addiction is coming to the fore that fits the evidence of history, social science, public health, and clinical research much better than the official view. I call it the "dislocation theory" of addiction. I believe that this way of seeing addiction is steadily replacing the official view.

Like the official view, dislocation theory is not drawn *de novo* from empirical facts but is an interpretation, with deep roots in Western history. It differs from the official view in almost every way, beginning with the people who support it. Its essential ideas are spreading *upward* in the addictions field, not propagated downward from officialdom. Its main proponents are the frontline addiction counselors, social workers, and public health advocates who respond pragmatically to people with serious addiction problems. Also, many addicted people gain strength for recovery by understanding their own addictive problems in accord with the dislocation theory, despite the omnipresence of the official view in the media. Within academia, support for the dislocation theory draws primarily from the work of historians, social theorists, and public health researchers rather than from the work of brain scientists and molecular biologists at the top of the academic pecking order. Given these characteristics of the spread of the dislocation theory, it is possible that high-ranking members of the media, government, medical, and academic hierarchies will be the last to learn about this re-conceptualization of addiction, despite the tectonic rumbles of a paradigm starting to shift.

The dislocation theory of addiction can only be sketched in this short chapter, in combination with a few gestures toward the supporting evidence. I have assembled more extensive reviews of this evidence elsewhere.[47] The theory is presented schematically in figure 8.2.

Instead of focusing all or most of its attention on drug and alcohol addictions, as the official view does, dislocation theory confronts the full range of destructive addictions at the outset. Although it applies to

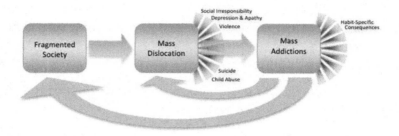

Figure 8.2. The dislocation theory of addiction.

drugs and alcohol addictions, it gives them no special significance, because there is no reason to separate their psychological manifestations or their potential for harm from those of other addictions.

Also in contrast to the official view, the dislocation theory focuses not on individuals but on the social causes of mass addiction in various societies and historical eras. Of course, each addicted individual has a unique story to tell, but the dislocation theory provides a framework within which individual struggles with addiction in the context of their own predispositions can be more deeply understood.

The dislocation theory fits comfortably with the evidence that perplexes the official view. This is easy to check, and, after being introduced to the dislocation theory, readers may want to systematically revisit the nine evidence-based and historical reasons given previously that the official view is now untenable. The remainder of the present chapter provides a brief overview of the dislocation theory and the evidence that supports it.

The Dislocation Theory and Supporting Evidence

The dislocation theory starts with the historical fact that social fragmentation has become ubiquitous in modern societies. Over the past few centuries, agricultural mechanization and the Industrial Revolution overwhelmed and crushed European agrarian communities and villages of every sort. Then, colonization crushed aboriginal cultures around the globe. This process was followed by the technological revolution and the rise of the all-powerful multinational corporations, developments that wreaked havoc with the industrial societies that were beginning to emerge from the ruins of agrarian and aboriginal cultures. The fragmentation of society that began in the early modern era has accelerated in the current period of globalization of free-market capitalism and neoliberalism. New technologies and products, and ever more subtle forms of manipulation for power and profit, sustain the strong force of social fragmentation.[48]

As shown in figure 8.2, dislocation is both the psychological consequence of social fragmentation and the precursor to mass addiction. The characterization of dislocation as the psychological consequence of social fragmentation refers to the rupture of enduring and sustaining connections between individuals and their families, friends, societies, livelihoods, rituals, traditions, nations, and deities, elements that form the basis of psychological wholeness. Erik Erikson is just one of the many psychologists whose holistic analyses have shown how this loss of social connections can destroy individual identity, purpose, belonging, and meaning.[49]

Dislocation is not restricted to geographic separation. Dislocation is a ubiquitous psychological malaise that afflicts people who stay home in disintegrating societies as much as people who are driven continents away from their roots. Dislocation also goes beyond material poverty. Although income inequality, hunger, and other material deprivations can crush the spirits of isolated individuals and families, these deprivations can be borne with dignity by people who face them together, as a psychosocially integrated society. On the other hand, dislocated people become demoralized and degraded even if they are wealthy. No amount of food, shelter, or money can restore their well-being.

Severe, prolonged dislocation is unbearable. It regularly precipitates anguish, suicide, depression, disorientation, and domestic violence, whether or not drugs are available. This is why forced dislocation (in such forms as exile, ostracism, and excommunication) has been a dreaded punishment since ancient times, and why social isolation remains an essential component of the contemporary technology of torture.[50] As figure 8.2 indicates, people who are suffering from dislocation display all the behaviors and other manifestations that in the official view are considered consequences of addiction, except, of course, the side effects of specific drug habits, such as cirrhosis of the liver and opiate-withdrawal symptoms.

Dislocation can have many causes besides social fragmentation. It can result from a tsunami that destroys a person's village or from a personal idiosyncrasy that his or her society cannot tolerate. It can be inflicted violently through abuse of a child or ostracism of an adult. It can be voluntarily chosen if a person turns from a balanced social life to the single-minded pursuit of wealth. But most significantly for the present chapter, dislocation can become the global norm if the steamroller of modernity systematically crushes societies everywhere. Sometimes, causes of dislocation are only superficially diagnosed as individual or family problems. For example, abuse of a child often turns out to be at least partially an effect of dislocation, when its origins are traced back a step further to unemployment or exploitation.

Just as a high prevalence of dislocation tracks societal fragmentation, a high prevalence of addiction tracks dislocation. A wealth of historical, clinical, and quantitative evidence shows that people who lose their identity or their sense of purpose, belonging, or meaning are very likely to become addicted, because addiction provides them with some relief and compensation. Severe addiction, as a kind of exaggerated devotion to an occupation or activity, provides a partial substitute for people who can otherwise be said not to "have a life."

Of course, addiction is not the kind of life addicted people anticipated, or that their societies anticipated for them, but it at least provides them with some meager sense of identity, purpose, belonging, and meaning. When street heroin addicts wake up in the morning, at least they know who they are and what they must accomplish that day. Without their addictions, many heroin addicts and other addicted people would have terrifyingly little reason to live. This is why people who cannot find better solutions to their dislocation cling so desperately to addictions—even very harmful ones.

The feedback arrows in figure 8.2 reveal two other reasons why addiction is so hard to overcome in modern society. When people adapt to dislocation by becoming addicted, the addictions often compound their dislocation by further undermining their families and communities. Many addicted people contribute in various roles to the further expansion of free-market capitalism and the social fragmentation that it entails, from wasteful "shopaholics" to insatiably greedy CEOs. In these ways, addiction has become a vicious cycle in modern times.

Although this self-perpetuating cycle is difficult to break in a global free-market society, many individuals do overcome their personal addictions. Adapting to dislocation by becoming addicted is not a form of "chronic" disease, as the official view maintains. If addiction does not prove to be a successful adaptation in the long run, many people eventually find some other way of reducing their dislocation, perhaps by changing to a less harmful addiction or by abandoning addiction altogether for another way of living. Thus, the literature on natural recovery that perplexes the official view fits comfortably with the dislocation theory. On the other hand, some people do not succeed in finding ways to ease their dislocation other than ruinous addictions. Their addictions are stubbornly resistant to treatment and punishment, although they can sometimes be managed successfully with intensive treatment, participation in self-help groups, and some unobtrusive coercion.

Although the dislocation theory puts primary emphasis on the social antecedents of addiction, it recognizes the moral courage and fortitude of individuals struggling to overcome or manage their addictions. It deepens the understanding of individual struggles and of the process of psychotherapy by showing that the more fragmented a society is, the more obstacles there are to prevent dislocated individuals from prevailing in these struggles, and the greater the likelihood that such individuals will lapse, or relapse, into addiction.

The dislocation theory also deepens understanding of the data on the genetic influences on addiction. Some people are genetically less suited than others to life in their particular culture or subculture and are therefore more likely to become dislocated and then addicted. Also, some people are genetically intolerant of alcohol and less likely to become addicted to it, because they cannot drink it for pleasure. The same kind of inherited intolerance (or tolerance) would probably apply to many of the activities and occupations to which people might become addicted. The available data on heritability of addiction, with several hundred genes showing some statistically significant relationship to one addictive habit or another, in one situation or another, is best understood in these complex ways, rather than by positing a simple "predisposition to addiction."[51]

Although the connection between dislocation and addiction is easily demonstrated in historical studies of aboriginal people and agrarian societies, it is by no means confined to premodern settings. Through-out the developed countries, dislocation plays havoc with delicate ties linking all classes of people to society, nature, and spiritual values. Al-though globalized free-market society produces both winners and los-ers as gauged by economic success, it ultimately produces only losers when dislocation is the measure. The political economist Karl Polanyi perceived the growing dislocation among rich capitalists as well as poor workers from the earliest beginnings of the free-market system, writing that "the most obvious effect of the new institutional system was the destruction of the historical character of settled populations and their transmutation into a new type of people, migratory, nomadic, lacking in self-respect and discipline—crude, callous beings *of whom both la-bourer and capitalist were an example*" (emphasis added).[52] As the basic markets in goods, labor, and capital have become securely established in the globalizing world economy, new kinds of markets for services, intellectual property, popular culture, and intimate relations have fur-ther amplified dislocation at every social level.[53] As these new markets further encroach upon social life, rich and poor people alike are find-ing themselves not only commodified but also capitalized. No longer commodified as "labor," many people now find themselves upgraded, dubiously, to "human resources." One's friends can be assessed, along with other assets, as "social capital." The tenor of one's inner life can be calculated by how rich it is in "emotional capital."

As markets extend their reach into society, governments extend their ability to manipulate social life in support of them, however much dis-location and addiction may result. The governments of rich countries employ carefully engineered techniques to keep people buying, selling, working, borrowing, lending, consuming, moving, learning, immigrat-ing, reproducing, and saving in ways that seem to maximally benefit the markets, increase gross domestic product, and support the latest eco-nomic "recovery."[54] This economic engineering invisibly undermines what remains of historical culture, as well as new traditions that might otherwise spontaneously arise, thereby further increasing dislocation and fostering addiction.

Free-market society not only manages people's personal and social lives in the interests of the economy; it also destabilizes the economy itself. For rich and poor alike, in great cities and small towns, people's jobs disappear on short notice, lifelong employees' pensions disappear, families and communities live with financial uncertainty, and people routinely change spouses, neighborhoods, occupations, co-workers, technical skills, status, reference groups, languages, nationalities, therapists, spiritual beliefs, corporate loyalties, and ideologies as their lives progress. Deregulation of financial capital in the 1980s enormously inflated the global free market in stocks, bonds, and debt obligations. Unregulated speculation in these global markets has brought devastating volatility and long-term uncertainty into local and national economies. The cataclysmic worldwide economic emergency that began in 2008 and continues today has compounded dislocation because many people who lost their jobs, homes, savings, or pensions found that they could no longer trust the institutions that had symbolized economic security, especially banks and regulatory agencies.

Clinical Testimony in Support of the Dislocation Theory

From the earliest days of clinical treatment of addiction to the present, many eminent practitioners have attested to the importance of the central ideas of the dislocation theory for understanding and treating their addicted clients. Naturally, they have described these ideas in their own vocabularies and with their own emphases, but the underlying concepts are evident. To illustrate this, I will use a brief example from the early days of psychotherapy and three from more recent history.

Sigmund Freud's *Civilization and Its Discontents* was published in 1929, near the end of Freud's long career of clinical practice and theoretical writing. Freud argued that for civilization to function effectively, it *must* deprive people of the instinctive satisfactions of pre-civilized life. He thought that people who could not find effective ways of dealing with this deprivation must inevitably resort to neurotic and even psychotic behaviors, among them the consumption of intoxicating amounts of psychotropic drugs and alcohol, in desperate attempts to cope.

Freud was not a revolutionary. He saw modern civilization as a magnificent accomplishment, with previously unimaginable benefits, in which civilized human beings did not have to live in fear of predators and hunger. Civilization, Freud observed, offers not only safety and food but also beauty, cleanliness, order, economic productivity, science, art, philosophy, and religion. But why does such a magnificent accomplishment produce so much unhappiness? Freud pointed out that to produce its many benefits, civilization must reorganize and regulate social relations so that everyone can work productively for the common good. But regulation inevitably creates pain by restricting many libidinal needs. Indeed, Freud saw civilization as almost at war with human nature, writing that "this cultural privation dominates the whole field of social relations between human beings . . . . [I]f the deprivation is not made good economically, one may be certain of producing serious disorders."[55]

Freud discussed many healthy ways in which people cope with civilization's stringent suppression of instinctual impulses. Healthy coping mechanisms include intense devotion to work, science, intellectuality, sexual love, and the development of refined cultural sensitivities.[56] But when people are chronically unsuccessful in dealing with civilized deprivations, the need for "palliative remedies" leads them to use psychopathological ways of coping, including addiction. He wrote that "those whose efforts to obtain happiness come to nought in later years still find consolation in the pleasure of chronic intoxication, or else they embark upon that despairing attempt at revolt—psychosis."[57]

Generally speaking, Freud believed that the psychological misery of civilized life must be accepted as the inevitable cost of civilization's bounty and that people could deal with the worst of their psychological problems through psychotherapy. Yet his thinking took an unexpected turn at the end of *Civilization and Its Discontents.* There, he raised the possibility that civilization makes people miserable because *civilization itself* is dysfunctional. Therefore, he suggested, the psychology of the future could be called on not only to diagnose pathological individuals reductionistically but also to diagnosis pathological civilizations, societies, and cultures and to offer social remedies: "To analytic dissection of the neuroses [of civilizations], therapeutic recommendations might follow which could claim a great practical interest. . . . [W]e may expect that one day someone will venture upon this research into the pathology of civilized communities."[58]

Freud belongs to the distant past of clinical theory and practice. However, many of his successors made use of similar ideas in their own approaches to understanding and treating addiction. When I give public speeches on dislocation theory, many addiction counselors, social workers, and professional psychologists and psychiatrists mention, with some excitement, that they are using the same ideas in their own work, even if they have not taken the time to make them explicit to their clients, their colleagues, or even themselves.

One partial concretization of the ideas of dislocation theory is called "community reinforcement." This approach, which emerged in the 1970s in the context of treatment for drug and alcohol addictions, is explicitly designed to help the client establish new drug- and alcohol-free social contacts and to strengthen and improve relations between clients and their families and friends.[59] Therapists enlist the help of members of clients' communities whenever possible. There is some evidence that the community reinforcement approach outperforms most conventional types of treatment that are not directed at overcoming dislocation, although these results have not been entirely consistent.[60]

Treatment of aboriginal people in Canada with addictions to alcohol and drugs often emphasizes the restoration of *cultures* that have been badly damaged by colonial practices as well as the re-establishment of interpersonal connections that have been ruptured through residential schooling and longstanding dysfunctionality within families. Perhaps the leading agency in this type of treatment is Round Lake Treatment Centre, in British Columbia, which has adapted as its slogan "Culture Is Treatment." S. R. Schaubel has written that "Aboriginal-led treatment facilities such as Round Lake Treatment Centre are utilizing reconnection to culture and community to ease the emotional pain of dislocation. The guiding philosophy at Round Lake [and its] ten sister centers across [British Columbia] is 'culture is treatment.' Programs focus on traditional values, cultural practices, spirituality, and activities that enhance positive views of Aboriginal peoples, feelings of self-esteem and identity."[61]

Marilyn Herie and Wayne Skinner are highly experienced Canadian addiction counselors and agency directors who are making dislocation theory more explicit in their conceptualization of treatment for addiction. In their introductory chapter to the newest edition of their text *Fundamentals of Addiction: A Practical Guide for Counsellors*, they introduce a conceptual framework they call "Biopsychosocial *Plus*." The *plus* stands for retaining the key elements of, but also going beyond, an older "biopsychosocial model" to include "culture and spirituality."

They write that they "also extend the social dimension to emphasize socio-structural and macro-societal factors, especially those rooted in historical and contemporary socio-economic inequalities. These are essential considerations for understanding and addressing the social determinants of health."[62]

The essential ideas of dislocation theory show up both in their discussion of prevention and in their discussion of counseling treatment. In discussing prevention, Skinner and Herie point out that "building healthy families and communities through effective health promotion policies and practices is the most fundamental step that can be taken to reduce addiction behaviours in a society."[63] Unfortunately, they stop short of exploring the political changes that may be necessary to make more effective health-promotion policies and practices possible.

In discussing treatment, Skinner and Herie stress the new trend in therapy toward building "recovery capital" in clients. Recovery capital is a concept drawn from research on natural recovery by Richard Granfield and William Cloud.[64] It refers to the personal and social resources that enable a person to put together a socially integrated life that reduces dislocation, thus reducing the need for addiction. This concept, Skinner and Herie say, "reflects a paradigm shift in addiction treatment from a focus on problems and illness to one directed toward solutions and recovery."[65]

Conclusion: Who Is Really Served by the Official View?

Addiction is more accurately and usefully conceptualized by dislocation theory than by the official view. The official view is an outdated construction that has led neither to a stable theoretical consensus nor to efficacious intervention.

I believe that the official view has maintained its status, despite all its problems, largely because it has served a protective function for the modern status quo from the nineteenth century to the present by narrowing the understanding of addiction. Its narrowed, reductionist understanding of addiction protects the modern status quo in two ways. First, it keeps constant attention on the need for individual correction rather than for societal reorganization, notwithstanding the obvious psychological devastation caused by social fragmentation in the modern world. Second, the official view effectively confines modern society's truly massive addiction problems to a relatively small group of drug users (viewed as pathological, morally irresponsible drug addicts), drug traffickers (viewed as morally depraved profiteers), peasant farmers (whose lack of cooperation with the War on Drugs means that their crops may be freely destroyed), and small-time growers and producers (often depicted as organized criminals). Oversimplifying a complex social problem in this manner keeps the spotlight turned away from a globalizing world economic system that maintains its power and profits by mass-producing dislocation, addiction, and a glittering array of products for addicted people to purchase. The spotlight is also turned from the great difficulties many people have in finding a satisfactory place in a dysfunctional society.

The modern status quo is thus shielded from the critical examination that the current global flood of addiction would otherwise provoke. With addicted people safely marginalized as diseased or immoral, or both, and with destructive addictions limited to drugs, there remains no possibility of conceiving addiction as an understandable response to an impossible social milieu or of seeing that successful intervention in the future will have to come more from societal change than from individual treatment.

NOTES

1 Nancy D. Campbell, *Discovering Addiction: The Science and Politics of Substance Abuse Research* (Ann Arbor: University of Michigan Press, 2007), 19.

2 David T. Courtwright, "The NIDA Brain Disease Paradigm: History, Resistance, and Spinoffs," *BioSocieties* 5 (2010): 137–47.

3 *Oxford English Dictionary*, Third Edition, s.v. "addiction."

4 "4. *Roman Law*. The formal delivery of a person or property to an individual, typically in accordance with a judicial decision. Cf. addict *v.* 1. Now *hist.*," Ibid.

5 It is sometimes argued that the idea of addiction was a new social construction or even a "fetish" that grew out of the economic tensions of the nineteenth century. See Harry G. Levine, "The Discovery of Addiction: Changing Conceptions of Habitual Drunkenness in America," *Journal of Studies on Alcohol* 39 (1978): 143–74; Gerda Reith, "Consumption and Its Discontents: Addiction, Identity and the Problems of Freedom," *British Journal of Sociology* 55 (2004): 283–300. However, instances of the use of *addiction* to describe destructive lifestyles centered on alcohol can be found much earlier than the nineteenth century. See Jessica Warner, "'Resolv'd to Drink No More': Addiction as a Pre-Industrial Construct," *Journal of Studies on Alcohol* 55 (1994): 685–91. It was the narrowing of the meaning of the word to apply *only* to compulsive use of alcohol and drugs, in a medical and moral framework, that was new in the nineteenth century.

6 Virginia Berridge and Griffith Edwards, *Opium and the People: Opiate Use in Nineteenth-Century England* (London: Allan Lane, 1987), xxiv–xxvii, chapters 3, 4.

7 Ibid., 51–54.

8 Ibid., xxvii.

9 Paul Starr, *The Social Transformation of American Medicine: The Rise of a Sovereign Profession and the Making of a Vast Industry* (New York: Basic Books, 1982).

10 Berridge and Edwards, *Opium and the People*, 154–55.

11 William L. White, *Slaying the Dragon: The History of Addiction Treatment and Recovery in America* (Bloomington, Ill.: Chestnut Health Systems/Lighthouse Institute, 1998).

12 Writing as a reporter under the pseudonym Boz, Charles Dickens assembled a composite description of nineteenth-century alcoholics in an article titled "The Drunkard's Death." It is available in *The Dent Uniform Edition of Dickens' Journalism: Sketches by Boz and Other Early Papers, 1833–1835*, ed. Michael Slater (London: J. M. Dent, 1994), 180–85. Jessica Warner has described the alcohol consumption of the British "Gin Craze," which began in the eighteenth century. See Jessica Warner, *Craze: Gin and Debauchery in an Age of Reason* (New York: Four Walls Eight Windows, 2002). Some of the descriptions of present-day alcoholics strikingly resemble those of Dickens and Warner in their writings about an earlier age; see, for example, Lorna Crozier and Patrick Lane, *Addicted: Notes from the Belly of the Beast* (Vancouver: Greystone Books, 2001).

13 Paul Aaron and David Musto, "Temperance and Prohibition in America: A Historical Overview," in *Alcohol and Public Policy: Beyond the Shadow of Prohibition*, ed. Mark Harrison Moore and Dean R. Gerstein (Washington: National Academy Press, 1981), 125–81 (see especially 138–39); Berridge and Edwards, *Opium and the People*, 160.

14 White, *Slaying the Dragon*.

15 Berridge and Edwards, *Opium and the People*, 154.

16 Alcohol was a drug according to definition 1b of *drug* in the *Oxford English Dictionary*.

17 *Drug-addiction* in this moralistic sense did not appear in the 1884 fascicule or in the main text of the 1928 edition. It first appeared in the 1933 supplement.

18 Berridge and Edwards, *Opium and the People*, chapter 13; White, *Slaying the Dragon*.

19 National Institutes of Health, *The National Institutes of Health: A Resource Guide* (Washington: Association of American Medical Colleges, 2005), 38, https://www.aamc.org/research/adhocgp/pdfs/nida.pdf.

20 Bruce K. Alexander et al., "The 'Temperance Mentality': A Comparison of University Students in Seven Countries," *Journal of Drug Issues* 28 (1997): 265–82; Christopher Russell, John B. Davies, and Simon C. Hunter, "Predictors of Addiction Treatment Providers' Beliefs in the Disease and Choice Models of Addiction," *Journal of Substance Abuse Treatment* 40 (2011): 150–64.

21 The book, *Addiction: Why Can't They Just Stop?* (New York: Rodale, 2007), is by John Hoffman and Susan Froemke. The national publicity campaign, the film series, the website, and the series of town hall meetings were described at an online

site (no longer accessible) sponsored by a group of prevention and treatment programs in association with HBO. The same ideas in more condensed form are available in a great variety of materials distributed free of charge in the United States—for example, National Institute on Drug Abuse, *Drugs, Brains, and Behavior: The Science of Drug Addiction* (Washington: National Institute of Drug Abuse), http://www.drugabuse.gov/sites/default/files/sciofaddiction.pdf.

22 Hoffman and Froemke, *Addiction*; David Sheff, *Beautiful Boy: A Father's Journey Through His Son's Addiction* (Boston: Mariner Books, 2009), 320–21.

23 Hoffman and Froemke, *Addiction*; Sheff, *Beautiful Boy*, 320–21.

24 See Gene M. Heyman, *Addiction: A Disorder of Choice* (Cambridge, Mass.: Harvard University Press, 2009), 65–67, for quotes from and references to American authorities stating this position.

25 This assumption is repeated throughout Hoffman and Froemke, *Addiction*.

26 Hoffman and Froemke, *Addiction* 17, 139, 148; Nancy D. Campbell, "Toward a Critical Neuroscience of Addiction," *BioSocieties* 5 (2010): 89–104.

27 Hoffman and Froemke, *Addiction*, 70–73, 90–92.

28 Ibid., 56; Courtwright, "The NIDA Brain Disease Paradigm," 137–47.

29 Jim Orford, *Excessive Appetites: A Psychological View of Addictions*, Second Edition (Chichester: Wiley, 2001); Bruce K. Alexander, *The Globalization of Addiction: A Study in Poverty of the Spirit* (Oxford: Oxford University Press, 2010), 34–36, chapters 9, 10; John Bradshaw, *Reclaiming Virtue: How We Can Develop the Moral Intelligence to Do the Right Thing at the Right Time for the Right Reason* (London: Piatkus, 2009); Benoit Denizet-Lewis, *America Anonymous: Eight Addicts in Search of a Life* (New York: Simon and Schuster, 2009). Dr. Gabor Maté has performed an invaluable service by documenting the severity and intractability of his own addiction to one of the most improbable of habits, buying recordings of classical music and listening to them at times that seriously interfered with his medical practice and family life. See Gabor Maté, *In the Realm of Hungry Ghosts: Close Encounters with Addiction* (Toronto: Knopf Canada, 2008).

30 See, e.g., Nora D. Volkow and Roy A. Wise, "How Can Drug Addiction Help Us Understand Obesity?," *Nature Reviews: Neuroscience* 8 (2005): 555–60.

31 Heyman, *Addiction*, chapter 4, 79–80.

32 Robert Granfield and William Cloud, *Coming Clean: Overcoming Addiction without Treatment* (New York: New York University Press, 1999).

33 Berridge and Edwards, *Opium and the People*, 156–57; Howard I. Kushner, "Toward a Cultural Biology of Addiction," *Biosciences* 5 (2010): 8–24.

34 Hoffman and Froemke, *Addiction*, 45.

35 Harold Kalant, "What Neurobiology Cannot Tell Us about Addiction," *Addiction* 105 (2009): 780–89; Laura Sanders, "Trawling the Brain: New Findings Raise Questions about Reliability of fMRI as Gauge of Neural Activity," *Science News* 176, no. 13 (2009): 16–20.

36 Paul Krugman, "How Did Economists Get It So Wrong?" *The New York Times Magazine* (2009, September 6): 36.

37 Ben Goldacre, "Cocaine Study That Got Up the Nose of the U.S.," *Guardian* (London), June 13, 2009, 8. World Health Organization, "Forty-eighth World Health Assembly, Committee B, Global Study on Cocaine Use." 1995. Retrieved October 7, 2014, from www.tnl.org/archives/docs/200703081419428216.pdf.

38 Christopher A. Bayly, *The Birth of the Modern World* (Oxford: Oxford University Press), chapter 12; Dwight B. Heath, "A decade of development in the anthropological study of alcohol use, 1970–1980," in Mary Douglas, ed., *Constructive Drink: Perspectives on Drink from Anthropology* (New York: Cambridge University Press, 1987), 16–69; Colin Samson, *A Way of Life That Does Not Exist: Canada and the Extinguishment of the Innu* (London: Verso, 2004). For an extensive review see Alexander, *The Globalization of Addiction*, chapter 6.

39 Alexander, *The Globalization of Addiction*, 158–60; Derrick Jensen, *Endgame: Volume 1, The Problem of Civilization* (New York: Seven Stones, 2006), 153. See also Carl Hart, *High Price: A Neuroscientist's Journey of Self-Discovery That Challenges Everything You Know About Drugs and Society* (New York: HarperCollins, 2013).

40 John B. Davis, *The Myth of Addiction: An Application of the Psychological Theory of Attribution to Drug Use* (London: Routledge, 1997).

41 Allan V. Horowitz et al., "The Impact of Childhood Abuse and Neglect on Adult Mental Health: A Prospective Study," *Journal of Health and Social Behavior* 42 (2001): 184–201; Cathy Spatz Widom, Naomi R. Marmorstein, and Helene Raskin White, "Childhood Victimization and Illicit Drug Use in Middle Adulthood," *Psychology of Addictive Behaviors* 20 (2006): 394–403; Carolyn E. Sartor et al., "Disentangling the Complex Association between Childhood Sexual Abuse and Alcohol-Related Problems: A Review of Methodological Issues and Approaches," *Journal of Studies on Alcohol and Drugs* 69 (2008): 718–27.

42 For an example, see Filmwest Associates, *From Grief to Action* (2002), documentary film, http://www.filmwest.com/Catalogue/itemdetail/2396/.

43 Courtwright, "The NIDA Brain Disease Paradigm," 137–47.

44 Hoffman and Froemke, *Addiction*, 56.

45 Jon Arrizabalaga, "(Re)emerging Diseases: A Global Threat to Public Health, Food Security and Human Development," paper presented at a conference of the Social Trends Institute, "Construction of New Realities in Medicine," Barcelona, April 15–17, 2010.

46 Some scholars are making efforts to broaden the field within the official view by paying greater attention to cultural factors that have shaped the official view and to the role of structural poverty as a risk factor in addiction. These include Caroline J. Acker, "How Crack Found a Niche in the American Ghetto: The Historical Epidemiology of Drug-Related Harm," *BioSocieties* 5 (2010): 70–88; Kushner, "Toward a Cultural Biology of Addiction"; and Courtwright, "The NIDA Brain Disease Paradigm," 137–47.

47 For a more extensive summary of dislocation theory and the evidence for it, see Alexander, *The Globalization of Addiction*, chapters 3–8, or my website, www.globalizationofaddiction.ca.

48 Karl Polanyi, *The Great Transformation: The Political and Economic Origins of Our Times* (Boston: Beacon, 1944); Dany-Robert Dufour, *L'Art de réduire les têtes: Sur la nouvelle servitude de l'homme libéré à l'ère du capitalisme total* (The art of shrinking

heads: On the new servitude of the free man in an era of total capitalism) (Paris: Éditions Denoël, 2003); Naomi Klein, *The Shock Doctrine: The Rise of Disaster Capitalism* (Toronto: Knopf Canada, 2007), chapter 1.

49 Erik H. Erikson, *Childhood and Society*, Second Edition (New York: Norton, 1963); Erikson, *Identity: Youth and Crisis* (New York: Norton, 1968).

50 Klein, *The Shock Doctrine*, chapter 1.

51 Kalant, "What Neurobiology Cannot Tell Us about Addiction."

52 Polanyi, *The Great Transformation*, 128.

53 Dufour, *L'art de réduire les têtes*; Dany-Robert Dufour, "Servitude de l'homme libéré: A l'heure du capitalisme total" (Servitude of the free man: In the hour of total capitalism), *Le Monde diplomatique* (Paris), October 2003, 3; M. Abley, "Where's the Rage When You Need It?," review of *The Defiant Imagination: Why Culture Matters*, by Max Wyman, *Globe and Mail* (Toronto), April 3, 2004, D4; B. Fawcett, "Saving Culture from the Market," review of *Blockbusters and Trade Wars: Popular Culture in a Globalized World*, by Peter S. Grant and Chris Wood, *Globe and Mail* (Toronto), April 3, 2004, D5; D. Ticoll, "Flatism Will Get You Everywhere," review of *The World Is Flat: A Brief History of the Twenty-First Century*, by Thomas L. Friedman, *Globe and Mail* (Toronto), April 30, 2005, D14.

54 James R. Beniger, *The Control Revolution: Technical and Economic Origins of the Information Society* (Cambridge, Mass.: Harvard University Press, 1986); Pierre Bourdieu, "L'essence du néolibéralisme" (The essence of neoliberalism), *Le Monde diplomatique* (Paris), March 1998, 3; Murray Dobbin, *The Myth of the Good Corporate Citizen: Democracy under the Rule of Big Business* (Toronto: Stoddard, 1998), chapter 3.

55 Sigmund Freud, *Civilization and Its Discontents* (Chicago: Great Books, 1929/1952), vol. 54, 767–802, at 781.

56 Ibid., 788.

57 Ibid., 776.

58 Ibid., 801.

59 The theoretical foundation of the community reinforcement approach is, however, entirely different from that of the dislocation theory, in that community reinforcement is based on Skinnerian behaviorism and cognitive behavioral therapy.

60 William R. Miller and Robert J. Meyers, "The Community Reinforcement Approach," *Addiction Research and Health* 23 (1999): 116–21; Michael Dennis et al., "The Cannabis Youth Treatment (CYT) Study: Main Findings from Two Randomized Trials," *Journal of Substance Abuse Treatment* 27 (2004): 197–213.

61 S. R. Schaubel, "Culture Is Treatment" (unpublished article, University of British Columbia, 2013), 10.

62 Wayne Skinner and Marilyn Herie, "Biopsychosocial *Plus*: A Practical Approach to Addiction and Recovery," in *Fundamentals of Addiction: A Practical Guide for Counsellors*, Fourth Edition, ed. Marilyn Herie and Wayne Skinner (Toronto: Centre for Addiction and Mental Health, 2013), 3–4.

63 Ibid., 13.

64 Granfield and Cloud, *Coming Clean*.

65 Skinner and Herie, "Biopsychosocial *Plus*," 23.

PART III

The Need for a More Holistic Ethical Discourse

9

Bioethics and Medicalization

JOHN H. EVANS

Medicalization is, according to its leading contemporary sociological analyst, "a process by which nonmedical problems become defined and treated as medical problems, usually in terms of illnesses or disorders."[1] Clearly this process is consistent with the rise of reductionism and the decline of holism. Classic examples of medicalization are the process whereby child misbehavior came to be defined as a medical problem, treatable with drugs like Ritalin, and where alcoholism (partly) changed from being a moral problem to a disease. The result is that we increasingly live in a society where more and more phenomena are under the ultimate control of the medical profession. We are the walking sick or potentially sick—much more so than our grandparents, who did not know that they had various medical problems that had not yet been invented, like ADHD, obesity, and hypertension. These were phenomena not under the aegis of medicine.

While scholars have examined medicalization for many decades, Peter Conrad argues that the "engines" of medicalization have shifted in recent years. Before the 1990s, medicalization was driven by the medical profession's pursuit of power and authority, the activities of social movements that have interests in phenomena being labeled "diseases," and struggles between professions. From the 1990s forward, the emergent engines of medicalization are, first, the pharmaceutical industry and other companies with interests in the expansion of medical categories like adult ADHD. The second engine is consumers' demanding medical interventions for personal and social "problems," like big noses solved through plastic surgery. Third is managed care, as these companies decide that medicalizing some problems (like obesity treated with bariatric surgery) is cheaper than paying for the negative health consequences of the phenomena.[2]

Medicalization thus continues unabated. Why? One part of the explanation is undoubtedly the social power of the various institutions that benefit from this process, like the pharmaceutical industry. While the medical sociologists who study medicalization have focused on this and similar explanations, I want to focus on another contributory facet. In the industrialized West, and in the United States in particular, many resources have been spent on developing the field of public bioethics as a "watchdog" of medicine and science. Because the profession of bioethics is "on the job" of safeguarding the public's ethics in medicine, this relatively new profession supplants other potential critics of medicine. In short, bioethics is supposed to be an external critic of medicine and science, and some people in this field have indeed raised questions about medicalization. However, in this chapter I will show that the nature of public bioethics as it has developed makes it largely incapable of offering an effective critique of medicalization. This is clear from the fact that while bioethics is capturing tasks from medical sociology one by one, one topic that remains the province of medical sociologists and not bioethicists is medicalization.[3] To use the terms I will develop in this chapter, the problem is that public bioethics has become a subordinate profession to science and medicine, and its dominant form of ethical argumentation is the same as that which would be used by science and medicine. Bioethics can then not discourage medicalization. For bioethics to contribute to a critique of medicalization, as well as to a broader critique of reductionism, would require severing public bioethics from science and medicine.

Medicalization as Professional Jurisdiction

Medicalization needs to be more precisely specified. I consider medicalization to be the same phenomenon as what sociologists of the professions would call medicine and science's "gaining jurisdiction." Andrew Abbott, in his influential book *The System of Professions*, argues that what is most important about professions is that they provide "jurisdiction," which is the link professionals make between themselves and what we would call their "work," but which can be more specifically thought of as a series of acts.[4] For example, and critically for this essay, physicians have established jurisdiction over healing disease in bodies through cutting into these bodies with knives. The reason this jurisdiction exists is that the audience for the profession thinks it should. For physicians and many other professions, the relevant audience is the general public—the public is convinced that physicians would do better at surgery than lawyers would. Similarly, they want lawyers, not nuclear engineers, to create their estate plans. Critically, a profession uses its "system of abstract knowledge" to legitimate its claim of jurisdiction over certain acts. Medicine has medical science, and lawyers have law. Professions are in constant competition with other professions over jurisdiction. While lawyers are not in competition with physicians over the same acts, physicians have been competing with chiropractors for years, and acupuncturists have recently joined the fray. However, medicine has been one of the most successful professions at gaining new jurisdictions over new acts by defeating competitors—in other words, medicalization. How the link is made between a particular "system of abstract knowledge" and acts is not so important for my present purposes, and the recent medicalization literature emphasizes that it is not only the profession that "benefits" from the link and that tries to make the link, but also activists and others. "Medicalization" is a specific instance of what most professions try to do—gain jurisdiction over acts.

The Emergence of the Jurisdictional Challenge to the Professions of Science/Medicine

To understand the role of the bioethics profession in the jurisdictional expansion of the medical profession, we must go back a number of decades. The 1960s was a time of great scientific innovation into areas of the human body, and these innovations seemed revolutionary. Scientists thought that humans would soon have technologies of mind control, human cloning, test-tube babies, artificial organs, human genetic engineering, and parthenogenesis. The transplantation of major body parts had already begun.[5] Ethical issues seemed to abound, and these issues seemed to concern the deepest holistic questions of human existence. For example, a prominent scientist wrote in the proceedings of a conference—appropriately titled *Man and His Future*—that "[T]he world was unprepared socially, politically and ethically for the advent of nuclear power. Now, biological research is in a ferment, creating and promising methods of interference with 'natural processes' which could destroy or could transform nearly every aspect of human life which we value. Urgently it is necessary for men and women . . . [t]o consider the present and imminent possibilities."[6]

These early conversations were dominated by scientists, who occasionally decided to let others in. In other words, scientists were attempting to obtain full jurisdiction over the ethics of scientific work. Of course, other professions had a long-established jurisdiction over ethics, most notably theology. Indeed, many of the scientists were interested not just in maintaining jurisdiction over the ethics of scientific work but in expanding their jurisdiction to cover tasks previously covered by the profession of theology. These scientists thought science should produce a sense of meaning and ethics for human society given that, from their perspective, religion had been made irrelevant by Darwin. As one interpreter of this era put it, some of these scientists thought that "the 'direction' of evolution, both biological and cultural, is the 'scientific' foundation upon which to reestablish our system of ethics and to rest 'our most cherished hopes.'"[7]

Similarly, the inventor of in vitro fertilization, Robert Edwards, complained that "many non-scientists see a more limited role for science, almost a fact-gathering exercise providing neither values, morals, nor standards. . . . My answer . . . is that moral laws must be based on what man knows about himself, and that this knowledge inevitably comes largely from science." He concluded by endorsing the views of the biologist Sir Julian Huxley that "Today the God hypothesis has ceased to be scientifically tenable, has lost its explanatory value and is becoming an intellectual burden to our thought."[8] In turn, the theologians recognized this attempt at jurisdictional expansion for what it was and fought back with a critique of the scientists, creating the first what we would now call "bioethical debate." For a number of reasons that I describe in depth elsewhere, the theologians succeeded in bringing public attention to these debates.[9] With public attention came calls for government action, and the government subsequently became involved with the ethics of science and medicine through the use of various executive branch agencies and commissions. In the terms of professional competition, the bureaucratic state became the ultimate consumer of these ethical claims, and it was then the bureaucratic state that conferred jurisdiction by listening to some professions and ignoring others.

This new consumer of ethical claims created a new environment for the professional competition, and soon a new profession emerged that was ideally suited for this new environment—bioethics. A new profession needs a distinct system of abstract knowledge, and events in the mid-1970s led to the creation of a distinct system from that used by theology (and other, more minor professional competitors). The degree of its actual (versus claimed) difference with the system of abstract knowledge used by scientists will be a central point below.

This new system of abstract knowledge started when, in response to the public's concerns, the government first focused on ethical problems in human experimentation and founded the National Commission for the Protection of Human Subjects of Biomedical and Behavioral Research, which first met in 1974. One of the mandated tasks of the commission was to "conduct a comprehensive investigation and study to identify the basic ethical principles which should underlie the conduct of biomedical and behavioral research involving human subjects" and "develop guidelines which should be followed in such research to assure that it is conducted in accord with such principles."[10]

In carrying out its mandate, the commission sought to identify the ethical principles that lay behind established practices. It found three principles that were "among those generally accepted in our cultural tradition": autonomy, beneficence, and justice.[11] The commission decided through scholarly reflection that these were the primary values held by Americans that were at stake in human experimentation. This was not itself a challenge to the theologians, as this would probably have been roughly equivalent to what they would have come up with on their own.

While the commission was deriving these principles, one of the commission's employees, together with another academic, was creating a principle-based approach to ethical problems that could be applied to any public issue.[12] This would be a problem for theology. This textbook, titled *The Principles of Biomedical Ethics* and first published in 1979, would come to be by far the most influential textbook, and the most influential system, in bioethics.[13] The book, now in its seventh edition, produced the same principles as the National Commission, except that the textbook split beneficence into beneficence and nonmaleficence.[14]

Principlism, as well as the other principle systems described by Veatch[15] and alternative methods in bioethics like casuistry, assume that the principles are drawn from "the common morality."[16] The "common morality" "comprises all and only those norms that all morally serious persons accept as authoritative."[17] Beauchamp and Childress also hold that it is "an institutional fact about morality, not merely our view of it, that it contains fundamental precepts" that function above the particularity of subcultures.[18] The four principles "can function as an analytical framework that expresses the general values underlying rules in the common morality."[19] Note the reductionistic quality to this claim—that morality can be expressed by four elements.

Common morality quickly became the system of abstract knowledge of the emerging bioethics profession. Depending on the context, different methods were used to determine the common morality. For example, some bioethics commissions claimed that consensus among diverse members resulted in the common morality. For instance, a report by the Congressional Office of Technology Assessment describes federal bioethics commissions as "mechanisms to articulate *common values* and foster consensus in the face of growing cultural and religious heterogeneity" (emphasis added).[20] However, the most dominant variant of the common morality system of abstract knowledge was principlism, which was often used by itself or in conjunction with other common morality methods.

Common morality principlism was not how theologians approached the ethics of science and medicine. They wanted a more holistic focus upon the "big questions," which tended to be the equivalent of asking what the principles of Western civilization should be for each scientific issue, instead of assuming a list of principles *a priori*. For example, thinking about germline human genetic engineering—the genetic modification of the "germ" cells (sperm and eggs), wherein modifications would be passed to future generations—was an opportunity to debate what the principles of Western civilization should be in relation to this technology. Should we try to maximize our health? Should we try to adhere to God's will for us? Should we keep ourselves genetically as we are? What sort of person should we engineer anyway?

However, the bureaucratic state does not want to have such fundamental ethical debates about principles. The use of the theologians' form of ethical reasoning by unelected government officials would seem to be perilously close to having unelected officials decide what the ethical principles of society should be. What would be preferable would be for unelected officials making ethical decisions on behalf of the public to be using a system of fixed principles. With fixed ethical principles, they are just following rules. Even better, these fixed principles are portrayed as the universal moral principles of Western civilization. That means that unelected government officials are simply following the implicit wishes of the citizens of the United States. Following fixed principles is also relatively easily for those without ethical or philosophical training and is therefore perfect for bureaucratic action in a variety of environments. To take but one example, every research university in the United States has an institutional review board (IRB), mandated to oversee all research with human subjects, staffed by interdisciplinary faculty members who do not have specialized training in ethics. They follow principlism as a way of ensuring that the public's ethics are not violated. Committee members do not have to debate what the ethics of the society they are representing actually are, but rather they have a checklist of pre-set principles, and they must ensure that the proposed research does not violate any of these principles. With this new system of abstract knowledge, and with the bureaucratic state promulgating this new ethics—often through public law—this new profession of bioethics slowly supplanted theology in the competition for jurisdiction with science and medicine.

The Professional Settlement between Bioethics and Science/Medicine

The motivation for the creation of the jurisdictional challenge to science/medicine by theology, and later by bioethics, was that science and medicine should not have jurisdiction over the ethics of science and medicine. The engine of change was to point to all of the bad ethical decisions that science and medicine had implicitly condoned, such as the infamous Tuskegee experiment, wherein poor black men were tricked into believing that they were being treated for syphilis when they were not, so that doctors could study the effects of the advanced stages of the disease. In that original moment, forty or so years ago, theology started the challenge and was quickly supplanted by bioethics.

Moreover, as many of the histories of bioethics have reported, bioethics took jurisdiction away from science and medicine on the specific topic of human experimentation.[21] Doctors and scientists wanted to retain control of their ethics, but bioethicists won in the court of public opinion and, quite critically, the bureaucratic state and forced the medical/scientific profession to follow the bioethicists' system of knowledge. This is evident today in that all medical research in the United States is essentially legally required to be vetted using the common morality principlist variant of the system of abstract knowledge of the bioethics profession.

However, the bioethics profession ended its challenge to science and medicine nearly as soon as it started. We need to import one last idea from the sociology of the professions—settlements in the jurisdictional space. Professions generally compete for full jurisdiction over particular work. Medicine is the classic case of full jurisdiction, where those not in the profession who engage in acts that the profession has jurisdiction over (like surgery) are put in jail. Some professions—perhaps seeing their limited chances for obtaining full jurisdiction in competition with a strong incumbent—reach settlements with one another regarding where the boundaries between two professions will lie.

The bioethics profession has a settlement with medicine/science that Abbott calls "subordination," wherein a dominant profession gives subsidiary acts to another.[22] The classic case of subordination is doctors and nurses, or doctors and X-ray technicians. Nurses and X-ray technicians do not have their own system of abstract knowledge but rather use that of their superior profession, and the superior profession essentially tells them what to do. If this assessment is right, then bioethics no longer is a watchdog—that is, vying for full jurisdiction—but has rather become part of the science/medicine profession.

Other scholars have claimed that bioethics was originally an oppositional profession dedicated to controlling science and medicine but is no longer. The historian Charles Rosenberg writes that "as a social movement, bioethics developed in the mid–twentieth century as a critical enterprise, a response to felt inhumanities in our system of health care and biomedical research. A response to specific abuses, bioethics has remained practice-oriented; society expects bioethics to solve or at least ameliorate insistently visible problems." However, "bioethics not only questioned authority; it has in the past quarter-century helped constitute and legitimate it. As a condition of its acceptance, bioethics has taken up residence in the belly of the medical whale; although thinking of itself as still autonomous, the bioethical enterprise has developed a complex and symbiotic relationship with this host organism. Bioethics is no longer (if it ever was) a free-floating, oppositional, and socially critical reform movement."[23]

Albert Dzur similarly concludes that "bioethics was born as a social-critical reaction" to developments in medicine but "grew up in a regulatory environment. . . . [I]t became clear, in the words of Daniel Callahan, a pioneer in the field, 'that the field was not going to be dedicated to whistle-blowing—bioethics has not turned out many Ralph Naders.' Rather than being a strong voice of critique, bioethics developed as a form of 'regulatory ethics,' something that allowed ethicists a more powerful internal role in organized medicine."[24] The sociologist Charles Bosk concurs, arguing that "[B]ioethics was a contemporaneous alternative to a more forceful challenge to medicine spearheaded by consumer and patient activists. This later challenge was more confrontational in tone, more insistent on structural change, and more focused on the politics of health care than was the bioethics movement. By assimilating bioethics, organized medicine was able to defang this other, broader challenge."[25]

Dzur sums this perspective up quite nicely with a political science term, referring to the "institutional capture" of bioethics by science and medicine. Linking institutional capture to the inability of bioethics as the supposed watchdog of medicine and science to raise issues that are contrary to the interests of the science/medicine profession, Bosk continues by writing that a captured bioethics has not raised a number of holistic "issues that also can be defined as ethical questions: the presence of so many millions of Americans without health insurance, the multiple ways the production pressures of managed care undercut the possibilities of the doctor–patient relationship that bioethics celebrates, the inequalities in health status between rich and poor, or the replacement of professional values with corporate ones."[26] To which I would add: "and medicalization, which serves the interests of the medical and scientific professions that bioethics is supposedly constraining."

In the House of Medicine

The transformation from an adversarial to a subsidiary jurisdiction with medicine/science is indicated by the fact that in the initial organizational moment of bioethics in the late 1960s and early 1970s, the first research centers were independent of the medical and scientific enterprise. The Hastings Center, arguably the first bioethics center, was free-standing, unrelated to any university or medical school. The Kennedy Institute of Ethics at Georgetown University, founded in the same era, was more associated with philosophy and theology than with the medical school. This has slowly changed over time until we have reached the point where bioethics centers are largely part of medical schools and dependent upon them for their funding.[27] Moreover, while I have not conducted an in-depth research project to demonstrate that this is the case, I believe that the bioethics centers that are part of medical schools are the most mainstream, adhering most closely to the common morality principlist system of abstract knowledge of bioethics, and the free-standing ones—like the Hastings Center—have retained a greater distance from mainstream bioethics.

If the arguments of bioethicists ever strayed far from the interests of the medical/scientific profession, the medical/scientific profession would have already tried to kill off bioethics. With many prominent bioethics centers embedded in medical schools, dependent upon their legitimacy and largess, it seems unlikely that if bioethics and the medical/scientific profession were really competitors, one competitor would allow the other to live in its house.

A great example of this institutional capture can be seen in a project conducted by the Stanford Bioethics Center, which is part of the Stanford School of Medicine. Recall that the original bioethics challenge to the science/medicine jurisdiction essentially claimed that scientists and physicians cannot decide ethics on their own but instead need an outside perspective, as exemplified by something like the institutional review board. As the historian David Rothman writes, "[D]ecisions that had traditionally been left to the individual conscience of physicians were brought under collective surveillance. Federal regulations, a compulsory system of peer review, [and other mechanisms] replaced the reliance on the researchers' good will and ethical sensibilities."[28]

Revealing how much the jurisdictional settlement has changed, the Stanford Research Ethics Consultation Model that the authors describe in a leading bioethics journal comes down squarely on the physicians and scientists' side of the debate with the early bioethics movement.[29] The authors describe a program wherein bioethicists go to "the benchside" of scientists to help them with ethical problems. Note, in contrast to the original bioethics critique, it is "advisory and collaborative rather than having decision-making authority."[30] This is what many scientists advocated during the early competition with bioethics—ultimately relying upon, to repeat Rothman, "the researchers' good will and ethical sensibilities."[31] Bioethicists argued that the public should control science through independent professions or commissions.

The scope of the Stanford consultation encompasses essentially all issues in science and medicine that are not currently covered by ethical regulatory authority such as IRBs and seems to include the sorts of issues that have been or would be of great concern to the public. An example the authors provide is "should research that would replace neurons in mouse brains with human neurons go forward."[32] This is essentially setting up an ethical mechanism for the residual field of all issues in medicine and science where there is no structural mechanism for public ethical input as with an IRB. Yet, in creating a mechanism to address these questions, scientists get to make their own decisions, in contrast to what happens with the human experimentation issue that bioethicists originally won jurisdiction over.

There is another similarity between the Stanford model and the scientists' proposals of the early 1970s. One scientist wrote in 1971 that "[W]hat is to be feared is that if the biologists do not invent a method of taking counsel of mankind, society will thrust its advice on biologists and other scientists and probably in a manner or form seriously hampering to science."[33] Other scientists voiced similar sentiments.[34] Scientists wanted to design ethical mechanisms not so that the public's ethics could actually have an impact on what scientists did but rather so that the public would be reassured and therefore not "thrust its advice on biologists" by regulating the ethics of science.

Although not explicit, a similar motivation seems to exist in the Stanford model. The authors write that "[c]onsultants will need to be familiar with at least some major areas of interaction among science, technology and society, such as incidents that have led to the development of research regulation or otherwise had major effects on the conduct of research. Awareness of areas of public concern about biomedical science and its application, including research events that have had a major influence on public perception of science, will also be important for consultants."[35] Throughout this statement, the authors' concern is to avoid the public's developing a negative perception of science—read: scientists—and not with what the actual ethical thought of the public is and how it could be brought to bear in scientific research. The last sentence in their article is also telling: "Measuring the value of such service should include . . . whether there is value to the public and any impact on public trust in science."[36] Part of the motivation here seems to be to keep scientists from doing things that will upset the public and so reinforce public trust in scientists. It is not an attempt to have public values influence science, as happened—however imperfectly—with IRBs. This is the instantiation of the scientists' original ethical decision-making model that bioethicists challenged, but now thirty-five years later it is proposed by bioethicists themselves.

The Stanford ethics consultation service reflects the powerlessness of bioethics in the face of its old nemesis and its new subsidiary role, akin to the relation of X-ray technicians to the superior profession of medicine. The new ethical consultation service is described by its authors as "providing a service (just as biostatistics does)" that best meets "the needs of those who request the service."[37] The authors write that it will be accepted only if it does not confront. They note that commentators have objected to strangers at the bedside as intruding into the domain of the physician. Even more tellingly, they reach back to a famous internal ethical critique of human experimentation written by a physician, Henry Beecher, in 1966 for an ethical model. Note that this critique was written *before* the theological jurisdictional challenge to science/medicine really took hold. They note, correctly, that Beecher's famous 1966 critique was not intended to set up independent oversight of medical researchers but to promote "the inculcation of virtue as an essential part of the practice of good science."[38] This rejects the lessons the early bioethicists took from Beecher's revelations—that physicians could not be trusted to make their own decisions and that ethics could reflect the public's values only if it were given regulatory teeth. Here a team of bioethicists is arguing for a return to an era before the original bioethics challenge to science and medicine ever happened. Institutional capture is complete.

The Identical Ethical Systems of Bioethics and Science/Medicine

Moreover, the current principles were largely derived from what were at the time "best practices" of scientists and physicians, so principlism is a system that scientists and physicians could have come up with on their own. The National Commission—which first articulated the principles—conducted a number of investigations of the treatment of human research subjects, examining whether, for example, subjects had actually given their informed consent, or whether the risk was actually as minimal as was claimed by the researchers. The nascent bioethics profession *did* innovate in creating the principle of "autonomy" to justify the by then longstanding practice of informed consent, but if one starts with informed consent, only a limited range of principles can be created. Similarly, "beneficence"—doing good and avoiding harm—has always been central to medicine as embodied in strictures like "First, do no harm," traditionally attributed to the Hippocratic oath. The conflict with bioethics was not over the content of the principles but rather that science and medicine—like all professions—wanted autonomy (e.g., jurisdiction), so that they could use their own discretion in their work. My reading of the early days of the nascent bioethics profession is that bioethicists forced the scientists and physicians to actually clarify and rigorously apply the procedures that were already in place.

One exception for medical research was the procedure of selecting research subjects. Many of the scandals that emerged in the 1960s and 1970s involved research on people who lacked social power, like orphans, prisoners, and poor African American men. The Belmont report emphasized a somewhat new and quite unarticulated practice of applying justice to the selection of research subjects. Researchers could not use orphans for research simply because the orphans were readily available. This restriction was justified with the principle of "justice." I think this principle did force some changes in medical research, but when principlism expanded beyond the clinical jurisdiction, justice was largely ignored. I concur with Albert Jonsen, one of the inventors of principlism, that "[J]ustice was the neglected sibling among the principles of bioethics, always acknowledged but seldom given significant tasks or much praise. Bioethics had so concentrated on the relationship between patient and physician that the wider world of fair and just institutions [was] neglected."[39] It is easy to see why "justice" would be ignored outside of clinical ethics, for many applications of this principle would seriously interfere with the modern medical research enterprise, dedicated as it so often is to helping the rich people on the planet and not the poor who lack drinking water, electricity, and other necessities.

In sum, while bioethics did force the science/medicine profession to rely in principle upon the ethics of the public (via bioethical systems of argumentation), the content of the most dominant bioethical system (principlism) closely follows what was then the existing scientific/medical ethics.

The Bioethics–Science/Medicine Jurisdictional Settlement and Medicalization

It is important to note that bioethics is reactive to the inventions of science and medicine. It is not the case that bioethicists dream up possible technological inventions or procedures that no scientist thinks are in the pipeline—like transplanting chimpanzee brains into humans—and then write ethical analyses of the scenarios. To the extent that participants in these debates engage in fairly pure speculation, they are probably not mainstream bioethicists and more likely hold a position as philosophers or some other not so applied profession. That said, it does not take much from a scientist to get a bioethical debate going. For example, at the height of a heated debate about germline human genetic engineering, it was not even possible to safely conduct the far less technically challenging genetic modification of human somatic cells.[40]

Instead, the way bioethical debate evolves is that some scientist says that his or her research shows that in X number of years, it will be possible to do Y. Y is not initially thought of as "part of" medicine or science, as it does not fit with the established system of ethics used by the bioethics profession. Debate ensues, and if Y is ethically acceptable, it becomes "part of" medicine and science. If it is deemed unethical, it does not. This is also a description of an important aspect of medicalization. For example, not too many years ago, face transplants were not possible. Then, they became so. Is this "ethical"? If so, then it becomes part of transplant medicine.

How about improving the genetic qualities of the human species? This has not been part of medicine, and such an expansion would constitute medicalization. However, a few decades ago scientists said that they were close enough to being able to engage in germline human genetic engineering that an ethical debate should begin. In this debate, scientists and bioethicists tended to argue that germline human genetic engineering fit with principlism—it forwarded beneficence, nonmalefi-cence, autonomy, and justice. Therefore, it was ethical and, by extension and following bioethics' relationship with science/medicine, germline human genetic engineering should be part of medicine. Somatic human genetic engineering was also not originally part of science and medicine, but it is now, with the common morality principlism solidly in place as its ethics.[41]

Similarly, the line between treating "disease" and engaging in "en-hancement" through genetic technology has been traditionally drawn at "normal functioning" of humans. Because it was part of normal human functioning to not have Tay-Sachs disease, engineering people to prevent them from getting this disease is treating disease, part of medicine, and is ethical. However, it is not part of normal human functioning to have ge-netic immunity from cancer, so despite this being a case of beneficence, it would have fallen on the "enhancement" side of the divide, not seen as ethically acceptable and so not part of medicine. This "normal function-ing" standard is not based on principlism, so we can expect it to come under pressure. Indeed, in these debates people have begun to articulate a divide between acceptable and unacceptable (part of medicine/not part of medicine) based upon whether it treats what the medical profession considers to be a disease. For example, while making people genetically less susceptible to cancer is not a "species-typical function," it has long been a goal of medicine.[42] Therefore, the therapy/enhancement divide is coming to be redefined from "normal functioning" to avoiding any condition that the medical profession defines as a disease. This would expand the permissible "therapeutic" uses of human genetic engineer-ing compared with the earlier distinction. "Beneficence" would be the primary principle, in contrast to the "normal functioning" distinction, which is definitely not part of the principles (but which might be called something like the principle of keeping things the way they are).

The system of abstract knowledge of the bioethics profession then becomes a mechanism by which interested people—be they bioethicists, scientists/physicians, or anyone else—can attach acts to "medicine and science" and thus make them socially acceptable. To take a final exam-ple: Is producing a baby with blue eyes, super-intelligence, and a gift for the piano part of medicine? Some ethicists argue that this is acceptable, essentially because it is required by the principle of autonomy and beneficence and does not violate the principle of nonmaleficence.[43] If it is morally acceptable, then it becomes part of the practice of reproductive health professionals. Indeed, in 2009 a clinic announced that it would start screening embryos for skin, eye, and hair color.[44]

The Features of Principlism That Articulate with Medicalization

Both the structure and the content of principlism make bioethics a force for medicalization. The most important structural feature is that the principles are claimed to be universally applicable to all problems in science and medicine. Let us consider the classic medicalization issue of the "problem" of small breasts, or the "problem" of childbirth. Obviously a more holistic approach would consider these to be social and cultural issues, not medical ones. Both of these can be analyzed using principlism: Who makes the choice to use medical technology (autonomy)? Will it help the person (beneficence)? Will it harm the person (nonmaleficence)? If we limit our ethical analysis to the principles, we can see that both of these "problems" are legitimately part of medicine.

The content of principlism—the four principles that are thought to embody the morality of all civilized people—seems almost designed for medicalization. The primary discursive move made in the medicalization process is to say that a task that has so far been outside of the jurisdiction of medicine causes suffering, and that medicine and science can help (and, in some cases, do a better job of relieving suffering than whoever, if anyone, has jurisdiction now). Misbehaving children cause suffering for themselves, their parents, and others around them. The medical profession gained jurisdiction over misbehaving children with the argument that various drugs like Ritalin can control this problem better than previously used methods. Similarly, the "problem" of short children was not a public problem before. But, undoubtedly short children suffer, and medicine had available a solution, the use of human growth hormone for these children.[45]

This urge to relieve suffering is a straightforward application of the principle of beneficence. Because all medicalization is framed as relieving suffering, the only way for the principlism of bioethics discourse to constrain medicalization is if one of the other principles were to do so. Nonmaleficence would seem to be such a constraint, in that medical treatments carry risks. For example, there is personal health risk from breast enhancement surgery. All drugs have side effects. Before a treatment is adopted by the medical/scientific profession, and so becomes available for a medicalized use, it must meet regulated standards for patient safety. Still, treatment risks always remain and must be balanced against potential benefits. There are some limited risks of hormone therapy for short kids, but then there is the benefit of not being the shortest one in the class.

The solution to this dilemma of whether the benefits outweigh the risks is provided by the final principle, "autonomy." It should be the patient who decides (autonomy) whether the benefit (beneficence) is worth the risk (nonmaleficence). It should be the person who wants a differently shaped nose who evaluates the risk/benefit ratio. Want to use Viagra despite the risks? It is for you to decide. Autonomy then offers no constraint whatsoever on medicalization, because if someone wants medicine to engage in an act—and medicine is willing—then it will happen.

In theory, the true constraint on medicalization within principlism is the principle of "justice." What would be required is a conception, for example, of where spending scarce medical and scientific resources on cosmetic surgery violates the principle of "justice" because it is more just that those monies be spent on the diseases of low-income countries. Needless to say, in at least American society, that is a total nonstarter. Americans already accept vast differential access to health care by socioeconomic class. If bioethicists really made arguments like this, nobody would take them seriously. There is a reason why "justice" as a principle is not used beyond recruitment into research studies. In sum, as long as bioethicists continue to use the common morality principlist system of abstract knowledge, there is no way to make an ethical argument against medicalization.

In a more indirect way, the bioethics profession fosters medicalization simply because it crowds out other professions that are more likely to critique medicalization, most notably the humanistically inclined faction of medical sociologists. The reality of the public sphere is that only so many stories about the ethics of science and medicine can be printed, only so many ethical experts can be in the Rolodex of the reporters, and only so much money is available for those who examine medicine and science from a social and ethical perspective. Quite simply, bioethics squeezes out others, so the existence of a bioethics profession that cannot critique medicalization limits the amount of critique that will occur.

Harnessing Principlism to Constrain Medicalization

Obviously, medicalization is the result of many social forces more powerful than ethics, such as the marketing power of pharmaceutical companies that help market diseases to the American consumer. However, ethics is a powerful component of medicalization, for if an act cannot be described as "ethical" by medicine, it will not become a part of medicine. Creating a form of ethics of medicine and science that does not inexorably lead to medicalization will go a long way toward combating medicalization.

I propose a solution that actually has the structure of principlism. Principlism is here to stay. It fits with the way bureaucracies work, and it is easily calculable and applicable by non-experts. However, it is in the interests of both the bioethics and medical/scientific professions for principlism as it is to continue, and this is what I propose to change. What I propose is a severing of the symbiotic relationship between science/medicine and bioethics by having bioethics derive principles that may not only not be held by scientific institutions, but which may not be in their interest. Bioethics would continue to operate as it has, albeit potentially without the largess of the medical and scientific establishment. Principlism can be modified in such a way that it does not automatically support medicalization. The first step would be to remove its claims to universality across all problems. There is no social reason for this aspect of common morality principlism, and it is a remnant of the birth of principlism from analytic philosophy. There is no reason why there could not be different principles for different medical and scientific phenomena. For example, the current four principles were created with human experimentation in mind. If we were to ask members of the public what they thought the underlying principles should be in deciding the ethics of human genetic engineering, they would be unlikely to create the same list.

The creation of more and different principles for each issue would be inherently more holistic and give people more ethical leverage with which to question and restrain medicalization. For example, let us say that we were to conduct a survey to find out what the deep ethical principles of the public are for germline human genetic engineering. Autonomy, beneficence, and nonmaleficence would probably be on the list. Perhaps too would something like "keeping humans as they are," which was implicit in the "normal human functioning" standard. This sort of principle was obviously not relevant to human experimentation, but in the context of the engineering of the future physical characteristics of the human species it would act as an ethical break upon the principles of autonomy and beneficence that would otherwise send this phenomenon down the medicalization track. It is not too difficult to imagine different principles, and the medical/scientific profession would be hard-pressed to argue against this move. If adopted by bioethicists, this new form of principlism would be an ethical constraint on medicine and science—but it would probably be a more forceful constraint than principlism is now, given that the current common morality principlism does not really constrain the medical profession.

Conclusion

Most scholars of medicalization seem to have reached the normative conclusion that they do not want to live in a world in which increasing swaths of human experience are under the logic of medicine. There are, or should be, experiences that use an older logic, that are under the jurisdiction of another profession or under no jurisdiction at all. We can all fear the medicalization of love.

How one would stop medicalization remains unclear, as it seems to be the result of broad and powerful social forces. In this chapter I have identified one contributing factor to medicalization, bioethics, and have outlined a reformist agenda for bioethics that constrains its use as an engine of medicalization.

NOTES

1 Peter Conrad, "Medicalization and Social Control," *Annual Review of Sociology* 18 (1992): 209–32 at 209.

2 Peter Conrad, "The Shifting Engines of Medicalization," *Journal of Health and Social Behavior* 46 (2005): 3–14.

3 Adam Hedgecoe, "Medical Sociology and the Redundancy of Empirical Ethics," 167–75 in *Principles of Health Care Ethics*, Second Edition, ed. R. E. Ashcroft, A. Dawson, H. Draper, and J. R. McMillan (West Sussex: Wiley, 2007).

4 Andrew Abbott, *The System of Professions: An Essay on the Division of Expert Labor* (Chicago: University of Chicago Press, 1988).

5 See, e.g., Albert R. Jonsen, *The Birth of Bioethics* (New York: Oxford University Press, 1998).

6 Gordon Wolstenholme, *Man and His Future*, ed. G. Wolstenholme (London: J. & A. Churchill Ltd., 1963), v.

7 Howard L. Kaye, *The Social Meaning of Modern Biology: From Social Darwinism to Sociobiology* (New Brunswick, N.J.: Transaction Publishers, 1997), 42.

8 Robert Edwards, *Life Before Birth: Reflections on the Embryo Debate* (New York: Basic Books, 1989), 165–66.

9 See John H. Evans, *Playing God? Human Genetic Engineering and the Rationalization of Public Bioethical Debate* (Chicago: University of Chicago Press, 2002). See also Evans, "After the Fall: Attempts to Establish an Explicitly Theological Voice in Debates Over Science and Medicine after 1960," 434–61 in *The Secular Revolution*, ed. Christian Smith (Berkeley: University of California Press, 2003). The previous three paragraphs are derived from this latter piece.

10 Cited in Albert R. Jonsen, "Foreword," ix–xvii in *A Matter of Principles? Ferment in U.S. Bioethics*, ed. E. R. DuBose, R. P. Hamel, and L. J. O'Connell (Valley Forge: Trinity Press International, 1994), xiv.

11 National Commission for the Protection of Human Subjects of Biomedical and Behavioral Research, *The Belmont Report: Ethical Principles and Guidelines for the Protection of Human Subjects of Research* (Washington: U.S. Government Printing Office, 1978), 4.

12 See Tom L. Beauchamp, "The Origins and Evolution of the Belmont Report," 12–25 in *Belmont Revisited: Ethical Principles for Research with Human Subjects*, ed. J. F. Childress, E. M. Meslin, and H. T. Shapiro (Washington: Georgetown University Press, 2005).

13 Renée C. Fox and Judith P. Swazey, *Observing Bioethics* (New York: Oxford University Press, 2008), 168.

14 While *principlism* generally refers to this four-principle system popularized by Beauchamp and Childress, many competing systems in bioethics employ the same logic. For example, Robert Veatch identifies single-principle theories, like utilitarianism and libertarianism, that maximize the values of beneficence and autonomy, respectively. Two-principle theories include the "geometric method" of comparing benefits and harms and Engelhardt's approach, which uses the principles of permission and beneficence. Other systems have five principles (Baruch Brody), six principles (W. D. Ross), seven principles (Veatch's own system), and ten principles (Bernard Gert). (Veatch outlines all this in his essay cited below.) For my purposes I can treat these as all the same in that they are based upon fixed principles that can be used for any bioethical issue. According to Tom Beauchamp, the staff person for the National Commission that created the Belmont Report where the principles were first articulated, while

he was writing the Belmont Report he was simultaneously writing the textbook on principlism which argued that principles are universally applicable (Beauchamp 2005). Therefore it should be said that principlism was invented in the context of a discussion of human experimentation but was not limited to this one issue.

15 Robert M. Veatch, "How Many Principles for Bioethics?" 43–50 in *Principles of Healthcare Ethics*, ed. R. E. Ashcroft, A. Dawson, H. Draper, and J. R. McMillan (West Sussex: Wiley, 2007): 49.

16 See Leigh Turner, "Zones of Consensus and Zones of Conflict: Questioning the 'Common Morality' Presumption in Bioethics," *Kennedy Institute of Ethics Journal* 13(3): 193–218 (2003).

17 Tom L. Beauchamp and James F. Childress, *Principles of Biomedical Ethics* (New York: Oxford University Press, 2001), 3.

18 Ibid., 4.

19 Ibid., 12.

20 U.S. Congress, Office of Technology Assessment, *Biomedical Ethics in U.S. Public Policy—Background Paper* (Washington: U.S. Government Printing Office, 1993), 7.

21 See Jonsen, *Birth*; David J. Rothman, *Strangers by the Bedside: A History of How Law and Bioethics Transformed Medical Decision Making* (New York: Basic Books, 1991).

22 In my earlier work I wrote that the bioethics profession had what Abbott labels an "advisory jurisdiction" with science wherein bioethics interpreted, buffered, or partially modified actions taken by science/medicine within science/medicine's own full jurisdiction. I no longer think this is quite right. (See Abbott, *System of Professions*, 75.)

23 Charles E. Rosenberg, "Meanings, Policies, and Medicine: On the Bioethical Enterprise and History," *Daedalus* 128(4) (1999): 27–46, at 37–38.

24 Albert W. Dzur, *Democratic Professionalism: Citizen Participation and the Reconstruction of Professional Ethics, Identity and Practice* (University Park: Pennsylvania State University Press, 2008), 212.

25 Charles Bosk, "Sociology and Bioethics," in *Handbook of Medical Sociology* (1999), 64.

26 Ibid.

27 In Bosk's description, "bioethics developed within the institutional structure and with the institutional resources of academic medicine, and this undoubtedly influenced its critical thrust" (see 61).

28 Rothman, *Strangers by the Bedside*, 90.

29 See Mildred K. Cho, Sara L. Tobin, Henry T. Greely, Jennifer McCormick, Angie Boyce, and David Magnus, "Strangers at the Benchside: Research Ethics Consultation," *American Journal of Bioethics* 8(3) (2008): 4–13.

30 Ibid., 8.

31 The following four paragraphs are largely taken from John H. Evans, "Keeping Society from the Benchside," *American Journal of Bioethics* 8(3) (2008): 14–16.

32 Cho et al., "Strangers," 9.

33 Robert G. Edwards and David J. Sharpe, "Social Values and Research in Human Embryology," *Nature* 231 (14/May 1971): 87–91, at 89.

34 Evans, *Playing God?* 80–85.

35 Cho et al., "Strangers," 10.

36 Ibid., 12.

37 Ibid., 8.

38 Ibid., 6.

39 See Jonsen, *Birth*; Rothman, *Strangers by the Bedside*, 413.

40 See Evans, *Playing God?*

41 Ibid.

42 LeRoy Walters and Julie Gage Palmer, *The Ethics of Human Gene Therapy* (New York: Oxford University Press, 1997), 109–11; Eric T. Juengst, "Can Enhancement Be Distinguished from Prevention in Genetic Medicine?" *Journal of Medicine and Philosophy* 22 (1997): 125–42 at 126; Erik Parens, "Is Better Always Good? The Enhancement Project," 1–28, in *Enhancing Human Traits: Ethical and Social Implications*, ed. E. Parens (Washington: Georgetown University Press, 1998), 5.

43 See John H. Evans and Cynthia E. Schairer, "Bioethics and Human Genetic Engineering," 349–66 in *Handbook of Genetics and Society: Mapping the New Genomic Era*, ed. P. Atkinson, P. Glasner, and M. Lock (London: Routledge, 2009).

44 Naik Gautam, "A Baby, Please. Blond, Freckles—Hold the Colic," *Wall Street Journal Online* (12 February 2009).

45 See Peter Conrad, *The Medicalization of Society: On the Transformation of Human Conditions into Treatable Disorders* (Baltimore: Johns Hopkins University Press, 2007).

10

The Dominion of Medicine

Bioethics, the Human Sciences, and the Humanities

JEFFREY P. BISHOP

Despite the extraordinary place that medicine and medical science play in our lives and culture, we routinely find fault with them for falling short of ethical standards. Medicine's influence does not reflect our unqualified approval of it: Indeed, we see signs of ethical lapses everywhere, whether in the cold, impersonal nature of an increasingly technological and bureaucratic medicine or in research practices that exploit the least-empowered members of society. Society's disquiet can be traced to several sources. The biological reductionism of modern medicine, also discussed elsewhere in this volume, is one such source. Another, more surprising, is the series of attempts to *reform* medicine. These reform efforts have been sometimes directed at the reductive nature of medicine and sometimes at the procedural/bureaucratic nature of modern practice. Yet each reform movement has failed because it assumes or has been subsumed into the same biomedical paradigm it set out to reform.

The first ethical critiques of modern medicine came from theologians, beginning in the 1950s, who challenged physicians and scientists on the grounds that they had forgotten that the patient or research subject was first and foremost a person. They also sharply challenged medicine's embrace of the technological imperative at the expense of assisting people in achieving or maintaining health. They raised the question of whether medicine had a sufficiently defined end or purpose and reflected on the human condition and the limits that were needed to keep medicine from violating the goods of persons. These theological critiques had teeth and were often at odds with the implied teleology and value assumptions of biomedicine. Because they were grounded in distinct theological languages, however, they were not easily translated into a secular idiom, a problem in a society whose fundamental conceptions of the human good were in flux and which was strongly susceptible to the growing capacity and promise of biomedicine's technological mastery over the body.

The early theological critiques were ultimately too threatening and too particularistic to have a broad social impact. A secular and pluralistic society was growing wary of any ethical critique of medicine that depended on theological premises. Surely, ran the unspoken consensus, the commonsense shared values of society should be sufficient to guide medicine. By the late 1960s, the very theologians who had called medicine to account began to drop the specifically theological content of their critiques in order to participate in the developing secular arena of bioethics. Bioethics did not work within the framework of the older medical ethics but within a public policy framework and newly emergent "common morality" theories. In this reform movement, theological and robustly metaphysical moral positions—whether Jewish, Christian, Muslim, or neo-Aristotelian—were progressively marginalized. Proponents of such positions were welcome to offer their perspectives on bioethical questions, to be sure, but the approved frameworks for policy and institutional purposes developed in far narrower terms of individual rights and organizational efficiency. Common morality theories have been ascendant in this reform movement ever since.

In addition to the theological and the common morality reforms of medicine, two other reforms arose from *within* medicine. The first, George Engel's biopsychosocial medical model, attempted to bring the social sciences to bear on medicine. In its own way, the biopsychosocial model made direct claims about the nature of human persons, but rather than in the language of dignity of persons, for example, it did so in the language of descriptive social science. Engel hoped that if medicine were attuned to a wider dimension of the human being through careful attention to social and psychological research, medicine would be better situated to meet the needs of the patient in a holistic and ethical way.

The second reform from within medicine was a new humanism in the form of the medical humanities movement. Its guiding principle toward a more ethical and richer quality-of-care was the education of physicians in the humanities. The humanities—literature, art, history, philosophy—would help physicians see more clearly the nature of the human person and allow human values to come to the fore in the clinical encounter. The prescription for medicine was that doctors read more great books, attend art shows, or learn narrative competency in order to reclaim the humanistic ends of medicine.

This chapter will examine each of these reform efforts—theological, public policy bioethics, biopsychosocial, and humanities—and demonstrate the ways in which all were subsumed under the dominion of biomedicine and reordered to serve its animating goods. In addition, I will argue that because bioethics, the human sciences, and the medical humanities live under the dominion of the medical technological complex, any strong challenge they might have represented to biomedicine's epistemology, ontology, and teleology is effectively silenced. They reproduce the very thing they seek to reform.

The "Theological" Reform of Medicine

Theologians were the first bioethicists.[1] In Albert Jonsen's historical account, which is largely noncritical and descriptive, he points to a "Trinity" of mid-twentieth-century theologians—Joseph Fletcher, Paul Ramsey, and Richard McCormick—as the founders of bioethics.[2] In 1949, well before the rise of bioethics as a professional field, Fletcher—an Episcopal priest and theologian—gave a series of important lectures on modern medicine and the kinds of moral and ethical conundrums to which it would give rise.[3] Fletcher was ahead of his time. In 1949, medical technology had not yet advanced to a point where ethical issues had come into clear relief. Fletcher's early work, written while he taught in a divinity school, was directly informed by Christian doctrine and challenged the emerging technological direction of biomedicine. Over time, however—and Fletcher continued to publish on medical moral issues into the 1970s—he moved away from Christian theology. He left his divinity school post and took up residence in a medical school. He eventually adopted an act-utilitarian ethical philosophy (the morality of an act or set of actions is evaluated on the principle of the greatest good for the greatest number of people, where good is defined as the greatest amount of pleasure), eschewing any prohibitive ethical claims that might halt or hinder research or treatment options.[4]

A similar revisionism can be seen in the second of Jonsen's "Trinity," Paul Ramsey, another esteemed Protestant theologian. Ramsey maintained that his Christian commitments shaped all of his work in medical ethics. Like Fletcher before him, Ramsey had great stature as a Christian ethicist long before he began to write on matters arising in medicine. If Fletcher's ethic was a utilitarian one, Ramsey's Christian ethic was a deontological one (the morality of an act or set of actions is evaluated in terms of its adherence to moral rules or duties).[5] Yet as Ramsey moved further into the realm of medical ethics, the actual theological content of his reflections began to diminish, though in a different way than did Fletcher's. In fact, with the exception of the preface to *The Patient as Person*, Ramsey made little appeal to theological themes as he wrestled with such questions as consent to the treatment of children, the definition of death and the care of the dying, vital organ transplantation, and scarce medical resources.[6] In addition, Ramsey turned to the Roman Catholic tradition of moral inquiry—especially its natural law threads. Most Protestant moralists do not embrace natural law approaches to ethics because these approaches do not appeal to special revelation. Natural law holds that norms of conduct are created into human nature and the natural order by God; they reflect His eternal law and can be known by human reason. In turning to natural law, Ramsey embraced a form of moral discourse without direct appeal to specific Christian doctrine.

Ramsey's turn to natural law brings us to the third moral theologian on Jonsen's list: Richard McCormick, a Jesuit priest. McCormick was a representative of the Roman Catholic arm of theological bioethics. Roman Catholic moral inquiry has long worked in the tradition of natural law. Drawing on natural law and the use of natural reason, McCormick and his Protestant friend Ramsey developed a fruitful dialogue in which each began to develop his own distinct ethic. But like Fletcher, Ramsey and McCormick did not appeal to doctrine or any exclusively Christian themes when speaking in the public square.

Each of these thinkers received some acceptance by the medical establishment precisely because they did not or ceased to speak in a specifically theological voice—whether Catholic or Protestant. An important question about these theologians is the one the theologian Stanley Hauerwas, in his characteristically brusque way, once asked of Ramsey: Was there anything distinctively theological in their approach to medical ethics? Hauerwas writes: "So medical ethicists, being the good priests they are, went to where the power is in liberal societies—medical schools. Kings and princes once surrounded themselves with priests for legitimation. Likewise, politicians today surround themselves with social scientists to give those they rule the impression that they really know what is going on and can plan accordingly. Physicians, in an increasingly secular society, surround themselves with medical ethicists. God no longer exists, the sacred universe of values has replaced God, and allegedly ethicists think about values and decisions that involve values."[7] Had, in other words, these theologians so attenuated their public arguments that they were no longer Christian ethicists but medical ethicists who merely subserved a secular medicine and gave it ethical permission? Ramsey, in his defense, believed that there was a remnant of Christianity in the political structures and social institutions in Western democracies, including the institution of medicine. It was this remnant that gave him the authority to do "public ethics," as he called it, even as he longed for the day when a richer Christian ethics would become the "dominant secular" viewpoint.[8] Perhaps the fact that the social and political structures of the West have their origin in Western Christian theological concepts meant that theologians could give voice to the metaphysical moral concerns felt by the public without further recourse to scripture or salvation history. Either way, these influential theologians tended to adopt public forms of reasoning in a nonsectarian, rational, and philosophical, rather than traditional theological, language.

At the same time, other theologians continued in the particularistic, non-universal language of traditional theology, and they came up against the powerful world of medical science, which demanded that theology and metaphysical concerns not get in the way of progress. This point is particularly well developed in another social history of the rise of bioethics: that by John Evans.[9] Evans's history is a different and more critical account than Jonsen's. In Evans's account, under the pressure of the medical/scientific establishment the robust picture of human meaning and purposes of theological ethics was condensed and simplified into broadly acceptable secular ends, and reasoning toward those ends took an increasingly secular form.[10] In other words, Evans holds that the "thick," substantive ends of theology were "thinned out" to accommodate the ends of a secular and rationalistic medicine. But *contra* Evans, the ends of medical technological science are not, in reality, thin.

From the beginning of the bioethical project, many physicians and medical scientists, anxious to protect their turf and prerogatives, perceived theological voices as threats. These scientific thinkers would increasingly marginalize the critical theological voices. For example, the Harvard microbiologist Bernard Davis believed that theologians had both exaggerated the dangers of genetic research and downplayed its possible successes.[11] He even drew an analogy between theological reflection on research ethics and Communist political ideology, arguing that theologians were stifling progress as much, in their way, as the Communists were.[12] The theologians, each of whom called for caution, were pitted against the progressive ideas that animate much of scientific research, with its promises to end suffering for humanity.[13]

The full story involves elements of both Evans's and Jonsen's accounts. The medical establishment insisted that theologians thin out their language in order to participate in the bioethical discussion, thereby marginalizing the distinctive theological contribution and challenge to the commitments and values of medicine and the life sciences. At the same time, when theologians, anxious to be heard, stopped using robust ontological or teleological language in their critiques of contemporary medicine, they ceased to constitute a challenge. An important alternative voice was muted, enabling biomedicine to proceed free of its challenge. In other words, as the morally thick language began to thin, and as theologians began to translate their arguments into secular, rationalistic terms, they forfeited debate about the ends of medicine and allowed medicine's own robust framework to carry the day.

That outcome leads me to disagree with Evans's thesis. Theological ends were not merely translated into generic secular ends. Medical science itself carries with it various kinds of ultimate ends, and these have more substance than is acknowledged. The purposes of biomedicine are veiled in an abstract and utopian language of beneficence, promising cures and a world in which there is no disease or pain or sorrow. It promises unabated happiness and an end to the limits of embodiment. The scientific apologists enacted a particular framework, not "thinner" than but very *different* from the framework of the theologians, and it was that framework which caused McCormick and Ramsey so much consternation. Biomedical science carries with it a very different understanding of the good life from the one reflected in Christian ethics. In fact, the battle between theologians like Ramsey and McCormick and scientists like Davis originated in different understandings of the ends and purposes of medicine.

The political battle between theologians and scientists set in motion two other reform trajectories. The first was an attempt to smooth over deep ethical differences through the development of various common morality theories, which emphasize what we can accept and endorse in common. This effort to reform medicine depended largely on political means, on the work of advisory commissions set up by branches of federal and state governments to negotiate political fights about values, ends, and means with respect to both research and clinical questions. Today, we think of this as bioethics proper. The second trajectory, with two major wings, was an attempt to reform medicine from within the practice itself. I will address the political reform first, and then the two internal reform movements.

Philosophers, Public Policy, and the Secularization of Bioethics

In a 2008 talk, given on the tenth anniversary of the founding of the American Society for Bioethics and Humanities (ASBH), the bioethicist Tod Chambers noted that of all the groups and disciplines—physicians, philosophers, lawyers, humanists from several disciplines, and theologians—that founded ASBH, the theologians were the only ones no longer active.[14] He bemoaned the fact that the substantive content of theological reflection had been lost from bioethics, as the discipline shifted to secular forms of reasoning. Others have made similar points.[15]

The exile was gradual. As already noted, the first era of bioethics began in the 1950s, when critiques of medicine and its ethics came almost entirely from theological circles. The second began in the late 1960s, when key theologians de-emphasized their theological premises in order to accommodate a bioethics grounded in the secular polity of the contemporary West. This overtly pluralistic approach gave way in the 1970s to the third era, when philosophers began to offer common morality theories as antidotes to both the theological bioethics filled with content (as I have claimed) and ordered by robust ends (as Evans claims), on the one hand, and a cacophonous and relativistic pluralism, on the other. The ship of the political establishment skippered in partnership with scientific research agendas would have to steer between the Charybdis of the theologians and the Scylla of relativistic pluralism. Common morality theory would serve as the map.

The most popular of these common morality philosophies found its articulation in Tom Beauchamp and James Childress's influential book *Principles of Biomedical Ethics*, which has gone through many editions. Their approach, known as principlism, is a prime example of the trend toward secular forms of reasoning.[16] They are not alone. There were many other philosophical appeals to secular forms of reasoning, such as those of Robert Veatch and H. Tristram Engelhardt Jr., that attempted to negotiate differences among those who did not share robust metaphysical moral commitments.[17]

Unfortunately, Evans's history focuses his critique of bioethics entirely on principlism, without engaging other theories of common morality or other theories of bioethics designed to negotiate difference. But he does do a good job of showing the ways in which theologians were marginalized by the establishment of various jurisdictional authorities. For a professional bioethicist to call herself a "bioethicist," he observes, she must have a set of tasks over which she can claim some sort of expertise: If bioethicists are professionals, there must be some jurisdiction over which they can claim authority. Evans argues that there have emerged three task spaces over which bioethicists claim jurisdictional authority. Those spaces are health care ethics consultation, also known as clinical ethics consultation; research ethics; and public policy bioethics.[18] Evans describes how each of these task-spaces emerged from this history. Those who do not occupy these jurisdictional task-spaces, he argues, should refer to themselves as "cultural bioethicists," a term that represents a group of thinkers and activists who attempt to place their agenda in the marketplace of ideas but who do not themselves have any political or public policy authority. These days, theological bioethicists would fall into Evans's category of cultural bioethicists.

Evans notes that the task-spaces of health care ethics consultation and of research ethics consultation find their jurisdictional authority in the hospital and in the establishment of the Institutional Review Boards that monitor research involving human subjects, respectively. The exclusion of theological voices from these spaces might be expected in that these spaces are public spaces where there is a commitment to procedural norms (i.e., accepted procedural means to achieve broadly secular ends) but where thicker value commitments are circumscribed and subservient to patient/research subject values and protections. Within these two task-spaces, the work of bioethicists is aimed at the procedural analysis of cases in ethics consultation and research protocols in IRBs. In theory, the clinical bioethicist and the research bioethicist help to clarify moral and ethical problems, but they also seek to rectify these problems through the deployment of various procedures or techniques. In other words, the clinical bioethicist and the research bioethicist do not deploy their own values but help to clarify the values of the various stakeholders and to find negotiated settlements at points of disagreement.

To secure their professional jurisdiction, bioethicists hoped that, just as clinical ethics consultation and research ethics consultation had focused on means and procedures rather than on ends, public policy bioethics would do likewise. However, as Evans notes, with the mobilization of activists bent on influencing public policy, public policy bioethics essentially moved into the political arena, where whoever held political authority would be courted to enact the goals of various partisan groups. Public policy bioethics thus became politicized, and the "predetermined ends" of those holding particular partisan commitments began to be portrayed "as universally held by all people." In other words, predetermined ends were dressed up in common morality language and put on display as the kind of public policy that ought to be implemented.[19]

As both Evans and Jonsen note, in the mid-1970s several public relations crises caused the federal government to assert its authority over the ethics of scientific research.[20] Arguably the first public policy bioethicists emerged with the establishment of the National Commission for the Protection of Human Subjects of Biomedical and Behavioral Research.[21] Out of their deliberations came the initial formulation of the "principles" of bioethics. These principles—respect for persons, beneficence, and justice—came to be thought of as the best means for governing public policy bioethics because they did not require theological or metaphysical content. These mid-level principles—mid-level because they required no foundational grounding—would later emerge as Beauchamp and Childress's four principles (changing respect for persons to autonomy, and adding nonmaleficence).

Philosophically speaking, principlism claims that because its principles are mid-level and do not require specific ontological or teleological commitments, we can negotiate means to achieve politically acceptable ends without getting bogged down by philosophy. Yet, as Engelhardt has shown, the common morality approach of principlism leads only to a veneer of agreement placed over a chasm of disagreement.[22] Moreover, Beauchamp and Childress *implicitly* introduce a good deal of moral content into a purportedly neutral set of principles, meant to help different moral communities negotiate their differences.

Thus, with the establishment of these commissions and the principles that grew out of them, two things happened. First, the robust ends that had typically animated older theological reflection on bioethical issues were pushed further to the margins, and the principlist position ushered in as a means to negotiate difference (while, in fact though not in theory, smuggling in its own moral content). In this way, bioethicists deploying common morality theories have become essential to the social apparatus of biomedicine. Second, the scientists on the commissions were able to protect their own authority over research without the input of theologians or others who would challenge their implicit ends and object to some practices and interventions.

What we see, then, is the birth of a relationship between government commissions and the research and medical establishment, a relationship mediated through public policy bioethics. The point of these politically motivated commissions is to guard against unethical research, while not hampering scientific progress. Virtually every congressional or presidential commission works to attenuate the fears of the public, while not interfering with science. The unwritten rules are that a commission should never question what counts as progress, let alone define that toward which science is progressing.

For example, in the examination of brain death, I have shown elsewhere the great pains to which a public policy commission will go in order not to appear as though it is dealing with ends or robust metaphysical-moral claims.[23] The 1981 President's Commission for the Study of Ethical Problems in Medicine and Biomedical and Behavioral Research examined the definition of death. In their publication, *Defining Death*, the commission stated that it did not want to engage in "arcane philosophy."[24] Yet at the same time the commission deployed a definition of death as whole-brain death, reasoning that the two central features of human life can be "located" in the brain. First, the higher brain is considered the seat of psychological functioning—that is to say, the seat of personhood; second, the brainstem is considered the integrating location of all physiological functioning, the seat of physiological life. The rationale for this definition of whole-brain death thus imported two very different philosophical positions about the nature of human life—personhood as a metaphysical category and vitalism—every bit as arcane as any philosophy the commission claimed it could escape.[25] The operational myth of these commissions, and common morality theories more generally, is that one can debate such questions while setting aside issues of what counts as real or what goals or purposes are in view.

These commissions go a long way toward assuaging public fears, both by establishing a kind of governmental legitimacy and by controlling and limiting discussion. By appealing to authorities outside the medical establishment, public policy bioethicists work to reassure the general public that those with the authority to stop unethical practices have scrutinized medical research and interventions. Meanwhile, those who can most readily critique the ends of medicine, medical science, and medical technology are marginalized as "religious" or engaged in "arcane philosophy." It is indicative that when the President's Council on Bioethics, commissioned during the George W. Bush administration, invited theologians to once again sit on a government committee, there was a great public outcry and much bitter criticism from mainstream bioethicists.[26] Religious voices sitting on such high-level committees were no longer easily tolerated, much less expected. This left the public policy bioethicists, with their common morality theory, neutral posture, and focus on the efficiency and effectiveness of means, to rule out of discussion and preserve untouched the predetermined and unexamined ends of biomedicine.

Human Science, Humanisms, and the Humanities

Attempts to reform medicine through bioethics have ended up reproducing the ontological and value commitments of biomedicine. Much the same can be said for the two movements to reform medicine from the inside, both focused on the doctor–patient relationship. The first internal reform was an effort to apply the social sciences to medicine, the second to apply the humanities. Both began at about the same time in the mid-1970s.

There is an obvious family resemblance among words like *humane*, *humanity*, *humanism*, and *humanities*. Those who use these terms with regard to medicine seem to imagine that if only we could increase "humanism" in medicine we could improve on the "humane" treatment of patients. The similarity of the words elides differences among the terms, differences that complicate their meaning. As Engelhardt has shown, for example, there are many different humanisms.[27] Which one do we mean—Renaissance humanism, French Republican humanism, or the many humanisms of the twentieth century? Both National Socialism and Soviet Communism were humanisms, philosophically speaking. Moreover, what counts as human, what traits or properties one assigns to the human, and what counts as humane treatment are contested. Talk of humane and humanizing and humanism leaves a lot unexplained.

The Biopsychosocial Reform

In 1977, George Engel called for a different model of medicine that promised to humanize an increasingly cold, technological, and reductionist medicine through a biopsychosocial approach.[28] He argued that the biomedical model which focuses on diseases and bodies could not do justice to "the scientific tasks and social responsibilities of either medicine or psychiatry." For both scientific and political reasons, the model had to change. At the time he was writing, Engel believed that medicine was in crisis. Psychiatrists, for instance, were not certain whether "the categories of human distress" that they treated were "properly considered 'disease,'" as other branches of medicine were being called on to avoid the "psycho-sociological underbrush" and to focus only on organic disease.[29]

A dogmatic biological reductionism had resulted in the exclusion of nonphysical disorders from medicine. Biomedicine, Engel claimed, was as much a cultural model of medicine, with its own historical development, as the folk cures of the shaman. Like other cultural models of disease and healing, Western biomedicine was a social response created to deal with the physical and psychological threats presented by diseases of the body and the mind.[30] Thus, the biomedical model of medicine had reached its limits. The biomedical model, in 1977, no longer served the needs of Western societies.

Engel's remedy to reductive biomedicine was the biopsychosocial model of medicine. Biomedicine's model of disease, he argued, must be broadened in order to adequately capture and attenuate the human experience of disease. Engel hoped to create a medicine that did not ignore the psychological and social components of disease.[31] The "boundaries between health and disease, between well and sick are far from clear," he wrote, and are "diffused in cultural, social, and psychological considerations." Engel noted that the doctor of reductionist medicine is not adequate to the task of diagnosing or treating illness.[32] Robust human sciences are necessary, because society and culture shape the meaning of disease and the patient's experience of it.

The biopsychosocial model of medicine requires the doctor to oversee all aspects of the disease and the complete illness experience. It also creates the tools necessary to address all of these needs. According to Engel: "The doctor's task is to account for the dysphoria and the dysfunction which lead individuals to seek medical help, adopt the sick role, and accept the status of patienthood. He must weigh the relative contributions of social and psychological as well as biological factors implicated in the patient's dysphoria and dysfunction as well as in his decision to accept or not accept patienthood and with it the responsibility to cooperate in his own health care."[33] Moreover, medicine must be able to address the social context within which the patient lives, and "the complementary system devised by society to deal with the disruptive effects of illness, that is, the physician's role and the health care system. This requires a biopsychosocial model."[34]

In short, Engel claimed that his model provided a better explanatory model and framework for therapy than the biomedical model. He stated, "Hence, the physician's basic professional knowledge and skills must span the social, psychological, and biological for his decisions and actions on the patient's behalf involve all three."[35]

For Engel, the biopsychosocial model would not be as dispassionate as the reductive biomedical model; it would not ignore the patient's moral position. It would be sensitive to patient values and be informed by the human sciences. Being so informed, it would not only be more humane but would allow medicine to better do what it claims to be doing: addressing the whole patient. In short, it would be more holistic. This new paradigm served as a tool by which medicine might penetrate into the broader life of the patient. She was not merely a body; she was a body with a psyche and a body within a social framework. Under the new biopsychosocial model of medicine, the whole human being could be engaged, the total person treated, and in a truly humane way.

The biopsychosocial model of medicine thus claimed to humanize biomedicine from within by providing a more scientific—even if social scientific—and comprehensive vision of the human person. While there is much to recommend this model, it goes too far. The model, drawing on the social sciences, purports to give a nearly total view of the human person and deploys normative judgments of normality/pathology not only about bodily disorder and disability but also about every possible social arrangement and psychological problem or coping strategy faced by patients and their families. What begins as a worthy effort to create a more comprehensive model of care becomes a kind of totalizing care— and one that actually remained committed to biomedicine's understanding of the human person and the purpose of human life.[36]

The Medical Humanities Reform

At the same time that Engel was formulating his model, another effort at holistic reform developed, this time through the activities of medical humanists. In the mid-1970s, several medical schools launched departments, centers, or institutes for the medical humanities.[37] Within a short time, many different types of scholars besides theologians, the common morality philosophers, and social scientists turned their attention to medicine. Humanities scholars, from historians to literary theorists, initiated a new and wide-ranging body of writing on the personal dimensions of medical practice. Besides new centers, new journals were launched, such as the *Journal of Medical Humanities* in the United States and *Medical Humanities* in the United Kingdom, and new professional associations established.

Whereas the sciences, natural and social, provide insight into the biology and behavior of human beings, the humanities promise something richer, less ordered to "mechanisms" and causal explanation than to sympathetic understanding. They offer to help illuminate human persons in their embodied complexity, situated within diverse culturally and narratively ordered meanings, practices, and relationships. Their orientation is almost the polar opposite of the reductionist biomedical model and, like theology, could offer an important counterweight to the model and its deployment in contemporary medicine and society.

Humanities in medicine programs, however, do not challenge the reductionism or individualism of biomedicine. Instead, they instrumentalize the humanities as so many tools to promote efficiency. For instance, a recent proposal on professionalism in medicine calls on medical educators to align the goals of education in ethics and the humanities with the goals of efficient and effective practice—goals that, of course, must be empirically measurable.[38] Rather than see humanities education or ethics as integral to discerning, balancing, and nourishing the framework of medicine, humanities education is made to serve the already regnant (and unexamined) commitments and values of biomedicine.[39]

The instrumental nature of humanities education can also be seen in the uses of the visual arts in medical education, which are believed to enhance the observational and communication skills of medical students and residents.[40] Likewise, the literature and medicine movement has mutated into a narrative competency movement.[41] Thus, where a humanities education was once an end in itself, education in the medical humanities is justified only insofar as it is instrumental in creating doctors who function better as doctors, more efficient and effective doctors.

I have elsewhere shown how the medical humanities, especially in their drive toward narrative competency, perpetuate the power inherent in medicine. For instance, Charon writes: "Along with the scientific ability, physicians need the ability to listen to the narratives of the patient, grasp and honor their meanings, and be moved to act on the patient's behalf. This is narrative competence, that is, the competence that human beings use to absorb, interpret, and respond to stories."[42] Through an appeal to competency language, narrative competency becomes a new framework or model for more responsible biopsychosocial medicine. Charon has been one of the most active advocates for education in narrative competency. She notes that narrative competency "enables the physician to practice medicine with empathy, reflection, professionalism, and trustworthiness."[43] Moreover, Charon notes that narrative medicine makes doctors more effective in their work with "patients, themselves, their colleagues and the public." She continues: "From the humanities, and especially literary studies, physicians can learn how to perform the narrative aspects of their practice with new effectiveness. Not so much a new specialty as a new frame for clinical work, narrative medicine can give physicians and surgeons the skills, methods, and texts to learn how to imbue the facts and objects of health and illness with their consequences and meanings for individual patients and physicians."[44] Study of the humanities generally and narratives specifically will, its advocates maintain, make for better physicians. Lurking beneath the surface, however, is the more foundational purpose for reflecting on narrative: It will increase the efficiency and effectiveness of practitioners. The humanities must contribute to the instrumental thinking of the physician if they are to be valued.

Moreover, there is a distinction in both the biopsychosocial reform and the medical humanities between the facts and objects of medicine and the meaning attributed to them, creating a dualism of material and meaning. With the social sciences—psychology, sociology, and most recently anthropology—one gets at the facts and objects of medicine. With the humanities—philosophy, history, the visual arts, literature, spirituality (no longer theology), and narrative—one gets at the meaning attributed to those facts and objects. Thus, we can more efficiently and effectively attenuate the fears that medicine has become unethical. Doctors, armed with the tools of social science and humanized through a dose of humanities education or narrative competency, can be trusted to behave in ethically responsible ways.

Yet in a way, the human sciences and the humanities are co-opted, made to focus on the best means to carry out the implicit and unexamined ends of biomedicine. Bioethics in its clinical ethics, its research ethics, and its public policy forms has made peace with the ends of medicine and justifies that peace by claiming that the ends of medicine are in fact the ends held by the patient or even the ends of society. Bioethics, the human sciences, and the humanities all come to serve at the pleasure of medicine and the medical technological complex. The radical critiques of biomedicine from the domains of theology, such as the work of Gerald McKenny, and the ontological critiques from the field of disability studies, including the work of Jackie Leach Scully, are no longer heard or understood by the biomedical complex.[45] To put it differently, biomedicine's framework is enacted without critique, precisely because the critics are marginalized as mere voices of "cultural bioethics," in Evans's term, as voices of "religious" people, or as voices of "arcane philosophy." Biomedicine's dominion is safe from those who would fundamentally challenge it.

Conclusion

Insofar as medicine has marginalized robust critiques of its ends, attempting to focus its ethics on procedures and means to achieve assumed ends, it has become the ordering discipline of all the human sciences from the biological sciences to the social and psychological sciences and even attempts to order the humanities themselves. For medieval thinkers, theology was the queen of the sciences. Theology itself was a science—a mode of knowing. (*Scientia* means simply "knowledge" in Latin.) Each domain of knowledge—philosophy, natural philosophy, politics, agriculture, and all manner of other sciences—could access certain truths and the accompanying notions of goodness and beauty that attended those truths. Because theology reflected upon the highest good, the highest truth, and the highest beauty—in other words, because theology was the science/knowledge of God—theology was in a position to order other goods, including political goods, economic goods, goods of the created world (the natural world), goods of agriculture, and so on. So theology—with its sight on the highest good—could, like a queen, order the other bodies of knowledge, transforming them into theological goods ordered to the ends of the salvation and redemption of each person and of all of Creation.

Within the domain of human bodily existence, medicine seems to have taken over that role. Medicine now thinks it knows the goods of the body—its function, its aesthetic, its ethics. Insofar as medicine is biopsychosocial, it purports also to know the goods for the psyche of each human and the social/political/public health circumstances within which humankind can flourish. To put it differently, medicine purports to know definitively the ontological ground of the body and human persons. The moral dimension—the assessment of the goods of medicine, and the assessment of the means to achieve those goods—has in recent decades become the domain of bioethics. But as we have seen, bioethics is the handmaiden to biomedicine and serves to support biomedicine's ends. Insofar as bioethics marginalizes robust critiques of medicine, it protects medicine's ends. As the handmaiden of medicine, bioethics itself has its attendant handmaidens: the social sciences and the humanities. The social sciences uncover the truth—the facts—about bodies, as well as the social and political aspects of medical care of the body. The humanities give us the meaning and purpose of those truths for humanity. Bioethics then assists medicine in achieving its goods.

I have shown the way in which bioethics, the human sciences, and the humanities are now instrumentally subservient to biomedicine. They elevate the ends of medicine above critique—ends that are, of course, almost exclusively mechanistic. Medicine aims to repair or improve the machine of the body. And yet improvement of the body leads to an unconditional effort toward alleviating the entire human condition without a sense of what counts as human, of what the human condition is, of why the human condition is in need of alleviation, or of what counts as alleviation. If, however, bioethics, the human sciences, or the humanities threaten the assumed ontology and teleology of medicine, they are marginalized along with the radical critiques of theologians or disability scholars. And so instead they serve like obedient minions, gaining comfort and glory through their subservience and protecting the kingdom of biomedicine from the heresies of other robust metaphysical moral commitments.

Yet radical critiques of biomedicine still arise, even if they are excluded from the official moral deliberation of biomedicine's bioethics. Certainly Foucault was a critic of what he already in the 1960s knew to be problematic about medicine.[46] Ivan Illich likewise in the 1970s continued the critique.[47] From theological circles one thinks of the works of Stanley Hauerwas, Hans Reinders, Gerald McKenny, and John Swinton.[48] The journal *Christian Bioethics* also attempts to give unabashedly Christian answers to bioethical questions. There have been robust critiques from the disability community, as well as from within medicine itself.[49] Granted, no radical voices are permitted within the halls of state-sanctioned public policy bioethics commissions. But the very act of making the fundamental ontological and teleological commitments of biomedicine more transparent is important. It illuminates the grounds on which a truly robust medical ethics should proceed.

NOTES

1 See John H. Evans, *The History and Future of Bioethics* (New York: Oxford University Press, 2012); and Albert R. Jonsen, *The Birth of Bioethics* (New York: Oxford University Press, 1998).

2 Jonsen, *Birth*, 41–42.

3 See Joseph Fletcher, *Morals and Medicine* (Boston: Beacon Press, 1960).

4 Jonsen, *Birth*, 42–47.

5 Paul Ramsey, *Basic Christian Ethics* (New York: Scribner's, 1950), 89. Ramsey as a Christian grounded the duties in the personhood of persons, whereas Kant grounded his in the categorical imperative. Contemporary deontologists tend to ground the duties in a social contract such as the fiduciary relationship between physician and patient.

6 Paul Ramsey, *The Patient as Person: Exploration in Medical Ethics* (New Haven, Conn.: Yale University Press, 1974).

7 Stanley Hauerwas, "How Christian Ethics Became Medical Ethics," *Christian Bioethics* 1, no. 1 (1995): 11–28, at 14.

8 Ibid., 17–18; and Paul Ramsey, "Tradition and Reflection in Christian Life," *Perkins Journal of Theology* XXXV, no. 2 (1982): 46–56, at 47.

9 Evans, *The History and Future of Bioethics*.

10 Ibid., 7–8.

11 See ibid.; and Bernard Davis, "Prospects for Genetic Intervention in Man," *Science* 170 (1970): 1279–83.

12 Ibid., 1283.

13 For an excellent analysis of the progressivist tendencies in medicine, see Gerald P. McKenny, *To Relieve the Human Condition: Bioethics, Technology, and the Body* (Albany: SUNY Press, 1997). Also see the related discussion in Joseph E. Davis, "Reductionist Medicine and Its Culture Authority," chapter 1, this volume.

14 Tod Chambers, "The ASBH: Future, Present, and Past Tense." American Society for Bioethics and Humanities Meeting, October 25, 2008. Cleveland, Ohio.

15 See, e.g., Carla M. Messikomer, Renée C. Fox, and Judith P. Swazey, "The Presence and Influence of Religion in American Bioethics," *Perspectives in Biology and Medicine* 44, no. 4 (2001): 485–508.

16 Tom L. Beauchamp and James F. Childress, *Principles of Biomedical Ethics*, Fourth Edition (New York: Oxford University Press, 1994).

17 H. Tristram Engelhardt, *The Foundations of Bioethics*, Second Edition (New York: Oxford University Press, 1996); Robert M. Veatch, *A Theory of Medical Ethics* (New York: Basic Books, 1981). The first edition of Engelhardt's *Foundations of Bioethics* argues that many forms of secular reasoning, such as Beauchamp and Childress's principlism, usher in too much unexamined moral content. Engelhardt once seemed optimistic that his libertarian cosmopolitanism was the best procedural ethics to govern relationships between moral strangers; his optimism has faded in recent years.

18 Evans, *The History and Future of Bioethics*, xxvii–xxxv.

19 Ibid., 68.

20 Ibid., 37–42; Jonsen, *Birth of Bioethics*, 90–122.

21 Evans, *The History and Future of Bioethics*, 40.

22 Engelhardt, *Foundations*, 56–58.

23 Jeffrey P. Bishop, *The Anticipatory Corpse: Medicine, Power and the Care of the Dying* (Notre Dame, Ind.: University of Notre Dame Press, 2011), 142–67.

24 President's Commission for the Study of Ethical Problems in Medicine and Bio-medical and Behavioral Research, *Defining Death: Medical, Legal, and Ethical Issues in the Determination of Death* (Washington: U.S. Government Printing Office, 1981), 56.

25 Bishop, *Anticipatory Corpse*, 142–67.

26 Jonathan D. Moreno and Sam Berger, *Progress in Bioethics: Science, Policy, and Politics* (Cambridge, Mass.: MIT Press, 2010); Arthur L. Caplan, "'Who Lost China?' A Foreshadowing of Today's Ideological Disputes in Bioethics," *Hastings Center Report* 35, no. 3 (2005): 12–13; Ruth Macklin, "The Death of Bioethics (As We Once Knew It)," *Bioethics* 24, no. 5 (2010): 211–17; Jonathan D. Moreno, *The Body Politic: The Battle over Science in America* (New York: Bellevue Literary Press, 2011).

27 H. Tristram Engelhardt, *Bioethics and Secular Humanism: The Search for a Common Morality* (London: Trinity Press International, 1991).

28 George L. Engel, "The Need for a New Medical Model: A Challenge for Bio-medicine," *Science* 196 (1977): 129–36.

29 All ibid., 129.

30 Ibid.

31 Ibid., 131.

32 Ibid., 132.

33 Ibid., 133.

34 Ibid., 132.

35 Ibid., 133.

36 For a fuller discussion, see Bishop, *Anticipatory Corpse*, 227–52.

37 Rita Charon, "Literature and Medicine: Origins and Destinies," *Academic Medicine* 75, no. 1 (2000): 23–27.

38 David J. Doukas et al., for the Project to Rebalance and Integrate Medical Educa-tion (PRIME) Investigators, "The Challenge of Promoting Professionalism Through Medical Ethics and Humanities Education," *Academic Medicine* 88, no. 11 (2013): 1624–29.

39 Ibid.

40 Gary E. Friedlaender and Linda K. Friedlaender, "Art in Science: Enhancing Observational Skills," *Clinical Orthopaedics and Related Research* 471, no. 7 (2013): 2056–67; Martina Kelly et al., "A Picture Tells 1000 Words: Learning Teamwork in Pri-mary Care," *Clinical Teacher* 10, no. 2 (2013): 113–17; Pamela B. Schaff, Suzanne Isken, and Robert M. Tager, "From Contemporary Art to Core Clinical Skills: Observation, Interpretation, and Meaning-making in a Complex Environment," *Academic Medicine* 86, no. 10 (2011): 1272–76; K. Karkabi, comment on "Visual Thinking Strategies: A New Role for Art in Medical Education," *Family Medicine* 38, no. 3 (2006): 158; Johanna Shapiro, Lloyd Rucker, and Jill Beck, "Training the Clinical Eye and Mind: Using the Arts to Develop Medical Students' Observational and Pattern Recognition Skills,"

Medical Education 40, no. 3 (2006): 263–68; Charles L. Bardes, Debra Gillers, and Amy E. Herman, "Learning to Look: Developing Clinical Observational Skills at an Art Museum," *Medical Education* 35, no. 12 (2001): 1157–61; Jacqueline C. Dolev, Linda Krohner Friedlaender, and Irwin M. Braverman, "Use of Fine Art to Enhance Visual Diagnostic Skills," *Journal of the American Medical Association*, 286, no. 9 (2001): 1020–21.

41 Jeffrey P. Bishop, "Rejecting Medical Humanism," *Journal of Medical Humanities* 29, no. 1 (2008): 15–25; Rita Charon, "Literature and Medicine: Origins and Destinies," *Academic Medicine* 75, no. 1 (2000): 23–27; Rita Charon, "Narrative Medicine: Form, Function, and Ethics," *Annals of Internal Medicine* 134, no. 1 (2001): 83–87; Rita Charon and Martha Montello, *Stories Matter: The Role of Narrative in Medical Ethics* (London: Routledge, 2002); Kathryn Montgomery Hunter, Rita Charon, and Jack L. Coulehan, "The Study of Literature in Medical Education," *Academic Medicine* 70, no. 9 (1995): 787–94.

42 Rita Charon, "Narrative Medicine: A Model for Empathy, Reflection, Profession, and Trust," *Journal of the American Medical Association* 286, no. 15 (2001): 1897–902, at 1897.

43 Ibid.

44 Ibid., 1898.

45 McKenny, *To Relieve the Human Condition*; Jackie Leach Scully, *Disability Bioethics: Moral Bodies, Moral Difference* (Lanham, Md.: Rowman and Littlefield, 2008).

46 Michel Foucault, *The Birth of the Clinic: An Archaeology of Medical Perception*, trans. A. M. Sheridan Smith (New York: Vintage, 1991); Foucault, *Madness and Civilization: A History of Insanity in the Age of Reason*, trans. Richard Howard (New York: Vintage, 1988).

47 Ivan Illich, *Medical Nemesis: The Expropriation of Health* (New York: Pantheon, 1976).

48 See, e.g., Hauerwas, "How Christian Ethics Became Medical Ethics"; Hauerwas, *Suffering Presence* (Notre Dame, Ind.: University of Notre Dame Press, 1986); Hauerwas, *Naming the Silences* (Grand Rapids, Mich.: Eerdmans, 1990); McKenny, *To Relieve the Human Condition*; John Swinton, *Dementia: Living in the Memories of God* (Grand Rapids, Mich.: Eerdmans, 2012); Hans S. Reinders, *Receiving the Gift of Friendship: Profound Disability, Theological Anthropology, and Ethics* (Grand Rapids, Mich.: Eerdmans, 2008).

49 Bishop, *Anticipatory Corpse*; Jackie Leach Scully, *Disability Bioethics*.

11

In Search of an Ethical Frame for the Provision of Health

ANA MARTA GONZÁLEZ

Almost from its introduction, the World Health Organization's definition of health as "a state of complete physical, mental and social well-being"[1] was a matter of controversy,[2] because it implied a strong connection between health and general happiness. Less known, however, is that this definition was inspired by the description of the "healthy individual" penned by the medical historian Henry Sigerist in 1941:

> A healthy individual is a man who is well balanced bodily and mentally, and well adjusted to his physical and social environment. He is in full control of his physical and mental faculties and can adapt to environmental changes, so long as they do not exceed normal limits, and contributes to the welfare of society according to his ability. Health therefore is not simply the absence of disease; it is something positive, a joyful attitude towards life, and a cheerful acceptance of the responsibilities that life puts on the individual.[3]

Such a broad definition might have heralded a movement toward a more humane medicine, but its primary effect has been to accelerate the naturalization of ethics—that is, the substitution of "the healthy" for "the good" as the starting point of ethical discourse. This happened not so much because "the number of life-problems that are defined as medical has increased enormously"[4] but because the biological model of medicine, for which disease is a purely organic event, remains by far the dominant one.

As a result, it is increasingly common to see the ethical dimension of human behavior described not in ethical terms but in medical language. Medical language has come to seem a more enlightened way to describe behaviors that in the past were described in explicitly moral terms. In certain cases, the neutral language of science provides a secure and respectful means to describe human behavior and action in language un-colored by subjective or normative connotations. In addition, no matter how much importance we place on the subjective and emotional aspects of health care, we modern and rational individuals appreciate the prom-ised efficiency and objectivity of biomedicine.

The preeminence of the biomedical model is also reinforced by the rationalized procedures of the health care system; only one manifesta-tion of the general rationalization of institutions that Max Weber argued was characteristic of modern societies. So even when psychosocial ele-ments are considered as possible components of health, they are concep-tualized and described in language suitable to a highly bureaucratized medical system—suitable, that is, to the quantification and standard-ization that facilitate rational, efficient decision making. In this way, the procedures of the health care system, like those of all bureaucratic systems, are made to conform as closely as possible to the verification protocols of the natural sciences.

This confluence of the biomedical model and bureaucratic rational-ity has firmly established the authority of an "objective" vocabulary for describing and explaining human experiences. This vocabulary seems more respectful of personal dignity than explicitly moralizing descrip-tions of behavior, but when it is used in such a way as to minimize the possibility of human freedom and choice, it effectively undercuts the foundations of human dignity. This transformation in language does not mean that the subjective—emotional—dimension of human behavior has disappeared. Indeed, from many perspectives we could affirm ex-actly the opposite: Ours is a highly emotional culture. Yet the language used to describe those emotions is often that of science.

The upshot of this cultural transformation is that the distinction be-tween the healthy and the good, a major basis for ethical reflection, has become increasingly blurred in the past few decades. This raises two concerns. First, it is difficult to avoid the suspicion that certain impor-tant elements of our self-conception are at risk. How long can we expect to keep a moral image of ourselves if ethical language is progressively replaced with scientific and technical language? Second, such a compre-hensive understanding and use of "health" runs the risk of becoming an ideology, a totalizing discourse, which, precisely because it secures our approval, easily becomes a form of social control.

In what follows, I want first to introduce the distinction between the good and the healthy as it has been conceptualized in the ethical tradition. Against this background, I will point out certain developments in nineteenth-century philosophy that, along with the scientific developments of that century, help us to understand the process of the naturalization of the good, which has resulted in our contemporary conflation of the good and the healthy.

I will then argue that while this process of naturalization has been reinforced by the desire to avoid ethical controversies, it fails precisely in that effort. Ethical controversies always return in the end, especially in times of scarcity. So, I argue, it is always better to address these potential controversies in explicitly ethical terms at the outset, even before they erupt.

Finally, I will argue that ethical problems surrounding the definition of "normality" and proper care, and the just distribution of health resources, can be tackled only to the extent we develop a comprehensive notion of the human good, and its relation to the common (ethical) good, which, given the present conditions of our world, needs to be formulated and articulated at the global level.

On the Difference between the Good and the Healthy

Comparisons between health and goodness are common among the writers of classical times. Plato often uses such comparisons to illuminate the nature of virtue. In doing so, he readily sees some similarities but also insists on fundamental differences.

An apprehension of the difference between health and goodness is also present in Aristotle's distinction between natural goods and laudable goods, introduced in Book 8 of the *Eudemian Ethics*. Here, health is counted among the natural goods, while virtuous actions, because they deserve praise, are among the laudable goods. It is important to note, however, that the category of "natural goods" is not necessarily restricted to "physical goods." Aristotle mentions health along with other goods— such as honors, wealth, bodily strength, good luck, and power—that cannot be understood in merely physical terms.

The significance of listing health and these other qualities among the "natural goods" can be adequately grasped only when we compare them with the "laudable goods." This latter category comprises goods that are "praiseworthy in themselves"—what might also be called "moral goods." Among these moral goods Aristotle lists the different virtues. Drawing on this distinction, he goes on to characterize two types of good men in terms of those two types of goods. The "good man" is simply someone for whom natural goods are truly good. In other words, the mark of the good man is that he knows *how to use* natural goods: He is practically wise. Aristotle then distinguishes the good man from the "noble man." The defining mark of the latter is that he values virtuous actions for themselves, not only or chiefly for the natural goods they may secure.

Thus, while one mark of the good is its desirability, the fact that something is desirable is not enough to render it good *in itself*—that is, good without restriction and in all circumstances. In particular, the fact that we all desire health is not enough to make it a moral good, even though that fact justifies our calling health a natural good. Being healthy does not make us good as human beings; instead, being good, as human beings, is the purpose of ethics. Indeed, implicit in Aristotle's text is that in certain cases in which practical wisdom is absent, being healthy can make us worse human beings—for instance, if we draw upon our health to commit acts of injustice, or if in some situation we prefer health over bravery, justice, or friendship. Aristotle's point is that health, like the other natural goods, is good only when subordinated to good ends, those that constitute a good human life, which, in Aristotle's view, is the life of a social and political being. Although he frames it in very different terms, Immanuel Kant expresses a similar thought:

> It is impossible to think of anything at all in the world, or indeed even beyond it, that could be considered good without limitation except a good will. Understanding, wit, judgment, and the like, whatever such talents of mind may be called, or courage, resolution, and perseverance in one's plans, as qualities of temperament, are undoubtedly good and desirable for many purposes, but they can also be extremely evil and harmful if the will which is to make use of these gifts of nature, and whose distinctive constitution is therefore called character, is not good. It is the same with gifts of fortune. Power, riches, honor, even health and that complete well-being and satisfaction with one's condition called happiness, produce

boldness and thereby often arrogance as well unless a good will is present which corrects the influence of these on the mind and, in so doing, also corrects the whole principle of action and brings it into conformity with universal ends.[5]

In counting health among the goods of fortune, Kant is underscoring a point that is implicit in Aristotle's discussion: Health is frail, because it depends on a number of variable causes. The progress of science can certainly help identify and (to some degree) control those causes. However, medical scientific knowledge does not solve the problem of how to integrate health into a fulfilled, meaningful human life. Neither does it change the relative and conditional nature of the good of health, unlike good will, which is not a relative but an absolute good.

Fruitful commonalities exist between Aristotle and Kant. For both, health is a good, but one whose relevance can be properly assessed only in the context of ethical reflection, aimed at clarifying the nature of the human good as such. This means that, in the absence of ethical reflection of this sort, the reach and limits of the good of health run the risk of being distorted. When this happens, we start qualifying as "healthy" and "unhealthy" practices and behaviors once qualified as simply "good" or "bad," or else we start praising or blaming behaviors merely because they are deemed healthy or unhealthy. In either case, the indefinite nature of the healthy results in a sort of collapse into each other of the healthy and the good. The adjectives *healthy* and *unhealthy* become ethically charged.

While this terminological revolution may be simply a sign of our inability to reason with moral norms and values without a strong cultural context that supports them—or even, in our case, a cultural context marked by an overriding concern with health—it is certainly indicative of the naturalization of our ethical language. Not only have all aspects of individual life become potential candidates for medical therapy; many social processes are also explained in medical terms. Thus, we no longer speak only of "social injustices" but also of "social pathologies"; and virtually everything, from obesity to sadness, may now be seen as a disease, requiring pharmacological treatment and efficacious public health policies. Far from being an isolated phenomenon, this process of naturalization is consistent with a more general social enthroning of health. This can be seen in other widespread phenomena, such as our obsession with fitness and bodily perfection, regarding which we may echo Le Breton's comment on the cult of sports: It suggests that "the physical limit has come to replace the moral limit that present-day society no longer provides,"[6] ultimately, because the naturalization of the good is by now deeply embedded in our cultural and social practices.

The Naturalization of the Good in Nineteenth-Century Philosophy

By "naturalization of the good," I mean the gradual substitution of the healthy for the good that is now evident in much of our public discourse. This transvaluation can be viewed as a late effect of a long cultural process, nourished by the confluence of three factors at the beginning of the modern era: skepticism about the nature of the good, a desire to avoid political controversy, and a fascination with natural science.

This process is rooted in the increasing tendency to approach the human good in terms of health and disease that permeated nineteenth-century thought. Especially after Hegel, philosophy began to incorporate medical metaphors. Kierkegaard, Freud, Nietzsche, and Marx can all be interpreted in therapeutic terms, because all of them think the human being suffers from some sort of chronic (though not necessarily organic) malaise. While each philosopher accounts for this ailment differently, all of them resort to medical and therapeutic language.

Thus, for Kierkegaard, the human being is threatened by a "mortal disease" that, though it may have bodily symptoms, is not a physical dysfunction but a radical spiritual illness. The illness is none other than despair; it is mortal because it cannot be overcome, even by death. According to Kierkegaard, the only cure for despair is faith in God. This requires recognizing that human beings cannot be cured by their own means.[7]

Nietzsche also thinks that "Man is more diseased, more uncertain, more changeable, more unstable than any other animal, there is no doubt of it—he is *the* diseased animal."[8] In Nietzsche's view, unhealthiness is the norm for human beings.[9] But the conclusion he draws is the opposite of Kierkegaard's. For Nietzsche, the problem is that widespread unhealthiness generates a resentment of the healthy that leads to an inversion of the ancient aristocratic ethos in the form of the Judeo-Christian world-view. For this inversion he offers a naturalistic account: Thus, moral and religious notions are rephrased in physiological terms.[10]

More generally, both Freud's diagnosis of "civilization and its discontent" and Marx's depiction of an alienated humanity represent reflections on the illness that afflicts us. Although each author may make a different diagnosis, sickness becomes the explanatory paradigm. In this situation, some sort of medicine inevitably becomes the *prima philosophia*.

There are many possible reasons for the prominence of medical metaphors in nineteenth-century philosophy. The advance of natural sciences surely played a significant role because it placed a scientific approach to human behavior at the forefront and accelerated a naturalistic approach to the human experience.

While consideration of the human being as a "sick animal" can be traced back to Protagoras's account of the human being as a "defective animal" in Plato's *Dialogue*,[11] there is more reason to think of such metaphors as naturalizations of the theological doctrine of original sin. This is clear, at least, in Kierkegaard's case. Thus, had we accepted Kierkegaard's diagnosis, the medicine would have been primarily spiritual. Yet the nineteenth century was rich in scientific discoveries, and a naturalistic ethos resonated with them.

Since then, while the echo of a dual response to human malaise persists even in today's popular culture—as evidenced by the self-help best-seller *Plato, Not Prozac!*—the move toward medicalization has become ever more apparent.[12] This is partly because the scientific/therapeutic ethos is so pervasive in popular culture, and partly because an affinity exists between medicalization and the dynamics of consumer society, which favors the reduction of medical services to standardized products.[13] As Leahy and colleagues note, the term *consumer* had an ordinary meaning before it became widely understood to mean a purchaser of goods in the market. With this conception now the general meaning,[14] its application in the context of health goods and services raises a number of problems.[15] While health is not "the" good, neither is it an external good, amenable, like others, to market transactions. Health's being so intertwined with the good life, taking care of human health amounts to taking care of the human being. Inversely, neglecting or damaging human health amounts to neglecting or damaging the human being.

Furthermore, because the good of the human being is at the center of social and political life, taking care of human health is never solely an individual matter, to be approached merely from the consumer's point of view; it is also a matter of interest for society as a whole, not merely because of potentially infectious diseases, which can disrupt communal life, but because of people's genuine concern for their fellow human beings. This explains why the ways to structure the social provision of health care remain controversial: How much responsibility for their own health should be placed on the shoulders of individuals? How much responsibility should be placed on families and civil society at large? How much on the government?

And yet, the good of health, which deserves our care, is not the same as the means we use to encourage health. These means, unlike health itself, constitute external goods and services, and as such are amenable to economic transactions. This mixed nature is at the basis of many ethical conflicts surrounding the delivery of health care. While the dignity of the human person justifies speaking of the good of health as a human right, the means of delivering that good are often very expensive. This means that unlike political rights, which can be recognized as belonging to everybody without restriction, social rights such as the right to health care are subject to many economic limitations at both the individual and political levels. The fact that the delivery of health care lends itself to economic transactions is also at the basis of its eventual marketization. Therefore, there is a permanent need for the ethical reminder that health products, because of their direct connection with human well-being, are not similar to other kinds of products.

It should be noted that the commodifying tendency implicit in market economies represents a powerful social drive in favor of the biomedical model of health—ultimately, in favor of a strictly naturalistic approach to health. The particular push toward the naturalization of the good implicit in this process is highlighted by the metaphor used by Antonio Maturo, who quotes Alessandra Parodi: Since the discovery of antibiotics in the twentieth century, the body has become a battlefield where "the good" (drugs) fights "the bad" (microbes).[16]

Fighting disease through biomedical research and innovation has a deep ethical dimension to it. Yet the ethical dimension we so readily recognize in this kind of research, because it serves the human good in an obvious way, is not enough to reverse the cultural trend that invites us to rephrase all aspects of human experience, ethical aspects included, precisely in medical terms. Although medical science no longer gives the impression of proceeding from triumph to triumph, as it did in the first half of the twentieth century, biomedical language maintains its status as a privileged way of articulating our problems and insecurities.[17] We feel comfortable using this language, especially to account for difficult emotional experiences,[18] a development that signals a progressive colonization of human subjectivity by the objectifying language of science.

As I have argued, from a cultural point of view this contemporary inclination to rephrase human experience in medical terms may be due to the fact that throughout the last century we assimilated a naturalistic reading of the ideals of happiness and human success already at work in nineteenth-century thought. Yet this process has also been furthered by the dynamics intrinsic to the market economy, which, in the absence of internal ethical checks, tends by itself to approach health products like any other products.

Summarizing both aspects, we could conclude that in the conditions of late-modern societies, marked by the prestige of the biomedical model, bureaucratic rationality, and consumer capitalism, the naturalistic reading of happiness advanced by nineteenth-century thought has resulted in the colonization of human experience by medical language.

The Desire to Avert Ethical Controversies

From the perspective of public policy, a further catalyst for the replacement of the good with the healthy, or, as Le Breton suggests,[19] the moral limit with the physical, is the notion that the healthy seems, at least at first glance, less controversial than the good. While this view is itself far from uncontroversial, the truth is that ethical pluralism could provide a convincing rationale for the social and political replacement of the good with the healthy. Far from being ethically neutral, however, this replacement represents instead the uncontested advancement of a particular ethical position by default—namely, ethical naturalism, which is usually combined with some sort of consequentialism.

"Ethical naturalism" denotes a position that reduces moral goods to natural goods, a process characterized by the current tendency to reformulate human experiences as much as possible in the language of the biomedical sciences. In one sense this stance is correct, because the goodness of any being is nothing other than the perfection of its nature. This also applies to moral goodness, the proper goodness of the rational being. Yet the case of moral goodness is also unique, insofar as reason's task is to introduce order into all the goods at hand, an order that cannot simply be derived from natural properties or adequately explained as a function of mere survival, if it is to explain what makes a human life valuable and meaningful.

Ethics is concerned with far more than mere survival. The difference between merely living and living well is a question not of satisfying our natural needs and desires with increasing sophistication but rather of living, according to reason, in the light of the good anticipated by reason. Living in accordance with reason, however, entails the discovery of qualitatively different goods; and the discovery, also, of the peculiarity of the human (moral) good, which cannot emerge unless reason introduces order among the other goods. Reason introduces order in the light of certain principles, and in anticipation of an ideal of the good life that cannot be understood simply as a combination of pleasure and utility. It is only because of this, its inherent openness to the idea of the absolute good, that human life has not only a natural but also an intrinsically ethical value.

But because life is a precondition of the good life, disagreements as to the nature of the good life have always represented a temptation to reduce the human good to the natural good, thereby introducing naturalist positions into ethical and political thought. Thus, at the beginning of modern times, confronted with conflicting accounts regarding the human good, Thomas Hobbes resolved to focus his political reflections on the establishment of security and peace, leaving more debatable questions about the good to the private sphere. Assuming as its point of departure the generalized fear of violent death,[20] he introduced the modern state as an artifact designed to warrant peaceful coexistence among its subjects. The search for happiness became a private matter, to be decided according to individual inclinations, about which the state had nothing to say, as long as such inclinations did not endanger civic life.[21]

However, since the seventeenth century, when Hobbes was writing, the sharp divide between the public and private spheres has become increasingly less distinct. While Hobbes thought of security as the *raison d'être* of the state and the foundation of civic life, security is now generally seen in terms of personal well-being, as an individual right to be granted by the state. In other words, security, once the primary effect of political order and the precondition for public life, has been conflated with the right to life. (Indeed, for both Hobbes and John Locke, life was an individual right to be secured by the state.)

To the extent that the right to life was regarded as one of the reasons for the institution of the state, the collapse of well-being and security suggests an important shift in the way we approach state legitimacy: A legitimate state is not merely one that, by holding the monopoly of force, secures a peaceful coexistence but also one that shows an ability to provide sufficient well-being to its citizens. While we could certainly recognize here a sign of the increasing individualization characteristic of late-modern societies, the institution of the state within this mind frame has also resulted in the consideration of individual health as the focus of primary political interest.

Yet in the context of contemporary risk societies, government responsibility for individuals' health and well-being becomes an almost unmanageable requirement, which at any rate entails a radical move from politics to biopolitics. Thus, in their desire to protect their citizens from certain diseases, governments may issue far-reaching hygiene directives that inevitably interfere with people's lives, in ways that blur the early modern frontiers between the public and private spheres.

Playing with the two-fold meaning of the French word *sécurité*, as communal security and personal safety, Robert Redeker brilliantly captures the dilemma posed by these two conceptions in his book *Egobody: La fabrique de l'homme nouveau* (The making of the new man):

> Highway safety, the war against tobacco, the fight against cancer and other diseases have all become national causes, promoted to the front rank of political causes. The contemporary promotion of security to the status of a major political theme is in fact quite translatable to health, since security is nothing more—despite what is generally believed—than one aspect of health. Security is now imagined not as a civic virtue but as a personal right, a right of the self like the right to health. Thus, security is perceived as a human right that the State has the duty to protect, parallel

with its prescribed duty to ensure health. According to this view, security is no longer what it was for Hobbes, the effective source of all the duties of citizens to their sovereign. For Hobbes, security puts an end to the war of all against all, and in so doing it is neither a right nor a duty, but the origin of civil life. It is not above duties and rights (as it is in despotisms, which justify all their abuses in the name of security), it is below rights and duties, as their foundation. In the political configuration of late modernity, security no longer plays this role. It is simply held to be a right to be added to the gamut of rights with which the citizen is equipped.[22]

While the political security foundational to the institution of the state is to be clearly distinguished from the personal safety and well-being that now is requested in terms of "rights," Redeker suggests an increasing conflation of both concepts. This conflation would be a mark of the individualization of society and, relatedly, of the increasingly instrumental view of its institutions.

Yet if serving as an instrument for satisfying the individual need for health and security were the whole point of the state, its very existence would be threatened as soon as we found more efficient ways of satisfying that need. Against this view we can argue that the state is interested not merely in efficiency but also in justice and the fair distribution of resources.

Justice, a simultaneous concern for individual rights and for the common good, belongs to the minimal ethical substance of the state. We cannot, therefore, judge its performance by the standards of pure instrumental reason. Insofar as the state takes up the role of preserving and promoting the health of its citizens, its main concern is also related to justice, which additionally entails a genuine concern for the structure of health care provision. But which principles should structure the provision of health care? Along with the centrality of the human being, it is important to stress individual responsibility, without neglecting or discouraging existing social bonds. It is important to ensure universal access to health care without excluding private initiatives.

Speaking of the (minimal) ethical substance of the state is very different from asserting that private initiatives necessarily lack that ethical substance. That would be nonsense. All I am saying is that state initiatives cannot focus merely on matters of efficiency but always, and at the same time, on matters of fair distribution of resources. By contrast, private initiatives can legitimately focus on advancing excellence in a very particular area of education, research, or health without this being considered unfairly preferential. Apart from that, it is clear that in matters of education and health, private initiatives are often guided by altruistic concerns and also play an important social role in advancing knowledge and health care. Those are private sources of public goods that often relieve the state of burdens it cannot take upon itself.

In searching for the proper balance between efficiency and fair distribution, and between the roles of the public and private sectors, it may be helpful to consider some of the questions raised by Gary Taylor in his book *Health and Society: Key Debates in Health Care*:

Who is responsible for the health of the nation?
Does this responsibility lie with each individual, or is health a social condition
    for which governments should assume social responsibility?
Should the state play a major role in the direction and provision of health
    care or should we rely rather more upon the private sector and upon the
    increasingly influential voluntary sector?
Is there a fair way to ration health care?
To what extent should the state tackle health inequalities?
Is prevention better than cure?
What kinds of rights should patients have?
What is the impact of professionalism upon the relationship between different
    sections of the health care system?[23]

These are ethical questions, and they need to be addressed in ethical terms. The fact that they are controversial, that we can invoke arguments for or against any of them, does not give us a reason to exclude them from the public sphere. The mere fact that issues of health are so closely linked to the reality of our bodies does not guarantee that those issues will be private. Public authority sees itself entrusted to design and implement health policies, and citizens are usually ready to accept those measures, to consider them justified by the good of health—even if there is no real agreement on the nature of health, and even if there are reasons to suspect that, in the name of health, some people are making a profit and others imposing their particular ideologies.

We see, then, that in spite of having been introduced to bypass ethical problems and thus foster political unity, the replacement of the good with the healthy is not a viable solution to the kinds of problems that inevitably emerge in political life, because these problems are ultimately ethical in nature. While nobody denies that health is a valuable good, the problem starts when we have to decide about the distribution of scarce resources: What sort of criteria are we supposed to use? At this very point, ethical issues can no longer be hidden in medical language. When it comes to criteria of distribution, is not helpful simply to insist on the value of health. What we need is an ethics that can balance the good of health against other goods, as well as the individual good against the common good.

To the extent that health is a good that enables human beings to lead good lives, taking care of human health counts, in principle, as a morally good action. Conversely, people may be ethically blamed for not taking proper care of their own health, and, in certain cases, even for not taking political action to preserve or promote it.

Yet what is the measure of "proper care"? How far should we go, both individually and socially, to defend and promote the good of health? Are there recognizable boundaries between health and the search for physical perfection, so passionately pursued by so many people today, often as a matter of individual achievement? Indeed, is there any way to differentiate between a reasonable concern for preventing disease and the obsession with hygiene highlighted by Ivan Illich four decades ago?[24] How far should we go in our efforts to prevent all risks to individual safety? Should risk-taking behaviors be generally forbidden? If so, on what grounds?

We cannot expect to derive a notion of "proper care" or "reasonable risk" solely from social standards. Neither can we expect those criteria to derive from the natural sciences, as if the universal knowledge provided by science and articulated by bureaucratic rationality could in itself be adequate for handling the contingencies of particular cases.

The questions arising from notions of "proper care" and "reasonable risk" are ethical questions that cannot be answered unless we develop an explicit ethical reflection that goes beyond naturalism so that it clarifies the status of the good of health and its relationship with a good life. In my view, this clarification cannot be accomplished unless we expand our ideas of a good human life to include reference to a common good that has now become global in many relevant respects.

All this is to say that we need a different ethics, one that overcomes the limitations of the naturalistic framework. Naturalistic approaches to the human good easily become allies of ideology: If, in the public sphere, the human good is tacitly reduced to biological functionality, then, little by little, human beings start to feel pressure to adjust to certain ideals of normality that can be achieved only through increasing medicalization.[25] From a social perspective, human problems are reconceptualized in medical terms and given medical solutions. When the good is naturalized in this way, the ideal of "health" easily becomes the basis for an ideology of social control, the gatekeeper of normality; and people feel compelled to devise individual medical solutions for what are actually social and ethical problems and to adapt to social arrangements however inimical to well-being.

By asserting that we need a different ethics, I am simply emphasizing the need to consider health and biological functionality in the light of a more comprehensive view of the human good. To the extent that we are social animals, this more comprehensive view of the human good requires going beyond individualistic approaches to happiness and viewing our individual lives in the light of a common political good. Unless we are able to do so, we will lack the language to discuss, for instance, the relative justice or injustice of limiting universal access to health care resources, or the radical injustice of undeserved privilege.

As noted earlier, Kant reminds us that human beings may be healthy and yet be failures as good persons. Such failures are not just a private matter; they often have serious social and political consequences. This suggests that public discussion should be open to broader conceptions of the human good and not just stick to seemingly uncontroversial notions that reduce the good to the healthy, or reduce the discussion to issues of justice, revolving around the criteria for distributing health care in the face of scarcity. Even if we were to agree on the soundness of a given theory, we would still need to apply it to the case at hand. In other words, we would still need the practical wisdom necessary to assess the importance of the good of health against other goods, the individual good against the common good. This means that, more than a theory of justice, we need an integrative theory of practical reason, and for that we need a comprehensive theory of the good.

The Need for a Different Ethics

Although replacing the good with the healthy appears attractive largely because it seems to bypass ethical problems and thereby foster political unity, this replacement is not, in actuality, a viable solution to the problems that inevitably emerge in political life. These problems are ultimately ethical in nature. Among them, the distribution of health resources occupies a prominent place. Nobody denies that health is a valuable good. The problem starts when we have to decide about the distribution of scarce resources: What sort of criteria are we supposed to use? At this point, ethical issues can no longer be hidden in medical language. When it comes to criteria of distribution, it is not helpful simply to insist on the value of health. That goes without saying; indeed, it is one of the premises of the argument. Again, what we need is an ethics able to balance the good of health against other goods, as well as the individual good against the common good.

Developing a comprehensive view of the human good would clear the way for an integrative theory of practical reason, able to articulate different goods in practice, at both the individual and social levels. This is so because practical reason demands that we make sense of individual and political decisions about health and health care in the light of an idea of the good life—that is, a life lived in a way that makes sense of each of its parts, including contingency and suffering.

While this approach to the meaning of a "good life" may sound very formal, it is not actually so. Making sense of a human life is not merely a formal proposal; human beings carry with them sensitivities toward certain goods that they learn to recognize and increasingly realize in a coherent and integral way through all the contingencies that necessarily accompany their lives. In this context, it is important to stress that, as social beings, humans are receptive to specific values that are unattainable by the individual alone. There are values that can be experienced only in the company of other human beings, in the family, in friendship, in social and political life. In principle, living in political units serves this purpose: Political units, articulated around the notion of a common good, are supposed to provide room for experiencing and developing values that could never be developed in any other way. To care for and be cared for by others is one of those values.

It is no accident that in recent decades the two dominant discourses of cultural modernity—those of liberalism and social democracy—have each had a significant impact on health policies and have evolved toward a certain convergence precisely in terms of values.[26] These developments highlight the ethical relevance of political institutions.

Still, the emergence of the ethics of care in the 1980s fostered the realization that approaching health-related issues merely in terms of justice is insufficient. A further step is needed: Dealing ethically with issues related to health is not just a matter of reflecting on a fair distribution of resources but also, and crucially, a matter of care. This, however, requires emphasizing the human dimensions of the provision of care.

The idea is not to minimize the problem of adequate distribution of resources but, rather, to realize that the provision of health care demands a new focus on the human dimensions of care that cannot be reformulated simply in biomedical terms. Neither, for that matter, can care be reformulated in merely psychological terms; indeed, the psychologization of caring relationships would again involve the reconstruction of a basic relational experience in individualistic terms, this time in terms of individual feelings. Yet in order to live a good life, people need something more than pleasurable feelings, which, again, could eventually be medicalized: People need the experience of shared common values, around which they can construct the idea of a common good.

Although speaking in terms of common good may sound too ambitious, especially when we project this notion into the political arena, it is true that reasonable decisions are made with, at minimum, the objective of avoiding "the common bad"—a process that is another way of thinking in terms of the common good. The mere idea of avoiding the common bad or realizing the common good constitutes an invitation to transcend the dialectical divide between individual liberty and collective solidarity inherited from modernity through the work of practical reason.[27] This is again particularly clear in the case of health care, for health is a good we should individually take care of in the light of an idea of what it means to lead a meaningful life. But our health, like our life itself, is also a good for those who care for us.

Indeed, part of what makes our life meaningful is that it is also meaningful for others. Caring for as well as being cared for by others is a way of constructing an ethical community—that is, a community revolving around the good of the human being. While political life also revolves around the good of the human being, it does so from a different perspective, and with a view to developing other dimensions of human life. Thus, although political life may certainly benefit from citizens' living this kind of ethical experience, it cannot provide it all by itself. All political life can do is ensure that human interactions occur with respect for minimal ethical standards—ultimately, standards of justice—even if the special character of care relationships may make it particularly difficult to approach them in terms of corrective justice.

What is clear, however, is that in the absence of explicit ethical reflection that takes upon itself the task of sketching an idea of the human good, there is no way of balancing the good of health against other goods that we expect as part of a normal human life. Unless we develop a theory of the good that makes room for different types of goods, advances a hierarchy of goods, and makes sense of the notion of a common good, at both the political and global levels, it will be difficult to articulate an argument about justice in regard to the most pressing issues in health and economics.

Indeed, while we reject the idea that only the rich may have access to health care, the problem of finding a fair way to ration health care remains. It is not my task to solve this problem here. However, in light of the preceding reflections, it is possible to highlight three relevant considerations, which I offer by way of conclusion.

First, we should remember that health cannot be identified with the human good as such. If health were synonymous with "the good," there would be no way to assess its relative importance in the context of human life. In that situation, the very word *health* would easily become, as I observed in the preceding section, a name for an ideology that would, among other things, legitimize the increasing use of medicine for social control. On the contrary, precisely because health is not synonymous with the good, a moral agent can decline the pursuit of his or her own health in certain circumstances. In other words, while there is a duty not to take one's own life, there is not a duty to keep oneself alive in all circumstances.

Second, from an ethical point of view, the provision of health care should not be approached merely from the perspective of justice but also from the perspective of care. Caring for someone and taking care of someone more easily follow the logic of friendship than the logic of justice. In this regard, it is important to note, with Aristotle, a significant difference between the way equality works in justice and how it operates in friendship: "Equality does not seem to take the same form in acts of justice and in friendship; for in acts of justice what is equal in the primary sense is that which is in proportion to merit, while quantitative equality is secondary, but in friendship quantitative equality is primary, and proportion to merit secondary."[28]

A little further on, Aristotle clarifies what he means by "quantitative equality," as opposed to "proportion to merit": "For friendship asks a man to do what he can, not what is proportional to the merits of the case; since that cannot always be done, e.g., in honors paid to the gods or to parents; for no one could ever return to them the equivalent of what he gets, but the man who serves them to the utmost of his power is thought to be a good man."[29]

In other words, friendship does what is possible, even if it is not always possible to reciprocate in material terms, or in strict proportion to merit, as justice requires. This distinction is relevant to the present discussion about health care insofar as, very often, people simply do not have the necessary means to take care of their loved ones. All that can be said in this regard is that no one is obliged to do what is not possible. The mark of friendship is doing whatever is *possible*.

But the general aspiration of a society marked by solidarity among its members should be to make sure that the required means for health care are available to those who need them most. This leads us to consider the third aspect to be taken into account in the search for fairness in the rationing of health care: the subsidiary role of the government in the provision of health care. In speaking in these terms, I am speaking already of one aspect of "social justice." This kind of justice builds upon the aristocratic idea of distribution according to merit, as well as the democratic idea that every human being deserves, at the least, a life free from want. Social justice cannot be equated either with mere distributive justice or with corrective justice. It would be a mistake to think of social justice merely as something to be provided by the government: All social agents, individuals as well as organizations, play a role in this kind of justice, depending on how they fulfill their duties and respond to the opportunities life has placed before them. Very often the role of the government in matters of social justice is merely to ensure that duties are fulfilled and the law is not broken. However, there are times when it has to take a more active role. Recognizing those times is also a matter—as Aristotle might have put it—of practical wisdom.

NOTES

1 Preamble to the Constitution of the World Health Organization, http://www.who.int/governance/eb/who_constitution_en.pdf (accessed February 4, 2014).

2 See Daniel Callahan, "The Concept of Health," *The Hastings Center Studies*, Vol. 1, No. 3 (1973), 77–87.

3 Quoted by Joshua A. Salomon, Colin D. Mathers, Somnath Chatterji, Ritu Sadana, T. Bedirhan Üstün, and Christopher J.L. Murray, in "Quantifying Individual Levels of Health: Definitions, Concepts, and Measurement Issues," in *Health Systems Performance Assessment: Debates, Measures and Empiricism*, ed. Christopher J.L. Murray and David B. Evans (Geneva: World Health Organization, 2003), 301–18, at 302.

4 Peter Conrad, *The Medicalization of Society: On the Transformation of Human Conditions into Treatable Disorders* (Baltimore: Johns Hopkins University Press, 2007), 3.

5 Immanuel Kant, *Groundwork for the Metaphysics of Morals* 4: 393.

6 David Le Breton, "Pasiones del riesgo y contacto con la naturaleza," *Educación Física y Ciencia*, 11 (2009): 13–14. Available at http://www.fuentesmemoria.fahce.unlp.edu.ar/art_revistas/pr.3977/pr.3977.pdf.

7 Despair admits of different levels: One is unconscious despair—not being aware of being a self. Another is conscious despair, whether weak (the will to be a different self, the will not to be anyone, or the will not to be oneself) or strong (the will to be oneself, either resignedly or obstinately). Despair shows itself in the characteristic symptoms of a superficial aesthetic life. Being cured of an aesthetic life requires two further steps. The first is into the ethical stage, which brings unity to the divided life of the aesthetic person; however, to be cured of despair, it is necessary to take the second step, into the religious stage. See Søren Kierkegaard, *The Sickness unto Death: A Christian Psychological Exposition for Upbuilding and Awakening*, ed. and trans. (with introduction and notes) Howard V. Hong and Edna H. Hong (Princeton, N.J.: Princeton University Press, 1980), 13ff.

8 Friedrich Nietzsche, *The Genealogy of Morals*, trans. Horace B. Samuel (Mineola, N.Y.: Dover, 2003) (First Edition Boni and Liveright, 1913), III, 13, 87.

9 See Nietzsche, *Genealogy*, III, 14.

10 Thus, human sinfulness—which for Kierkegaard is the foundation of despair—is a moral interpretation of a physiological fact (*Genealogy* III, 16, 93). Likewise, from a genealogical point of view, Nietzsche says that it was his bad health that brought him to philosophy, although from a normative point of view he defends an ethics of distinction, which would preserve the healthy from the infectious company of the unhealthy.

11 See the myth of Prometheus in Plato, *Protagoras*, ed. Malcom Schofield, trans. Tom Griffith, *Gorgias, Menexenus, Protagoras* (New York: Cambridge University Press, 2010), 157–58.

12 Lou Marinoff, *Plato, Not Prozac! Applying Eternal Wisdom to Everyday Problems* (New York: HarperCollins, 1999).

13 Eva Illouz, *Saving the Modern Soul: Therapy, Emotions, and the Culture of Self-Help* (Berkeley: University of California Press, 2008); and Frank Furedi, *Therapy Culture: Cultivating Vulnerability in an Uncertain Age* (New York: Routledge, 2004).

14 Michael Leahy, Hans Löfgren, and Evelyne de Leeuw, "Introduction: Consumer Groups and the Democratization of Health Policy," in *Democratizing Health: Consumer Groups in the Policy Process*, ed. Hans Löfgren, Evelyne de Leeuw, and Michael Leahy (Northampton: Edward Elgar, 2011), 1–14, at 2.

15 Not every aspect of health can be approached from a market perspective, and even for the purposes of developing a theory of health economics, it may be necessary to differentiate several categories of health products. See Thomas Grebel, *Innovation and Health: Theory, Methodology, and Applications* (Northampton: Edward Elgar, 2011), 156–57.

16 Antonio Maturo, *Sociologia della malattia: Un'introduzione* (Milan: Franco Angelli, 2007), 26.

17 Timothy Milewa, "Health Activism in the Age of Governance," in Löfgren, de Leeuw, and Leahy, *Democratizing Health*, 15–29.

18 Joseph E. Davis, "Emotions as Commentaries on Cultural Norms," in *The Emotions and Cultural Analysis*, ed. Ana Marta González (Farnham: Ashgate, 2012): 31–50.

19 David Le Breton, "Pasiones del riesgo," 13–14.

20 "The passions that encline men to Peace, are Feare o Death; Desire of such things as are necessary to commodious living; and a Hope by their Industry to obtain them." Thomas Hobbes, *Leviathan*, vol. 2, ed. Noel Malcolm, in *The Clarendon Edition of the Works of Thomas Hobbes*, vol. IV (Oxford: Clarendon Press, 2012), 196.

21 Hobbes wrote:

> By Manners, I mean not here, "Decency of behaviour" . . . But those qualities of man-kind, that concern their living together in Peace, and Unity. To which end we are to consider, that the Felicity of this life, consisteth not in the repose of a mind satisfied. For there is no such Finis ultimus (utmost ayme,) nor Summum Bonum (greatest Good) as is spoken in the Books of the old Moral Philosophers. . . . And therefore the voluntary actions, and inclinations of men tend not onely to the procuring, but also to the assuring of a contented life; and differ onely in the way: which ariseth partly from the diversity of passions, in divers men; and partly from the difference of the knowledge, or opinion each one has of the causes, which produce the effect desired.

Hobbes, *Leviathan*, 150.

22 The French original:

> La sécurité routière, la guerre contre le tabagisme, la lutte contre le cancer et d'autres maladies sont devenues des causes nationales

promues au rang de causes politiques. L'accession contemporaine de la sécurité au rang de thème politique majeur est d'ailleurs tout à fait articulable à la santé, la sécurité n'étant rien d'autre—à l'inverse de ce que l'on pense généralement—que l'un des aspects de la santé. La sécurité en effet n'est pas aujourd'hui revendiquée comme vertu civique, mais comme un droit personnel, égotique, un droit de l'ego comme un droit à la santé. Ainsi, la sécurité est vécue comme un droit de l'individu que l'État aurait le devoir de garantir, parallèlement au devoir que lui est prescrit de garantir la santé. Dans cette perspective, la sécurité n'est plus du tout ce qu'elle fut chez Hobbes, la source effective de tous les devoirs des citoyens envers le souverain. Mettant fin à la guerre de tous contre tous, la sécurité n'est chez Hobbes ni un droit ni un devoir, mais l'origine qui engendre la vie civile. Elle ne se situe pas au-delà des droits et des devoirs (comme c'est le cas dans les despotismes, qui justifient tous leurs abus par l'argument de la sécurité), elle se situe en deçà de ces mêmes droits et devoirs, elle leur sert de fondement. Dans la configuration politique de notre modernité tardive, la sécurité ne joue plus du tout ce rôle. Elle est simplement tenue pour un droit venant s'ajouter au chapelet de droits dont le citoyen est doté.

Robert Redeker, *Egobody: La fabrique de l'homme nouveau* (Paris: Fayard, 2010), 121–22.

23 Gary Taylor and Helen Hawley, *Health and Society: Key Debates in Health Care* (Maidenhead: Open University Press, 2010), 2.

24 Illich wrote:

To a point, modern medicine was concerned with therapeutic engineering—the development of strategies for surgical, chemical, or behavioral intervention in the lives of people who are or who might become sick. As it appears that these interventions do not become more effective just because they become more costly, a new level of health engineering has been pushed to the foreground. Health systems are now biased in favor of curative and preventive medicine. New health systems are proposed that are biased in favor of environmental health management. The obsession with immunity gives way to a nightmare of hygiene. As the health-delivery system continually fails to meet the demands made upon it, conditions now classified as illness might well soon be classified as criminal deviance. Imposed medical intervention might be replaced by compulsory re-education or self-criticism.

Ivan Illich, *Toward a History of Needs* (New York: Pantheon, 1978), 97.

25 In their book *Against Health: How Health Became the New Morality* (New York: New York University Press, 2010), Jonathan Metzl and Anna Kirkland make this point, referring to Ivan Illich, Talcott Parsons, and Irving Zola, who first spoke of health, in Metzl and Kirkland's words, as a "normativizing rhetoric," 5.

26 Kearsley Stewart, Gerald T. Keusch, and Arthur Kleinman, "Values in Global Health Governance," in *Global Health and Global Health Ethics*, ed. Solomon Benatar and Gillian Brock (Cambridge: Cambridge University Press, 2011), 304.

27 Leahy et al., "Introduction: Consumer Groups," 1.

28 *Nichomachean Ethics* 8.7.1158b29–34.

29 *Nichomachean Ethics* 8.7.1163b14–17.

Conclusion

Limits in the Interest of Healing

JOSEPH E. DAVIS

Throughout this book we have used the reductionism/holism distinction as a heuristic for evaluating features of medicine across a broad continuum of concerns, from patient care at the "micro" end of the spectrum to global health disparities at the "macro" end. Neither term, as I noted in the Introduction, has a univocal meaning. In the various chapters, we describe different things as problematically "reduced," whether treating illness as merely a physical malfunction, recasting social problems and differences as dysfunctions of individual bodies, limiting risk factors to the modifiable behaviors of individuals, diminishing medical care to a marketplace commodity, narrowing ethical concerns to matters of individual autonomy or preference, or restricting the articulation of the human good to the naturalistic terms of the physical sciences. Similarly, "holism" includes multidisciplinary and integrative approaches, as well as attention to the patient as person; to the existential and dependency aspects of illness and suffering; to the environmental, social organizational, technological, and community influences on health and illness; to the relative place of health in a well-lived life and a just political order; to the perspectives and involvement of local citizens; and more.

The distinction between reductionism and holism is also not zero-sum, a contest between irreconcilable positions. The issue is an imbalance that results when a partial perspective, not wrong in itself, becomes the *only* perspective. Framing problems and treating them in atomistic, technical terms ("fixing") is certainly not always insufficient. As the physician Atul Gawande notes in his recent book *Being Mortal*, the medical profession has succeeded because of "its ability to fix. If your problem is fixable, we know just what to do."[1] In dealing with specific,

discrete problems—"hernias and heart valves and hemorrhaging stom-
ach ulcers"[2]—there is an obvious and appropriate place for this practical,
instrumental orientation. And, to turn things around, not everything
that passes for a holistic response is sufficient. The consumer approach,
discussed by Robert Dingwall (chapter 4), for instance, which is championed by certain social movements and patient advocacy groups in
the name of a more humane "patient-centeredness," rests on a flawed
conceptualization of medicine and the denial, in effect, of our shared
dependency.[3] Consumerism makes patient autonomy the only perspective and so strips out the necessary empathy and appropriate authority
of a genuine doctor–patient partnership. Both technical skill and patient
autonomy are important, but neither is a full picture of good health *care*.

What we need is a far richer balance. Given the dominance of reductionistic and individualistic approaches, this means finding ways to limit
their influence by bringing more substantive and holistic orientations to
bear. Efforts to "humanize" medicine and reform the curricula are not
enough. The problem runs deeper, and so must the response.

Drawing Limits and Countervailing Goods

For the most part, we have concentrated here on the biomedical model
as the symbolic and normative framework that dominates the practice
of medicine. This framework, as discussed in detail in several chapters,
is held together by a set of specific commitments that structure how
problems are characterized and remediation is pursued—a natural science way of objective and measurable knowing, an ontology with a sharp
dichotomy of the physical and the mental, a technocentric orientation, an
ethic of detached concern, and so on. But more than that, we have argued,
the model draws upon and projects a background of tacit, normative
assumptions of personhood, nature, and society that extends well beyond
fixing the body.[4] These include understandings of the real and the imaginary, the blameworthy and the blameless, the normal and the deviant,
the rational and the irrational, the controllable and the uncontrollable—
what, in short, is "normal, proper, or desirable."[5] This value background,
as we have further observed, is largely unacknowledged, hidden behind
medicine's language of scientific rationality, value-neutrality, universality, and beneficence. In every chapter, we find the same paradox: moral

judgments about personal responsibility being made in an abstract, scientific, and instrumental language of facts and findings.

We have tried to draw out elements of the value background in order to see what makes the reductionist biomedical orientation so powerful, so sought after for dealing with social issues and enforcing social norms, and so useful a tool for circumventing complex social, political, and economic problems. Just speaking of reductionism, even in its plural meanings, can fail to convey that power or shine a light on the mutually constitutive relationship of biomedicine and key features of the prevailing social order. As we have shown, medicine is a repository for a utopian project of eliminating suffering, a project that has been steadily extending to include more aspects of well-being, projects of self-determination, and ambitions for the enhancement of cognitive powers and other valued traits and capacities. Biomedicine's reductionist mode is also interlinked with additional goods and entrenched patterns and imperatives with respect to bureaucratic efficiency, economic incentives, and personal accountability. Moreover, and critically, we have argued that the very governing model of liberal democracies, which now address their citizens far less as the bearers of duties and obligations than as autonomous individuals with rights and freedoms, is implicated in the pull toward reductionist and individualist strategies to secure order and conformity through the right—"healthy"—personal choices. What makes the reductionist model compelling is not captured in what it "reduces" or omits, but in what goods that reduction makes possible or helps to secure.

Because there are cultural and moral goods at stake, efforts toward a more holistic balance must take those goods into account and seek to limit and contain their claims. This limiting task necessarily requires countervailing goods, modes of practice, and institutional arrangements. In key respects, we have argued, the dominant approaches in bioethics and public health have embraced too many of biomedicine's commitments, tacit values, and institutional imperatives. The substantive alternative they can offer has been stifled. Too often, they extend and reinforce rather than challenge and balance and so make the task of articulating limits more difficult. Too often, they help naturalize and normalize a skewed reductionism and individualism, and so make the status quo appear more inevitable and resistance more quixotic and even illegitimate.

But there is nothing natural or normal about the distorted focus on reductionism and individualism. In very basic ways, we have shown, it fails to address or acknowledge contextual realities that deeply influence health and health care. Concentrating disease prevention, for example, on personal lifestyle change neglects a large body of epidemiological evidence on the crucial influence of such factors as socioeconomic status, cultural practices, technological interventions, and environmental conditions. We have further suggested that the distortion rests on and perpetuates an inadequate picture of the human condition. The biomedical paradigm represses realities—our need for meaning in suffering, the irreducibly complex interaction between mind and body, our frailty and finitude, our shared sociality and bonds of interdependence, and so on—that we know facilitate and influence the efficacy of care, both provided and received.[6]

Moreover, the "fix" orientation is not monolithic. Our critique is indebted to holistic work in social medicine, social epidemiology, sociology, medical ethics, philosophy, and other fields. If often marginal, there are robust traditions of thought and empirical research in these fields that make us more attuned to the social and environmental underpinnings of health and illness, help us recognize the limits of therapeutic intervention, and highlight questions of meaning and morality that are too often concealed. Further, we have argued, new developments— for example, the resurgence of infectious disease, globalization, social fragmentation, aging populations, new forums for the voice of the patient, a renewed focus on prevention, the rapidly rising cost of medical care—are challenging the overreliance on and inappropriate application of reductionistic and atomistic modes of explanation and intervention. While none of what we have written portends a seismic shift toward holistic approaches, it does offer hope for change. And it suggests values, practices, and arrangements that could have some countervailing force in medicine, bioethics, and public health. To each of these I briefly turn.

Medicine

Any discussion of limits to medicine must begin with the question of its proper ends. The goals of medicine include at least the following: restoring health, relieving suffering, ameliorating illness (where health cannot be achieved), caring for the sick, and promoting the health of the community.[7] The realization of these goals, in turn, necessitates and is centered in a doctor–patient relationship, characterized by a physician's obligation to the good of the patient and a professional authority rooted in the ethical commitment to promote health and healing. Of course, speaking of the goals or proper ends of medicine does not answer complex questions of what these goals entail. Concepts of health and illness, suffering and care can be and are defined differently, with implications for how the domain of medicine and the doctor–patient relationship are conceived. But these concepts are not endlessly malleable; the proper ends of medicine provide some (not all) normative criteria for thinking about and adjudging appropriate interventions.

In our view, medicalization, as we have discussed it—an "insidious"[8] extension of reductionist medicine—is corrosive to medical practice and contrary to its legitimate goals. At first glance, this position appears counterintuitive to a holistic orientation. It would seem that if we are calling for an increase of attention to the social aspects of health and illness and the experiencing person, we are also calling for an extension and larger jurisdiction of medicine. While many in the holistic tradition say as much, that is not our position. We do affirm, with the holistic literature, that in some contexts an enlarged scope of medical attention is needed, that a practice of healing, for instance, looks beyond bodily dysfunction to the patient's experience and understanding of "illness-as-lived."[9] However, medicalization, as driven by commercial forces and cultural imperatives, is a process that extends reductionist medicine well beyond legitimate boundaries. Any effort to achieve a more holistic balance must find ways to constrain this relentless expansion and reaffirm the goods inherent to medical practice.

Our discussion suggests at least two avenues of resistance. The first concerns putting some space between "health" and "health care." Medicine is devoted to restoring health, which raises the important question of "What is health?" Is it primarily a freedom from bodily illness or infirmity—the traditional view—or is it something far wider, such as the World Heath Organization definition quoted by Ana Marta González in chapter 11: "a state of complete physical, mental and social well-being"? While the traditional definition seems too narrow, the WHO definition is too wide. We haven't offered any precise definition, but we have suggested that a broader, holistic conception of health does not necessarily imply an expansive domain of medicine. There is far more to health than professional health care, and part of our predicament, which medicalization has fostered, is a conflation of the two.

Several chapters, notably those by Christina Simko (chapter 2), Jon Arrizabalaga (chapter 7), and Bruce K. Alexander (chapter 8), point toward the importance of local, vernacular understandings and practices as a check on the biomedical orientation. Reductionist and high-tech medicine, embedded in expert systems and bureaucratic organization, is generally inimical to mutual aid, self-care, culturally mediated arts of suffering, traditional values, "natural recovery," public deliberation, and other forms of local sufficiency. In fact, it has done much to undermine these practices and the confidence people have in their own judgment.[10] Biomedicine promotes a subjectivity in which people turn the clinical "gaze" on themselves and participate in their own surveillance, as Deborah Lupton (chapter 6) notes. The crises we have highlighted, however, on both an individual and a collective level, can be moments in which self- and community-efficacy, nonmedical theodices, a more judicious use of low technology, the awareness and acceptance of finitude, the return of some care to ordinary people and mutual-aid societies, and so on can be entertained and re-envisioned anew. Medicalization is not a one-way process, and problems and struggles do not have to end up at the doctor's office or refracted through the biomedical model. Supporting alternatives can help counteract such dependence, and in the name of a richer conception of health and practice of healing.

A second avenue of intervention might be the mobilization of physicians and other health professionals to defend the integrity of their own practice. In light of our discussion of the processes of medicalization and the commodification of health and health care, it might seem that medicine possesses no framework of its own from which limits might be drawn. Both I (chapter 1) and Luis E. Echarte (chapter 3) document a slow accommodation to claims being made on medicine in the name of lifestyle consumerism, enhancement, and emancipation. The accommodation, sometimes under the pressure of vigorous polemics, such as the wholesale attack on paternalism, has both reflected and fostered the progressive loss of a language and a standard by which to resist. Less indirectly, some, such as the proponents of the enhancement uses of medical technology discussed by Echarte, call for a reconsideration of the goals of medicine that make that accommodation explicit.[11] However, if our analysis has merit, this erosion has troubling implications for medicine as an ethical profession.

For example, we noted that people can now do all sorts of things with and to their bodies, and further possibilities are on the way. To gain access to these interventions all they really need do is present themselves before a physician. The doctor will discuss the individual's experience and reasons for the desired medical intervention, to be sure, but, assuming the reasons are "reasonable," the decision belongs to the patient, the autonomous subject who alone is the judge of his or her quality of life.[12] It may be that the patient's ends are oriented to healing, but in principle there is no reason they must be, and in practice, as we noted, there are many uses to which medical technology is being put that have little connection to illness or infirmity. In these circumstances, doctors become mere "service providers." In not determining what ends their work serves, they contravene one of the very distinguishing marks of a profession and what defines it as ethical. Further, as Paul Starr argues: "The ideal of the market presumes the 'sovereignty' of consumer choices; the ideal of a profession calls for the sovereignty of its members' independent, authoritative judgment. A professional who yields too much to the demands of clients violates an essential article of the professional code. . . ."[13] Serving projects of self-determination might give patients what they want, might address burdens for the patient or enable or enhance his or her pattern of life, but unless what is provided aims at realizing some end or ends of medicine, then it is inconsistent with an ethical understanding of patient care. There are grounds, rooted in the constitutive and regulative values of the profession, for physician resistance to medicalization, a resistance that a substantive, humanistic bioethics could help to articulate.[14]

Bioethics

While the goals of medicine can provide some substantive guidance, our discussion has also highlighted the need to go further. Not only are the goals plural and not self-defining—health, illness, and so on can have different meanings—but they must also be situated in some larger ethic or public philosophy of the human and common good. We have emphasized throughout this book that health and illness are public as well as private matters, and that ethical questions are ineradicable from health and health care. As Dingwall (chapter 4) observes, "[T]he moral and the collective dimensions of medicine seem to be genuinely inescapable." The premise, and the great cultural appeal, of the reductionist biomedical approach was that the messy business of social interests, moral questions, and communal ends could be largely avoided. Bioethicists, John H. Evans (chapter 9) avers, to the degree that they have embraced a principlism centered heavily on autonomy, effectively reinforce this illusion, despite talk of the "common morality." But while we certainly recognize and affirm that citizens have plural purposes, we also believe there is a shared public responsibility to reflect on the meaning of health and the appropriate means to promote it, as well as on the just allocation of resources. These are community matters and they require some degree of social consensus, a consensus that is not pre-given but achieved.

An important place to begin, we believe, is with making the ethical values and assumptions in medicine more transparent. As noted above, there has been a tendency to conflate health and professional health care. Several chapters, particularly mine (chapter 1) and González's (chapter 11), have also noted the conflation of health with the good. Not only has health become a surreptitious moral language, obfuscating its prescriptive value assumptions, but it has also become nearly synonymous with the good life, obscuring the question of the place of health in a well-lived life and well-ordered community. An important work of ethics here is to help challenge this conflation by drawing out the implicit background assumptions and implications and rendering them discussable and open to deliberation. In this, the default naturalistic language will have to be replaced with ethical/political language, a task that will be contested. As I note in chapter 1, making judgments transparent makes them open to controversy.

This is a price that must be paid. Not only can a naturalized language of health become a kind of repressive ideology—a "healthism" (Lupton, chapter 6)—but the reductionistic and individualistic mode also closes off the sociopolitical analysis of troubles and blinds us to wider social responses and responsibilities. Especially in dealing with the complex questions surrounding the provision of health care, ethics needs to make justice central, not peripheral (Evans, chapter 9); rearticulate, not evade, our mutual obligation to one another (Dingwall, chapter 4); and work toward, not against, a larger ethical frame of human flourishing (González, chapter 11). Over the past half-century, as the disease burden has shifted from infectious to chronic conditions and medicine has moved from relatively low to high technology, the cost has spiraled upward at a staggering rate.[15] Allocation issues will not solve themselves. We need an ethical and public philosophical framework, attentive, as Dingwall (chapter 4) suggests, to the dynamics of the sick role, in order to confront directly burden sharing and questions of legitimacy and limits.

An ethics, as Jeffrey P. Bishop (chapter 10) argues, that can serve as a check on reductionist biomedicine cannot be one that works from the same underlying premises. Both in protecting the goods internal to the practice of medicine and in balancing the biomedical perspective, other perspectives and traditions, with a richer sense of the human condition, shared obligation, and flourishing, must be brought into the conversation. We have discussed a number of important resources that are or could be available. I mentioned above reinforcing local communities and the resources of vernacular practices. Both Evans (chapter 9) and Bishop (chapter 10) argue that the progressive marginalization of theology, with its "thick" substantive languages of human goods and rich traditions of reflection, has left the field of bioethics depleted. While there are no easy answers, they suggest that opening up the field by cultivating institutions outside medicinal centers and political tutelage could create a space for a stronger, less biomedical bioethics. This bioethics might re-engage theology, as well as the distinctive contributions of political philosophy, disability studies, and other fields, including the humanities, realized in terms less instrumental to satisfying needs or accomplishing pre-defined goals.[16]

While some reform of bioethics is important, it is not nearly enough. All the chapters situate medicine within the larger world. Medicine is embedded, influencing but also being influenced and positioned by forces well beyond its confines. Whatever its internal dynamics, a reductionistic and individualistic medicine also reflects deep reductionistic and individualistic tendencies in the liberal political and cultural order.

The ethics and public philosophy we are gesturing toward is aimed not just at internal reforms to medicine or bioethics but also at resisting these tendencies in the wider society. We need a broad public deliberation that inquires into human goods, the good life, our shared purposes and obligations to one another, and the common challenges we face. This is a conversation that does not presuppose a default set of stealth goods, or any monistic vision of *the* good, but deliberates in the recognition that the goods at stake—from our relation to biomedical technology to the just allocation of resources—are not private matters or questions of personal preference but inescapably matters of the common good. If we hope to challenge and counterbalance the biomedical orientation and its extension, then we must also work toward a public philosophy, anchored in public deliberations open to diverse viewpoints and pushing beyond liberal individualism.[17] This is a work that a robust, holistic public health could also help to articulate.

Public Health

As is often said, while the sick person is the doctor's patient, "public health regards the community as its patient."[18] This does not mean that doctors have no concern for the community, or that public health professionals have no concern for individuals, just that because they have different "patients" their primary focus is different. The goal of public health is the health of the general community, and rather than cure or ameliorate illness, it concentrates on prevention. While in theory complementary, the power, prestige, and cultural authority of biomedicine have subordinated public health, weakening its distinctive character and purpose. The biomedical model, as we have noted, detaches disease from social conditions and social inequities, the very factors that it is public health's purpose to explore and address. Evans (chapter 9) argues that the absorption of bioethics into medical centers has been an important factor in undermining its independence. That has not been the problem for public health; it has always maintained separate schools. Yet, it too has been co-opted in important respects.

If physicians need to defend the integrity of their own practice, so too must public health professionals. At issue is not a violation of its standing as an ethical profession but an accommodation with biomedicine that is costing public health its distinguishing orientation. All the chapters in Part II document the basic insight of social medicine, which, in Anne Hardy's (chapter 5) words, perceives "the health and welfare of the wider environment, the household, and the individual to be interconnected within one system of well or ill being." While public health has not abandoned this inclusive vision, we have argued, its current prevention philosophy, centered on individual risk factors, leaves its reformist voice largely silent. Its effort to identify and work toward changing social and environmental conditions that produce disease is lost. Its attention to the stresses of life in modern society that harm people and create new vulnerabilities to illness is diverted.

The implication of our analysis is that public health needs to reconnect with its social medicine roots, reintroducing a tension with medicine that brings its research and practical agenda back into a complementary (not subservient) relationship that works as a balance to the equally valuable but different goals of medicine. This public health would aim to improve and promote population health by again focusing on life conditions and social inequities and not just on individual behaviors and predispositions. Rather than promote the wide use of self-surveillance technologies, such as those described by Lupton (chapter 6), for example, public health could help lead the critical exploration she calls for of their social and political implications, especially for the disadvantaged. This public health, Arrizabalaga (chapter 7) argues, would be in a much better position to again recognize the technical limits and iatrogenic effects of biomedicine, to offer a more dynamic and systemic perspective on disease and global health, and to foster a multidisciplinary and critical approach that integrates research from the biomedical and social sciences. And this public health would be far better equipped to take account of the social fragmentation, community dysfunction, and other cultural and economic factors noted by Alexander (chapter 8) as contributing to social dislocation and rising levels of addiction. Rather than serve the status quo with efforts to "fix" individuals in need of repair, this public health would turn the spotlight back on the power of structural determinants and intervention through social changes, including those designed to address destabilization, discrimination, and the social determinants of vulnerability.

Finally, a public health re-linked to the social medicine tradition could contribute to the public philosophy we are calling for. Its holistic orientation is outward-looking and focused on the wider, indeed global, community and offers alternative values and approaches to the reductionism and individualism of biomedicine and liberal society. Among the possibilities that we have alluded to here are an emphasis on a larger notion of health and social goods to temper the nearly exclusive concern with individual choice and preoccupation with the body; a greater openness to vernacular and local practices of self-care and meaning-making and more attentiveness to and humility in the face of cultural variation and difference; a greater acceptance of the limits and finitude of the body and less susceptibility to illusions of control and inevitable progress through intensive technology use; and a greater recognition of the ill effects "induced and introduced" by modern practices and technologies themselves.[19] While the ascendant reductionistic and individualistic orientation in medicine and bioethics virtually forecloses addressing questions of harm to the common good, this is surely a line of inquiry public health might embrace.

Conclusion

"Short-term solutions are insufficient" is one of the lessons that Arrizabalaga (chapter 7) draws from the troubled response to (re)emerging diseases over recent decades. It is a lesson that also applies to all the cases discussed in this book, from prevention to quality-of-care, the problem of suffering to the medicalization of everyday life. Yet another appeal of the fix orientation is that it promises some finality. No other work need be done or solutions sought once the broken mechanism or vulnerability—in individuals—is identified and some change or technical repair initiated. To heal, by contrast, is less efficient and more open-ended, more personal to a life and involving conditions and social arrangements less tractable to simple solutions. It is never *just* a fix to a technical problem because it involves the human things, which resist being instrumentalized as means, reconfigured as abstract systems, or engineered as commodities. In the end, these are the things that we need to re-appropriate for the task of resisting an invidious and one-sided reductionism and drawing limits on its expansion.

NOTES

1 Atul Gawande, *Being Mortal: Medicine and What Matters in the End* (New York: Metropolitan Books, 2014), 8.

2 Ibid., 70.

3 See also Ana Marta González, "In Search of an Ethical Frame for the Provision of Health," chapter 11, this volume; Alison Pilnick and Robert Dingwall, "On the Remarkable Persistence of Asymmetry in Doctor/Patient Interaction: A Critical Review," *Social Science and Medicine* 72 (2011): 1374–82.

4 See Deborah R. Gordon, "Tenacious Assumptions in Western Medicine," in Margaret Lock and Deborah R. Gordon, eds., *Biomedicine Examined* (Dordrecht: Kluwer, 1988), 19–56.

5 Ivan Illich, *Medical Nemesis: The Expropriation of Health* (New York: Pantheon, 1976), 45.

6 For example, the physician Danielle Ofri, in her *What Doctors Feel: How Emotions Affect the Practice of Medicine* (Boston: Beacon, 2014), reports on a study correlating physician empathy with patient outcomes. The study found that "[t]he rate of severe diabetes complications in patients of high-empathy doctors was 40 percent lower than that of patients with low-empathy doctors." Ofri adds, "This is comparable to the benefits seen with the most intensive medical therapy for diabetes, except that those treatments also cause significant side effects" (p. 57).

7 Ezekiel J. Emanuel, *The Ends of Human Life: Medical Ethics in a Liberal Polity* (Cambridge, Mass.: Harvard University Press, 1991), 16.

8 Irving Kenneth Zola, "Medicine as an Institution of Social Control," *Sociological Review* 20 (1972): 487–504, at 487.

9 S. Kay Toombs, *The Meaning of Illness: A Phenomenological Account of the Different Perspectives of Physician and Patient* (Dordrecht: Kluwer, 1992); see also my "Introduction: Holism Against Reductionism," this volume, for additional sources.

10 It is worth noting that Ivan Illich anticipated all of these points much earlier in *Medical Nemesis*.

11 For a particularly clear example, see also Henry Greely et al., "Towards Responsible Use of Cognitive-Enhancing Drugs by the Healthy," *Nature* 456 (2008): 702–5.

12 For an interesting discussion of these points with respect to beginning- and end-of-life interventions, see Dominique Memmi, "Governing through Speech: The New State Administration of Bodies," *Social Research* 70, 2 (2003), 645–58.

13 Paul Starr, *The Social Transformation of American Medicine* (New York: Basic Books, 1982), 23.

14 Here again, the applied ethics tradition, such as the principlist approach discussed by Evans (chapter 9) and Bishop (chapter 10), will be of no help. In this tradition there is no notion of intrinsic norms to a profession.

15 And the future does not look bright. In late November 2014, for example, the first-ever gene therapy drug was set to go on sale in Germany. The drug, Glybera, produced by a Dutch biotechnology company for the treatment of a rare genetic

disorder called lipoprotein lipase deficiency, was priced at €1.1 million ($1.4 million). http://www.reuters.com/article/2014/11/26/us-health-genetherapy-price-idUSKCN0JA1TP20141126.

16 For an important example of a substantive bioethical interdisciplinarity, see President's Council on Bioethics, *Being Human: Readings from the President's Council on Bioethics* (New York: Norton, 2004). On the President's Council and its more holistic approach to bioethics, see Adam Briggle, *A Rich Bioethics: Public Policy, Biotechnology, and the Kass Council* (Notre Dame, Ind.: University of Notre Dame Press, 2010).

17 See, for example, the discussion of such a public philosophy in Michael Sandel, *Democracy's Discontent: America in Search of a Public Philosophy* (Cambridge, Mass.: Harvard University Press, 1996).

18 Mary-Jane Schneider, *Introduction to Public Health*, Fourth Edition (Burlington, Mass.: Jones & Bartlett Learning, 2014), 6.

19 Ulrich Beck, *Risk Society: Towards a New Modernity* (London: Sage, 1992), 21.

ABOUT THE CONTRIBUTORS

Bruce K. Alexander is a psychologist and Professor Emeritus at Simon Fraser University. His primary research interest has been the psychology of addiction. His well-known "Rat Park" experiments helped to demonstrate that simple exposure to narcotic drugs does not cause addiction. He is the author of *The Globalization of Addiction* (2010) and *A History of Psychology in Western Civilization* (2015).

Jon Arrizabalaga is Research Professor in the History of Science at the Institución Milá i Fontanals, Spanish National Research Council, Barcelona. His works include *The Great Pox: The French Disease in Renaissance Europe*, with John Henderson and Roger French (1997); *Health and Medicine in Hapsburg Spain: Agents, Practices, Representations*, edited with Teresa Huguet-Termes and Harold Cook (2009); and *War, Empire, Science, Progress, Humanitarianism: Debate and Practice within the International Red Cross Movement from 1863 to the Interwar Period* (2014).

Jeffrey P. Bishop is Professor of Philosophy and holds the Tenet Chair of the Albert Gnaegi Center for Health Care Ethics at Saint Louis University. He serves on the editorial board of the *Journal of Medicine* and is the author of *The Anticipatory Corpse: Medicine, Power, and the Care of the Dying* (2011).

Joseph E. Davis is Research Associate Professor of Sociology and Director of Research at the Institute for Advanced Studies in Culture at the University of Virginia and publisher of the *Hedgehog Review*. He is the author or editor of three books, including *Accounts of Innocence: Sexual Abuse, Trauma, and the Self* (2005), as well as many articles and essays.

Robert Dingwall is a consulting sociologist and Professor at Nottingham Trent University. He has published widely on aspects of medicine, law, science, and technology. Among his many books are *Essays on Professions*; *Qualitative Methods and Health Policy Research*; *An Introduction to the Social History of Nursing*; and *The Protection of Children: State Intervention and Family Life*.

Luis E. Echarte is Assistant Professor of Philosophy of Medicine at the University of Navarra School of Medicine. Since 2009, he has also led a project on neuroethics for the Culture and Society Institute. He is the author of *Emotional Habits of Health and Beauty* (2014) and also of many papers on the relation of neurological research to questions of habits, identity, and agency.

John H. Evans is Professor of Sociology at the University of California, San Diego. He is the author of *Playing God? Human Genetic Engineering and the Rationalization of Public Bioethical Debate* (2002); *Contested Reproduction: Genetic Technologies, Religion and Public Debate* (2010); and *The History and Future of Bioethics: A Sociological View* (2011), as well as articles in many leading journals.

Ana Marta González is Associate Professor of Moral Philosophy at the University of Navarra (Spain). She is Director of the Emotional Culture and Identity project, based in the Institute for Culture and Society at the University of Navarra, where she serves also as Scientific Coordinator. She is also the academic leader of the Culture and Lifestyles branch of the Social Trends Institute.

Anne Hardy is Honorary Professor at the Centre for History in Public Health, London School of Hygiene and Tropical Medicine. Her publications include the *Epidemic Streets: Infectious Disease and the Rise of Preventive Medicine, 1850–1900* (1993) and *Salmonella Infections, Networks of Knowledge and Public Health in Britain, 1880–1975* (2015).

Deborah Lupton is Centenary Research Professor at the University of Canberra in the Faculty of Arts & Design. She is the author or co-author of fourteen books on topics including the sociology of medicine and public health, risk, the emotions, food, obesity politics, and digital technologies. Her recent books include *Digital Sociology* (2015); *Fat* (2013); and *The Social Worlds of the Unborn* (2013).

Christina Simko is Assistant Professor of Sociology at Williams College. She is the author of *The Politics of Consolation* (2015). Her work has also appeared in the *American Sociological Review*.

INDEX

Abbott, Andrew, 242, 248
aboriginal addictions, 219–20, 227, 231
activism. *See* patient activist movements
act-utilitarianism, 265
acupuncture, 2
addiction, 20, 21; as a brain disease, 214; as
a chronic disease, 217; as a compulsion,
212; definition of, 208, 209–10; dislocation theory of, 20, 200, 208, 223–32,
317; genetic influences on, 227; as managed but not cured, 214, 217; as medicalized, 210–13, 215, 222; non-alcoholic
or drug related, 216; official view of,
208, 213–23, 232–33; social causes of,
219–20, 224, 227; as social construction, 233n5; as vicious cycle, 226–27;
and willpower, 214, 218, 200, 221
agricultural revolution, 96, 98, 224
AIDS, 21, 145, 183–84. *See also* HIV/AIDS
alcohol addiction, 210, 211
alcoholism, as a disease, 241
Alexander, Bruce K., 20, 21, 200, 312, 317
algorithmic calculation for health care,
165–67, 169
Alzheimer's disease, 214, 217
American Board of Addiction Medicine,
213
American Psychiatric Association, 7
American Society of Addiction Medicine,
213
American Society of Bioethics and Humanities, 269
amphetamines, 86–87, 219
antibiotic drugs, 46, 179, 185, 291

antidepressants, 63, 65, 74, 75, 78, 90
anti-drug movements, 211
antimicrobial drugs, resistance to, 180
antipsychotics, 9
antiretroviral therapy drugs, 195–96
antiseptic surgery, 38, 44
Aristotle, 286–88, 302–3
Aronowitz, Robert, 10
Arrizabalaga, Jon, 19–20, 21, 222, 312, 317,
318
asthma, 214, 217
"at risk" groups, 166, 168–69
Attention Deficit Hyperactivity Disorder
(ADHD), 56, 57, 59–60, 65, 93, 241
Aubert, Vilhelm, 114
autoimmune diseases, 181
autonomy, 54, 56, 57, 87, 95, 100. *See also*
self-determination
autonomy (principlism), 107n34, 253, 255–
57, 271, 314
avian flu, 187
Awbrey, David, 63, 77

Bacon, Francis, 34, 35–41, 52, 54–55, 59n18
bacteriology, 44, 133, 136
barbiturates, 86–87
bariatric surgery, 241
Barry, John M., 188
Bauman, Zygmunt, 66
Beard, George, 53
Beauchamp, Tom L., 246, 260n14, 271, 272,
281n17
Beck, Ulrich, 197
Beecher, Henry, 252

Printed in the United States
By Bookmasters